LOST FREEDOM

Lost Freedom

*The Landscape of the Child and the British
Post-War Settlement*

MATHEW THOMSON

OXFORD
UNIVERSITY PRESS

OXFORD
UNIVERSITY PRESS

Great Clarendon Street, Oxford, OX2 6DP,
United Kingdom

Oxford University Press is a department of the University of Oxford.
It furthers the University's objective of excellence in research, scholarship,
and education by publishing worldwide. Oxford is a registered trade mark of
Oxford University Press in the UK and in certain other countries

Published in the United States of America by Oxford University Press
198 Madison Avenue, New York, NY 10016, United States of America

British Library Cataloguing in Publication Data

Data available

Library of Congress Cataloging in Publication Data

Data available

ISBN 978–0–19–967748–1

Acknowledgements

The origins of this book lie in watching my own children grow up, and in thinking about the differences between their experiences and my own growing up in the Britain of the 1960s and 1970s. In that sense, Grace and Joe both have played a key formative role in the development of this book. The experience of being brought up by my parents, David and Anne, and by aunts, uncles, and grand-parents, mostly now departed, of hearing about their childhoods, and of sharing and deciphering this with siblings Kate and Rachel, has also shaped my thinking. The book is dedicated to this family, past, present, and future.

Research for the book was assisted by the funding of the Wellcome Trust, who supported a Strategic Award on the theme 'Situating Medicine' at Warwick's Centre for the History of Medicine. In the Centre for the History of Medicine, Katherine Angel provided assistance at an early stage of the research, and both she and Jonathan Toms were invaluable and encouraging sounding boards for my half-formed ideas. For insights, leads, and in some cases sharing of unpublished work, I would also like to thank Sally Alexander, Stephen Brooke, Hugh Cunningham, Angela Davis, Rhodri Hayward, Harry Hendrick, Hilary Marland, Alan Prout, Denise Riley, Carolyn Steedman, John Stewart, Rachel Thomson, and John Welshman. The arguments of the book were tested and improved through papers presented at the Universities of Bergen, Durham, Glasgow Caledonian, Greenwich, Manchester, Oxford Brookes, and Warwick, at the History of Psychoanalysis seminar of the IHR, and at two History and Policy meetings at the Department of Education. I am grateful for the hospitality but also the valuable feedback I received within these settings. Towards the end of the project, I also had the pleasure of assisting Rhian Harris at the Museum of Childhood in London in preparing 'Modern British Childhood', an exhibition on the history of childhood of Britain since the Second World War, which encouraged me to think about communicating in a different way.

The History Department at Warwick has provided a supportive environment, wonderful colleagues, and the stimulus of outstanding undergraduate and post-graduate students. In particular, I would like to thank Heads of Department Margot Finn and Maria Luddy for support and guidance at different stages of this project. Sarah Hodges has provided always entertaining company on drives up and down the M40. And Carolyn Steedman read and commented on a draft of the book and has offered generous encouragement. At Warwick's Modern Records Centre, Helen Ford and her team provided assistance in the final stages, for which I'm grateful. At Oxford University Press, Christopher Wheeler was receptive to the idea of the book and offered valuable advice on its framing and title, Cathryn Steele and Emma Barber saw the book through the Press, and Charles Lauder, Jr and Andrew Hawkey were a pleasure to work with as copy editor and proofreader. I particularly thank the anonymous readers who generously gave up their time to provide the Press with detailed reports on the book proposal and the final manuscript. The book is much better for having been able to respond to their thoughtful suggestions and criticisms.

Finally, the period of writing this book would have been much less fun without the release of Surreal Madrid every Thursday at 9pm. I have enjoyed every minute of this. Thanks in particular to John Hunt for helping to make this possible. I have also been fortunate to find two such faithful companions in Leo and now Cairo, who have provided me with a regular diet of walks, and with time to think. And last but not least, Michelle O'Callaghan has been a wonderful mother to Grace and Joe, has put up with me, and has provided essential support and company throughout the research and writing of this book.

MT
Wolvercote, 2013

Contents

List of Figures

All images are from loose orphan photographs in a box within the Lady Allen of Hurtwood papers at the Modern Records Centre, University of Warwick: MSS.121/AP/40.

List of Abbreviations

BBC	British Broadcasting Corporation
BMA	British Medical Association
DSM	Diagnostic and Statistical Manual of Mental Disorders
ESN	Educationally Subnormal
ILEA	Inner London Education Authority
ITA	Independent Television Authority
ITV	Independent Television
JEP	*Journal of Environmental Psychology*
MRC	Modern Records Centre, University of Warwick
NCCL	National Council for Civil Liberties
NSPCC	National Society for the Prevention of Cruelty to Children
OMEP	World Organisation for Early Childhood Education
PAL	Paedophile Action for Liberation
PIE	Paedophile Information Exchange
RoSPA	Royal Society for the Prevention of Accidents
SEPEG	Semaines Internationales d'Etude pour L'Enfance Victime de la Guerre
UNESCO	United Nations Educational, Scientific, and Cultural Organization
UNICEF	United Nations Children's Fund
UNRRA	United Nations Relief and Rehabilitation Administration
WAC	BBC Written Archives Centre, Caversham
WHO	World Health Organization

Introduction

LOST FREEDOM

It seems natural that there should be a sense of lost freedom when we look back to our own childhoods. However, this book argues that the sense became more deeply entrenched in the decades after the Second World War and moved from being an individual feeling to a subject of public anxiety and social policy. There is now a widespread belief that childhood is not what it once was, and in particular that children have lost the freedom to roam beyond the confines of family and home, to explore the nooks and crannies of the urban landscape, to subvert this environment creatively, and to test themselves in the face of danger, exercise their imagination and bodies, and thereby develop real independence, resilience, and an understanding of their world. Children, according to this logic, have been confined, trapped indoors, cocooned by anxieties about traffic and paedophiles and by increased pressures, demands, and expectations, caught in a vicious circle in which such cocooning leaves them poorly equipped to cope in the outside world. Even those who grew up as recently as the 1970s will commonly look at what it is tempting to regard as the increasingly house-bound, screen-tied existence of their own children and feel this loss. No doubt, such feelings are partly a product of nostalgia. They run the danger of overlooking new freedoms, particularly those of technology and of a virtual world that has radically expanded in the intervening years. They sit alongside a permissive revolution in what children can do, how they are listened to, and what adults can do legally to control them. And they exist within a context of greater affluence and a consumer revolution that have given children far more freedom to be actors in a world of commodities (albeit alongside a new set of pressures and expectations). Nevertheless, when it comes to the child's freedom to explore a physical landscape beyond the home, there is compelling evidence that both belief in loss and a reality of loss were important features of the social and cultural history of the post-war era. One of the aims of this book is to examine these histories of lost freedom.

The book argues that the period from the Second World War to the 1970s saw much of the groundwork for a segregation of the child from the outside world, particularly urban world. For instance, it saw increased concern about child safety, an idealization of home and family, and new efforts at providing special environments for the child. It was also a period that saw a resulting heightened sense of loss. The move towards the prizing of the child, an idealization of domesticity, and efforts to provide special environments that would foster child development all had longer term roots, but the Second World War was a significant influence in making security of the child more important. Though recalled as Britain's good war, it had a darker side in which anxiety about human nature and cruelty was played out on the figure of the child. This had three results. It strengthened the case for removing children from dangerous environments such as the street. It turned attention to the provision of specially designed spaces such as the playground or the virtual landscape of children's television. And it lay behind the idealization of home, family, and maternal attachment as providing essential psychological security for child development. By the early 1970s, this post-war cocooning of the child was fostering mounting concern about loss of freedom, and this in turn spawned a radical vision of children's liberation and efforts to reintegrate the child in the urban environment. However, the radical vision was short-lived, and it was followed by a more profound closing down of the physical spaces of childhood than had been seen in the post-war decades. As such, another way of reading the post-war period is that despite mounting concern over security this remained a period of comparative freedom. Therefore, the period from the Second World War to the 1970s was one that saw the making of our idea of lost freedom, but it is also one which we now look back to fondly in search of that lost freedom. The book offers an account of how this paradox arose.

Recent concern about the well-being of British childhood is exemplified in the furore that surrounded the publication of a 2007 UNICEF Report on 'Child Well-Being', which placed the United Kingdom at the bottom of its league of twenty-one leading economic nations. Only in one area did the UK come near the top of the rankings: second in its record on safety, judged in terms of numbers of accidents and injuries. When it came to 'subjective well-being', it was at the very bottom. Unsurprisingly, the Report attracted considerable attention.[1] The UNICEF data seemed consistent with concern about childhood alcohol and drug use, as well as high rates of teenage pregnancies in the UK, risky behaviour that sits intriguingly alongside the one striking 'success' in the area of child safety. In this climate, even the culture of safety found itself increasingly open to criticism. Perhaps part of the problem was that British children were too penned in by over-anxious adults? According to such thinking, the cosseting of childhood led to lack of independence, anxiety, and social isolation, and this left such children unprepared and 'unresilient' for the stresses that lay ahead, or likely to react to overprotection through risk. A picture emerged of a cycle of psycho-social and physical childhood pathology: children were left to sit in front of television or computer screens because it seemed safer than leaving them to play on their own outside in the face of the dual dangers of traffic and predatory paedophiles; as a consequence, they lacked the environment, the social contact, and the situations for play necessary for healthy development, and were left to be seduced by the violent fantasy of the video game, or were abandoned to a premature virtual encounter with the adult world of consumerism and sex; while a lack of exercise through screen-tied, house-bound life,

---

[1] UNICEF, *Child Poverty in Perspective: An Overview of Child Well-Being in Rich Countries* (2007).

and the fast food diet of the atomized household, fostered obesity; and children emerged as a result at increasing risk from mental illness manifest in attention deficit and eating disorders, anxiety, depression, self-harming, drug abuse, educational failure, and general unhappiness.[2]

The debate drew on public and parental anxieties about managing children in the midst of rapid social and technological change, a twentieth-century culture of advice on child-rearing fuelling rather than alleviating parental anxieties.[3] And anxieties gathered momentum in an era of politics and policy that was increasingly interested, on the one hand, in child well-being in relation to a new economics of happiness, and, on the other, in psycho-social, behavioural, and possibly biological or neurological insight to address the apparent failings of the welfare state when it came to issues of personal conduct and well-being—a failure that seemed to be exposed in the threat of rioting 'feral' children in the summer of 2011.[4] Of course, the historian would tend to regard the novelty of such anxieties with a good deal of scepticism: just the latest in a long series of social panics centred on youth and cycles of deprivation.[5] They could also point out areas of huge progress in ensuring child well-being by the second half of the century: the rescuing of the child from the abuses of economic exploitation;[6] the creation of a space for the child to be a child through the discovery of the child mind and a cultural shift from a parenting culture of discipline to one centred on play;[7] the development of a welfare state with one of its central aims to foster the 'prized' child through education, medicine, social services, and economic policy;[8] the recognition and policing of child abuse not just outside but within the family, and not just in the form of physical

---

[2] Sue Palmer, *Toxic Childhood: How Modern Life Is Damaging Our Children and What We Can Do about It* (London, 2006).

[3] Peter Stearns, *Anxious Parents: A History of Modern Childrearing in America* (New York, 2003).

[4] In fact, the spectre of 'feral' children had already exploded into public consciousness in 2002 to the background of the murder of Damilola Taylor and New Labour's launch of a policy of Anti-Social Behaviour Orders: Jo-Ann Goodwin, 'The Savages', *Daily Mail*, 23 March 2002; 'The Time for Sentimentality Is Over: Let us Tame These Feral Children', *Independent*, 29 April 2002.

[5] For an example of gangs earlier in the century: Andrew Davies, *The Gangs of Manchester: The Story of the Scuttlers, Britain's First Youth Cult* (Preston, 2008). On delinquency: Victor Bailey, *Delinquency and Citizenship: Reclaiming the Young Offender, 1914–1948* (Oxford, 1987); Kate Bradley, 'Juvenile Delinquency, the Juvenile Courts and the Settlement Movement 1908–1950: Basil Henriques and Toynbee Hall', *Twentieth Century British History*, 19 (2008), 133–55; Abigail Wills, 'Delinquency, Masculinity and Citizenship in England, 1950–1970', *Past and Present*, 187 (2005), 157–85.

[6] On the importance of child labour: Jane Humphries, *Childhood and Child Labour in the Industrial Revolution* (Cambridge, 2010).

[7] Carolyn Steedman, *Margaret McMillan, Childhood, Culture and Class in Britain* (London, 1990); Carolyn Steedman, *Strange Dislocations: Childhood and the Idea of Human Interiority, 1780–1930* (London, 1995); Sally Shuttleworth, *Mind of the Child: Child Development in Literature, Science and Medicine, 1840–1900* (Oxford, 2010); Christina Hardyment, *Dream Babies: Childcare from Locke to Spock* (London, 1983).

[8] The literature is extensive. It includes V. A. Zelizer, *Pricing the Priceless Child: The Changing Social Value of Children* (New York, 1985); Roger Cooter (ed.), *In the Name of the Child: Health and Welfare, 1880–1940* (London, 1992); and Harry Hendrick, *Child Welfare: England 1872–1989* (London, 1994). And on the problem child (and family): Alysa Levene, 'Family Breakdown and the "Welfare Child" in 19th and 20th Century Britain', *History of the Family*, 11 (2006), 67–79; John Welshman, 'In Search of the "Problem Family": Public Health and Social Work in England and Wales 1940–70', *Social History of Medicine*, 9 (1996), 447–65.

abuse, but also mental and sexual;[9] and the move, particularly in the last decades of the century, to see children not just as deserving subjects of care but also as having rights and a voice of their own (a shift with major implications—some described it as a 'paradigm shift'—for how social science, medicine, and even history had to approach the subject of the child in future).[10] The historian would also highlight the need to be cautious about the way that nostalgia is likely to colour views of the world of childhood freedom that we feel we have lost and particularly memories of our own even relatively recent childhoods as significantly more free but also less troubled than those of today: nostalgia perhaps nowhere more powerful than in relation to memories of childhood; and nowhere more challenging than in a history that involves contextualizing our own childhoods.[11] Yet, for all this, the current anxiety about childhood does cry out for historical investigation that addresses the apparently paradoxical story of relatively recent real or imagined 'decline' (to put it crudely) as well as 'progress'. The aim of this book is to set one aspect of the current debate—that which centres on the changing psycho-social spaces of childhood, or what I have called here the landscape of the child, and thereby the balance between safety and danger, protection and freedom, the home and the outside world—into historical perspective.

THE LANDSCAPE OF THE CHILD

The book adopts two frameworks for thinking about the landscape of the child. First, it breaks this landscape down into three symbolic spaces: the institution, the home, and the outside world. The struggles, debates, and visions of the landscape of the child that this book considers can all be related to at least one of these spaces, and often to the interplay between them; indeed, it is the relationship and the tensions between these different landscape settings, rather than a social history of any one, that is at the centre of the discussion that follows. Of the three landscapes, that of the institution will receive the least attention. This is partly because of the book's argument about its shifting significance. But it is also because fuller coverage has not been possible within the scope of this study. Those in search of more detailed history of nurseries, schools, care homes, penal institutions, and hospitals can turn

[9] George K. Behlmer, *The Child Protection Movement in England, 1860–1890* (Stanford, 1997); George K. Behlmer, *Child Abuse and Moral Reform in England, 1870–1908* (Stanford, 1982); Lionel Rose, *The Massacre of the Innocents: Infanticide in Britain, 1800–1939* (London, 1986); Lionel Rose, *The Erosion of Childhood: Child Oppression in Britain, 1860–1918* (London, 1991); Hendrick, *Child Welfare: England 1872–1989*.
[10] The key work in announcing this paradigm shift in the British context was Alison James and Alan Prout (eds), *Constructing and Reconstructing Childhood: Contemporary Issues in the Sociological Study of Childhood* (1990). The historian most clearly associated with this new agenda is Harry Hendrick, who contributed an historical essay to the Prout and James volume. His position is further developed in *Child Welfare: England 1872–1989*; *Children, Childhood and English Society, 1880–1990* (Cambridge, 1997); and *Child Welfare: Historical Dimensions, Contemporary Debate* (Bristol, 2003).
[11] The theme of nostalgia is explored in George K. Behlmer and F. M. Leventhal (eds), *Singular Continuities: Tradition, Nostalgia, and Identity in Modern British Culture* (Stanford, 2000).

to several useful efforts in extending the well-established history of institutional care into this period; however, this a field still in need of further development.[12] Of these spaces, the book does cast light on criticism about school, which was the most important institutional landscape for children in the second half of the period, though there is of course far more to say on this important subject and those in search of this will need to turn to what is already an extensive literature on the history of post-war education.[13] At several points it also touches on the history of children in residential care. However, the relationship between the landscapes of home (and family) and the outside world is more central in the analysis that follows. Again, the book does not attempt to offer a social history of home, but it hopefully does add something to our developing understanding of the post-war reconfiguration of this site.[14] The book is particularly interested in the third landscape space of the outside world, especially the urban landscape and the space of the street. This was the landscape faced by a majority of children in what was already predominantly an urban society by the second half of the century. And the street was central symbolically in thinking about the outside world. This focus means that a history of the rural landscape is by contrast given relatively little attention within the book. This is not to say that there is no place in future work for more nuanced comparative, regional studies that highlight different types of urban, suburban, and rural landscapes of the child. The point is that the central terms of the debate emerged out of thinking about a particular sort of urban landscape, hence the focus here.

One of the reasons for starting the study with the Second World War is that it marks an important shift in thinking about which of these three spaces offered

[12] On the penal system: Wills, 'Delinquency, Masculinity and Citizenship'. On hospital care: Harry Hendrick, 'Children's Emotional Well-Being and Mental Health in Early Post-Second World War Britain: The Case of Hospital Visiting', in M. Gijswijt-Hofstra and Hilary Marland (eds), *Cultures of Child Health in Britain and the Netherlands in the Twentieth Century* (Amsterdam, 2003), 213–42. On nursery care: Denise Riley, *War in the Nursery: Theories of the Child and Mother* (London, 1983). On children's homes: June Rose, *For the Sake of the Children: Inside Dr Barnardo's: 120 Years of Caring for Children* (London, 1987); Christian Wolmar, *Forgotten Children: The Secret Abuse Scandal in Children's Homes* (London, 2000); Katherine Holden, 'Other People's Children: Single Women and Residential Childcare in Mid-Twentieth Century England', *Management and Organizational History*, 5 (2010), 314–30; Janet Fink, 'Inside a Hall of Mirrors: Residential Care and the Shifting Constructions of Childhood in Mid-Twentieth Century Britain', *Pedagogia Historica*, 44 (2008), 287–307; Tom Shaw (Scottish Government), *Historical Abuse Systemic Review: Residential Schools and Children's Homes in Scotland 1950 to 1995* (Edinburgh, 2007).

[13] There is brief discussion of this subject in Chapter 3. Much of Chapter 7 focuses on arguments about the need to recast schooling in light of interest in the perspective of the child and radical concerns about limitations to children's freedom in this institutional setting. For the argument that interest in child psychology was initially important in the development of progressive education: Mathew Thomson, *Psychological Subjects: Identity, Culture and Health in Twentieth-Century Britain* (Oxford, 2006), Chapter 4. For the history of post-war schooling: Roy Lowe, *Education in the Post-War Years, 1945–1964* (London, 1988); and Roy Lowe, *Schooling and Social Change, 1964–1990* (London, 1996). On the history of school design in the period: Andrew Saint, *Towards a Social Architecture: The Role of School Building in Post-War England* (New Haven, 1987). And for the emerging history of space in education, see the special edition of *History of Education*, and the opening editorial: Catherine Burke, Peter Cunningham, and Ian Grosvenor, '"Putting Education in its Place": Space, Place and Materialities in the History of Education', *History of Education*, 39 (2000), 677–80.

[14] For instance, Claire Langhamer, 'The Meaning of Home in Post-War Britain', *Journal of Contemporary History*, 40 (2005), 341–62.

a good landscape for child development. Until the middle of the century, the institution (and separation from the home: partial, in the case of the school; temporary, in the case of the reformatory and hospital; or even absolute, in the case of children's homes) was regarded as an often ideal solution to problems of childhood.[15] This confidence was never the same again after the war, even if the institution survived—in part by adopting the rhetoric of home and family. The war in turn would see home, for some of the same reasons, idealized to a new degree as the space essential for well-being, and the outside world viewed increasingly as a danger or something to be replaced by new specially designed outside spaces (both physical and virtual) such as the adventure playground and children's television.[16] As such, the book indicates that a significant part of the ideological work in the delimiting of the landscape of the child in fact took place over half a century ago, even if the reality for some time thereafter remained very different.

The second framework is one of thinking not about different landscape settings— the institution, the home, and the street—but of outlining three different and over- lapping relationships between landscape and the child. The first is the history of the child as a figure *in* the landscape (to coin a phrase used by Richard Hoggart in his *Uses of Literacy*—itself indicative of the landscape perspective that would be increas- ingly prevalent as a mode of social understanding in this period).[17] This is foremost a social history project of mapping where children spent their time, where they could go, and what they saw, though it is also potentially a history of cultural land- scape—of what they read and viewed.[18] Secondly, there is a history of ambition, design, and policy: a history of making a landscape *for* the child. Finally, there is the history of the way children saw, or were understood to see, their world: a landscape *of* the child. It is the impact of this last landscape that is at the centre of the analysis that follows. The recognition that children had their own landscape vision would fundamentally affect visions of designing a landscape *for* the child and attempts by social scientists, writers, and photographers to represent this landscape.

This idea of a triad of landscape perspectives coming together in the social pro- duction of space in some ways mirrors the influential model of space as conceived,

---

[15] The commitment to institutional solutions was particularly marked in the Victorian period; however, it continued into the first half of the twentieth century, evident, for instance, in the energy invested in a new system of institutional care and control for those described at the time as mentally defective and feeble-minded: Mathew Thomson, *The Problem of Mental Deficiency: Eugenics, Democ- racy, and Social Policy in Britain, 1870–1959* (Oxford, 1998).

[16] The movement to design special spaces reflected a long-standing emphasis on the value of the garden as a space combining protection and freedom. Within the context of the welfare state the opportunities to design such spaces reached a new level. For analysis of this phenomenon from an international perspective: Marta Gutman and Ning de Coninck-Smith (eds), *Designing Modern Child- hoods: History, Space, and the Material Culture of Children* (London, 2008).

[17] Richard Hoggart, *The Uses of Literacy* (London, 1959), p. 8.

[18] It is partly in this rich sense of social and cultural historical location that the 'landscape' term was used by my colleague Carolyn Steedman in her influential *Landscape for a Good Woman* (London, 1986). Given Steedman's interest in autobiography and psychology, her use of landscape also extends to the question of how historical actors saw their own worlds: the landscape *of* (the third of the land- scape relations set out here).

perceived, and lived, put forward by the French sociologist Henri Lefebvre in 1974.[19] Such an interest in the interplay of landscape and subjectivity, in the project of understanding the landscape *of* man as well as resulting efforts to design a landscape *for* the cultivation of this subjectivity, is characteristic of new approaches to the history of landscape in the field of historical geography. Such work still tends to focus on the countryside, the traditional terrain of landscape study, but it invites us to engage in a much broader history of ways of seeing. It steers us from a history of observation (landscape at a distance, the object of pictorial aesthetics) to one also of inhabitation, from a history of the land to one also of the eye.[20] When it comes to the history of twentieth-century Britain, the most important work in this vein is David Matless's study of *Landscape and Englishness*. Focusing on the period up to the end of the Second World War, Matless is particularly illuminating on the ways in which contemporary consciousness of the importance of seeing the landscape propelled a series of projects of modernization, regulation, education, and control. Rather than dismissing the appeal of the countryside and its preservation as products of nostalgia and anxiety about social change or national decline, he recasts this phenomenon as part of a modernizing project of cultivating citizenship, an example of the governmental trajectory towards control and management of environment and its population.[21]

Moving beyond preoccupation with the rural landscape and its ongoing importance in relation to citizenship and national identity, *Lost Freedom* concentrates instead on the urban landscape encountered by the majority of the population. Through its engagement with psychology and psychologically informed social science, it also pushes further the implications of a consciousness that landscape was in the eye of the beholder. In developing this line of analysis, it builds upon Mike Savage's important recent work on the influence of social science reaching into everyday life and the constitution of identities in the post-war period.[22] As Savage demonstrates, sociology in particular became increasingly influential from the early 1960s onwards.[23] However, when it came to children, psychology had a powerful foothold, and in this area it is less easy to locate a clear turning point from individual to social understanding in the 1960s.[24] In part this is because the psychological models that had come to the fore to address childhood subjectivity

---

[19] Henri Lefebvre, *The Production of Space* (Oxford, 1991).

[20] John Wylie, *Landscape* (Abingdon, 2007).

[21] David Matless, *Landscape and Englishness* (London, 1998).

[22] Mike Savage, *Identities and Social Change in Britain since 1940: The Politics of Method* (Oxford, 2010). The work of Peter Mandler on social science particularly in relation to ideas of national character and identity is also significant in this regard: Peter Mandler, 'Margaret Mead amongst the Natives of Great Britain', *Past and Present*, 204 (2009), 195–233; Peter Mandler, 'One World, Many Cultures: Margaret Mead and the Limits of Cold War Anthropology', *History Workshop Journal*, 68 (2009), 149–72; Peter Mandler, 'Being His Own Rabbit: Geoffrey Gorer and English Culture', in Clare Griffiths, James Nott, and William Whyte (eds), *Classes, Cultures and Politics: Essays on British History for Ross McKibbin* (Oxford, 2011).

[23] Savage, *Identities and Social Change*, pp. 112–34. Savage notes Nikolas Rose's work on the influence of psychology during the period (for instance, *Governing the Soul* (London, 1999)), but suggests that this has been overplayed compared to the role of sociology (*Identities and Social Change*, p. 12).

[24] Thomson, *Psychological Subjects*, Chapter 4.

in the middle decades of the century were already invariably social in orientation. But it also reflects the fact that the sociological studies of the 1960s and 1970s did often recognize that understanding children entailed an attempt to see the world from their perspective. Indeed, as Savage has demonstrated, this reorientation towards a landscape perspective, and one in which meaning and fantasy became an increasingly important dimension, was one of the most significant features in the development of British sociology in the period.[25] In other words, both psychological and sociological science in this period from the Second World War to the 1970s tended to frame childhood experience as psychological *and* social, and as an issue of perspective as well as surroundings; both fields seeing a move towards what we might call landscape thinking. This phenomenon was particularly marked when it came to the subject of the child, where the challenge of perspective was so difficult to ignore (it was no coincidence that new disciplines and theories of space such as environmental psychology and psycho-geography would also find one of their seminal subjects in the landscape of the child).

The account that follows also argues that landscape thinking extended beyond social scientists themselves. In particular, it uncovers the roles of groups such as teachers, social workers, town planners, television producers, photographers, and environmentalists in drawing on social science in conceptualizing and shaping a landscape of the child. But we also see how the subjects of policy—the children— could come to understand themselves in this new language: social scientific language and understanding, and particularly the language of perspective and, developing out of this, of rights, becoming an integral part of the landscape of the children themselves; and the histories of subjectivity, social science, and social policy as a result coming together in an explosive mix by the 1970s. The book also considers the extent to which landscape assumptions about the roles of freedom and social relationships in the fostering of subjectivity were embedded in family life through the diffusion of psychological theory and its popularization in child-care literature. Finally we see the media emerging as an increasingly important arena for publicizing social science, though often as an object of critique rather than admiration.[26] The permeation of society by this language and its ways of understanding by the 1970s is a phenomenon that is only now beginning to attract the attention that it merits, and the book aims to contribute to this process.[27]

It is also worth clarifying that this is a study that casts more light on the landscape of *the child* (an idealized and sometimes abstract figure), rather than on *childhood* or *children*. The history of childhood—the framework which has dominated work in this field over the past few decades—has entailed a focus on the process by which children come to be defined as children, and pays particular attention to the

---

[25] Savage, *Identities and Social Change*, pp. 22–47.

[26] For an example of the role of the press in this area: Adrian Bingham, 'The "K-Bomb": Social Surveys, the Popular Press, and British Sexual Culture in the 1940s and 1950s', *Journal of British Studies*, 50 (2011), 156–79.

[27] The popularization of psychological language and ways of thinking is also developed in my *Psychological Subjects*.

way in which the meaning and demarcation of age has changed over time.[28] From this perspective, the use of the category of the child in this book, which at times may obscure important differences between different stages of childhood, may be frustrating.[29] It reflects, not a denial of the importance of this type of history, but an acceptance which provides an opportunity to shift our focus to the place of the child in space. In examining this relationship, the book draws on examples ranging from the very young infant (for instance, in relation to debates over attachment), to the adolescent (for instance, in relation to issues of sexuality and vandalism). In general, the child is taken as anyone in this period up to the age of sixteen; however, at times in relation to institutional contexts that defined childhood, like children's homes or schools, or in relation to debates over lack of adult rights, it has been necessary to extend this parameter by several years.

The decision to describe this as a history of the child, rather than of children, is an acknowledgement that at its centre this is a study of patterns of ideas and that it therefore pays relatively little attention to the story of individual children. It offers a picture of how a range of academic disciplines, professions, and administrators came to develop an understanding of the child's view of the world and of how this informed their efforts at designing spaces for the child to grow and develop. It also casts some light on the ways in which the class, ethnicity, and gender of the child affected this process. But it does not generally turn to the narratives of children themselves—in contemporary diaries and essays, and reflection back in memoir and oral history—in an effort to reconstruct the way the world was seen from the perspective of the individual children who lived through it, and in order to 'particularize' their landscapes.[30] In short, the book uses the figure of the child to think with and in order to uncover a history of the how the child developed as an object of study and policy. In doing so, it is nevertheless important to acknowledge that, to paraphrase Margaret Mead, the child doesn't exist, only children exist (they are all individuals, and all in the process of change), and thus that a good deal is also lost in the process of thinking in this way.[31] Of course, the history of how children themselves viewed and experienced their landscape is not without its own

[28] Philip Ariès, *Centuries of Childhood* (London, 1962); and Hugh Cunningham's 'Histories of Childhood', *American Historical Review*, 103 (1998), 1195–208; *Children and Childhood in Western Society since 1500* (London, 2005); and *The Invention of Childhood* (London, 2006); and Colin Heywood, *A History of Childhood* (Cambridge, 2001).

[29] In particular, work on childhood in the twentieth century has pointed to important developments in differentiating between children and adolescents, to new concerns about youth culture, and to the coining of a new language of the 'teenager' in the post-war period: Harry Hendrick, *Images of Youth: Age, Class, and the Male Youth Problem 1880–1920* (Oxford, 1990); Bill Osgerby, *Youth in Britain since 1945* (Oxford, 1998); Jon Savage, *Teenage: The Creation of Youth Culture* (London, 2007); and David Fowler, *Youth Culture in Modern Britain, c.1922–c.1970* (Basingstoke, 2008).

[30] One of these intriguing sources is a body of essays written by eleven-year-old children in 1969 reflecting on what they would be doing when they reached twenty-five: Jane Elliott, 'Imagining a Gendered Future: Children's Essays from the National Child Development Study in 1969', *Sociology*, 44 (2010), 1073–90.

[31] Mead made this point at the symposium on 'Children, Nature and the Urban Environment', in Washington, DC, in March 1975. She is quoted in this sense by Colin Ward in his seminal *The Child in the City* (London, 1978), p. vi. Ward's book is a key landmark in the history that *Lost Freedom* sets out and is discussed in Chapters 1 and 7.

challenges and potential shortcomings. The idea of an unmediated voice is open to question; there is difficulty in generalizing from the sometimes atypical voices that survive; and there is the challenge of extrapolating the voice of children from that of adults remembering childhood, and of screening out the effects of nostalgia, reinterpretation, and faulty memory. This is not to say that impressive work on this subject has not engaged with these issues in an increasingly sophisticated, illuminating, and moving manner.[32] Hopefully, however, a history of how a landscape *of* the child came to be recognized, but also of how this voice and perspective came to be valued, imagined, collected, and organized at the time, and of how this conceptualization changed over time—a history that this book hopes to develop—will provide an important aid in further developing a history of the landscape as seen by children themselves.

RETHINKING THE POST-WAR SETTLEMENT

The story of lost freedom set out in the book begins against the backdrop of the emergence of a welfare state, and of what tends to be seen as a new war-born relationship between state and people. It then takes this story up to the 1970s, a time when the social, economic, and ideological settlement forged out of the experience of war, and maintained through cross-party consensus in the 1950s and 1960s, was showing signs of breaking down. The emergence of this settlement, and debate about its exact nature, has been one of the dominant themes of modern British history. The question of its end or its realignment has attracted less attention to date, and is fraught with difficulties given that there is less confidence now than there once was about its original and ongoing coherence. However, as historians move forward in time, this issue of retreat or renewal in the 1970s and beyond will attract more attention.[33] One of the aims of this book is to reflect on these issues from a fresh perspective.

It is important to preface these efforts with the caveat that the idea of a fundamental and clear-cut transformation of the British polity in the aftermath of the Second World War—as the term 'settlement' might be taken to suggest—finds far less support in the historiography than was once the case. In its starkest form, the idea of a post-war settlement suggests that Britain fundamentally changed as a

---

[32] For an example of how such a particular history can challenge generalized assumptions about working-class children's lives: Steedman, *Landscape for a Good Woman*, p. 11.

[33] For reflections on the importance of attending to this story: James Vernon, 'The Local, the Imperial and the Global: Repositioning Twentieth-Century Britain and the Brief Life of its Social Democracy', *Twentieth Century British History*, 21 (2010), 404–18. Whereas Vernon implies some kind of closure to the life of post-war social democracy, a historiography focusing on the welfare state (perhaps inevitably given its ongoing life) has tended to assume a more evolutionary language of 'renewal'. In his 'biography' of the welfare state, Nicholas Timmins, for instance, ended his story in the early 1990s with the prospect of renewal and a 'potential new settlement over the welfare state': *The Five Giants: A Biography of the Welfare State* (London, 1995), p. 519. Nevertheless, this literature on the welfare state tends to share the view that there was a moment of crisis and an 'historic break' in the 1970s: Rodney Lowe, *The Welfare State in Britain since 1945* (Basingstoke, 1993), pp. 301–29.

result of the Second World War; that liberal democracy made way for social democracy, spurred on by the collectivist spirit of a 'people's war'; and that this was cemented, not just in the terms of the new welfare state, but also in the linked acceptance of Keynesian economics and of the need for full (male) employment. The notion of a post-war settlement also implies that war established a consensus on these ends and means which reached across the political spectrum in the decades that followed. Since the 1980s, a period which saw a loss of confidence in the welfare state but also in the economics of the post-war era, there has been a tendency to chip away at this narrative. Historians have questioned both the idea of a wartime revolution in values and expectations among the public, and the extent to which war led to a radical shift to the left. The economic basis of the welfare state settlement has been recast as part of a longer evolutionary process, a continuation of William Beveridge's work on national insurance begun some three decades earlier and maintaining his expectations that welfare was to run alongside and not replace or undermine personal responsibility.[34] In education, we see behind the tripartite system an ideology of meritocracy rather than social levelling.[35] In health care, we have come to recognize the ways in which radical development was hampered by the vested interests of the medical profession.[36] And in social welfare more generally a picture of the rise of the state has made way for one of an ongoing mixed economy of welfare in which voluntarism adapted but persisted.[37] We have also been reminded of the way that this settlement only partially destabilized the British establishment and class system, and of the consequent limitations of post-war social democracy.[38] Equally, when it comes to the post-war consensus, closer analysis has begun to reveal far more political tension and division over expenditure, the level of state interventionism, and the defence of individual liberties than was once apparent.[39] We are more alert to the degree to which a fundamental shift of direction for economic and social policy was already being signalled in the 1970s. And close analysis of the history of the post-war welfare state is producing

---

[34] Jose Harris, 'Political Thought and the Welfare State 1870–1940: An Intellectual Framework for British Social Policy', *Past and Present*, 135 (1992), 116–41; Jose Harris, 'Political Ideas and the Debate on State Welfare 1940–45', in H. Smith (ed.), *War and Social Change* (Manchester, 1986), pp. 233–63; Jose Harris, 'Did British Workers Want the Welfare State? G. D. H. Cole's Survey of 1942', in J. Winter (ed.), *The Working Class in Modern British History: Essays in Honour of Henry Pelling* (Oxford, 1983), pp. 200–14.

[35] Adrian Wooldridge, *Measuring the Mind: Education and Psychology in England, c. 1860–1990* (Cambridge, 1990).

[36] Charles Webster, 'Conflict and Consensus: Explaining the British Health Service', *Twentieth Century British History*, 1 (1990), 115–51.

[37] G. Finlayson, *Citizen, State, and Social Welfare in Britain, 1830–1990* (Oxford, 1990); G. Finlayson, 'A Moving Frontier: Voluntarism and the State in British Social Welfare, 1911–1949', *Twentieth Century British History*, 1 (1990), 183–206; Jane Lewis, 'Family Provision of Welfare in the Mixed Economy of Care in the late Nineteenth and Twentieth Centuries', *Social History of Medicine*, 8 (1995), 1–16.

[38] Ross McKibbin, *Classes and Cultures in England, 1918–1951* (Oxford, 1994), pp. 553–6.

[39] Rodney Lowe, 'The Second World War: Consensus and the Foundation of the British Welfare State', *Twentieth Century British History*, 1 (1990), 152–82; Ben Pimlott, 'The Myth of Consensus', in L. M. Smith (ed.), *The Making of Britain* (London, 1988), 129–42; Martin Francis, 'Set the People Free? Conservatives and the State, 1920–1960', in Ina Zweiniger-Bargielowska and Martin Francis (eds), *The Conservative Party and British Society* (Cardiff, 1996), pp. 56–77; Brian Harrison, 'The Rise, Fall, and Rise of Political Consensus in Britain since 1940', *History*, 84 (1999), 301–24.

a more complex, nuanced, and shifting terrain that takes into account not the just the struggles between different visions of welfare, but also changing attitudes towards the motivations and agency of welfare providers and recipients.[40] The idea of a post-war settlement centred on the welfare state is not wholly abandoned in this historiography, but the contours of this settlement have emerged as far more subtle, its nature less monolithic.[41] And with post-war historical focus shifting to issues such as affluence and consumption, permissiveness, and post-colonialism, as well as the social changes associated with shifting attitudes towards class, gender, race, and age, there are further challenges in rethinking the nature of the post-war settlement.

Lost Freedom offers a fresh perspective to contribute to this ongoing process of reassessment. In doing so, one of its starting points is a classic issue in work on the wartime settlement: the impact of war-born concern about children. In his influential official history of wartime social policy, Richard Titmuss had argued that revelations about child ill-health and poverty, particularly through the process of evacuation, had been an important factor in a change of consciousness necessary in accepting the need for a welfare state.[42] Subsequently, historians have been more divided over the meaning of the wartime concern over evacuees. There is a recent tendency to argue that it reveals not just a new consciousness about need, but also a gulf of understanding between the classes, with middle-class hostility complicating notions of war-born social solidarity and a revolution in values and expectations.[43] The analysis of the war's impact on thinking about children that follows shares this tendency to recognize the complexity of war-born attitudes. It points to the importance of considering attitudes towards children who lived through the Blitz, and not just the evacuees (whose experiences in turn varied radically). And in casting light on the influential nature of psychological interpretations of well-being, it indicates the need to engage with attitudes towards fantasy as well as revelation about material circumstances. It also argues that a focus on the child's need for protection, which in some respects went beyond the evidence, emerged as particularly influential because adults often played out their own war-born anxieties on the figure of the child. The suggestion here is that the effect of such thinking was important in establishing

---

[40] Lowe, *The Welfare State in Britain since 1945*; Julian Le Grand, 'Knights, Knaves or Pawns? Human Behaviour and Social Policy', *Journal of Social Policy*, 26 (1997), 149–62; Julian Le Grand, *Motivation, Agency and Public Policy: Of Knights and Knaves, Pawns and Queens* (Oxford, 2003).

[41] Though recently it has been provocatively argued that the Britain of this settlement was a warfare as much as a welfare state: David Edgerton, *Warfare State: Britain, 1920–1970* (Cambridge, 2006). And even analysis of the development of the welfare state places emphasis on the importance of war as an escalator of state expansion: James Cronin, 'The British State and the Structure of Political Opportunity', *Journal of British Studies*, 27 (1988), 199–231; James Cronin, *The Politics of State Expansion* (London, 1991).

[42] Richard Titmuss, *Problems of Social Policy* (London, 1950). Confirming the idea that evacuation did increase consciousness of social problems: John Welshman, 'Evacuation and Social Policy during the Second World War: Myth and Reality', *20th Century British History*, 9 (1998), 28–53.

[43] An important early intervention in this direction was John Macnicol, 'The Effect of Evacuation of Children of School Age on Attitudes to State Intervention', in H. L. Smith (ed.), *War and Social Change: British Society in the Second World War* (Manchester, 1986), 3–31.

a particular sort of post-war framework for understanding and caring for the child: one which shaped certain new social policies in the realm of childcare; which also proved highly influential in the attitudes and assumptions of a generation of childcare workers in a range of professions; and which perhaps most crucially contributed to a set of assumptions about the child's need for a balance of home and family, on the one hand, and freedom to explore, play, and thereby grow, on the other. Moreover, because of an emphasis on the psychological importance of relationships, and on the need to grow through the freedom of play, it was a vision that was in origin inherently both social and democratic in its outlook. As such, it provides us with an indication of how the social democratic ideology of the era could extend from the realm of social policy into a broader set of expectations about the fostering of healthy emotions in social life. In other words, this analysis of wartime attitudes towards the child points to an emotional and social dimension to the post-war settlement: one that sat alongside and interacted with the stories of social and economic policy which dominate our accounts of the subject; and one which helped to shape family and social life in the decades that followed. This was important in contributing to the broader social settlement that emerged out of war. In particular, psychological ideas about the necessity of attachment between children and their mothers (based on a social democratic argument about the need for loving social relations, but also tolerance and freedom within this setting) helped to justify and make possible the combination of what was in reality a limited welfare state (depending on the family in childcare) and full (male) employment at the heart of the post-war settlement. The social democratic ethos is also evident in post-war efforts to provide managed, specially designed freedoms for the child, often beyond the realm of statutory social policy, for instance in children's television programming, in adventure play and voluntary playgroups, but also in raised expectations about freedoms within the home. In short, *Lost Freedom* suggests that it may be helpful to extend our view of the post-war settlement beyond the traditional territory of social and economic policy to include powerful structures of feeling, such as that emerging in response to the wartime child, and to trace their influence in shaping social life in war's aftermath.

If one outcome of setting the story of *Lost Freedom* within the context of the post-war settlement is to open up consideration of a social and psychological dimension in our thinking about the formation of this settlement, the other is to cast light on some of the problems and limitations that it subsequently encountered in realizing its aspirations. Firstly, an analysis of photography points to the way in which the figure of the street child who had escaped the protective grip of family and welfare state emerged as symbol of a freedom that was perhaps lost in this settlement. Secondly, the book argues that that the recognition that the child saw the world through a child's eyes provides us with an opportunity to explore a limitation of, and a fault line within, the broader settlement that was attracting attention by the 1970s. The tendency within the broader settlement had been to ignore the challenge of taking into account perceptions and subjectivity, and to approach recipients of welfare as passive victims rather than active agents, an undifferentiated mass rather than subjects in their own right.[44] By contrast, the vision of the child's needs that came to the fore in the Second World War was one that had subjectivity at its very heart, even if this could often be overlooked in policy and practice because it was such a potentially subversive idea and was only fully acted upon in the context of a broader critique of the neglect of subjectivity in welfare in the 1970s. Children were the initial fault line for such thinking because by mid-century theories of child development, and hence of fundamental child difference, were rapidly becoming part of a new psychological common sense. However, this also helped to justify a position in which children lacked a voice or what would later be talked about as rights. As a consequence, this was a fault line that, although an area of tension in acting in the name of the child, could be largely covered up until the explosion of debate in the seventies. Instead, subjectivity was turned into a target for expert understanding and management. Several of the chapters that follow consider these responses. And the final chapter in particular develops the argument that by the late 1960s and early 1970s, not only do we see the radical implications of this way of understanding children, but we see what we might call landscape thinking—an interest in the way in which recipients of welfare understood things from their own perspective—encouraging a rethinking about the issue of subjectivity within the broader post-war settlement. This had the potential to democratize social policy, and this was evident for instance in the aspiration to take into consideration the mental maps of the child in town planning. However, in the longer term an understanding and mapping of subjectivity also had the potential to provide the basis for more pervasive forms of governance.

Although this idea of the making and then the faltering and realignment of a post-war social settlement provides the dominant chronological frame for the book, there are two qualifications to this model that also need to be highlighted. Firstly, in order to make a point of contrast, and sometimes in order to acknowledge a degree of continuity with earlier developments, most of the chapters in fact also include significant analysis of the first half of the twentieth century. Moreover, in an effort to explain the changes that came at the end of the period, and in order to offer some reflection on the relationship between the historical study and the debates of our time, the final three chapters, particularly the concluding chapter, look forward to developments after the 1970s. So although this is primarily a study of the landscape of the child in the period from the Second World War to the 1970s, it also offers some insight on developments across the century as a whole. Secondly, there is a different type of periodization that also shapes the book. This is a periodization that reflects the process of generational change. The effect of generation is something encountered in all historical work, but it is particularly acute because of the subject matter of this book. Certain historical moments—the evacuation and the Blitz of the Second World War are obvious examples—did not only profoundly shape contemporary thinking about the landscape of the child,

---

[44] This problem is also highlighted in Le Grand's account of the post-war shift from thinking about welfare recipients as 'pawns' to active agents: *Motivation, Agency and Public Policy*.

but they directly affected the children who lived through them and this could have a long-term generational legacy. The children of the Second World War would also grow up to discover their own childhoods and the efforts of their own parents in public narratives of the war, and this would result in a resurfacing and reworking of feelings and memories much later and in changed circumstances. The children of war would then often play out the effects of that remembered childhood in the way that they too attempted to represent and design a landscape for the next generation of children. In these ways the articulation and effects of experience could be delayed, emerging only as one generation passed into the next. The effect of generation is also evident in the explosion of radical thinking about the liberation of childhood in the late 1960s and early 1970s, a generation who had been the subjects and recipients of post-war protection now apparently reacting against this culture. It resurfaced towards the end of the century as the children of war became objects of public fascination, the remaining survivors, not just of this central moment of national memory, but also of a generation who now paradoxically came to be looked back upon nostalgically as the last beneficiaries of a seemingly disappearing landscape of childhood freedom. It is even played out in the way that popular but also academic history has come to frame and picture the post-war era, with the image of the child in the bombed city a symbol of the mission of the welfare state but also of nostalgia for lost freedom. Finally, the book will hopefully provoke reflection on the role of generation in shaping our own preoccupations, as historians, sociologists of childhood, policy makers, and parents, about lost freedom, the changing landscape of the child, and the nature and boundaries of the post-war settlement.

STRUCTURE OF THE BOOK

The last part of this Introduction will summarize the structure of the book, the relationship between the chapters, and the main arguments of each in turn. The book begins with two chapters that act as starting points for the analysis that follows. These two chapters, together with the third, also address the relationship between the mid-century social settlement and the landscape of the child. In the second section of the book, the fourth, fifth, and sixth chapters all provide case studies of responses to what have now come to be seen as key dangers and causes of a loss of childhood freedom. The final section of the book consists of a single longer chapter on developments from the late 1960s onwards, with a particular focus on the 1970s.

The book opens with a chapter on photography and the child. One of the purposes of this chapter, and of this starting point, is to establish the strikingly visual, social fact that the urban street was initially a central feature of the post-war landscape of the child, but also that it has become through nostalgia a central image of lost freedom within the writing of modern British history. In these two respects, the image at the heart of the chapter—of the child at play in the city, and in which 'the words spell deprivation but the pictures spell joy'—acts as a trigger for the enquiry as a whole.[45] One of the main objectives of the remaining chapters is to make sense of the symbolic importance of this image and to explain and chart the subsequent disappearance of children from British streets. The second function of the chapter is to use the subject of photography, and a shift from portrait to landscape visualization, as a vehicle for opening up the story of how we have come to represent and understand the landscape of the child. In particular, it highlights the way that interest in the child's perspective transcended the domain of social science to influence the way that professional photographers but also amateurs came to represent children. In that sense, the chapter begins a broader line of argument within the book about ways of understanding associated with social science being diffused, popularized, and entering common sense. It also foregrounds a tension in understanding landscape which would be at the heart of debates across the post-war period. It points to the existence of what Stuart Hall has described as the 'social eye' of mid-century, social democratic, documentary photography alongside and in interrelation with what one might call by contrast the subjective eye.[46] Although this landscape photography of the child might be at pains to set the child in a social setting, it was a social setting that only had meaning in relation to the viewpoint of the child. As such, there were limits to the power of such photography as authoritative statement about social situation. This was a photography that raised questions about meaning rather than closed them down. And, increasingly, this was a photography in which its subjects were recognized as looking back. It pointed therefore towards a new understanding of the landscape of the child in which the social observer no longer had all the answers. And it opened up a landscape vision in which the child was no longer mere victim of the environment and social deprivation but was recognized by the 1970s as a purposive agent in subverting and giving meaning to surroundings.

The second chapter of the book takes us to a different starting point: the mid-century period of the Second World War, the emergence of the welfare state, and the process of reconstruction. In doing so, it introduces a line of argument about the post-war settlement which is taken forward in the remainder of the book. The unique circumstances of war provided a kind of laboratory for understanding of the landscape of the child. Evacuation turned attention towards the impact on children of being taken away from their own homes and families. The Blitz offered an experiment in exposing children to a landscape of danger, violence but also freedom, symbolized by the figure of the child playing in the bombsite. And in meeting the challenges of wartime European dislocation there was a final experiment in the relationship between landscape and the child and one that put British thinking on an international stage. Two conclusions emerged out of this cauldron of theory, experimental practice, and raw events. On the one hand, the story of evacuation in particular came to be seen as providing evidence of the damaging effect of separation of children from families and home, and this provided crucial

---

[45] Colin Ward, *The Child in the City* (London, 1978), pp. 80–1.
[46] Stuart Hall, 'The Social Eye of *Picture Post*', *Working Papers in Cultural Studies*, 2 (Spring, 1972), 71–120.

ammunition for a domestication of the landscape of the child after the war. On the other hand, the story of children in the Blitz, and in fact some of the evidence on evacuation, pointed in a radically different direction, emphasizing the resilience of children and the appeal of new freedoms in war. The dominant resulting message was that which highlighted the need for protection and in particular the need for home, family, and emotional security. Through advice on childcare, through the work of social workers, and through new standards on protection of children, what we see therefore is the extension of the wartime social settlement to embrace the emotional security of the child. But this reflected war-born anxieties experienced by adults just as much as evidence based on the children themselves. And it was in some respects ill-timed in that war also placed considerable strains on the stability of the family. Despite the lasting image of this as Britain's good war and of wartime stoicism and social solidarity, children provided an object for the playing out of deep anxieties about human nature, cruelty, and emotional damage. This was a hidden story of the war that nevertheless cast a long shadow, lying behind the efforts to cocoon childhood in post-war childcare policy, surfacing in the anger of the children themselves in early accounts of the evacuee experience, and part of the context for the post-war generation's enthusiasm for child liberation in the 1970s in reaction against protection. Most recently, in the unearthing of stories of damage at the end of the century (which, it should be emphasized, do not reflect what we know of the evacuee experience as a whole), it has led to efforts to position the evacuee as the equivalent to the shell-shock victim of the Great War. The war, then, has a crucial position in the post-war story of lost freedom. In particular, the shadow of war helped to turn freedom from an assumed natural state of childhood to something that had to be nurtured and protected and as consequence to something that came to be seen and experienced as in perpetual danger of being lost.

The third chapter of the book examines the idea that the post-war settlement extended into the realm of domestic childcare and emotional security. Though we benefit from several studies of the work and life of psychologist John Bowlby and one important study of the popularization and influence on policy of his ideas in the context of the Second World War, there has been little attention given to the story of influence after the war or to the nature of what we might call 'Bowlby-ism'.[47] The chapter offers the first account of this important subject. It argues that the diffusion of such psychological theory is a key to understanding much post-war thinking on the landscape of the child in Britain. In particular, it helped to extend war-born anxiety about child protection, and a focus specifically on the importance of attachment between mothers and their young children, into the post-war decades. As such, it was an important element of the broader post-war settlement. It helped to justify reliance on the family, and women in particular, as the central providers of childcare. And in its emphasis on the importance of social relations but also play and freedom it offered a vision of child development that was peculiarly suited to an era of social democracy. However, the second half of the chapter examines the problems with this model. It traces the emergence of a feminist critique of

---

[47] Riley, *War in the Nursery*.

Bowlbyism. It also considers the difficulties of sustaining an idealized landscape of home in the face of social changes including the problems of life in high flats, the realities of increasing levels of employment for women, and post-war immigration. Finally, it argues that the figure of the home-bound, isolated child was emerging as a symbol of deprivation and lost freedom by the 1970s, and it suggests that this entailed a loss of confidence in the position of home and family within the post-war settlement.

The fourth chapter of the book offers a case study of how the post-war era reconciled recognition of the importance of a protected environment to nurture the child's developmental needs with appreciation that the child could only fully develop through play and exploration. It shows how children's television programming emerged as one solution to this dilemma of providing both protection and freedom. Children's television would offer a virtual landscape, bringing the outside world into the home, and communicating this to the child in a language that reflected an understanding of the child mind. It would offer the child a managed freedom for the cultivation of social democratic growth. This at least was the theory. In reality, it proved far more difficult to confine children in such a manner. In particular, the boundaries between child and adult programming proved inherently permeable. On the other hand, although the child's attraction to programmes involving violence attracted some concern, just as remarkable is the complacency about exposing children to a landscape of programming that reached beyond the idealized developmental sanctuary. The chapter pays particular attention to what was in fact the largest scale British psychological study of its day, a survey undertaken by Hilde Himmelweit on television viewing amongst British children in the 1950s.[48] The very scale of the research indicates the importance of the issue, and although Himmelweit downplayed her findings she did reveal that an increasing proportion of British children's time was being spent in this virtual landscape, and invariably not in the way that the paternalists of the BBC had envisaged. In retrospect, the modest degree of contemporary alarm is striking. The chapter suggests that this needs to be attributed not only to opposition towards interference from television producers and liberals but also to the physical landscape of the child being cut back in the same period and thus the virtual landscape of television emerging as an increasingly important alternative.

The fifth chapter turns to the physical landscape of the child and in particular to the relationship between rapidly increasing levels of traffic and outside play. Again, it considers the potential of specially designed landscapes, this time in the form of playgrounds, and highlights the limitations of such spaces. It also draws on another major social scientific survey, the study of parental attitudes towards young children undertaken by John and Elizabeth Newson.[49] It indicates that although the Newsons were alert to changes in the degree to which parents were willing to allow very young children to roam about in the urban environment, the level of freedom

[48] Hilde Himmelweit, A. N. Oppenheim, and Pamela Vince, *Television and the Child: An Empirical Study of the Effect of Television on the Young* (London, 1958).
[49] John and Elizabeth Newson, *Four Years Old in an Urban Community* (London, 1968); and *Seven Years Old in the Home Environment* (London, 1976).

that these children had even at the start of the 1970s now appears striking.[50] As with the debate over television, we find arguments about the danger of traffic, but little willingness to challenge the commercial interests and freedoms that lay behind the democratization of driving in the post-war era. Instead, psychology suggested that children involved in accidents were vulnerable because of unsatisfied emotional needs. Psychological insight also indicated that, for all the efforts to educate children in road safety, the act of crossing the road was in fact simply too complex for the young child, suggesting that the focus instead needed to be on preventing parents from allowing children to be exposed to such danger. In short, in the period from the war to the 1960s, social science and the argument that children saw the world differently to the adult once again may have pointed to the importance of freedom for the child, but it often in practice acted to reinforce segregation of the child from the broader urban landscape on the grounds of developmental capacity and needs.

The sixth chapter turns from traffic to the other high profile fear surrounding modern childhood: the threat of the sexual molester and paedophile. It demonstrates that up until the 1970s this was a far less significant factor behind lost freedom than was traffic. Indeed, the language of paedophilia and widespread alarm over sexual abuse of children only became commonplace after the mid-1970s. The chapter is particularly significant in relation to the influence of social science. Again, psychology initially tended to downplay danger, accepting the sexuality of the child as a factor in such cases, viewing criminal procedures as psychologically damaging, and casting suspicion on the reliability of the child voice. The second half of the chapter looks at how this situation changed in the 1970s. In particular, it examines an extraordinary moment in which a paedophile rights lobby mistakenly saw an opportunity to publicize their cause and did so by drawing on social scientific theory. The resulting outcry was one significant factor in helping to draw to a close a radical stream of thinking about child liberation that came to the fore in the early 1970s and in heightening anxieties about child safety.

The final chapter of the book is its longest and perhaps the most important given the relative scarcity of historical work on the period which it covers—the 1970s—as well as the novelty of its four linked case studies of environmental education, the children's liberation movement, the politics of play, and the rethinking of vandalism within radical criminology, and its reflections on the interplay between social policy, subjectivity, and social scientific thinking. It situates the late 1960s and early 1970s as seeing a surge of interest in a human environmentalism: a model of seeing people in a landscape setting that had first emerged in the seminal recognition that children had their own perspective and which now encouraged a broader rethinking of the relationship between democracy and planning. When it came to children, pessimism about earlier efforts to respond to their viewpoint through planning, and a growing concern about social isolation, linguistic failure, and environmental deprivation, began to encourage a reaction against the idealized

[50] Mayer Hillman, John Adams, and John Whitelegg, *One False Move: A Study of Children's Independent Mobility* (London, 1990).

landscape of home, family, and protection that had dominated the post-war decades. Instead, the full implications of the idea that children had their own landscape vision, which until now had been largely held in check, exploded into areas of public debate. The results were fascinating: at times, outrageous and probably misconceived; at times, perhaps offering a vision that we might still hope to work towards. To a large extent, the important place that thinking about the landscape of the child had within the counter-cultural revolution of the late 1960s and early 1970s has been lost from view. The child was recast from a state of innocence to knowingness, a subject with a voice that needed to be listened to and acted upon even when it clashed with adult interests. And although there was anger that the forces of planning and capitalism had largely ignored or failed in addressing the child's viewpoint, there was a reluctance to accept the idea that the working-class child was to be written off as a passive victim of environmental deprivation. Instead, radical theory and politics looked towards children subverting the city environment, using play, fantasy, and even forms of resistance to fashion a landscape for living and growing in modern, urban times. Indeed, in this context, and with a gesture to future anxieties, it now began to be recognized that the overprotected middle-class child was perhaps just as likely to become a victim of 'experiential starvation'. The chapter concludes with a survey of some of the reasons for the collapse of this radical moment in thinking about the landscape of the child. It also briefly reflects on the relationship to developments since the 1970s.

1

The Image of Lost Freedom

Photographs of the child in the city, and particularly in the space of the street, compel us to recognize a social fact in a way that is rarely so powerfully apparent through the written record alone. This is not to deny that we also need to think critically about the evidential value of such images as representations of social reality. The problem is that we too readily dismiss the significance of the visual record in conceding that images necessarily manipulate reality. In doing so, we risk neglecting a type of evidence that links us to the past with an immediacy and power often lacking in the written record. The photographic record shows us, again and again, young children, alone, or at least without obvious adult supervision, in the streets of the city. Apart perhaps from the novel—a source of course with its own challenges—it is difficult to think of any written document that could make the same point, and certainly make it so clearly and powerfully. The question of where the child was in a particular instance of time is simply not one that would normally gain the attention of anyone making a written record. The act of playing on the streets might be documented by way of social observation by social workers or social anthropologists, or it might be possible to reconstruct its probability through inference based on records of crime.[1] But there is a huge difference between the recorded passing comment on such play and seeing it. The first is transient and forgettable, and could have a variety of meanings: it leaves the historian with considerable work to do. The second is, by contrast, both striking and concrete. We know, of course, that photographs offer us an image of reality, not reality itself. We know that the look of the photograph is the result of genre and stylistic convention, as well as technical issues such as the camera's focus, the filtering of light, and the chemical processes of development. We know that the framing of the image cuts it off from a broader context. We know that the subject of photographs reflects the interests of the photographer rather than being a representative picture of social reality. And we know that the human subjects of the photograph were often conscious of being shot and that this means that photographs are often capturing people in the act of being photographed rather than in a natural state. Yet, the photograph still compels us to recognize a simple social fact: children used to

[1] Indeed, this approach has recently begun to bear fruit, with a study of juvenile justice in Dundee and Manchester indicating the high proportion of cases in the period 1945–60 which related to conflict over the use of streets and 'play gone wrong': Louise Jackson and Angela Bartie, 'Children of the City: Juvenile Justice, Property and Place in England and Scotland, 1945–60', *Economic History Review*, 64 (2011), 88–113.

Fig. 1. Boys playing football in street (photographer unknown)

occupy the streets of our cities. For all the important caveats about needing to read these images critically, this central fact is difficult either to dispute or not to be in some way moved by.[2]

It is in seeing such images that the subject of historical difference and change becomes most strikingly apparent. The image also provides us with detail, but perhaps more importantly an emotional impression, about past everyday life that we are very unlikely to find anywhere else. It is one thing to be told that traffic has increased; another to see this and to see the possibilities for the child in the absence of the car. It is seeing that children are playing and passing time on the pavement, street and wasteland without any sign of adult supervision that highlights a fundamental change in the history of child freedom.

It is the fact that very young children would contemplate sitting in the street, facing away from any possible oncoming traffic—caught in a single shot—that enables the viewer to know something about the past in a glance that would only be possible through conjecture after trawling through reams of statistics of urban traffic volume. And it is the fact of children deep in concentration, chalking the road, exploring the ripples of a puddle, or trying to look and reach through the

---

[2] As Roland Barthes put it: 'Photography never lies; or rather, it can lie as to the meaning of the thing, being by nature tendentious, but never as to its existence' (*Camera Lucida* (London, 1982), p. 87). For reflections on photography as a source: Gillian Rose, 'Practising Photography: An Archive, A Study, Some Photographs and a Researcher', *Journal of Historical Geography*, 26:4 (2000), 555–71.

Fig. 2. Chalking the street (photographer unknown)

metal bars of street drain covers that opens our eyes to a lost landscape of the child, the landmarks of which are now largely hidden from view and touch.[3]

THE PROBLEM OF NOSTALGIA

Because these are images of children, they also have a powerful emotional resonance. We have all been children, and many of us have been the parents and carers of children. For both reasons, it is difficult if not impossible to view these pictures without connecting them to personal histories of childhood. Partly for this reason, partly too because of a process of social change over the course of the century that

---

[3] Colin Ward, *The Child in the City* (London, 1978), pp. 80–1. Figures 1–4 are all from a large collection of orphan photographs in a box within the Lady Allen of Hurtwood papers. Figure 3's photograph of the girl walking in a puddle was taken by photographer Valentine Rylands, possibly for the Save the Children Fund. The photographers of the boys playing football (Figure 1), the girl 'chalking' the street (Figure 2), and the boys in pedal cars: (Figure 4) are unknown. Most likely they were considered by Lady Allen for one of her many publications on the need to provide proper play facilities for children and were probably set in London: Modern Records Centre, Warwick (MRC), MSS.121/AP/12/40.

Fig. 3. Girl and street puddle (photographer: Valentine Rylands)

will be reviewed in this book, for the audience today it is also difficult not to read these photographs nostalgically, projecting into them echoes of what we feel to be our own lost freedom and innocence. Here, the figure of the urban working-class child has had particular appeal to a middle-class and intellectual audience who romanticized childhood freedom yet became more anxious about giving their own children this freedom in the outside world. Working-class children attracted attention because they found less freedom and opportunity for play in the discipline and limited spaces of their own homes and sought this for longer outside and particularly in the spaces of the city. And even though the post-war figure of the working-class adult would become harder to sentimentalize in the context of greater affluence, this remained easier when it came to children floating free from this context in the spaces of the city.[4] This is why, as Colin Ward already reflected in reviewing the photographs of his seminal book *The Child in the City* of 1978, we find it so hard to view these images, even those designed as rallying calls for social reform, in a wholly negative light:

> There is an ultimate paradox about the lives of city children. Readers must have had the experience of watching television documentaries exposing some social evil, and of

[4] On the dominance of pre-1940 imagery: Chris Waters, 'Autobiography, Nostalgia, and Working-Class Selfhood', in George K. Behlmer and Fred Leventhal (eds), *Singular Continuities: Tradition, Nostalgia and Identity in Modern British Culture* (Stanford, 2000), 178–95. For reflections of the relationship between affluence and class in post-war Britain, see the 'Contesting Affluence' special edition of *Contemporary British History*, 22 (2008).

Fig. 4. Pedal cars in the street (photographer unknown)

contrasting the solemn words of the Social Problem Industry with the evidence of the cameraman. You hear about the inhuman living conditions of the slums of Naples, but you see wonderfully vivacious and happy people who never stop to worry about whether they or their children are well-adjusted or whether they are deficient in the capacity to form 'meaningful social relationships.' They are too busy living or keeping others alive. You hear about the wickedness of child labour, but you see children who are resentful that interfering reporters and officials are making it even harder to spend the long summer holiday earning their purchasing power instead of indulging in petty theft which is a statistical norm of juvenile life. Similarly, although throughout this book you read about the deprivations of the city child, you see through the eyes of the photographers how children colonise every last inch of left-over urban space for their own purposes, how ingeniously they seize every opportunity for pleasure. The words spell deprivation but the pictures spell joy.[5]

[5] Ward, *Child in the City*, p. 210.

Lost Freedom

Ward was highlighting a paradox at the heart of post-war photographic representation of the British child. The same tension is evident in the history of a photograph taken by Bill Brandt, one of the most significant figures in the history of twentieth-century British photography. *East End Girl Dancing the Lambeth Walk*, taken in London in 1939, presented a theme developed in a series of his photographs from this period: children engrossed in their own world, here represented by a young, confident girl, skirt hitched up, head held high, as she steps out to perform in front of a line of admiring, laughing friends.[6] In reality, as Brandt noted, she was showing off not just to her companions, but also to the photographer and the camera; indeed, it seems from his own writing that the photograph was initially a statement about something that he recognized as joyful, playful, and assertive in the child. It was also, however, an image within the context of a broader body of documentary photography that set out to expose conditions of poverty. In the Second World War, with the child emerging as a key symbol of past social injustice and of the potential for renewal through state intervention, the photo-journal *Picture Post* used Brandt's *Lambeth Walk* to illustrate one of its articles in this light. The caption read: 'In the Days before Youth Clubs: with no club to go to, they spend their time playing juvenile games in the street.'[7] Yet, as early as 1950, in a new *Picture Post* article on 'Street Play and Play Streets', we see a more positive reading of the same picture. A new caption evoked the rhythms of song and dance: 'O Then She Was a Lady and this is the Way She Went: the imitation game, performed by the rising talent of the playstreets.'[8] It was difficult to sustain a negative reading of a picture of playing and laughing children, the emotional power of the image readily overriding the narrative of material constraints. The distance in time made this easier. It was a relatively short one, but we should not underestimate the gulf in feeling between 1943 and 1950 that the *Picture Post* itself had played a key role in cementing within the national imagination: one looking to escape from interwar social misery; the other within the brave new world of the welfare state and emerging affluence. The reframing of the image indicates, in fact, that there was already nostalgia for a time when poverty had meant that children could more easily colonize the street; that something may have been lost in the advance of material comfort and social protection. In short, nostalgia is not just something that shapes our own view of these pictures; it is also an integral part of the history of the pictures themselves. Both will be important themes in what follows.

THE IMAGE OF SOCIAL HISTORY

Although historians have been slow to recognize or embrace the value of photography when it comes to twentieth-century social and cultural history, the child in the city has emerged as one of the key images in representing the period as a whole.

[6] Paul Delany, *Bill Brandt: A Life* (Stanford CA, 2004), pp. 140–3. This well-known image can be viewed at <http://www.billbrandt.com/>.
[7] *Picture Post* (2 January 1943).
[8] 'Street Play and Play Streets', *Picture Post* (8 April 1950).

This is true even of histories in which the child is only a minor subject of concern. The image, in this case, is hardly illustrative. It acts as a symbol, and often appears on front covers. However, rarely, if ever, do these historians explain or directly address their use of the image. For instance, the ambiguities of Brandt's Lambeth girl resurfaced on the cover of Ross McKibbin's influential 1990 collection of essays on the nature of class relations in Britain during the first half of the century.[9] And drawing on the allusion to deprivation but joy, Robert Colls placed a Salford-set image of five working-class boys sitting, precariously but happily, on a high wall, on the front cover of his 2002 exploration of meanings of the nation, *Identity of England*. It is an intriguing image. Though the gas masks evoke the Second World War, the photographer, Shirley Baker, took the picture in 1962. Colls' publishers framed the image in nostalgic sepia tones, whereas the original was black and white. But even Baker's original was part of her broader project of capturing a disappearing world.[10]

Why does this type of image of the child, and a particular type of image of the child centred on the poor, urban child, adorn the covers of books on the social history of the twentieth century? Perhaps it is an issue of the child emerging as a central object of state and professional concern, in child study, childcare, and most crucially child welfare. However, as already noted, many of these histories pay little direct attention to children. For instance, Colls' *Identity of England* includes only a few passing references. The relationship, one is left to assume in the absence of discussion, is less direct, and both more symbolic and personal. The poor urban child acts as visual shorthand for a broader narrative of reform and social improvement that has come to dominate our view of the period, a story centred on the triumph of the working class or 'the people'. But the power of the image also relates to the particular challenges yet opportunities of recent history. The image confronts us with the otherness of the recent past, and thus the drama of the story as history. Yet, at the same time, it takes advantage of this proximity, linking readers (and authors) into the story through association with their own childhoods and family histories. In doing so, it implies that amidst the progress something has been lost: our own childhoods, but also innocence, freedom, and community. Crucially, it is the ability of the image of the child to touch upon this paradox that makes it such an important one for representing our ambiguous feelings about this history of social change. The objective of this chapter is to develop a more nuanced appreciation of this key image of our recent history: to explain why and how the words have come to spell deprivation but the pictures have come to spell joy.

---

[9] Ross McKibbin, *The Ideologies of Class: Social Relations in Britain, 1880–1950* (Oxford, 1990).

[10] As well as illustrating the cover of Robert Colls' *Identity of England* (Oxford, 2002), this image also appears as plate 20, between pages 212 and 213. Shirley Baker, herself born in Salford, was best known for her pictures of a community that was being demolished. This is highlighted by plate 22 in Colls' book, also taken by Baker and set in Salford just two years later, in which two children stand alongside their mother and her pram (perhaps in contrast to the earlier freedom) in what was once a street of houses. Now the street leads across a barren wasteland to a horizon of high-storey flats. At no point does Colls himself directly interrogate these pictures, though the juxtaposition is probably intentionally suggestive. On Baker's work in this area: Shirley Baker, *Street Photographs: Manchester and Salford* (Newcastle, 1989).

Although the majority of the analysis that follows will concentrate on professional photography, it will first turn briefly to the story of the amateur. In doing so, it will point to a crucial development, which would make this image such a powerful one in representing ambiguous feelings about our social history, which would spill over from the sphere of the professional to the amateur, and which would make the landscape image of the child one that opened up uncertainty about projects of control and regulation: the recognition that children saw the world differently to adults.

POPULARIZATION OF THE LANDSCAPE VISION

By the 1920s, with light, unobtrusive cameras increasingly inexpensive, photography had emerged as a popular pastime and hobby, and mass production was putting the technology of the 'snapshot' into the hands of millions.[11] At the same time, the family was being encouraged to prize, study, and scientifically manage the development of the child.[12] It is unsurprising that the two should have come together. They were both modern with a scientific or technological sheen, and they both reflected the passage into the domestic sphere of an amateur, scientific and perhaps secularized evangelical compulsion to monitor and give order to everyday life. The hobbyist could turn to camera clubs and specialist magazines and books for advice on all sorts of photographic challenges. Among them was photographing the child. Here, the act of photography was presented as no mere whim but as having genuine aesthetic and social value. Theories of development projected a vision of the child in constant flux. Without the camera, the stages in this history would fade from sight; with the camera, it became a responsibility to capture them for memory.

Children, asserted one guide (a naked young girl posed naturalistically in sand on its cover), ought to be photographed much more than they were.[13] However, gone were the days of needing to troop children off to the studio of a professional photographer. For the child, the studio visit was often akin to the dreaded trip to the dentist, and when children found no pleasure in having their photographs taken there could be no genuine pleasure from the pictures themselves. At best the

---

[11] John Taylor, *A Dream of England: Landscape Photography and the Tourist's Imagination* (Manchester, 1994), pp. 131–4; Don Slater, 'Consuming Kodak', in Jo Spence and Patricia Holland (eds), *Family Snaps: The Meanings of Domestic Photography* (London, 1991), pp. 49–59. The family album and its relationship to memory and identity has attracted more attention than the advice literature: Annette Kuhn, *Family Secrets: Acts of Memory and Imagination* (London, 1995); Marianne Hirshch, *Family Frames: Photography, Narrative and Postmemory* (Harvard, MA, 1997); Deborah Chambers, 'Family as Place: Family Photograph Albums and the Domestication of Public and Private Space', in Joan M. Schwartz and James M. Ryan (eds), *Picturing Place: Photography and the Geographical Imagination* (New York, 2003), pp. 96–114; Gillian Rose, *Doing Family Photography: The Domestic, the Public and the Politics of Sentiment* (Farnham, 2010).

[12] C, Hardyment, *Dream Babies: Child Care from Locke to Spock* (London, 1983); Rima Apple, *Mothers and Medicine: A Social History of Infant Feeding, 1890–1950* (Madison, WI, 1987); Lyubov Gurjeva, 'Child Health, Commerce and Family Values: The Domestic Production of the Middle Class in Late-Nineteenth and Early-Twentieth Century Britain', in Marijke Gijswijt-Hofstra and Hilary Marland (eds), *Cultures of Child Health in Britain and the Netherlands in the Twentieth Century* (Amsterdam, 2003), pp. 103–26.

[13] John Wells, *Child Photography* (London, 1927).

result was artificial. Photographic naturalism and an appreciation of child psychology were the keys to capturing real child development.[14] Studio photography made its own efforts to accommodate this new taste—placing children in a nursery-style environment amidst toys and against outside backgrounds, setting children at their ease by talking to them, and concealing cameras behind toys—but the amateur, particularly the amateur who knew the child, could do a better job, capturing children unaware and absorbed in play in their own environment.[15] The truly successful photograph also depended on a leap of imagination towards seeing the world like the child. In a guidebook published in 1945, at the height of war-born interest in child psychology, we see the child as a consequence being repositioned as subject rather than object of photographic enquiry:

> Unlike the adult, who sees only what he expects to see, the child uses his eyes and sees with rapture. Success depends first of all on re-entry into the child's world; and to be accepted as a friend by children one must respect them as real people. It is hopeless to look down on them as quaint amusing things to be coaxed into action by absurd baby talk.[16]

The aim of such photography was to capture how children looked at, and even felt about the world: the rapture of the child in the act of perception.[17]

In these injunctions to capture the child's perspective, we see that a move from portraiture to a landscape vision of childhood was not simply a product of professional photography but was also becoming integrated into popular culture. This was also evident in the enthusiasm for taking the camera into the outside world. One guidebook admonished readers to make sure they never left home without it.[18] This was not just the case when setting off as a family. There was no hesitation in encouraging strangers to roam parks, playing fields, and zoos in order to capture children unaware and unselfconscious on film.[19] The problem for the stranger was the affectedness of children if they realized a picture was being taken (and in that sense, parents did have an advantage); hence the advice to lurk in environments in which the child was fully preoccupied. Striking here is the absence of any apparent concern about such clandestine photography. The display of photographs in this advice literature—for instance, the young girl sitting naked playing in the sand—offers further indication of a gulf in anxieties towards childhood safety between our own time and the mid-twentieth century.[20]

The family photographer and the social realist clearly occupied very different situations; nevertheless, channels of photographic as well as psychological advice,

---

[14] Mary Arnheim and Rudolf Arnheim, *Phototips on Children: The Psychology, the Technique and the Art of Child Photography* (London, 1939), pp. 7–8.

[15] Rosalind Thullier, *Marcus Adams: Photographer Royal* (London, 1985); Robin Lenman (ed.), *The Oxford Companion to Photography* (Oxford, 2005), p. 115.

[16] Frank Partington and Molly Partington, *The Art of Photographing Children* (London, 1945).

[17] See, for instance, the images of 'The Child's World' in Partington and Partington, *The Art of Photographing Children*, following p. 40.

[18] Arnheim and Arnheim, *Phototips on Children*, p. 13.

[19] Arnheim and Arnheim, *Phototips on Children*, p. 14.   [20] Wells, *Child Photography*.

but also examples in hugely popular magazines such as the *Picture Post*, brought connections and parallels to encourage a landscape reorientation at the popular as well as the professional level. This had implications for the role of photography within the private sphere of the family that merit further attention, and it also had implications for the reception of professional imagery, helping perhaps to explain why the public have seen joy and not just deprivation in photography of the working-class child in the city. In turn, with the coming to the fore of this sort of domestic photography, and at a time when home and family in the context of both interest in child development and war-born anxieties about security and attachment had a heightened appeal, professional photographers were themselves likely to see the child in a new, more psychologically individual and vulnerable way. The second half of this chapter turns to the story of how professional photography changed in response to such influences and concerns, why it turned to the subject of the street child, and how this resulted in the images of lost freedom that have come to be such powerful symbols in narrating our recent social history. It divides this analysis into three sections: firstly, the emergence of the street child as a subject, and its significance in opening up a more psychological perspective within photography; secondly, the impact of the Second World War on this mode of representation; and finally, the post-war child in the city and the increasingly radical and subversive nature of this imagery by the 1970s.

THE STREET CHILD AS SUBJECT

By the late nineteenth century, the fact of the photograph, what John Tagg has called its 'evidential force', was making it a natural tool of governance. It was linked to a series of new practices associated with record keeping and classification, identification, and anthropological and social investigation as well as journalistic exposé.[21] The power of these images lay in the claim to authenticity and exactitude; it also, however, depended on a potential to appeal to the emotions of the viewer.[22] There were technical as well as stylistic reasons why the effectiveness of the photograph in this regard remained limited: lack of portability; the need for a static subject because of the long shutter speeds; and the difficulty of working with natural light. These problems are apparent in the earliest major photographic study of street life, John Thomson's *The Street Life of London*, where children were self-consciously posed in an attempt to convey a series of moral messages.[23] It was in the interwar era, with the emergence of a social-realist documentary style, that emotion and narrative drama gave the social fact a new power, soon reaching a mass audience through the medium of the photo-journal. New technology of lighter weight and portable cameras and faster shutter speeds made this possible. Photography could

---

[21] John Tagg, *The Burden of Representation: Essays on Photographies and Histories* (London, 1988).

[22] For an account: Seth Koven, *Slumming: Sexual and Social Politics in Victorian London* (Princeton, 2004), pp. 88–137.

[23] Colin Westerbeck and Joel Meyerowitz, *Bystander: A History of Street Photography* (London, 1994), pp. 73–4.

move outside to its subject and catch it in action, rather than having to stage it and present it against an artificial background. Children were a central theme, ideal through their innocence in highlighting the inequity of the urban landscape.[24] They had always been keen to have their pictures taken, crowding inquisitively around the camera and indeed making it difficult for photographers to work in the environment of the street, but now there was a greater opportunity to capture them innocent of the camera.[25]

The shift was also an ideological one. The documentary style aligned itself with progressive and socialist politics which set individual suffering within a social and economic context, and it could make this point through the ability now to capture its subjects within a landscape: typically, the landscape of urban poverty and the street.[26] However, in bringing its subjects to life in such a way, animating them through relationship to a landscape, and provoking feelings of emotional identification between viewer and image, such photography also brought to the fore a tension in meaning that had always been there even in the most objectifying images of identification and classification: there was a person, a life, and a world beyond the flat black and white image, and it was increasingly hard not to feel that the face looked back. This also began to raise the question of whether the subjects of such photography saw the projected landscape in the same way as the viewer. So, although documentary photography fundamentally depended on realism, it also had the potential of challenging the authority of representation, often perhaps unconsciously, though at times with clear links to an avant-garde and surrealist exploration and subversion of everyday life.[27] Such tensions were particularly likely to emerge when it came to photography of the child. The basic idea that the child psychologically apprehended the world in a rather different way to the adult and that play was crucial in such exploration was becoming part of common sense. By the 1930s, it was difficult for any documentary photograph of the child to be immune from such assumptions. Such photographs already offer us, therefore, not just insight into the whereabouts of children within the landscape, but also a sense of how the child's own relationship to and perspective on that landscape was understood at the time.

An early example of such a shift is provided by Humphrey Spender's 'Worktown' photographs, taken as part of Mass-Observation's study of everyday life in Bolton in 1937–8. Mass-Observation aimed to reveal what lay beneath the surface of everyday life through a combination of diaries and social observation. The Worktown project fell into the latter category, though alongside the written report it also provided the visual report of Spender's camera. Spender would find that working-class subjects tended not to welcome the intrusion of the camera (hence the absence of

---

[24] Alan Marcus, 'The Child in the City', *History of Photography*, 30 (2006), 119–33; Tony Birch, '"These Children Have Been Born in an Abyss": Slum Photography in a Melbourne Suburb', *Australian Historical Studies*, 35 (2004), 1–15.

[25] Lenman (ed.), *Oxford Companion to Photography*, p. 115.

[26] Tagg, *Burden of Representation*, p. 12.

[27] For the latter: John Roberts, *The Art of Interruption: Realism, Photography and the Everyday* (Manchester, 1998). The work of both Humphrey Spender and Bill Brandt exemplifies such a link between social documentation and the avant-garde.

pictures involving adult eye contact or domestic interiors). One of the reasons a large number of his photographs focused on children may be that they were much happier to cooperate. Indeed, this is a point to bear in mind more generally in gauging the significance of the social fact of the child in street photography. Spender offers us a picture of stark dichotomy between the landscapes of the working-class and the middle-class child.[28] The image of the latter is confined to the 'elite' dance class, the boating pool, and the leaf-dappled park in the company of adults, with the child's natural spirit for play both channelled and regimented. The working-class child by contrast appears uncontained, colonizing the empty and decaying spaces of the city—the building sites and wastelands and the crumbling pavements—but also having no fear or restraint in a carnivalesque intervention in electioneering, the most symbolic of adult activities. One of the most intriguing of these photographs is that of two small boys, distant figures in the midst of a huge arena-like wasteland, close enough though to see that one has his shorts down around his knees, and that they are determinedly focused on targeting the puddle at their feet, with jets of pee arching out in comparative admiration and defiance of their social situation.[29] In several others, little children are peering through the hole of a broken fence on a railway bridge. The high fence cuts off their freedom, but they subvert this space using their size to look through it. And the indecipherable graffiti that decorates the fence suggests that they have colonized this run-down landscape, giving it a meaning that the adult can only guess at.[30] The camera and the viewer are spying on the boys, just as the working class feared. In doing so, however, and in apparently capturing such moments of secret spontaneity, Spender's images look under the surface of everyday child life, exposing its strangeness and ungovernability. They open up a history of photography as a window, not just on the position of the child in the landscape, but also for contemporary understanding of, and a struggle to represent, the way children themselves saw, experienced, and gave their own meaning to this landscape.

THE IMPACT OF THE SECOND WORLD WAR

Particularly significant in terms of projecting the documentary-style image of the child to a mass audience was the weekly photo-journal *Picture Post*, founded in 1938 by the German refugee Stephan Lorant, who had pioneered a new approach to the marriage between picture, text, layout, and typography in the *Workers*

---

[28] These images are collected in Jeremy Mulford (ed.), *Worktown People: Photographs from Northern England, 1937–38 by Humphrey Spender* (Bristol, 1982). A similar class contrast was drawn by Bill Brandt in his *The English at Home* photographs: Stephen Brooke, 'Children and Streets: Class, Childhood and the City in 1950s and 1960s Photography', NECBS Paper, 2009.

[29] Deborah Frizzell, *Humphrey Spender's Humanist Landscapes: Photo-Documents, 1932–42* (New Haven, 1997), plate 26. This image and many of the other Worktown photographs are also visible at <http://boltonworktown.co.uk/photo-collection/>. It is given the title 'Boys Peeing on Wasteland': <http://boltonworktown.co.uk/photograph/boys-peing-on-wasteland/>.

[30] The image can be seen at <http://boltonworktown.co.uk/photograph/children-playing-2/>. There is also a series of photographs on the graffiti itself: <http://boltonworktown.co.uk/themes/graffiti/>.

Illustrated paper in Munich. *Picture Post* was selling 1,350,000 copies within four months and 1,500,000 by 1940, when Lorant departed for the United States. Tom Hopkinson took over as editor, bringing with him a British tradition of social reporting, and remained until 1950. During this time, *Picture Post* continued to attract a mass audience, though in the 1950s sales fell off and the journal closed in 1957. There has been a temptation to explain its popularity and then its demise in terms of a window of opportunity before television. But we also need to recognize that its success was due to an ability to capture the mood of the time.[31] From the mid-1930s, there was a new appetite for looking hard at society, and this came to a head in the Second World War. What Stuart Hall calls the 'social eye' of *Picture Post* flourished in this context, and made its own contribution towards a 'moment of transparency' in which the roots of social experience were rendered visible.

The power of the *Picture Post*'s documentary-style photography, argues Hall, lay in its ability to transfer the significance of wartime events to the image on the page. It gave readers a feeling of having been there. But in its choice of subject matter and in its style, it also made everyday events and experiences just as crucial to a feeling of involvement in an historical moment as would have been news of meetings between the leaders of the great powers. Characteristically, it took a major event, but then used this as a pivot to shift the focus to the ordinary onlookers and bystanders. In doing so, the everyday assumed a greatly intensified significance. Of course, the *Picture Post* photograph did not represent an unmediated reality. As Hall explains, its power lay not just in its relationship to a particular historical moment but also in its honing of a style of representation suited to this moment. The uncomplicated layout and aesthetic, with an absence of poetic language and black and white pictures square on to the reader, gave an impression of straight-talking rather than artifice. The pictures rarely drew attention to their own technique and style, and this had the effect of emphasizing content and message instead. Yet, the unusually large pictures and their frozen-in-time quality contributed to the sense of a more immediate line of communication than was normally the case in magazines and newspapers. Indeed, through their prominence and immediacy, the photographs often commanded the text, reversing the normal relationship in illustrated articles.

One of the *Picture Post*'s key subjects in making a link between the political and the everyday, and between war and the social, was the child. It was no accident that the front cover of the famous 'Plan for Britain' edition in January 1941, in which the *Picture Post* advanced the case for planning as the route to a better post-war society, showed infants on a slide.[32] How did one represent the vision of the planned society through photographic realism? One could focus on the ills of the present, but more positively one could focus on an element of the present that embodied the potential to make a better Britain. In both respects, the child on the

---

[31] Stuart Hall, 'The Social Eye of *Picture Post*', *Working Papers in Cultural Studies*, 2 (Spring, 1972), 71–120. Tom Hopkinson also questioned the role of television in *Picture Post*'s decline, suggesting instead that there had been a loss of confidence in the identity of the magazine as it tried to compete with a new generation of more glossy and frivolous picture magazines: Tom Hopkinson (ed.), *Picture Post, 1938–50* (London, 1970), 20–1.

[32] *Picture Post* (January 1941).

slide was an ideal subject. Indeed, the image would become increasingly prevalent by the end of the war, with the playground emerging as the planned alternative to the neglect and danger of the street and as a symbol of the new society.[33]

However, in foregrounding the child as a symbol both of devastation and of future hope, the Second World War could also encourage photography to focus less on the child in a social setting and to highlight instead the individual face and behind it a landscape of emotion and suffering. We find this sort of trajectory if we trace the evolving imagery of the Save the Children Fund. Soon after its foundation in 1919, the Save the Children Fund had appealed for public support with dramatic line drawings of the tragedy of disease and famine in Russia, sometimes accompanied by contrasting drawings of comfort in Britain. The captions—'the most awful spectacle in history', 'the appalling tragedy of suffering childhood', or 'thousands of children in immediate peril of death'—but also the narrative approach made possible by the freedom of drawing gave little doubt that the images were to be read as tragic drama. In one, an empty bowl signifies hunger. In another, the winding trail of people signifies homelessness. In another, a girl collapses on a street in the rain with a crowd looking on. It was not only the narrative orientation and the medium of the line drawing that set these images apart from representation of similar subjects in the Second World War. It was also an issue of focus. Mothers, in the Save the Children imagery of the early 1920s, had in fact been even more central than their children, strikingly so, given the title of the charity. Hunger, disease, suffering, and homelessness were rendered less by a focus on the defects of the body (these were gaunt, but far from the emaciated forms that would emerge later), and not by the expression of the face, as it would be in the Second World War, but by the ragged and tattered garments, the bare feet, and the posture. Frequently, the head-in-hands, face-hidden, pose conveyed the emotional distress of the mother and child.[34] The line drawings may have been 'crude', but this perhaps underestimates their strength when it came to situating the child within a story.[35] When the Save the Children Fund began using photography in its publicity from 1921, the subject matter was similar—a mother holding her child—but the drama and the message were harder to sustain. Photography revealed the clothing as thicker and thus warmer, and hats and boots were in evidence. The subjects were now, for the first time, obviously ethnic. The expressions were harder to decipher. Words had to play a more central role in conveying meaning. In doing so, they resorted to emphasizing that the power of the image lay in its authenticity.[36]

---

[33] The *Picture Post* would also play an important role in bringing the idea of transforming bomb-sites into adventure playgrounds to a British audience: 'Why Not Use Our Bombed Sites Like This?', *Picture Post* (16 November 1946).

[34] These images were regularly displayed in *The Times*, and this discussion is based on a survey of the fund-raising pleas from 1919 to 1921; for instance: 'The Starving Children of Europe' (23 December 1919); 'The Most Awful Spectacle in History' (5 March 1920); 'Hopeless Dawn of a New Year' (1 January 1921); 'The Appalling Tragedy of Suffering Childhood' (24 February 1921); 'Russia Swept by Famine and Cholera' (12 August 1921).

[35] The 'crude' description is Seth Koven's: *Slumming*, p. 135.

[36] 'Thousands of Children in Immediate Peril of Death', *The Times* (18 November 1921); 'Unparalleled Distress', *The Times* (23 February 1922).

The contrast to the visual strategy of the Second World War is striking. The early photographs may have lacked the narrative power of the line drawings, but they still depicted a similar sort of narrative subject.[37] In the Second World War, the focus of the camera shifted to the child's face. Previously, we had an image of children in relation to mothers, to a story, and to a landscape; now we have the child in close-up, an image of both innocence and emotional need. Such images located suffering internally, in relation to the psychological circumstances of the child, identified through the face rather than material markers such as clothes or a narrative situation; or if there was a landscape, and thus a narrative, it was one of absence and thus separation.[38] The removal of a surrounding landscape acted to intensify the focus on the child as a universal symbol of war's devastation: a landscape would have located the object of concern in a particular place and country; the point was that all children suffered yet offered hope in relation to war. The shift reflected anxiety about the devastating psychological effect of the loss of a landscape when it came to children: not just that experienced by the refugee, but also by the British evacuee and orphan of war, and more generally by 'the child who has never known peace' chosen to represent the impact of war and the prospects for the future on the cover of *Picture Post* in 1945. The image of the child in isolation from context emphasized the need for protection, the need for a mother perhaps, but crucially the need for the absent landscape of home.[39] This was why a *Picture Post* special edition on the child refugees of war in 1948 struck such a chord, attracting the largest correspondence of any in the magazine up until that date.[40] As the next chapter will discuss at greater length, the high level of interest in these images was related to the way that the child and the landscape of the child emerged as one of the main channels for working through the most horrific features of the war.

THE CHILD IN THE POST-WAR CITY

War and its resultant hopes but also insecurities had concentrated photographic focus on the figure of the child. It also ensured that this image was a deeply psychological one, particularly interested in the perspective of the child. It meant that though interest in the landscape of the child remained, this was increasingly one

[37] 'Unparalleled Distress', *The Times* (23 February 1922).

[38] 'Keep Faith with the Children', *The Times* (25 October 1943); 'Austerity—Christmas—But Love and Sacrifice are not Controlled', *The Times* (9 December 1942).

[39] By the 1950s and 1960s, the visual focus of Save the Children Fund publicity had shifted back to the foreign child. See, for instance, the imagery in Kathleen Freeman, *If Any Man Build: The History of the Save the Children* Fund (London, 1965). The focus on the child continued to be a way to highlight the problems of psychological trauma, homelessness, and separation; however, it now also depicted the starving body of, for instance, the Korean child (in the 1950s) and the African child (in the 1960s): *The Times* (1 November 1956; 24 May 1958; 17 January 1966). As Seth Koven has highlighted, it was not until the 1980s that Save the Children took a self-critical approach to its use of photography. At this point, it drew up a code of guidelines that aimed to protect the rights, dignity, and humanity of its subjects (*Slumming*, p. 135).

[40] 'Europe's Children', *Picture Post* (24 April 1948). For response: *Picture Post* (8 May 1948; 15 May 1948). The context for this response is discussed in Chapter 2.

understood in terms of psychological need rather than serving a role of social critique. As the reframing of Brandt's *Lambeth Walk* suggests, the post-war vision of the child of the city would increasingly be one in which nostalgia for a freedom that was in the process of being lost would complicate a message of social reform. Moral outrage was now more likely to be expressed through the type of picture arrived at by the Save the Children Fund in the Second World War, in which the camera would focus in close-up on the personal wounds of neglect and abuse, and in which the absence of the good home continued to be the fundamental landscape statement.[41] By contrast, the photography that came to focus on images of children at play in the streets of the city began to lose its inherent political, social reforming message. Such photography looked at its subject in a new way, or at least it was free to bring to the fore elements that had perhaps always been there in an image like Brandt's *Lambeth Walk* but which had been overshadowed while such photography served as a reforming 'social eye'. In particular, it was now free to turn children into its subjects, rather than its passive victims and objects of inquiry. So the new post-war photography of the street went much further in raising questions about the perspective of the child. It asked whether an adult vision of reform was one that failed to understand the street from the child's perspective, and one that in fact eroded the freedom of the child and cut away at the child's world. It also went further in challenging the gaze of the viewer and reader with the returning gaze of the child: its child was both less knowable and more knowing.[42]

Photographer Roger Mayne, born in 1929, part of a generation coming to maturity on the cusp between the pre-war world of economic depression and its striking poverty and the post-war world of affluence, and also one that had experienced war through the eyes of childhood and adolescence, had made his own professional debut in the *Picture Post* in 1951.[43] As a young man, he was influenced by the new photojournalism and by photographer Henri Cartier-Bresson's idea of the 'decisive moment'. Bresson had emphasized that the essence and unique value of photography, in contrast to the dominant artistic media to date, in particular painting, was that it provided an opportunity to recognize in a fraction of a second what was truly significant and thus to capture the form that gave this moment its true expression. The street was a perfect environment for such an approach to photography. Famously, Bresson covered his small camera in black tape so that he could catch his subjects unaware. Mayne came to public prominence through a series of photographs of young people—children but also the new phenomena of the teenager and the teddy boy—in Southam Street in London, a remaining relic of pre-war urban slum life, which was to be demolished in 1968–9.[44] By the late

---

[41] See, for instance, the photographs that illustrate Ann Allen and Arthur Morton, *This is Your Child: The Story of the National Society for the Prevention of Cruelty to Children* (London, 1961).

[42] This theme of the child's challenge in looking back is developed in Anne Higonnet, *Pictures of Innocence: The History and Crisis of Ideal Childhood* (London, 1998).

[43] The article, 'Between Two Worlds', was about the making of a ballet film by the Oxford University Film Group (*The Street Photographs of Roger Mayne* (London, 1993), p. 67).

[44] His work can be compared to that of Shirley Baker, who photographed the disappearing slums of Salford. Baker later reflected on the problems of nostalgia: Baker, *Street Photographs*, pp. 15–18.

1950s, he had emerged, as one retrospective of his work put it, as the 'photographic laureate of teenage London'. Mayne's photographs adorned the front covers of the *Observer* magazine as well as Colin MacInnes' seminal 1959 novel of life among London youth, *Absolute Beginners* (whose central character and narrator, like the figure at the heart of Antonioni's 1966 London-set film *Blow Up*, was appropriately himself a young photographer, roaming the city on the hunt for the decisive moment). Mayne provided an image that served for the childhood of the future: MacInnes' teddy boys and girls, assertively staring back at the camera. But he also provided images that served as a link to the past and a lost, pre-commercial world of childhood folk culture, and he provided the cover for Iona and Peter Opie's *The Lore and Language of School Children* of 1959.[45]

Mayne's inspiration had come from an incident in the 1950s, when he found a group of children playing on one of London's many remaining bombsites. The location is highly significant, and the next chapter will explore the meaning of the bombsite in relation to the thinking about children, freedom, and danger in the post-war world. What Mayne found on this site of destruction were children in their element: assertive, in command of their own time and pleasure, in a seemingly natural state. When they saw him, they were distracted, but not hostile; they were keen to have their photographs taken.

From 1955, he replicated the technique in his Southam Street pictures, which were taken over a period of five years, and which carried the theme of children and adolescents in a landscape of freedom from bombsite to the site of the street. The photographs of Southam Street presented a world in which the boundaries between the home and the street were blurred, and in which home could not contain the energy of the child: signalled in the slippers worn outside, in the steps to the house as a meeting place, and most fundamentally in the street as a communal playground. The car was almost completely absent, as was the responsible adult. Children creatively transformed the material of this rundown urban environment: kerbs became seats; the street provided a canvas for chalk, a pitch for football, or a track for homemade go-karts made out of junk; and the lamp posts were transformed into swings.[46]

There is no obvious message about the need for social reform, or for lamp posts to make way for playgrounds. Instead, it would soon be difficult not to read such black and white images nostalgically. Certainly, this would be the case when the photographs began to attract renewed interest in the 1990s. It was evident in letters from former residents themselves, but also in the popularization of the images after the singer Morrissey used them on record sleeves and tour backdrops.[47] Even at the

---

[45] *The Street Photographs of Roger Mayne*, pp. 78–9.

[46] As one resident recalled: 'Fun was made up of not so much toys because we didn't have many, but by swinging around the lamp post on a long skipping rope' (*The Street Photographs of Roger Mayne*, p. 84). This and other reminiscences were provided by letters from former residents in 1992–3.

[47] For details on the images used for the sleeves of his singles 'Interlude' (with Siouxsie, 1994) and 'Roy's Keen' (1997), and on the 1997 tour: <http://www.morrissey-solo.com/people/mayne.htm>. Morrissey himself, born in Manchester in 1959, was part of the generation relocated from streets akin to Mayne's Southam Street. In earlier work, as part of the Smiths, he had reflected on less comfortable memories of childhood freedom in relation to the nearby 1965 Moors Murders, discussed in Chapter 6 ('Suffer Little Children', *The Smiths*, 1984).

time, Southam Street was something of a relic of the type of terraced, Victorian, inner-city working-class street that was fast disappearing as such areas of London were turned over to the planners and developers. In that sense, nostalgia was a factor from the start. However, Mayne's central aim was an artistic one: an experiment in using what might be seen as an anthropological method of working in the one site for a long period of time in order to capture the child in the 'decisive moment' of action and expression.[48] In adopting this approach, his photographs in truth captured something far more ambiguous and unsettling than a nostalgic vision of childhood innocence. The children often looked back at the camera, challenging the viewer. Moreover, the focus was often not so much the child as the figure of the adolescent—an increasingly threatening figure.[49] There is some indication that Mayne was here also working through feelings about his own childhood, and as the next chapter will suggest this was characteristic of the war-child generation.[50]

Mayne's pictures captured children in the landscape of the street in order to frame an essential and untamed quality of childhood, and in doing so implicitly challenged the social documentary vision of the child as mere object of suffering. But in 1964 a lesser-known book of photographs accompanied by a striking text went even further in shifting the focus of attention to the landscape as seen and experienced by the child. *Street Children* was one of a series of projects under the hand of writer B. S. Johnson during this period, including novels and several other documentary projects, which broke new ground in experimenting with forms of representation.[51] Another was an exploration of the experience and memory of the evacuee, which will be discussed in the next chapter. Johnson was himself an evacuee and felt scarred by the separation and by the resulting fear for his mother left to face the bombing. His interest in the way that the child could see the world in a very different way to the adult emerged out of this experience. As a writer, he was also aware of the challenge in bridging this divide. One of his strategies was to collaborate with a photographer, Julia Trevelyan Oman, who again cast the street child in the language of black and white film, though now of a more grainy and less

[48] In the British context, Mayne was recognized already in the mid-1950s as a significant figure in the move from photography as social comment to photography as art: 'The Photographer as Artist', *The Times* (13 July 1956). And for an early review of his street landscapes: 'A Camera in the Back Streets', *The Times* (17 February 1959).
[49] On anxieties about immigration in the period: Wendy Webster, *Imagining Home: Gender, Race and National Identity, 1945–64* (London, 1997); Chris Waters, '"Dark Strangers" in our Midst: Discourses of Race and Nation in Britain, 1947–1963', *Journal of British Studies*, 36 (1997), 207–38; and Wendy Webster, 'There'll Always be an England: Representations of Colonial Wars and Immigration, 1948–1968', *Journal of British Studies*, 46 (2001), 557–84. On anxieties about youth: Bill Osgerby, *Youth in Britain since 1945* (Oxford, 1998).
[50] Martin Harrison, *Young Meteors: British Photojournalism: 1957–65* (London, 1998), p. 35; *The Street Photographs of Roger Mayne*, p. 80. Mayne moved on from his urban landscapes of the child to rural, more abstract landscape when he moved to Dorset with his young family.
[51] For background on Johnson, see Jonathan Coe's *Like a Fiery Elephant: A Life of B. S. Johnson* (London, 2004). Coe dedicated the book to Oman, whom he had interviewed but who died before the book's publication. Coe offers only limited discussion of the *Street Children* book; however, he suggests that the photographs preceded the text, that Oman and the publishers had wanted the less gritty title of *Pavement Children*, and that the book met with a muted response (pp. 141, 180). Johnson committed suicide, aged just 39.

sharply focused texture that evoked the blurring of the real and the remembered in Johnson's text.[52] A second was to deploy an innovative typographic strategy. *Street Children* used three typefaces: bold roman text to represent the spoken words of the child; roman for the conscious thoughts; and italics for the subconscious.

Again, Johnson's children were far from the passive victims to environmental deprivation of social realism. Through text and image, Johnson attempted to portray their 'absorption in the immediate; and, above all, their enormous confidence, their curiosity about living, and their acceptance and transcendence of their environment'.[53] The photographs reflected this shift of focus towards the perspective of the children themselves. There were no close-ups of faces, but instead there was an attempt to focus in on the details of an environment that only the child saw or noticed: 'split stucco, flakeworn pavingstone, cobble gutters, disintegrating rendering, cracked and peeling wood', all part of the physical texture of a landscape in which these working-class children grew and developed.[54]

As with Mayne's photographs, occupation of the street and the independence of the children—adults are wholly absent—were dominant themes. However, there was now no sense in the text, or indeed in the imagery, that the book was attempting to capture a lost or departing world. Indeed, certain aspects, such as the high number of immigrant children, but also the shift away from focusing on such an old-fashioned community and landscape as Southam Street, make the Johnson/Oman pictures far less open to nostalgia than Mayne's. This is highlighted, for instance, in Johnson's inscribing of an italicized subconscious to the book's first photographic subject, a young boy with a dummy in his mouth (but a mother nowhere in sight) on the pavement of an urban street:

> *They don't have to tell me about this human condition: I'm in it. They don't have to tell me what life's about, because I know already, and it's about hardness. Hardness and being on my own, quite on my own. You understand that much right from the beginning, from the first time the pavement comes up and hits you, from the first time you look round for someone you expected to be there and they aren't. Oh, I know you can get close to people, but that's not the same. In the end, you're just on your own.*
>
> *But that's not the point. The point is that you have to go on living it, life, and not only just put up with it, either, but let it see that it doesn't matter to you. That you're going to go on living however many times things come and knock you flat, however many people aren't there when you expected them to be.*
>
> *So they don't have to tell me about it: I'm in it, right in it. You just have to go on.*[55]

So rather than evoking a lost world, Johnson's attempt to imagine the landscape of the child evokes the freedom, in the face of deprivation and alienation, of the child who looked back. However, what is also striking about this landscape vision is the contrast to the home-centred ideology that we have come to associate with the post-war decades. Johnson's child is one who feels quite starkly the absence of security and attachment.

---

[52] Oman went on to be a leading costume and set designer. Her papers, including a large number of photographs of children taken in preparing for *Street Children* are now held at the University of Bristol Theatre Collections: JTO/005/001-9. She married Roy Strong.

[53] B. S. Johnson, *Street Children* (London, 1964), p. 1.

[54] Johnson, *Street Children*, p. 1.   [55] Johnson, *Street Children*, p. 3.

As this highlights, we may have come to assume too readily that the rhetoric of attachment theory, family values, and consumer-driven domesticity was necessarily a reflection of social practice and experience, or that the working-class and immigrant child was as protected as was perhaps the case within the middle-class home. This is a theme that will be explored in the third and final chapters of this book.

Colin Ward's *Child in the City*, published after a further decade of rapid social change in 1978, provides us with a final version of the image of the urban child that has been traced throughout this chapter. This was a book with far more text than Johnson's and with a far more overt political message: children were being deprived of a social environment. However, as the quote from the start of the chapter highlighted, the photographs that richly illustrated the text throughout told a slightly different story: children could still be found creatively exploring and playing in the spaces of the city, however inappropriate.[56] The photographic images are at the heart of an argument that children were not passive victims of environmental deprivation, but were subjects who could subvert and manipulate an inadequate urban landscape (and at the same time resist governance and control, as captured in one image of boys playing street football against a wall with the graffiti 'ed' appended to the sign Wandsworth Child Guidance Unit).

The context for Ward's study will be considered in more depth in the final chapter of the book. The discussion here will concentrate just on the images. Many of the photographs were taken by Ann Golzen, though Ward also drew on other photographers and picture libraries. Throughout the book, the images tended to follow and support the text. One result of this was that they were far more varied in subject than the others discussed in this chapter. The fact that the photographs were all still in black and white links them with the past, but this perhaps is unfortunate because the underlying message was more dynamic. It offers us two central landscape images and arguments. On the one hand, it provides us with a single striking image, out of line with the focus of most of the others, of a small child, head squeezed up in front of net curtains, just high enough to peer out of the 'privacy and isolation' of the home onto the street.[57] This type of image marks both a loss of confidence in the landscape of home, attachment, and protection that had come to fore in the aftermath of the Second World War, and a recognition that children were in danger of being deprived of access to a world of outside freedom.[58] On the other hand, the child of the city was still there, and predominated in the images of the book, but was radically recast and updated. The book presented its readers with a series of traditional images of the street child, though as an historical artefact, evoked through picture-library photography. The street child also now appeared in new, comparative form, through drawing on recent images from poorer countries in the developing world.[59] However, when it came to the British

---

[56] Ward, *Child in the City*, p. 210.   [57] Ward, *Child in the City*, p. 43.

[58] This theme is explored in greater depth in Chapter 3.

[59] Ward's interest in the history of such photography is later evident in Colin Ward and Tim Ward, *Images of Childhood: Old Photographs* (Stroud, 1991). In this book he argues that old photographs are a valuable source in revealing the much greater presence of children on streets in a period of high density cities, when children left school earlier, and before the advent of television (p. 4).

Fig. 5. Adventure playground (photographer unknown)

urban landscape of the 1970s, rather than a pessimistic vision of children confined in houses and evacuated from the city, the book offers us a powerful photographic statement about the child's capacity to find new freedom in a subversion of waste-land, derelict sites, and even the car-dominated street. We encounter children explor-ing the new opportunities, spaces, and obstacles provided by the urban landscape of the 1970s: using the cardboard boxes that now littered shopping streets; or using the slopes of the concrete jungle of post-war urban reconstruction for roller skates and skateboards. We also find a picture of a host of other spaces of and for the child in the modern city, some deliberately designed, such as the urban farm or the adventure playground, others indicating how children were able to find opportuni-ties in an adult landscape, such as in shopping or public transport. In short, Ward offers us, not nostalgia for a lost landscape of the child, but a landscape under challenge and in the midst of a struggle for reformation.[60]

We find an intriguing insight into the evolution of this view of the landscape of modern British child in the remaining papers of the woman who pioneered the adven-ture playground in the period, Lady Marjorie Allen of Hurtwood. Allen appears to have recognized that nothing could be more powerful than the photograph in making an argument about the potential and the needs of the child. Over a period from the Second World War to the 1970s, we find her seeking out and collecting images of the variety of playgrounds that started to emerge during this period, and which will be discussed in Chapter 5. In particular, we find a powerful visual statement about adventure playgrounds emerging out of the wartime rubble, jammed right up against busy inner-city streets to create radical zones for child freedom (Figure 5).

[60] Indeed, taking up the story of images of childhood in Britain from the 1970s to the present, Patricia Holland has pointed to the classic image of childhood innocence falling away and coming under more critical scrutiny: *Picturing Childhood: The Myth of the Child in Popular Imagery* (London, 2004).

Fig. 6. Boy climbing in adventure playground (photographer unknown)

Yet we also find the image of the child looking back, challenging the viewer with the fact of the child's-eye perspective and the joy of freedom even amidst the junk of wartime damage and urban development: an image that pointed beyond nostalgia for innocence to an untameable dimension of the child that needed the danger of the adventure playground space to thrive (Figure 6).[61]

---

[61] Both images are to be found in MRC MSS.121/AP/12/40.

Fig. 7. Woman and child looking down from flats (photographer unknown)

We also find Allen being drawn through the power of the image to the challenges posed by a modern urban environment. This was captured for instance in one image of a penned-in mother and child looking down anxiously from the balcony of a high-rise flat (Figure 7).[62]

But we also see Allen, like Ward, finding visual evidence of the child's ability to overcome, and perhaps subvert, barriers to freedom. This was symbolized in one image of boys making a tree house in one of the few remaining trees in Kennington

---

[62] MRC: MSS.121/AP/12/40. Several other photographs in this box attempted to capture the rules that restricted play in such settings, with signs from the 'city architect' outlawing play on balconies or on the garage forecourts below.

Fig. 8. Tree-house, St Agnes Place, Kennington, London, May 1962 (photographer unknown)

in inner-city London, within the wasteland shadow of the high-rise buildings that were springing up all around (Figure 8).[63]

Freedom in the face of urban development is also captured in an image of a group of boys climbing onto a roof (Figure 9). Behind the last boy on his way up the ladder there is an official sign declaring that nobody under age can go onto the roof. The message has been repeated on the wall in chalk. But all this is subverted, not just by the fact of the boys' climbing, but also by the way they have chalked their own instruction to 'kick the window hard' on the way up.[64]

The location of such images within the files of the social reformer takes us from the world of the photographer to the world of practical policy, and in doing so it reveals the close link in this period between the two ways of seeing. This is a further reason why the development of an image of lost freedom in this chapter has important implications for the chapters that follow.

---

[63] The exact location is given as St Agnes Place, Kennington, London, and the photograph is dated May 1962 (photographer not named): MRC MSS.121/AP/12/40.

[64] A note suggests that the setting is Notting Hill, a location discussed in some detail in Chapter 7. The photographer is not named: MRC MSS.121/AP/12/40.

Fig. 9. Boys climbing onto roof (photographer unknown)

CONCLUSION

Although photography presents us with the striking social fact of children inhabiting the spaces of the city in a way that we now feel we have lost, this chapter has also directed us towards a series of other cultural and political factors behind the power of this image. In the interwar period and in the context of plans for a welfare state, the image came to the fore as a symbol of what was wrong about an old world and what was possible through social reform. Wartime anxieties about child safety encouraged such thinking. And it was encouraged by new technology that made it possible to capture the child in the 'decisive moment' and by new forms of dissemination such as the photo-journal. However, the prominence of the image was also a product of a romance about child freedom that readily turned it into a symbol of nostalgia. The appetite for such a reading of the image was encouraged by a widespread interest in the psychology of the child that emphasized the importance of freedom in development and which was a factor in shaping the way that the camera looked at and framed the child within popular culture and not just amongst an artistically orientated photographic elite. However, it came to the fore particularly powerfully in the photographic vision of a generation who had been the children and adolescents of war and who now saw in the child and adolescent of the city an image of a freedom and resistance that attracted them within the context of post-war affluence and social security. Rather than a mere tool of nostalgia, this image challenged satisfaction in an image of domesticity at the heart of the post-war settlement and came to centre on outlying figures within that settlement such as the immigrant child and the teenager. It hinted at the child as a figure, not of pity, but of anger, resentment, and even danger. And in Ward's full articulation of its political implication, it presented a fundamental challenge to the success of post-war planning, with the child as a symbol for a new politics of resistance and renewal. It is because the image of the child in the city provides a vehicle for our sense of achievement about this post-war settlement, but also our ambivalence about its effects, that it has become such a central image for our social history as a whole. This trajectory from the insecurities and heightened security of war to the radical challenges of the 1970s provides a model for more detailed examination in the remainder of this book. Starting with the Second World War, subsequent chapters will turn from visual to written records to explore the reality and myth of lost freedom.

2

The Shadow of War

The landscape of the child in modern Britain, and the history of lost freedom, can only fully be comprehended set within the shadow of the Second World War. One of the reasons for the war's importance was that it presented new and to a large extent unique evidence on the relationship between child well-being and environment. Four episodes in particular attracted attention, two well-known, two less so: the evacuation of children from bomb-threatened towns, and their separation from home and family; the life, by contrast, of the children who stayed behind, and their ability in particular to cope with the threat to danger, epitomized by the Blitz; the wartime exposure of conditions in residential children's homes; and the observation of and direct contact with the children of war-torn Continental Europe, who had often lost homes, parents, and homelands altogether. Each offered a perspective on the comparative value of home, institutional care, and independence outside of such adult constraints. The war therefore provided a unique laboratory, and a set of large-scale experiments, for thinking about the landscape of the child. The main body of this chapter assesses each of these experiments in turn.

The Second World War has in fact had a surprisingly minor place in a history of childhood whose primary focus has been changing attitudes towards age. This is because the war, in this regard, appears to see a continuation of trends from the interwar period: in particular, a 'prizing of the child'; and an appreciation that the child progressed through a series of psychological developmental stages, and that child care needed to be shaped accordingly.[1] The war's position emerges as more significant, however, if we conceptualize the history of childhood instead in relation to space. A clue to this is to be found in the recent framing of the nation that emerged out of war as 'family Britain', a title that reflects the considerable importance that historians have come to attribute to the spaces of family and home in defining what sort of society Britain was in the post-war decades.[2] In a spatial sense,

---

[1] See, for instance, the handling of the war in Hugh Cunningham's survey of the subject, *The Invention of Childhood* (London, 2006). On the development of concern about psychological health: Harry Hendrick, *Child Welfare: England 1872–1989* (London, 1994); Roger Cooter (ed.), *In the Name of the Child: Health and Welfare, 1880–1940* (London, 1992); John Stewart, 'Child Guidance in Inter-war Scotland: International Context and Domestic Concerns', *Bulletin of the History of Medicine*, 80:3 (2006), 513–39; Mathew Thomson, *Psychological Subjects: Identity, Culture and Health in Twentieth-Century Britain* (Oxford, 2006), Chapter 4. The 'prizing of the child' phrase comes from V. Zelizer, *Pricing the Priceless Child: The Changing Social Value of Children* (New York, 1985).

[2] David Kynaston, *Family Britain, 1951–57* (London, 2009). Increasingly, set against emerging evidence of the instability of family in earlier centuries and the social changes to come, the mid-century decades have come to be seen as somewhat unique in their fostering of the 'normal' family.

war was a factor in three fundamental shifts in the history of British childhood. Firstly, it acted as the catalyst for a critique of the institution as a solution to problems of childhood, and as providing a good landscape for the child. Faith in large institutions—an inheritance from the Victorian era, and which had been backed up by what was in retrospect a hugely impressive willingness to spend on buildings and the cost of care—would never be the same again. Secondly, the period saw a heightened idealization of home as a landscape for child development and the extension of this ideal across society. Finally, the war brought to the fore a dilemma over the relationship of the child to a landscape beyond the protection of the home: on the one hand, in highlighting the psychological need for attachment and the importance of an imaginative landscape, it encouraged the idea that home could provide all that the child needed and directed concern towards the need to protect children from outside dangers that threatened such security; on the other, it exposed the energies of children, their attraction towards and ability to cope with the dangers of war, and the need to provide access to a broader landscape or to design special spaces to satisfy these drives. This chapter explores the relation of the Second World War to the first two of these transformations in the landscape of the child: thinking about the child's relationship to the institution and to the home. It also points to the significance of the war in sowing seeds for the third transformation: the closing down of access to the outside world.

RETHINKING THE 'GOOD WAR'

A further objective of the chapter is to use this subject of the landscape of the child to contribute to a more general re-evaluation of the war's meaning for modern British society, and it will introduce this theme before turning in more detail to the

This is explored in Pat Thane, 'Family Life and "Normality" in Postwar British Culture', in Richard Bessel and Dirk Schumann (eds), *Life after Death: Approaches to a Cultural and Social History of Europe during the 1940s and 1950s* (Cambridge, 2003), pp. 193–210. On the idealization of home: Clare Langhamer, 'The Meanings of Home in Post-War Britain', *Journal of Contemporary History*, 40 (2005), 341–62; Wendy Webster, *Imagining Home: Gender, 'Race', and National Identity, 1945–1964* (London, 1998); Denise Riley, *War in the Nursery: Theories of the Child and the Mother* (London, 1983). As Langhamer notes, such an idealization was not wholly new and is better described as a realization of aspirations already emerging in the 1930s. In this respect, see also: J. Giles, 'A Home of One's Own: Women and Domesticity in England, 1918–1950', *Women's Studies International Forum*, 16 (1993), 239–53. Langhamer also points out that even in the 1950s the working class saw only a partial material realization of the ideal, with many young couples still forced to live with their parents. Nevertheless, contemporary consciousness of a new ideal was captured in the words of a leading post-war British sociologist: 'for the first time in modern British history the working-class home, as well as the middle-class home, has become a place that is warm, comfortable, and able to provide its own fireside entertainment—in fact pleasant to live in. The outcome is a working-class way of life which is decreasingly concerned with activities outside the house or with values wider than those of the family': M. Abrams, 'The Home-Centred Society', *The Listener* (26 November 1959), 914–15, quoted in Langhamer, 'Meanings of Home', 341. Langhamer's article on the meaning of home is in the context of a special edition of the *Journal of Contemporary History* on 'Domestic Dreamworlds: Notions of Home in Post-1945 Europe'. Though Langhamer questions the significance of the war, pushing attention back to social aspirations that already existed in the 1930s, other contributions in this collection do point to a war-born desire for domestic security. See in particular the introduction by Paul Betts and David Crowley: pp. 213–46. A striking absence in these essays, despite the focus on home, is the figure of the child.

wartime discoveries. Through aerial bombardment and evacuation, the war directly affected the lives of British children in a way that is unique in British history. In that sense, children are an important component in making this what historians have described as a 'total war', or as more recently figured a 'people's war'.[3] Yet this literature leaves children only partially examined: objects of concern, a population for evacuation, pity, and planning, rather than an active constituency of the 'people' whose feelings and voice merit attention in their own right.[4] The child provides two powerful and contrasting images that have frequently been deployed in illustrating what has become the dominant narrative of Britain's war. On the one hand, there is the evacuee: distraught and abused, torn from home and family. On the other, there is the child of the Blitz, playing in the ruins of the city, a symbol of hope amidst destruction. Both illustrate a view of the war as a catalyst for positive change on the home front, an opportunity to learn lessons, and a moment for heightened public consciousness of social problems to encourage reform. In this way, the story of British children in the Second World War has tended to merge into the broader, dominant narrative of this era as one of new social solidarity and the coming of the welfare state. We have come to see the evacuation experience as a spur to mounting concern about the condition of children, a factor in the case for better healthcare, mental welfare, and social services, and leading to a more comprehensive childcare system under the 1948 Children Act. And we recognize revelations of the damaging effect of wartime separation from home, family, and mothers as almost certainly an important trigger for a post-war idealization of family and home. This chapter re-examines this idea of war heightening the importance of home, and it opens up the subject of the war's impact on the child's relation to public space—a line of enquiry that has attracted less attention. In doing so, it suggests that the story of the landscape of the child in wartime Britain, and the implications of this for the post-war era, can be figured rather differently than it has been to date. In particular, it places greater emphasis on the projection of war-born anxieties about human nature onto the figure of the child, and on the ways in which this resulted in sensitivity towards the difficulties of home and family life that have been underestimated in accounts of a war-born golden age of stable family life.

Developing such a line of argument about childhood sits uncomfortably alongside a tendency of looking back on Britain's wartime experience in positive terms. This is a war that has attracted immense attention to the subject of suffering on the one hand and to a human capacity for violence on the other. Yet, this has left the portrayal of war on Britain's home front relatively untouched, or even highlighted

---

[3] Arthur Marwick took up the banner of 'total war' from sociological and economic analysis: *Britain in the Century of Total War* (1968). The shift of focus towards a history of experience, but also continuing interest in the relation between such experience and the post-war political settlement, helps to account for its replacement in recent debate by the idea of a 'People's War'. The seminal text for the latter was Angus Calder's *The People's War, 1939–45* (London, 1969).

[4] This is even the case in a recent study that sets out to be more alert to social divisions that continued to cut across the nation despite wartime pressure for unity: Sonya Rose, *Which People's War? National Identity and Citizenship in Britain, 1939–1945* (Oxford, 2003).

it as a story of positive human values by way of contrast. Subsequent theoretical development has seen the horrors of the war tied to broader processes of modernity.[5] Yet this has done little to challenge a British story that already found in the emergence of the welfare state a strong and largely celebratory narrative of modernization. Equally striking is the contrast in historical writing about the legacy of the two world wars in Britain itself. We find a vast literature on loss, mourning, individual and collective trauma, and the problems of memory and repression when it comes to the First World War, but far less literature on the cultural legacy of war after 1945, let alone work exploring loss, trauma, and the need to repress the memory of certain aspects of war.[6] We have a picture of Britons struggling emotionally to recover from the First World War, but implicitly doing so rapidly and without great difficulty after 1945, perhaps thanks to the healing balm of the welfare state and then increasing affluence.[7] A shift of attention towards the social and cultural history of the post-war era has yet to change this situation. This contrast may be justified to some extent, but the subject at the very least deserves more serious consideration than it has received to date. Tony Kushner has argued that even when it came to the horrors that others had endured and experienced, in the Holocaust in particular, there was very little appetite within Britain for dwelling on such matters as people attempted to put war behind them.[8] As a study of post-war British art and literature puts it, 'the reaction from the war began in the first weeks of the peace, a wish for oblivion, a denial of the past as soon as possible, a search for whatever pleasure and laughter could still be found'.[9] For all the advance of psychotherapy—by now far more readily available and culturally significant than in the First World War—this was still a culture in which the best way to deal with difficult experiences was to move on, certainly not to dwell on the morbid; to put aside, forget, and repress.[10]

[5] Z. Bauman, *Modernity and the Holocaust* (Cambridge, 1989).

[6] The literature on memory, loss, and remembrance in response to the First World War is vast and still emerging, reaching back to Paul Fussell's seminal literary analysis of the war as foundational for thinking about such subjects: *The Great War and Modern Memory* (New York, 1977). Subsequently, the focus of social and cultural historians has extended to specific sites of memory and mourning such as battlefield tourism, and war memorials, for instance: A. Gregory, *The Silence of Memory* (Oxford, 1994). There is also now a large literature on 'shell-shock' in the Great War, as well as popular literary representations of the phenomenon such as Pat Barker's *Regeneration* trilogy, which has tended to present the episode in terms of a language of trauma (an approach that has several problems): Thomson, *Psychological Subjects*, 182–6. Study of memory and the Second World War has tended to emphasize, by contrast, recall of the positive and a resistance to dwelling on the negatives. See, for instance, the essays dealing with Britain in Martin Evans and Ken Lunn (eds), *War and Memory in the Twentieth Century* (Oxford, 1997).

[7] A partial exception here, taken further in this chapter, is: Joanna Bourke, 'Going Home: The Personal Adjustment of British and American Servicemen after the War', in Bessel and Schumann (eds), *Life after Death*, pp. 149–60.

[8] Tony Kushner, *The Holocaust and the Liberal Imagination* (Oxford, 1994), pp. 219–55; Tony Kushner, 'The Impact of the Holocaust on British Society and Culture', *Contemporary British History*, 5 (1991), 349–75. See also Dan Stone, 'The Domestication of Violence: Forging a Collective Memory of the Holocaust in Britain, 1945–6', *Patterns of Prejudice*, 33 (1999), 13–29.

[9] Andrew Sinclair, *War Like a Wasp* (London, 1989), p. 191.

[10] Kushner, *The Holocaust and the Liberal Imagination*, pp. 242–3.

The more painful side of this wartime history, and the place of the child within this, has also been obscured by the formation of public memory. The war has been democratized and domesticated: an era in which images of battle were an everyday part of popular culture has given way increasingly to a story of the 'People's War'. Yet, as Geoff Eley has indicated, the latter, albeit with different emphases, has tended to be just as comfortable a way of dealing with the period as the earlier celebration of victory: it remains Britain's 'good war'.[11] As part of this process of remembering the People's War, there has been an explosion of popular history dealing with children on the home front.[12] Partly this is an issue of timing. By the end of the century, as a desire to remember the war came to the fore, the main survivors were people who had been children at the time. Indeed, as we lose our last Great War veteran, the children of 1939–45 have emerged as the pre-eminent survivors of one of our great national sagas, whose stories are relayed in books and through television and museums. Like Great War veterans, their individual recollections of the period are shaped by a relationship to public memory.[13] They are intensely personal yet also universal, examples of the spirit of Britain in adversity, and consequently rarely challenge the dominant narrative of the good war. The popularity of history, spurred on by genealogy and television, has turned this generation into keen historians of their own past, using memoir, oral history, and diaries.[14] They have clearly found an audience among their own generation but also beyond it, with schools and museums keen to use such material in the hope that it will be of interest to children.[15] It provides a picture of a time in which children experienced dangers and challenges, but also freedoms and responsibilities, that are in striking contrast to the experience of those growing up half a century later. This may help to account, not just for the telling, but also for the appeal of these stories. However, it is in the nature of this literature, in its particularity, its detailed narrative mode, its focus on the everyday, that such a message remains implicit and under-analysed: these are exercises in personal memoir and nostalgia, rather than social analysis.[16] Because of the emphasis on the experience of the ordinary citizen and child, and

---

[11] Geoff Eley, 'Finding the People's War: Film, British Collective Memory and World War II', *American Historical Review*, 106 (2001), 818–38.

[12] The literature is extensive; some examples include: Pam Schweitzer, *Goodnight Children Everywhere: Memories of Evacuation in World War II* (Age Exchange, 1990); Kate David, *A Child's War: World War II through the Eyes of Children* (Peterborough, 1989); David Childs and Janet Whorton (eds), *Children in War: Reminiscences of the Second World War* (Nottingham, 1989); Susan Goodman, *Children of War: The Second World War through the Eyes of Generation* (London, 2005).

[13] For insight on this phenomenon in relation to the Anzac veteran of WWI: A. Thomson, *Anzac Memories: Living with the Legend* (Melbourne, 1994).

[14] The history of this popular literature awaits more attention. One early work on childhood during the Blitz notes the influence of a new popular history from below of the First World War, the upbeat tone compared to George Coppard's *With a Machine Gunner to Cambrai* (London, 1969): Colin Perry, *Boy in the Blitz* (London, 1972). For reflections on the popularization of history in late-twentieth-century Britain: Peter Mandler, *History and National Life* (London, 2002).

[15] Lucy Noakes, 'Making Histories: Experiencing the Blitz in London's Museums in the 1990s', in Evans and Lunn (eds), *War and Memory*, 89–104.

[16] For a valuable academic and analytical approach to this narrative of children's wartime contribution to the war effort, and one which demonstrates a potential of the child for independence: Berry Mayall and Virginia Morrow, *English Children's Work during the Second World War* (London, 2011).

the narrative of coping, un-fussily, in the face of adversity—the story of 'Britain can take it'—the genre of writing sits happily within the frameworks of the People's War and the good war.

The analysis that follows presents a less comfortable story of the British child and the Second World War. It argues that the figure of the child provided a focus for an anxiety about human nature, a story of suffering, and a feeling of loss that emerged out of war.[17] In particular, it highlights evidence and contemporary anxiety regarding the personal damage resulting from the war. This is evident in views regarding the evacuee, but also the child of the Blitz, children in care, and the children of wartime Europe. What we also see, however, is a tendency for such feelings about damage and danger to be extended from children in particular states of danger and deprivation to all children who had experienced war. And although the dominant message of popular child psychology was one that emphasized the importance of home and family as a haven, this also carried within it other less comfortable messages about the internal anger of separated children, about the darker side of childhood fantasy, and about the gulf between child and adult understanding of the world. The war-born anxieties were one of the reasons for the vigour of attempts at reintegration of the child within the home; but the damage to children and families who had been through war meant that such a vision of home would be difficult to realize. The resulting tensions, played out eventually as the children of war and of post-war security reached maturity and began to react against the war-born culture of protection, offer an example of the way in which we might begin to rethink some of our comfortable assumptions about the good war and its post-war legacy.[18]

EVACUEES

The history of British children in the Second World War is dominated by the story of evacuation. Pre-war concern about the potentially devastating effect of aerial bombardment led to an extraordinary effort to move vulnerable people out of

---

[17] This is also the subject of recent work on psychoanalytic study of anxiety in the war: Michal Shapira, 'The Psychological Study of Anxiety in the Era of the Second World War', *Twentieth Century British History*, 24 (2013), 31–57. Richard Overy has also argued that psychoanalysis was at the heart of an increasingly morbid view of human nature in the lead-up to war: *The Morbid Age: Britain between the Wars* (London, 2009). For a more positive view of the way in which wartime psychoanalysis could be turned towards the construction of a social democratic subjectivity: Thomson, *Psychological Subjects*, Chapter 7, 'Psychology and the Mid-Century Crisis', and Chapter 3 of this book.

[18] It speaks to Eley's suggestion that there is a more troubling social history of 'family secrets' that needs to be uncovered to disrupt the narrative of the good war: 'Finding the People's War: Film, British Collective Memory and World War II', *American Historical Review*, 106 (2001), 818–38. Significantly, several of his examples relate to the figure of the child as being a symbol of damage as well as hope. A key example is the Alexander Mackendrick film *Mandy* (1952). Here, he is influenced by Annette Kuhn's *Family Secrets: Acts of Memory and Imagination* (London, 1995). See also Jay Winter, 'Film and the Matrix of Memory', *American Historical Review*, 106 (2001), 104–24; and Pierre Sorlin, 'Children as Victims in Postwar European Cinema', in Jay Winter and E. Sivan (eds), *War and Remembrance in the Twentieth Century* (London, 1999), pp. 104–24. For a recent example of the turn to a darker history of the British wartime home front: Amy Bell, 'Landscapes of Fear: Wartime London, 1939–1945', *Journal of British Studies*, 48 (2009), 153–75.

major cities, and in particular out of London. The process began on 1 September 1939, two days before the outbreak of war. In the first phase, around 1.5 million were evacuated, over half of them unaccompanied school children. A second wave of evacuation came in response to the fall of France in the summer of 1940 and the onset of the Blitz. A smaller wave came late in the war, in response to rocket attacks on London in 1944. In addition to the official schemes, evacuation also took place independently and on ad hoc basis. In total, over 3.5 million people were evacuated over the course of the war, the vast majority children.[19]

The literature recounting this story is extensive, some of it academic, but now even more of it popular history written by those involved at the time or drawing directly on their memories. The earlier literature concentrated on the implications of evacuation for social policy. The recent literature has turned in particular towards the evacuee experience. Much of this work on experience continues to conform to the good war narrative: stories of new excitements, new discoveries, and new freedoms. However, evacuation has also been an issue that has exposed a fault-line in the good-war narrative. This has been encouraged by a revisionist academic literature on the relationship between evacuation and class relations, which emphasizes the difficulties in integrating urban working-class children into middle-class homes in the country, the prevalence of negative imagery around the evacuee, as well as a tendency to cast the health problems encountered amongst these children as signs of a broader social pathology.[20] But drawing on personal testimony, some, like Martin Parsons, have gone further to look at this uncomfortable encounter from the perspective of the evacuee and to cast it in the later twentieth-century language of the 'trauma of separation, insecurity, abuse in all its forms'.[21] Like many other such traumatic experiences, suggest Parsons and Penny Starns in their account of the 'true story' of evacuation, this had remained hidden for a long time and was only now finding a voice as the evacuees retired and reflected back.[22] James Roffey, founder and General Secretary of the Evacuees Reunion Association, thanked Parsons for drawing attention to a problem until then overlooked and for helping surviving evacuees to understand something long repressed: 'many of these former evacuees try to avoid speaking or even thinking about this crucial part of their lives. Most cannot help doing so without finding long repressed emotions welling up inside them, emotions that have affected them throughout their adult lives and which will never go away'.[23]

Clearly, the emergence of this perspective must be seen within the context of a late-twentieth-century explosion of interest more generally in emotional well-being, trauma, and abuse.[24] However, a similar sort of perspective did in fact surface three

---

[19] For an authoritative account of evacuation that captures the variety of experience: John Welshman, *Churchill's Children: The Evacuee Experience in Wartime Britain* (Oxford, 2010).

[20] John Macnicol, 'The Effect of Evacuation of School Children on Attitudes to State Intervention', in H. Smith (ed.), *War and Social Change* (Manchester, 1988), pp. 3–31.

[21] Martin L. Parsons, *'I'll Take That One': Dispelling the Myths of Civilian Evacuation, 1939–45* (Peterborough, 1998), p. 249.

[22] Martin Parsons and Penny Starns, *The Evacuation: The True Story* (Peterborough, 1999), p. 196.

[23] Parsons, *'I'll Take That One'*, pp. 12–13.

[24] Frank Furedi, *Therapy Culture: Cultivating Vulnerability in an Uncertain Age* (London, 2004).

decades earlier in one of the most interesting studies of evacuation, largely lost sight of among historians perhaps because of its literary form. Published in 1968, *The Evacuees* was an edited collection of first-person narratives, but its driving force was the radical literary modernist B. S. Johnson, whose work on *Street Children*, published four years earlier, had already signalled his interest in experimenting with form in exploring the perspective of the child.[25] Though the experience of the individual contributors was varied, some recalling aspects of evacuation with fondness and as offering new freedoms, Johnson's editorial line highlighted both a troubling tension between child and adult perspectives and a resulting anger towards the older generation—those who 'ordered our saving and suffering'—for instituting a policy, albeit with good intent, that wrought deep psychological damage in the children concerned.[26] Evacuation was doubly difficult. Not only were the children deposited in an alien world and separated from their families, but they later faced the perhaps even greater, but less well-recognized, challenge of having to readjust to what was a changed home on their return:

> For many of the children the return was evacuation all over again. They came back to a mother whom they probably remembered, but she was sleeping with a stranger who insisted he was their father. In some cases they came from a comfortable middle-class home to a crowded flat in slum or near-slum conditions; from friends, again to an alien society where they had to make friends all over again; from a situation in which they had perhaps been neglected, but had learnt independence, to one in which they were petted, fondled, embraced with a devotion perhaps guiltily over-compensating for the deprivations of the earlier years.[27]

As an evacuee, Johnson had been particularly distressed when his own mother had returned home without him after the first stage of evacuation. Was she deserting him? Almost certainly not: she was surely doing it for his benefit. But did she realize his worry about what would happen to her if she was returning to the danger?[28] For Johnson, the psychological damage caused by evacuation was more serious than that of the Blitz. More startling is his claim that it could be worse than that experienced by children in occupied Europe.[29] Evacuation may have saved lives, but it should never have been allowed. Its full after-effects for the millions who had been involved and upon a generation still to come to power were yet to become apparent.[30]

Johnson's remarks offer an intriguing insight into the way in which the war could be a source of intergenerational conflict. In particular, it suggests a link between feelings of wartime childhood emotional damage and some of the anger of the

---

[25] B. S. Johnson (ed.), *The Evacuees* (London, 1968). His work on street children is discussed in Chapter 1. Johnson's thinking about evacuation also gained publicity through a 1968 BBC television documentary on the subject as well as radio discussion: BBC WAC, 'When the Children Had to Go', on *Woman's Hour*, 31 October 1968. The television documentary was broadcast as part of the programme *Release*: Jonathan Coe, *Like a Fiery Elephant: A Life of B. S. Johnson* (London, 2004), pp. 259–60.

[26] Johnson, *The Evacuees*, p. 20. Nick Hubble has suggested that Johnson was alone in his negative view of evacuation: '"An Evacuee For Ever": B.S. Johnson versus Ego Psychology', in Philip Tew and Glynn White (eds), *Re-Reading B. S. Johnson* (London, 2007), p. 144. The analysis that follows indicates a more widespread ambivalence among his evacuee memoirists.

[27] Johnson, *The Evacuees*, p. 17.   [28] Johnson, *The Evacuees*, pp. 149–59.

[29] Johnson, *The Evacuees*, p. 18.   [30] Johnson, *The Evacuees*, pp. 19–20.

'angry young men' of the post-war era, particularly by the 1960s when the children of the war were coming to maturity. Written by figures on the cusp of careers, mainly in the arts, Johnson's collection of retrospective evacuee memoir and reflection raises far more challenging questions about the problems of memory and the child's perspective in mapping the effects of evacuation than does the later literature on the ordinary evacuee experience. It is particularly significant for the fact that it offers an insight into a period that was largely silent on the difficult events of war. Very little else was published between the more psychological and policy-orientated efforts of wartime itself and the popular publishing phenomenon towards the end of the century. Clearly, the fact that the book partly reflects the feelings of the period from which the memoirists looked back must modify the way that we interpret its findings about the children of 1939–45 themselves. It reflects a growing sense in the late 1960s that children should have a voice and that child and adult interests and perspectives could be in conflict, and this is projected back into the handling of memory. However, it also indicates the potential importance of the war experience as a trigger to such thinking. Moreover, the book's effort to think critically about the problems of reconstructing the child's view are so unique in the literature on evacuation, and the use of imaginative life writing in some ways so much more probing and uncomfortable than conventional biographical and oral history narrative, that Johnson and his fellow memoirists' views of how children experienced and understood evacuation at the time merit more attention than they have received to date.

The *Evacuee* memoirists were now in the age-range of 30–45. Most had been children, though a few were young adults in the war, for instance in the capacity of teachers evacuated with the children. Invariably, they adopted a strikingly disjointed style of writing to evoke both the gaps of memory and the confusion of the child's mind. War itself was represented as being largely hidden from view; beyond the physical horizon of the countryside, but also beyond the landscape of child comprehension. Yet the memoirists recalled the challenge nevertheless of having to negotiate the adult meanings of war, not the least because of their own involvement in what people were calling 'evacuation'. As former footballer and England captain Johnny Haynes put it: 'To a five-year-old, it was an alien word which belonged to the strange and mysterious world of the adult vocabulary: Evacuation. It was one of those words which I had already learned to be wary of, words that ended with "shun", like immunization and conscription and mobilization.'[31]

Born in 1934, Jonathan Miller is now one of the best known of Johnson's evacuees.[32] Given that his father was one of the leading child psychologists of the period and a pioneer in establishing child guidance practice before the war, and that Miller went on to study medicine at Cambridge and to become a leading cultural commentator on the history of mind, it is unsurprising to find him reflecting back highly conscious of the psychologically stressful nature of evacuation, the unconscious wounds that could be carried into later life, and the need to appreciate the child's own perception of the situation. Like many such middle-class children, he was not an official evacuee, but he still shared much of the evacuee experience,

---

[31] *The Evacuees*, p. 135.   [32] *The Evacuees*, pp. 199–204.

leaving London and travelling around the countryside with his family as his father, Emanuel, was posted to a series of hospitals. 'Existence seemed quite provisional', he recalled, 'and although I never knew any real danger or discomfort the restless inconstancy of those four nomad years have left traces which can never be rubbed out.'[33] Miller was not separated from his family, but he recalls that even the prospect of separation through a train journey provoked horror.[34] Like other contributors, his account evokes a picture of wartime mobilization as incredibly confusing for the child, exacerbated by an atmosphere of secrecy that was epitomized by the removal of names from train stations as Miller and his family arrived at yet another strange temporary home. However, as an example of the older child's experience, his story is also one of growing understanding of this broader world. This includes an appreciation of the 'real evacuees', who took on a tragic role in his imagination. Knowing nothing about the violence of war, they came to represent 'the absolute of misfortune and loss'. Yet, stronger and more aggressive than middle-class children like Miller, they also seemed dangerous; 'despite their pallor and weakness and their grief. Possibly because of it.' Approaching puberty by the end of the war, Miller's account is one of dawning adolescent comprehension, and of a move beyond the limited, personal horizon of childhood: 'The social landscape stretched out to the horizon on either side and I knew perfectly well by then where I was both in space and time.'[35] As we will see in the final chapter of this book, this growing recognition of how older children made sense of their landscape in social and even social scientific ways was one of the important developments in understanding of the landscape of the child in the later part of the period.

Miller had not experienced the separation from family that was often at the heart of the evacuee experience. For those who did, the return home was in fact invariably recalled as at least as difficult as the initial separation. The future television presenter Michael Aspel, born in 1933, found the landscape of home fundamentally changed: diminished physically but also emotionally; everything seeming much smaller, and war turning his mother into a nervous wreck. His brother Alan, just four when he left and nine on his return, did not even remember 'home' and took years to adjust.[36]

With powerful imagery, focusing in particular on the symbolic objects of the identifying label around the evacuee's neck and the gas mask, cartoonist Mel Calman, born in 1931, offered a still raw picture of abandonment and of the alienation and sense of lost identity that resulted from being thrown into the midst of this huge bureaucratic machine of evacuation:

> I have this image of a small boy with a label tied round his neck. The boy has no features and is crying. He is carrying a cardboard box, which contains his gasmask.... I remember that labels with names on were pinned to our clothes before we left London. I think I felt that I had no identity and was a parcel being posted to the country. The labels frightened me as much as the idea of leaving my parents. A child of seven, if lost, can tell people his name. A label assumes that he does not know his

[33] *The Evacuees*, p. 199.   [34] *The Evacuees*, p. 202.
[35] *The Evacuees*, p. 203.   [36] *The Evacuees*, p. 33.

name, or worse, has no name and is given one at random from a list of names.... Perhaps the gasmask felt like a second face, a mask that would replace my own face as soon as I left London. I remember that the gasmask looked inhuman with its celluloid eyeshield and metal snout. I remember that it smelt like rubber and that I could not breathe properly inside it.[37]

Calman's evacuee, torn from a social landscape and cut adrift, is a pitiable figure, and one whose gut feelings would prove impossible to leave behind. 'Even nowadays whenever I travel anywhere and have to say goodbye to my own children', admitted Calman, 'I identify with that small boy. I remember the label and the gasmask and feel anxiety gripping my bowels. I write my name on the luggage labels and hope I do not return to find my home bombed to ruins and my identity lost somewhere underneath the rubble.' These ongoing feelings would be played out in the figure of the vulnerable 'little man' of Calman's cartoons and in the depression that dogged his later life.[38]

Leslie Dunkling, born in 1935, recalled his evacuee experience as a 'mental minefield', and one that he still disliked thinking about.[39] He noted a painful disjuncture between this personal feeling and the fact that society seemed to speak only in positive terms about evacuation; indeed, he could not 'remember hearing a single unhappy story.' Again Dunkling was pointing to a forgotten tension between the child, who experienced the confusion and hurt, and the adults, who, relieved of responsibility and confronted by the excitements of war, often lived more than ever before and who therefore tended to plant a very different picture in public memory. As Dunkling saw it, this was a longer term tension based on separation that the war was now extending across the class spectrum: the well-to-do having 'evacuated' children for years via nannies and boarding schools. 'Suddenly, in 1939, it was the working-class mothers who were offered temporary freedom, the very mothers who had seen years of unrelieved slavery stretching before them.' And this was made possible because they could convince themselves it was in the interests of the child. Separation, as such, was reflected back upon as something that was not simply a case of unfortunate wartime circumstances, but which also related to some far more fundamental tensions when it came to the interests of children and adults, and to a problem of feelings of neglect and physical but also emotional 'evacuation' that existed in peace as well as war.

This tension was exacerbated by the adult view of the child mind. It was difficult for adults to appreciate that even though children might not appear to understand or even know about the public war, they could still be deeply affected by their experience. Poet Barry Cole, born in 1936, could only remember war through a series of disjointed snapshots, but he emphasized the emotional intensity of these images. Children, he reflected, had lived in the moment. The broader landscape of the war was largely beyond comprehension, and so it was understood in terms of the half-grasped feelings of surrounding adults, and it was translated or mapped onto events and things that had a more concrete presence within the landscape of

---

[37] *The Evacuees*, p. 35.   [38] *The Evacuees*, p. 36.
[39] Dunkling was a lecturer at Leicester College of Education: *The Evacuees*, pp. 73–8.

the child: the enemy, for instance, finding representation in Cole's childhood fears of an unpleasant local gamekeeper. What this meant, however, was that children could still experience the intense emotions of war, even if this was through the projection of its fears and hates onto unsuspecting figures. This was difficult for adults to understand. Moreover, evacuation turned from snapshot and experience in the moment to meaning, via the contrast to home and the adult narrative of home: evacuation generally had to be bad in the end, because home was good, even if in fact this was the adult's as much the child's story.[40]

The gap in understanding between what adults thought children were experiencing and what they in fact saw and felt was a common theme. And this helped to explain why the evacuee voice itself had struggled to assert itself until now. The problem was that the sheer intensity of child experience, but also the emotional difficulty in the memories, inhibited the sort of recollection that would make sense in terms of the adult world of public record. As another memoirist recalled:

> There aren't any dates as far as I'm concerned. I have attempted at various times of more than average courage to sit down and try to arrange events into some chronological order. I have failed. The important point is that there was no chronological order to me as to many children during a childhood others called 'the war'. I have failed because this particular exercise in discipline is one which might disturb too many impressions. There are too many frightening combinations, unpleasant possibilities and unexplained emotional responses. I need to fail. There's a safety in the knowledge that I don't know.[41]

John Furse, a painter born in 1932, recalled his confusion about the place of his return home in the grown-up story of victory:

> It's not the going, the being taken away, the leaving London that I remember most, it's the coming back. I was brought back, I suppose, to make sure I tasted the fruits of victory, brought back but not home. They took me from my home and brought me back to a strange city I knew nothing about and I felt out of place.[42]

This could foster bitterness and even anger that lingered into the post-war era. Children had been drawn into the war emotionally, but to provide an object for playing out of adult anxieties. The meaning of the war for the children themselves had been overlooked, and this was now at the root of the bitterness within the evacuee generation. The adults, reflected one of the memoirists:

> just didn't understand why we felt like we did, and they still don't. They didn't understand it was their war and not ours... That's the whole point about evacuation, they got us involved in something we knew nothing about, a game we weren't ready for. We played but were too young to fight and we didn't know what they were fighting for—we thought they just wanted to win. The fighting stopped and the game went on and they didn't tell us the new set of rules. I'm glad they won but I'd like to know where we were wrong.... I'd like to know why they brought me back when I wanted

---

[40] *The Evacuees*, pp. 45–9   [41] *The Evacuees*, p. 80.   [42] *The Evacuees*, p. 105.

to go on fighting—brought me back safely I suppose. That's the whole point of being an evacuee. You're hidden away and saved, that's what to evacuate means—'to withdraw'. I wonder what they saved me for.[43]

In other words, evacuees may have half-grasped that they were expected to belong in some kind of grander landscape of a war that was more than a war, a war that in some way had something to do with saving them, but evacuation was recalled as a process of 'withdrawal', damage, and loss, feelings that could run alongside many more positive memories of the experience but which were not as readily dissolved by the return home and the building of a better future (the war that was more than a war) as the heroic narratives of the good war might suggest.

WARTIME CHILD PSYCHOLOGY

The Evacuees provides us with an indication of a growing interest in the child's perspective by the end of the 1960s, an issue with radical implications which will be considered at some length in the final chapter of this book. It also, however, suggests that the experience of evacuation was perhaps particularly suited to bringing such thinking to the fore. This section of the chapter will explore the extent to which wartime child psychology had already paved the way in this regard, and if so how this interest in the landscape *of* the child (the way the child saw the world) affected recommendations on how best to forge a landscape *for* the child in the post-war era. It will focus on two of the most important reports on the psychological effects of evacuation. Firstly, it will turn to a study of evacuation from London to Cambridge in the first stages of the war, which was headed by the child psychologist Susan Isaacs. Secondly, by way of contrast, it will turn to a study from later in the war, undertaken by Sigmund Freud's daughter, psychoanalyst Anna Freud, and American psychoanalyst Dorothy Burlingham. This second study was able to build upon the experience of the earlier phase of evacuation and could also take into account how children had responded to the bombing of a city such as London. The analysis will conclude by turning to post-war radio broadcasts that centred on the return home of the evacuated children.

Susan Isaacs' *Cambridge Evacuation Survey* was primarily concerned with evaluating evacuation as a social policy. It looked to the immediate challenges of protecting these children and of maintaining wartime morale. It also had a clear eye on the lessons that might be learnt when it came to planning social services in peacetime. With regard to the latter, it is important to recognize that although evacuation did function as a kind of laboratory for studying the effects of separation, it did not present a wholly new set of problems; even before the war substantial numbers of children were 'boarded out' with private families, and there was a clear consciousness that lessons needed to be learnt in continuing to address this challenge.[44] Of course,

---

[43] *The Evacuees*, p. 114.
[44] Susan Isaacs (ed.), *Cambridge Evacuation Survey: A Wartime Study in Social Welfare and Education*, with cooperation of Sibyl Clement Brown and Robert H. Thouless (Methuen: London, 1941), p. 13.

the type of children boarded out in war was rather different than in peacetime, but the experience could throw valuable further light on the challenges of separating children from families and might also uncover individuals who had a capacity for mothering (as potential foster parents) which could be useful in the longer term for children currently in institutions.[45] The report was highly critical of the preparations for evacuation: the overemphasis on logistics, the inadequate consideration of human arrangements, and the failure to utilize psychological expertise in considering the likely psychological implications of the policy.[46] It was written in part in response to the return home of a high proportion of these initial evacuees, regarded in itself as a sign of the failure of the policy. And it noted the misgivings and distress of those involved on either side, which lay behind this drift back: 'The town was ill at ease in the country. The country was shocked at the manners and morals of the town.'[47] On the other hand, it did not offer a wholly negative picture. It acknowledged, for instance, that 'from every quarter, also, there came stories of new health, newly discovered pleasures among those dispersed, of generous care and devotion among foster families'. Evacuation was not yet seen as inevitably damaging, as would be the norm by the end of the war. Instead, Isaacs and her colleagues looked to improve the policy by better use of expertise, selection of the right billets, and proper management. Study of children who had returned home suggested that this was not so much the result of the child's psychological distress as of the fact that the parents were missing them and anxious, or simply that the billets had been inappropriate.[48]

As well as downplaying the distress of the children at separation (and emphasizing that of adults instead), the Cambridge survey offers us intriguing insight into the children's views about their surrounding physical landscape. This was captured in essays in which they were asked to write on the theme 'what I like in Cambridge/ what I miss in Cambridge'. Rather than necessarily welcoming the space of the countryside, they often emphasized how much they missed the freedoms and facilities of the city, especially its parks and playgrounds.[49] Turning conceptions of city traffic on their head, they saw the Cambridge roads—busier and narrower—as more dangerous, and more restrictive of freedom.[50] The report observed that because the children had arrived in Cambridge in summertime it had not seemed necessary to worry about 'recreation'. But as winter set in, and it became too cold to swim in the river, the streets dark and silent, it became clear that there was a need to organize leisure to keep the evacuees occupied. However, Cambridge itself had no such tradition. The very concept of 'recreation', the report suggested, was something that only really applied to city dwellers, children included.[51] In short, taking into account the child's view led to an appreciation of the importance not just of home—indeed, here the evidence was mixed on the feelings about separation—but of the way children

---

[45] *Cambridge Evacuation Survey*, p. 14.   [46] *Cambridge Evacuation Survey*, pp. 4, 11.
[47] *Cambridge Evacuation Survey*, p. 2.   [48] *Cambridge Evacuation Survey*, p. 132.
[49] A similar point in relation to evacuated slum children struggling to adjust to the lack of freedom away from the town was made by Edna Henshaw, 'Some Psychological Problems of Evacuation', *Mental Health*, 1:1 (1940), 8.
[50] *Cambridge Evacuation Survey*, pp. 63–87.   [51] *Cambridge Evacuation Survey*, p. 156.

experienced a separation from the broader urban landscape that surrounded home, and not just its greater freedoms and opportunities but also its sites equipped and designed with the child at least partly in mind.[52]

Anna Freud and Dorothy Burlingham's research focused on a later stage of the war, from December 1940 to February 1942, and was based on the children they had encountered in their nurseries in Hampstead, North London. The timing and location meant that many of the children had direct experience of air raids and bombing, an issue that was not a factor in the Cambridge study of first-wave evacuees. By this stage of the war, there was also a stronger consciousness of the damage that could result from evacuation (damage now seen as normal, not just something that would be experienced by the neurotic child). However, the evidence was also beginning to suggest that children were remarkably resilient in the face of air raids, able to translate the danger in the 'long accepted way of the traditional fairy story', via imaginative games and drawings, to limit anxiety: 'the shelter is the den or the magic carpet, the gas mask is the magic wand or ring which gives security over overwhelming odds. Hitler is a bogey, like the giant or the dragon.'[53] Or as Mass-Observation put it, suggesting a broader provenance of such thinking: 'Hitler is an evil vision: no ice cream is a horrid fact.' As a consequence, parents were being advised not to be too concerned by the fact that their children were so swept up by games of commandoes, bombing raids, and concentration camps; in doing so, they were simply externalizing and playing out their inner doubts and fears.[54] Indeed, adults would tease children with Hitler hiding on the local common or targeting them personally if they had been naughty.[55]

There is indeed plenty of contemporary and retrospective evidence to support the view that children were surprisingly psychologically robust when left alongside their families in Britain's bombed cities. 'What's the use of worrying? That's what I say. People who worry, especially kids like us, who have got to grow up strong, are fighting Hitler's battle for him.'[56] These were the opening lines of the novel *Blitz Kids*, written by Elinor Mordaunt in 1941. Accompanied by light-hearted illustrations, it told the upbeat story of a working-class family of children getting on without their mother and despite their drunken father, undeterred by bombing and the destruction of their home, and resisting evacuation. Over half a century

---

[52] For similar recognition of the psychological difficulties in adjusting to the loss of an urban landscape: Henshaw, 'Some Psychological Problems of Evacuation', 5–10. And on the increase of neurotic symptoms and delinquency following evacuation evident in Cyril Burt's research: *Mental Health*, 1:3 (1940), 88.

[53] On the shift to seeing evacuation as bad for all: Edna Henshaw, 'Observed Effects of Wartime Conditions on Children', *Mental Health*, 2:4 (1941), 97, 93–102. The view on air raids is apparent in coverage of the issue in *Mental Health* by early 1941, for instance: Priscilla Norman, 'Some Preliminary Notes on Mental Health Work for Air Raid Victims', *Mental Health*, 2:1 (1941), 1–7; Doris Odlum, 'Some Wartime Problems of Mental Health', *Mental Health*, 2:2 (1941), 33–7. For a more sober view, acknowledging possible longer term problems: H. E. Howarth, 'Impressions of Children in a Heavily Bombed Area', *Mental Health*, 2:4 (1941), 98–101.

[54] Mass-Observation, 'What Children Think about the War', *Nursery World* (16 September 1943); Mass-Observation, File Reports 1910 and 1662.

[55] David Thomson, *Try to Tell the Story* (New York, 2009), pp. 3–9.

[56] Elinor Mordaunt, *Blitz Kids* (London, 1941), p. 7.

later, film director John Boorman, born in 1933, recalled a more middle-class, suburban, wartime childhood that had formed the basis for his film *Hope and Glory* and its equally upbeat view: 'How wonderful was the war!…We kids rampaged through the ruins, the semis opened up like dolls' houses, the precious privacy shamefully exposed.'[57] In accounts from the time and in the literature of post-war recollection it is hard in fact to find many dissenting voices. In his retrospective review of Mass-Observation's wartime work, Tom Harrisson noted the relative lack of information regarding the response of children to the Blitz, as opposed to that of adults (or of adults' views of the child). In part, he attributed this to their absence as evacuees. He suggested that of those who stayed, some were excited, some nervous, but on the whole they coped as well or perhaps slightly better than their parents.[58] This is a more downbeat summary than is often the case. As already noted, the psychologists recognized that the attractions of war for the child had its darker side, but they too tended to agree that children could generally cope as long as they had the security of a family.[59] Likewise, recent retrospective analysis undertaken by epidemiological psychiatrists appears to confirm the contemporary view that the war was notable for the low level of psychological breakdown among the civilian population, even if it pays no specific attention to the impact on children.[60]

The coming together of concern over the damaging effect of separation through evacuation and of air raids for those left behind provided the rationale for nurseries, like Freud and Burlingham's, designed to offer day and residential care within easy reach of mothers. Again, what is striking about these efforts, and tends to be somewhat hidden in a historiography that emphasizes intervention in the name of the child, is the attempt to understand and take into consideration the child's view. And here one does see a significantly darker picture than the 'Blitz kids' image that has come to illustrate our narratives of the good war. In particular, such research casts light on the ways in which close proximity to bombing and its destruction brought the violence of war into the heart and internal psychological dynamics of the landscape of the child. Research on these children revealed their interest in planes, bombs, and anti-aircraft guns. Children realized that houses were flattened by bombs and that people were killed. And they recognized the absence of their fathers as soldiers. They understood this, and by and large could cope with it. What confused them—echoing the later memoir material in the Johnson volume (even if the London children had a strikingly stronger grasp of the public landscape of war than the evacuees to the countryside)—was why they did not stay behind in

[57] John Boorman, *Adventures of a Suburban Boy* (London, 2003), p. 19.

[58] Tom Harrrisson, *Living through the Blitz* (London, 1976), pp. 321–2.

[59] However, it was recognized that a small number of children were seriously affected by the air raids and in particular by prolonged periods of blitz. Of more concern was the unknown long-term affect: H. E. Howarth, 'Impressions of Children in a Heavily Bombed Area', *Mental Health*, 2 (1941), 98–101; Doris Odlum, 'Some Wartime Problems of Mental Health', *Mental Health*, 2 (1941), 33–7.

[60] Edgar Jones, Robin Woolven, Bill Durodié, and Simon Wessley, 'Civilian Morale during the Second World War: Responses to the Air Raids Re-Examined', *Social History of Medicine*, 17 (2004), 463. See also Emmy E. Werner, *Children Witness World War II* (Oxford, 2000), pp. 211–19, which supports the idea that the level of adult upset rather than the child's experience was a more likely determinant of the emotional damage to the child in the war and later life.

London with their mothers, having been there during the worst stage of the Blitz. If it was unsafe for them, what did this mean for their mothers? There was no sign that children exhibited traumatic shock, even in the worst of the Blitz, if accompanied by their mothers or a mother substitute and assuming that those around them remained calm. Indeed, instead of turning away from destruction in horror, young children were excited. However, in the psychologists' view, this did not make the situation benign. The fact that children could cope did not mean that they went undamaged. Children needed to be guided to restrict and then repress natural aggressive impulses. Instead, they found confirmation of these impulses in the outside world. The playground of the bombsite was therefore a mixed blessing: 'Children will play joyfully on bombed sites and around bomb craters with blasted bits of furniture, and throw bricks from crumbled walls at each other. But it becomes impossible to educate them towards a repression of or a reaction towards a repression against destruction while they are doing so.'[61] It was very hard for children to fight their own death wishes while people were being killed all around them. Young children had to be safeguarded from war, not because it was strange and horrific for them, but because it was so close to the 'primitive and atrocious wishes of their own infantile nature'.[62] Older children who understood war were no better off as the bombing provoked intense anxiety about their maturing efforts to repress and control destructive instincts.[63]

One might think that this pointed to the psychological need to evacuate children from such an environment. Here, there was something of a quandary for Freud and Burlingham. For they also now recognized, far more acutely than had been the case in the first stage of the war, the psychological damage that could result from separation of the child from the family. Yet clearly, and particularly in light of their own observations about the psychic world of the child of the Blitz, it was an unfortunate fact of wartime that some form of evacuation could be a necessity. They arrived at the conclusion that it was not simply separation but the form of separation that was the problem. Therefore psychological expertise, and an appreciation of the child's perspective, as with the earlier Cambridge study, opened the possibility of a less extreme position on separation than often assumed. The abruptness of the initial mass evacuation had been particularly damaging. Children needed to be eased into the situation, with visits from the mother. This might be traumatic, but it was far better than the alternative of the situation of the 'artificial war orphan'.[64] Here, their diagnosis was damning. The very young child might appear to be coping with separation, the grief apparently short-lived, but the absence of the love object in the present was most devastating at an age when projecting into the future was impossible. Reactions included a refusal to eat and to be handled, clinging to a toy as a substitute, 'withdrawal' (that term which resonated in the memories of Johnson's *Evacuees*) into a dazed state or illness, and a refusal to

---

[61] Dorothy Burlingham and Anna Freud, *Young Children in War-Time in a Residential Nursery* (London, 1942), p. 31.
[62] Burlingham and Freud, *Young Children*, p. 31.
[63] Burlingham and Freud, *Young Children*, pp. 34–5.
[64] Burlingham and Freud, *Young Children*, p. 79.

recognize the mother when she did appear. Beyond the age of three, children were more able to hold on to the hope of memory. But this was also a time when they were going through the conflicts of reining in their natural savagery and had to cope with severely negative thoughts directed at their parents. The guilt that arose led to an overstressing of love and made feelings of separation even more intense. The very youngest children could forget or become indifferent to their parents, shifting their focus to a new object of attention if this was available. Those beyond the age of three didn't forget but still shifted their affection and struggled to readjust. In both situations, there were likely to be serious problems of readjustment at the end of the war.

Burlingham and Freud's influential study reveals an appreciation of the confusion and damage recalled by Johnson and his fellow memoirists. It offers us in fact a strikingly bleak picture of the British child of the Second World War, and of the difficulties that would have to be overcome in healing psychological wounds, much more so than Isaacs' study at the start of the war. It is a view of the war that again highlights its darker side and the way that this would leave its mark on the post-war family. And it is a view in which efforts to understand the way the child saw the world, in fact but also unconscious fantasy, were central. It was this that made anxieties about the child, concern about separation, and expectations of the role of family relationships and home environment as a salve all so powerful towards the end of the war. What this tended to overlook was the fact that such investigation had also made it clear that children in fact thrived in the danger, missed the broader freedoms of the city, often resented home, and might not so readily readjust to the sanctuary that the new psychological common sense was suggesting should be their proper place.

In terms of a popular audience, Donald Winnicott was one of the most influential psychological voices of the war, but also crucially its aftermath. Winnicott spread his message through a famous series of BBC Radio broadcasts, the subsequent publication of these talks in magazines and paperbacks, and the use of his clear prose in the training of a post-war generation of social workers and teachers. Broadcast from 1944, the radio talks in fact focused far more on the problems of reintegrating the child within the family than on evacuation itself.[65] However, they now assumed a general understanding that evacuation had been a huge mistake from the perspective of the child's well-being: 'There are some curious people—optimists, I suppose—who heralded evacuation as something that would bring new life to the poor children of the cities. They could not see evacuation as a great tragedy...it could never be a good thing to take children away from their ordinary decent homes.'[66] Although this view overestimates the weight of evidence and assumes too readily the universality of the experience, it is nevertheless important

---

[65] These talks are collected together in two volumes: D. W. Winnicott, *The Child and the Outside World* (London, 1957); *The Child and the Family* (London, 1957). The volumes contain a single earlier talk from 1939 on 'The Deprived Mother'. The others come mainly from 1944–6 and 1949–51.

[66] D. W. Winnicott, 'Home Again' (Broadcast on the BBC in 1945), *The Child and the Outside World*, p. 94.

in heralding, and placing into such common sense and accessible language, a conclusion that seems to have been increasingly axiomatic.[67]

Winnicott did appreciate that children returned not just to home, but to the surroundings of home. In doing so, he provided his audience with a striking picture of how the urban landscape was transformed in the move from war to peace:

> Here are the children home again, filling our ears with sounds that had long been almost dead. People had forgotten that children are noisy creators, but now they are being reminded. Schools are reopening. Parks are spreading themselves for the reception of their old customers: mothers and prams, and children of all sizes, shapes and colours. Back streets have become cricket pitches, with the children generally adapting themselves to town traffic. Round the street corners come bands of Nazis or other kinds of gangsters, complete with guns improvised out of sticks, hunters and hunted alike oblivious of the passers-by. Chalk marks reappear on pavements, to let little girls know where to hop, and when the weather is good, and there is nothing else afoot, boys and girls can be seen standing on their heads or on their outstretched arms, with their feet up against the wall.[68]

But, as Winnicott saw it, this space had to be an extension of the psychic security of home, opened up by having a bath, a bed, and a kiss to run back to. Ultimately, the landscape of home provided all that the child needed. Out of the seemingly little things of home, the child would find 'all that a rich imagination can weave'. Recognizing that the broader landscape of the child was a landscape of fantasy, and that this provided a terrain for playing out the central emotional dynamics of home and family, Winnicott effectively downplayed the importance of a physical and social landscape: 'The wide world is a fine place for grown-ups looking for an escape from boredom, but ordinarily children are not bored, and they have all the feelings they can stand feeling inside their own house or within a few minutes from the doorstep.'[69] For the evacuee, home had been transformed in absence into a wholly imagined and psychic space. The physical spaces of home had lived on in the memory as symbols of attachment: one room would be associated in the child's mind with mother and father, another with siblings, another with the family cat.[70] The physical landscape of this domestic space might seem limited, but it was vast and complete in responding to the child's psychic need for location, providing all the emotional moorings necessary for an essential social identity. For the child whose psychic need for security was met in loving domestic family life, the imagination offered sufficient opportunities, radically yet safely, to expand the horizons of home: 'enriching the world out of his own head'.[71]

However, analysis of this internal landscape also revealed that war presented unique challenges for such an idealized vision of home. The evacuees had had to

---

[67] Winnicott, 'Home Again', p. 94.   [68] Winnicott, 'Home Again', p. 93.

[69] Winnicott, 'Home Again', p. 94. As Lyndsey Stonebridge has argued, Winnicott's interest in space was translated into the vocabulary of the psyche: 'Bombs, Birth, and Trauma: Henry Moore's and D. W. Winnicott's Prehistory Fragments', *Cultural Critique*, 46 (2000), 91, 80–101.

[70] Winnicott, 'Home Again', p. 94. See also the analysis of home as a psycho-social space by sociologist Charles Madge, 'Private and Public Spaces', *Human Relations*, 3 (1950), 187–99.

[71] Winnicott, 'Home Again', pp. 94–5.

act, effectively, as their own strict mothers and fathers. Relieved of this burden with the return home, they would now turn to naughtiness. The parents' unconditional love would provide something to be defied and even hated as the child discovered the deepest parts of his childish nature. Though this was to be regarded as a healthy step, it would offer a difficult challenge for adults unused to tackling such problems during the war, insecure about the child's affection, and used to having life more to themselves. Parental care would need to be strong as well as loving, and not least for this reason there was a need for the return home not just of the children but also of their fathers. Winnicott acknowledged that some children would be so damaged that the parents would be unable to cope.[72]

THE BROKEN HOME

The irony was that psychologists such as Winnicott were reifying the home as a sanctuary at a time when its emotional foundations were being rocked by war.[73] This made their project of familial reconstruction all the more urgent, yet also more difficult. As Dr Alan Maberly, Director of the Provisional National Council for Mental Health put it in 1945, the problem was not just evacuation: 'it was necessary to realise that the vast majority of children in the country had lived in broken homes for nearly five years, if not longer.'[74] And looking forward, the wartime destruction of housing and the heightened importance of providing emotional security for children made the problem of the broken home seem acute.[75]

    This subject of the emotional damage left by war has in fact attracted little scholarly attention, and less so in a British context than in relation to other combatant nations in the Second World War.[76] One of the few accounts to adopt such an argument arose from a *Sunday Times* enquiry into the fiftieth anniversary of D-Day, which invited readers to write in response to the question 'What happened to you when Daddy came home?'[77] What emerged was a story of men returning home and struggling to adjust or to be accepted, and of the unhappiness that resulted. As Alan Ross had noted in his 1950 account of *The Forties*, 'For a great many, the end

---

[72] Winnicott, 'Home Again', p. 96.
[73] Sir James Marchant (ed.), *An Enquiry with Recommendations* (1945), p. 135.
[74] Discussion on 'The Maladjusted and Delinquent Child', *Mother and Child*, 15:10 (1945), 158.
[75] Leslie Housden, 'The Effect of Modern Home Conditions on the Rearing of a Family', *Mother and Child*, 19:8 (1948), 176–8.
[76] The contrast is noted in Thane, 'Family and "Normality" in Postwar British Culture' in Bessel and Schumann (eds), *Life after Death*, particularly in relation to work on post-war Germany that is covered in the rest of the volume.
[77] Barry Turner and Tony Rennell, *When Daddy Came Home: How Family Life Changed Forever in 1945* (London, 1995), p. 222. Wendy Webster gives the subject brief attention, though in part by drawing on this study, when she asserts the increasing importance of an ideal of home in response to the Second World War: Webster, *Imagining Home*, pp. 6–14. A recent publication offers us a picture based on compilation of first-hand accounts relating to returning soldiers: Alan Allport, *Demobbed: Returning Home after World War Two* (London, 2009).

of the war marked the beginning of their decline. The war had been an emotional pinnacle from which, subconsciously, they would have liked to look down from for ever.'[78] The public response confirmed that many of these returning men had struggled to readjust, experiencing not just depression but a degree of jealousy and resentment towards those who had remained at home. Those with fathers who fought in the war often recalled the return of a man who was a stranger.[79] Greater emotional expectations, in terms of both fatherhood and marriage, may not have helped. At the time, psychiatrist Tom Main drew some attention towards the psychological difficulties of returning soldiers.[80] However, consciousness never approached the widespread concern and sympathy for the troubles of the shell-shocked soldier following the First World War.[81] With civilians effectively now on the frontline, it was perhaps harder for the returning soldier to make special claims on sympathy.[82]

In the popular imagination, the Second World War has come to be seen as fostering something of a golden age for domestic stability, but there are in fact some indicators that challenge this picture. The period 1938–55 saw a rise in homosexual offences. There were widespread fears that the wartime absence of fathers was leading to an epidemic of juvenile delinquency. There was a backlog of 25,000 divorce cases by 1944. Maintenance orders to cover for marital separation rose from 10,538 in 1938/9 to 25,400 in 1945/6. And Mass-Observation reported that one in four husbands and one in five wives had experienced extra-marital sexual relations in the war.[83] We should, of course, be cautious about the meaning of such evidence, which sometimes reflected rising expectations.[84] But these expectations compounded war-born strains to store up problems for post-war family life. Research by psychiatrist Eliot Slater and psychiatric social worker Moya Woodside found that although marital breakdown in war itself had been remarkably rare, war-born neurosis was proving a factor in post-war marriage patterns. In other words, people who had been psychologically changed and damaged by the war might have been able to stand strong in the face of wartime adversity but they sometimes struggled when faced by the mounting familial expectations of the peace.[85]

---

[78] Quoted in Turner and Rennell, *When Daddy Came Home*, p. 224.

[79] Turner and Rennell, *When Daddy Came Home*, pp. 72–108, 223. See also Germaine Greer, *Daddy We Hardly Knew You* (London, 1989).

[80] T. F. Main, 'Clinical Problems of Repatriates', *Journal of Mental Science*, 93 (1947), 354–63. See also T. A Radcliffe, 'The Psychological Problems of the Returned Ex-Service Men', *Mental Health*, 7:1 (1947), 2–5.

[81] Michael Roper, 'Between Manliness and Masculinity: The "War Generation" and the Psychology of Fear in Britain, 1914–1950', *Journal of British Studies*, 44 (2005), 343–62.

[82] Turner and Rennell, *When Daddy Came Home*, pp. 56–7.

[83] Turner and Rennell, *When Daddy Came Home*, pp. 144–58.

[84] Clare Langhamer, 'Adultery in Postwar Britain', *History Workshop Journal*, 62 (2006), 86–115. Also on the rising emotional expectations in relation to fathers: Laura King, 'Hidden Fathers? The Significance of Fatherhood in Mid-Twentieth-Century Britain', *Contemporary British History*, 26:1 (2012), 25–46.

[85] Eliot Slater and Moya Woodside, *Patterns of Marriage: A Study of Marriage Relationships in the Urban Working Classes* (London, 1951), p. 219.

British psychologists did recognize the difficult situation left by war for the re-establishment of family life.[86] Because of this they did in fact recognize that there would sometimes be a need for alternatives. Even that central text on the importance of home, Freud and Burlingham's *Infants without Families*, recognized that there was still likely to be some need for residential nursery care which would supplement that of the family.[87] And as already noted, although Donald Winnicott's post-war broadcasts provided a powerful endorsement for the re-establishment of normal family life, they also acknowledged that this would take place in very difficult circumstances. In this regard, it is also important to recognize that Winnicott's key wartime work was in the development of hostels for maladjusted children, a legacy that would be taken forward in the post-war years in therapeutic communities for children whose families simply could not cope. Indeed, his evidence to the influential Curtis Committee inquiry into childcare in 1945–6 would be in support of such hostels.[88] At the same time, war-born heightened expectations about the emotional environment of home would make it difficult to find appropriate fostering situations that could replicate the family, particularly since the experience of unsuccessful billeting of evacuees had left concern about 'an impulse of hostility' among potential foster parents 'often deeply unconscious', to children who were 'not actually or emotionally their own'.[89]

Perhaps the strongest indication of the difficulties left by war, and of a public anxiety about family life that sits awkwardly alongside stereotypes of social stability, is the post-war debate over child cruelty in the home.[90] Concern was in part the result of changing expectations and of a shift of focus from physical to 'mental cruelty' that reflected increased awareness of psychology, but it also resulted from the social challenges of the wartime situation. For instance, we find the National Society for the Prevention of Cruelty to Children and the *Daily Mail* raising concern over children left alone to cope with the terror of night-time bombing, or left to find their own way to a shelter. Part of the problem was that the demands of war could mean that it was more difficult than before to ensure parental care at all times. However, the NSPCC claimed that the war had also seen real deterioration

---

[86] Susan Isaacs, 'Fatherless Children', in New Education Fellowship, *Problems of Child Development* (London, 1948), pp. 3–15. This volume also contained a series of essays exploring the difficulties in post-war family life: Joan Riviere, 'The Bereaved Wife' (16–23); Ella Freeman Sharpe, 'What the Father Means to the Child' (24–32); Frank Bodman, 'Aggressive Play' (38–43); and D. W. Winnicott and Clare Britton, 'The Problem of the Homeless Child' (65–73). The challenge of the return of the father also attracts consideration in Allport, *Demobbed*, pp. 66–74.

[87] *Infants without Families*, pp. vi, 107–8.

[88] D. W. Winnicott, 'Children's Hostels in War and Peace', in Symposium on 'Lessons for Child Psychiatry', *British Journal of Medical Psychology*, 21 (1948), 175–80; D. W. Winnicott and Clare Britton, 'Residential Management as Treatment for Difficult Children', in D. W. Winnicott, *Deprivation and Delinquency*, ed. Clare Winnicott et al. (London, 1984); Judith Issroff, *Donald Winnicott and John Bowlby: Personal and Professional Perspectives* (London, 2005), pp. 196–7.

[89] Theodora Alcock, 'Conclusions from Psychiatric Social Work with Evacuated Children', *British Journal of Medical Psychology*, 21 (1948), 181–4.

[90] Another area in which this anxiety surfaced was in public stories of child murder cases. See, for instance: 'Missing Children Dead in Wood', *The Times* (24 November 1941), a case involving the murder of two girls by a soldier.

in the standards of family life, particularly amongst the socially maladjusted, and that this lay behind a rise in prosecutions.[91] The publicity at the start of 1945 surrounding the abuse and death of a fostered boy named Dennis O'Neill had brought this issue to a head. The case has been seen as a trigger in the calls for the public inquiry, often known as the Curtis Committee (after its Chair Myra Curtis), which led to the Children Act of 1948. The Committee recommendations and the eventual Act would focus on children, like O'Neill, who were in care.[92] However, as far as the NSPCC was concerned, this left a huge problem of abuse, cruelty, and neglect within the ordinary home, where according to their estimate 6–7 per cent of all children needed help. Indeed, the NSPCC calculated that just 6 per cent of its total workload came under the new legislation. By the end of the 1940s, the NSPCC's workload was approaching 100,000 cases, an equivalent figure to numbers covered by the Children Act.[93] The British Medical Association and the Magistrate's Association agreed that an investigation into children within the family home, comparable to the Curtis Report on children in institutions, was now urgently needed.[94] Prosecutions for cruelty or neglect of children had almost doubled in the period 1933 to 1953.[95] But these influential bodies also now backed the argument that existing definitions of cruelty and neglect needed to be extended to embrace the child's emotional environment:

> the effect on the child's mind of constant exposure to domestic strain, immoral behaviour, insecurity and anxiety; deliberate actions on the part of the parent or guardian which are calculated to frighten the child excessively or reduce him to an unbearable state of mental or emotional tension; [and even] the denial of adequate affection or means of self-expression.[96]

Anxieties about the impact of wartime social change added to the concern. New wartime freedom for women, not just through paid employment, but also because of release from the everyday duties of motherhood through evacuation, raised the spectre of maternal resentment and a damaged emotional environment on the children's return. There was also fear that rushed wartime marriages were crumbling in the different circumstances of peace. Against such a background of raised expectations and alarm over social change, there seemed a real prospect of a generation of unwanted and emotionally crippled children.[97]

[91] Anne Allen and Arthur Morton, *This is Your Child: The Story of the National Society for the Prevention of Cruelty to Children* (London, 1961), pp. 50–4.

[92] The committee declined to accept that children cared for in the home but deprived of a 'normal' home life fell within its remit: *Report of the Care of the Children Committee*, Cmd. 6922 (HMSO, 1946), p. 6.

[93] Allen and Morton, *This is Your Child*, p. 62; NSPCC letter, 'Children in Distress', *The Times* (12 July 1948); Letter from Eva Hubback, 'Children Neglected in Their Own Homes', *The Times* (6 July 1949); Editorial on 'Cruelty to Children', *The Times* (12 December 1949).

[94] Report of the Joint Committee of the BMA and the Magistrate's Association, *Cruelty to and Neglect of Children* (London, 1956), p. 7.

[95] Rising from 559 to 913: *Cruelty to and Neglect of Children*, p. 10.

[96] *Cruelty to and Neglect of Children*, p. 12.

[97] Eustace Chesser, *Unwanted Children* (London, 1947), pp. 56, 115; *Cruelty to and Neglect of Children*, p. 15.

The post-war concern about cruelty to children can also be understood as a result of broader war-born anxieties about human nature, anxieties which were otherwise largely repressed by a population keen to put war behind them but which found a form for expression in the figure of the abused child. As psychiatrist and social reformer Eustace Chesser put it in his post-war work on child cruelty: 'Our consciences were aroused by concentration-camp horrors. In recent times, we have thanked God we were not as certain other nations are.' But the mounting evidence about the extent of cruelty to children allowed no such complacency: 'Are we, perhaps, after all, not so very different in kind but only in degree?'[98] Such transferral of broader feelings of anxiety and horror can perhaps help to account for the extraordinary explosion of public conscience in response to Lady Marjory Allen of Hurtwood's exposure of conditions in children's homes in the midst of war. How to respond to the violence of war was a particular dilemma for pacifists such as Allen, and again protection of the child appears to have provided a focus for psychological resolution. The moral case for contributing to the national effort was much stronger than it had been in 1914–18. It was also harder to maintain an identity as opponents of a state that treated conscientious objection in a more liberal manner.[99] Many pacifists responded by finding cause, free of the taint of militarism, in social service. This was notably the case in the work of the Pacifist Service Units established in 1940, whose social work with 'problem families' they intriguingly described as giving 'active expression to their pacifist values'.[100] The child, as the innocent bystander and victim of war, was the central focus of attention in such work.

As a 'total pacifist', Allen could take no part in the war effort, but she did not see helping children as infringing this requirement. Early in the war, she became involved in the movement to establish nurseries to assist in the care of evacuated young children, and in 1942 she became chair of the Nursery School Association. War and childcare were again integrally linked in Allen's scheme to use the debris of the Blitz to make children's toys and furniture. Quakers and other conscientious objectors provided the necessary labour and craftsmanship. Within four months there were over a hundred work parties, and in 1943 there was an exhibition of the work at Harrods opened by President of the Board of Education, R. A. Butler, and visited by the Queen. Subsequently, the scheme extended to involve Scouts, Guides, the Women's Institute, and even prisoners. Not only was this an act of cathartic physical alchemy, with Hitler's bombs supplying the fabric for objects of innocent play, but it also emerged as having a therapeutic value for those involved in production. By the end of the war, some three million toys and other items had been distributed.[101]

---

[98] Eustace Chesser, *Cruelty to Children* (London, 1951), p. 24.

[99] Martin Ceadel, *Pacifism in Britain 1914–1945: The Defining of a Faith* (Oxford, 1980), pp. 304–8; James Hinton, *Protests and Visions: Peace Politics in Twentieth-Century Britain* (London, 1989).

[100] Alan Cohen, *The Revolution in Post-War Family Casework: The Story of Pacifist Service Units and Family Units, 1940–1959* (Lancaster University, 1998), p. 7; Tom Stephens (ed.), *Problem Families: An Experiment in Social Rehabilitation* (London, 1945).

[101] Marjory Allen and Mary Nicholson, *Memoirs of an Uneducated Lady* (London, 1975), pp. 150–9.

Allen was particularly concerned about the way that nursery centres often came under the authority of the Ministry of Health or the Ministry of Labour rather than the Board of Education. This led to administrative confusion. More crucially, there was no justification not to offer all children the same standard and type of care. The fear was that the new nursery care centres, as opposed to the nursery schools, were little more than 'dumps' or 'cloakrooms' for children. In order to get more women into industrial work, the government was encouraging full-time nursery care for children from birth in centres staffed by nurses. Allen objected to the removal of babies from their mothers but also to the lack of specialized staff for infants. She tried to convince the government that the cost and extra staff needed to care for babies outweighed any advantages of getting their mothers into work. On the other hand, looking to the future, she added her support to the case for extending nursery school provision under the 1944 Education Act. This story and that of the limited realization of hopes for post-war nursery schooling has been told elsewhere.[102] More significant here is that it was through this campaign for reform of nursery provision that Allen came to recognize a group of children who looked different to the others: 'They were fat, flabby and listless and wore heavy, ill-fitting clothes and boots so clumsy they could only shuffle along. They looked overfed and unhappy, and never seemed to join the others in the playground.' It is an intriguing combination of characteristics and reflects the way that an inability to play emerged in the context of the war as a key marker of damage: play seen as essential to a child's successful adaptation of inner needs and drives to wartime circumstances.[103] Allen's children turned out to be the residents of homes and institutions for orphans. In her memoirs, Allen offered a striking account of her first visit to one of these places. Her emphasis was on the 'unhomely' atmosphere. This was figured in terms of physical and emotional sterility and a uniformity that undermined individual identity: 'drab walls and identical dull grey bedcovers... no personal treasures... no sign that anyone had tried to create a warm, cherishing atmosphere.' Children had withdrawn into themselves—withdrawal once again the symptom that she, like the child psychologists, and later Johnson's memoirists seemed to feel that the war had been particularly important in exposing. She found children standing around unoccupied, shy, and with little curiosity. Such neglect was made worse by a discipline that verged on cruelty. In one home the nun in charge was happy to announce that bed-wetting was cured though confinement for three weeks or 'correction in front of the others' in the chapel.[104] The situation was no better in homes made up of groups of 'cottages', even though she had hoped that this model might offer some kind of family atmosphere. She found places cut off from the outside world, with such an emphasis on uniformity and order—a 'conspicuous lack of tone, interest and spontaneity'—that there was no room for children to express themselves or develop as children.[105]

---

[102] Riley, *War in the Nursery*.

[103] Clare Britton, 'Children Who Cannot Play', in New Education Fellowship, *Play and Mental Health* (London, 1945), pp. 12–17. Republished in Joel Kanter (ed.), *Face to Face with Children: The Life and Work of Clare Winnicott* (London, 2004).

[104] Allen and Nicholson, *Memoirs*, pp. 171–2. [105] Allen and Nicholson, *Memoirs*, p. 173.

In 1944, Allen produced a memorandum on her findings. Significantly, rather than talking simply of orphans, she announced herself as uncovering the problem of 'children deprived of a normal home life'. She sent copies to the relevant government departments and another, accompanied by a letter, to *The Times*. The public response to publication in *The Times* was so great that when the paper's editor Sir William Haley gave a lecture on 'The Formation of Public Opinion' in 1958 he chose Allen's letter and the resulting furore as the perfect example. There was a torrent of letters in immediate response, and even after the normal correspondence had been closed the paper was forced to publish six round-ups of further letters, with the total response an all-time record.[106] This was an extraordinary expression of public feeling, particularly in the midst of war and its other worries. By the end of the year and after mounting concern in Parliament, the government was forced to announce its own public inquiry. In early 1945, Allen kept the pressure up with publication of *Whose Children?* This pamphlet quoted from the correspondence she had received since first raising the issue and was written, as she put it, in a style 'to stir the human heart'.[107] It painted a stark and distressing picture of emotional neglect, highlighting in a series of snapshots an emphasis on discipline and order which often approached cruelty: 'meals in compulsory silence—children forcibly fed, by holding noses—a three-year old child put to bed in a dark room as punishment for temper tantrum—child forcibly put to rest by holding blankets over their heads—children compelled to walk in crocodiles, although surrounded by suitable playing space.'[108] Such images attracted a vast amount of press coverage, the pamphlet reportedly reviewed in some fifty papers.[109] Further debate followed the death of Dennis O'Neill, who with his younger brother, Terence, had been abused by his foster parents. Allen had presented such 'boarding out' as preferable to institutional care. It was shortly after this, in February 1945, that the government announced the appointments to its committee of inquiry. Allen was regarded as too involved, and by many to have overstepped the mark in the emotive *Whose Children?* She was surprised and upset not to be included, though she was invited to submit evidence and was interviewed by the chairman, Myra Curtis.[110]

In histories of social policy and childhood, it is the Curtis Committee and the ensuing Children Act of 1948 that attract attention.[111] The remarkable wartime furore surrounding Allen's revelations, which forced the government into action, has attracted surprisingly little comment. Much of the drama in fact is in the Allen story and in the popular appeal, in the midst of war, of its central character, the emotionally withdrawn child: the child deprived of a normal home life who could not as a result be a child. It was the power of this figure that was seminal for the history of lost freedom that followed, and this needs to be understood in the context of the shadow of war.

---

[106] Allen and Nicholson, *Memoirs*, pp. 180–2.   [107] Allen and Nicholson, *Memoirs*, p. 185.
[108] Lady Allen of Hurtwood, *Whose Children?* (London, 1945), p. 7.
[109] Allen and Nicholson, *Memoirs*, p. 186.
[110] Allen and Nicholson, *Memoirs*, pp. 188–9.
[111] Stephen Cretney, *Law, Law Reform and the Family* (Oxford, 1998).

THE INTERNATIONAL DIMENSION

The figure of the emotionally withdrawn child that appeared in Allen's exposé, in Freud and Burlingham's account of separation, and then in the evacuee memoirs was also to be found in accounts of the children of the Holocaust and of war-devastated Europe that emerged at the end of the war. The striking similarities raise questions once again about the relationship between domestic concerns and tragedy on the international stage. Were the contours of this domestic figure, and the sympathy and concern attending this figure, a product in part of dawning understanding of the terrible impact of war on many European children, and a projection of guilt, sympathy, and horror over the human dimension at the heart of the international situation onto an object of protection that lay more comfortably close to home? Or was the British figure of the child without a normal home life in fact projected outwards, helping to domesticate and make sense of the horror encountered on the European stage?

What is clear is that the children of Europe assumed an increasingly prominent position in British public consciousness as the war approached its conclusion. In particular, the European child was mobilized as a figure of sympathy in efforts to steer the British public to accept a shift in emphasis from warfare to international peace, aid, and welfare.[112] Pacifist publisher Victor Gollancz used photographs of starving German children in pamphlets attempting to gain support for his Save Europe Now campaign, and to convince a British people hoping for an increase in their own rations to support instead the purchase of food for the recently defeated enemy.[113] The problem of the concentration camps was initially publicized through drawing attention to the child population.[114] A prohibition on British troops fraternizing with the occupied German population made an exception when it came to playing with children, and this attracted further attention to their plight.[115] Aid for Palestine found a focus in the Children and Youth Aliyah Movement campaign on the plight of Jewish orphans.[116] And a film of Belsen concentration camp provided images of children at play to engage the sympathies of a domestic audience, with the child acting as a symbol of the survival of humanity and the innocence of the victims (while British children themselves were to be protected from seeing

---

[112] On the latter, and the 'spiritual and sometimes physical pornography' of coverage of the enemy in the British press: Victor Gollancz, *Our Threatened Values* (London, 1946), p. 25.

[113] Victor Gollancz, *Is It Nothing to You?* (London, 1945). See also Victor Gollancz, *Leaving Them to Their Fate: The Ethics of Starvation* (London, 1946). Gollancz argued that the Germans were on a diet of 1,000 calories per day compared to the British intake of 2,850 (p. 20). His biographer estimates that 75,000 copies were distributed free of cost, and a further 75,000 sold: Ruth Dudley Edwards, *Victor Gollancz: A Biography* (London, 1987), p. 422. On Save Europe Now: Matthew Frank, 'The New Morality—Victor Gollancz, "Save Europe Now" and the German Refugee Crisis, 1945–46', *Twentieth Century British History*, 17 (2006), 230–56; and casting doubt on Gollancz's claims about starvation: John Farquharson, '"Emotional but Influential": Victor Gollancz, Richard Stokes and the British Zone of Germany, 1945–9', *Journal of Contemporary History*, 22 (1987), 501–19.

[114] 'Children from the Camps', *The Times* (7 May 1945); 'Jewish Children', *The Times* (26 June 1945).

[115] 'British Forces in Germany—Permission to Play with Children', *The Times* (15 June 1945).

[116] Children and Youth Aliyah, *Behold the Child of Our Time* (London, 1945).

such images—for instance, they were barred from visiting the *Daily Express* exhibition on Belsen—lest it unleash a potential for sadism).[117]

Looking back with a sense of disappointment from the 1970s and a society of battered babies, maladjustment, and increasing youth violence, social worker Agatha Bowley recalled the 1940s as heady days, a time when it seemed that English child welfare could teach the world about the way forward for family life.[118] The British experience of evacuation, in particular, was influential in shaping attitudes towards the core problems and challenges in dealing with the displaced children of Europe. Freud and Burlingham, for instance, extended the approach developed in relation to wartime British children to children from Theresienstadt Concentration Camp who arrived in Britain after the war.[119] And British psychologists and social workers brought an understanding developed in relation to the evacuation and Blitz in Britain into the work of international aid organizations such as the United National Relief and Rehabilitation Agency (UNRRA), set up in November 1943 to organize international efforts to help 'displaced persons'.[120] Here, British psychoanalyst John Rickman headed the Inter-Allied Psychological Study Group, which reported on 'The Psychological Problems of Displaced Persons' in June 1945. As editor of the *British Journal of Medical Psychology*, Rickman was very familiar with the findings on evacuation, a subject that attracted extensive attention in his journal. He was assisted by H. V. Dicks, G. R. Hargreaves, and A. T. M. Wilson, part of a generation associated with Britain's Tavistock Clinic, psychiatrists who were to the fore in bringing the fruits of a psychodynamic approach to assist Britain's war effort and then post-war domestic and international reconstruction. After the war, Hargreaves would become Deputy Director of the World Health Organisation, a position which would enable him to deploy John Bowlby from the Tavistock to write his influential WHO report on maternal attachment in 1952. And alongside these medical psychologists was Gwen Chesters, who acted as Advisor on Child Psychology to the UNRRA and who brought an expertise in play and experience of working in the field of social work in Britain.[121] The 'Psychological Problems of Displaced Persons' report provided an extensive forty-page analysis of the psychological

---

[117] Hannah Caven, 'Horror in Our Time: Images of the Concentration Camps—The British Media, 1945', *Historical Journal of Film, Radio, and Television*, 21 (2001), 229–31, 247.

[118] Agatha Bowley, *Children at Risk* (London, 1975), preface.

[119] Anna Freud and Sophie Dann, 'An Experiment in Group Upbringing', in *The Psychoanalytic Study of the Child* (New Haven, CT, 1951), pp. 127–68.

[120] Jessica Reinisch, 'Internationalism in Relief: The Birth (and Death) of UNRRA', *Past and Present*, 210 (2011), 258–89; Ben Shephard, 'Becoming Planning Minded: The Theory and Practice of Relief, 1940–1945', *Journal of Contemporary History*, 43 (2008), 405–19. For an account of UNRRA activities across Europe: Ben Shephard, *The Long Return Home: The Aftermath of the Second World War* (London, 2010).

[121] Chesters had contributed an essay on play therapy in a book edited by Jonathan Miller's father, psychiatrist Emanuel Miller: *The Growing Child and Its Problems* (London, 1937). She would also produce a report for the Home Office on the needs of displaced children and offered a picture of boys who feared that they might kill and others who feared they had lost feeling: Dorothy Macardle, *Children of Europe: A Study of the Children of Liberated Countries: Their Wartime Experiences, Their Reactions, and Their Needs, with a note on Germany* (London, 1949), p. 244.

dimensions of rehabilitation. It drew directly on the example of British evacuation, but now extended its implications first to European children and then to the problem of reintegrating displaced persons more generally (on the principle that adults displaced from their social backgrounds tended to return to the dependent attitudes of childhood in their relationship to authority). The report argued that a 'need to be loved and valued', and therefore issues of attachment and security, lay at the heart of the problem:

> It is a basic fact in working with refugees and expatriates that many of their attitudes and much of their behaviour can only be understood if we assume that they feel themselves to have been proved unworthy of the affection and tolerance of friends. Examples of this mechanism at work were frequent among evacuated children in England in 1939–40. Devoted parents who had evacuated their children to protect them from air raids found after return the child interpreted the evacuation as a sign of being unwanted and unworthy to remain in the family. In consequence, the child is at once anxious to be reassured of its place in the family and angry over the humiliation of having been 'cast out', which behaviour is naturally very disturbing to the average parent.[122]

As Tara Zahra has put it in her account of post-war efforts to tackle the problem of 'lost children', the workers of the UNRRA, 34 per cent of a staff of nearly 13,000 by her estimate British, 'typically sought and found confirmation of a set of universalist psychoanalytic principles'.[123] Specifically, she points to the importance of a concern about separation developed during the war in relation to children faced by British evacuation (with the Freud and Burlingham research particularly influential), but which could readily be extended in an emerging 'psychological Marshall plan' to the subject not just of the refugee child but of the displaced adult.[124]

Attending a meeting of the international child welfare organization SEPEG in Zurich in September 1945, Lady Allen noted how the representatives from other countries looked to England for a lead, and how differences in experience were overlooked as 'all children, without distinction of nationality, were the victims of war'.[125] Reflecting back on the post-war efforts in 1949, Dorothy Macardle emphasized once again the importance of the British research in shaping understanding of the problems of refugee children: on the one hand, the remarkable ability of children, as shown in the Blitz, to survive hardship and violence; on the other, the importance of attachment and the conclusion therefore (drawing on Freud and Burlingham) that institutional care was no solution.[126] However, the picture that emerged, and which was now brought to a broader audience in Macardle's account but also through a popular medium such as *Picture Post* (attracting record correspondence in response), was one of real tragedy, of the deep psychological wounds of even those children who appeared resilient, and of the potential damage stored

---

[122] UNRRA, 'Psychological Problems of Displaced Persons' (June, 1945), p. 3: Wiener Library, HA5-4/3.

[123] Tara Zahra, 'Lost Children: Displacement, Family, and Nation in Postwar Europe', *Journal of Modern History*, 81 (2009), 45–86, 48.

[124] Zahra, 'Lost Children', 48–59.

[125] 'Impressions of SEPEG', MRC MSS.121/CH/3/1/24.i.

[126] Macardle, *Children of Europe*, pp. 13, 252–3, 270.

up for the future.[127] The full realization of the horror of what children had been through, and of how this marked them, was made apparent as publicity seeped out about the disturbed behaviour of refugee children in homes set up in post-war Britain.[128] At the same time, the new cultural arm of the United Nations, UNESCO, advanced the case for internationalism in the field of education and mental health care on the grounds that war had handicapped and mentally starved a whole generation of children: the horror of war universalized but also displaced through the figure of the child of the future.[129]

Yet, as with studies of the British children of war, the European situation provided a second message that was less compatible with an emphasis on the importance of home and attachment. Just as the Blitz, or even the freedoms of the countryside in evacuation, would point to the value of a broader landscape and to the child's appetite for exploration, freedom, and even danger, the European experience could likewise point to the need for something more than a future of cocooned life in the family home. Lady Allen became involved in one of the new international organizations, the World Organisation for Early Childhood Education (OMEP), which carried forward the message of interwar progressive education. Here she encountered the message of the Swedish expert in social welfare Alva Myrdal that children as young as two had a strong urge to strike out on their own, and that just as home was crucial to psychological well-being so were routes to enable the young child to reach beyond the home to explore a wider environment.[130] If the war taught that security was crucial for well-being, it also taught that children needed to be reared in a way that encouraged independence and an ability to live in groups: both were crucial to a healthy democracy.[131] Allen would find a perfect practical route to develop this philosophy in her discovery of a pioneer adventure playground in Emdrup, Denmark, which had been set up under Nazi occupation to divert the rebellious energies of local children. It was quickly recognized that this provided a welfarist rendering of the freedom, risk, and thrill that British children had found in the bombsites of the Blitz, and Allen would establish a campaign to make such playgrounds widely available in post-war Britain.[132] The psychological need to play,

---

[127] Macardle, *Children of Europe*, p. 257; 'Europe's Children', *Picture Post* (24 April 1948); 'Europe's Children—How Readers Responded', *Picture Post* (8 May 1948); 'Europe's Children: A General Response', *Picture Post* (15 May 1948).

[128] Macardle, *Children of Europe*, p. 245; Mollie Panter-Downes, 'The Children Who Don't Trust Anybody', *Sunday Dispatch* (7 April 1946); Margot Hicklin, *War Damaged Children: Some Aspects of Recovery* (Thornton Heath, Surrey, 1946).

[129] Thérèse Brosse, *War-Handicapped Children* (UNESCO, 1950); Elisabeth Rotten, *Children, War's Victims: The Education of the Handicapped* (UNESCO, 1949); Thérèse Brosse, *Homeless Children: Report of the Conference of Directors of Children's Communities Trogen, Switzerland* (UNESCO, 1950); *Children of Europe* (UNESCO, 1949); *The Influence of Home and Community on Children under Thirteen Years of Age* (UNESCO, 1949).

[130] As well as a foundational figure for the Swedish welfare state, Myrdal was another woman who took a lead in the post-war internationalization of welfare as Head of the United Nations section on welfare policy in 1949 and then Chair of the UNESCO social science section from 1950 to 1955.

[131] Allen and Nicholson, *Memoirs*, p. 205.

[132] Allen and Nicholson, *Memoirs*, pp. 196–7; 'Why Not Use Our Bomb Sites Like This?', *Picture Post* (16 November 1946).

therefore, emerged out of war as just as much a dictum as was attachment: a vital medium for working through the inner problems of the child and for coming to terms with reality; and an inability to play now coming to be seen as a marker of deep-rooted problems.[133] The power of play was what made it possible for children to turn public violence into safe fantasy. The tension between the two visions—of providing children with a security centred on home and family on the one hand, and of offering them the freedom of genuine play on the other—would be at the heart of efforts to provide a landscape for the child in the decades that followed.[134]

CONCLUSION

This chapter has argued that narratives of the 'good war' neglect a set of deep anxieties about human nature that came to the fore in wartime British thought and feeling and found a vehicle for expression in the figure of the psychologically damaged and vulnerable child. One result of this was a heightened concern about protection, and in particular about the need for the emotional security that could be provided by the landscape of home and family. War also, however, offered evidence on the importance of a broader landscape beyond the home and of the child's appetite for play, freedom, and the exploration of danger, and it left the challenge of reconciling these two messages. And although it exposed the inappropriate nature of much institutional care, it would in fact leave scope through the cultivation of a more homely manner of care for the persistence and even expansion of such settings right up to the 1970s. This was also a consequence of the fact that the emphasis on home came at a time when the family was rocked by the stresses of war and exposed by the new expectations of emotional security.

The war was also important in encouraging interest in the way that the child saw the world differently to the adult. This invariably entailed efforts to understand the inner, psychic world of the child. Children's apparent delinquency or bed-wetting in response to evacuation could be explained in terms of the rupture to the child's psychic world, but also the ongoing anxieties about the landscape of home that mushroomed through absence. And children who apparently coped under air raids and against a backdrop of public violence could be seen as translating this experience into narrative that made sense within their own limited horizon. This might mean that such experience was safely handled via the imagination and play; but it could also mean that children were damaged at a deeper emotional level, and this made the challenge of emotional reconstruction even more acute. Because Britain

---

[133] Britton, 'Children Who Cannot Play'.

[134] Annette Kuhn has highlighted this tension in her analysis of the film *Mandy*, directed by Alexander Mackendrick in 1952, centring on the story of a deaf girl and her family's dilemma of whether to send her to a special school or to care for her at home. The bombsite—still a key part of the landscape in the early 1950s—located just behind the family house, reminds the viewer of the proximity of war and conflict. It is also, however, the place where the local children play and the place that promises release from the love but claustrophobia of the family home, and a world shaped by adults, for the disabled child (*Family Secrets: Acts of Memory and Imagination* (London, 1995), pp. 21–39).

was confronted with these issues from the very start of the war, it was influential in a broader international debate on the children of war. Domestically, the wartime importance of understanding this internal world of the child meant that this was a crucial period for the advance of psychoanalysis but also of professionals within education and social work who took on the lessons of psychoanalysis. Indeed, it was so important that in the midst of war British psychoanalysis would descend into acrimonious dispute over the degree and ways in which it might access this perspective of the child: whether through applying theories derived from adult psychoanalysis; whether through listening to the child; or whether though simply watching them play or draw. What is striking now is less the differences between these positions than the way the psychoanalytic interest in the landscape of the child gained purchase in the context of war.[135] The next chapter will begin to consider how the lessons of war adapted to the challenges presented by the welfare state and became embedded within the social fabric of the post-war settlement. Here, as the anxiety about child cruelty in the aftermath of the war already indicates, the welfare state settlement in relation to child welfare was only a partial one, leaving the question of whether home could indeed provide an ideal landscape for the child open to challenge in the years to come.

As the evacuee memoirists reflected, the project of their saving, first in evacuation and then in the return home, had been one in which they had been ciphers in a broader battle, the purpose of which they little understood. And as this chapter has indicated, these wartime anxieties had a tendency to turn all children into victims of war and into objects for saving. It was this shadow of war that helped to turn freedom from an assumed natural state of childhood to something that had to be nurtured and as consequence to something that came to be seen and experienced as in perpetual danger of being lost.

---

[135] The dispute, known as the 'controversial discussions', had complex roots and was personal as well as theoretical. It set a group headed by Melanie Klein, which believed in the ability to use psychoanalysis on young children, against a group headed by Anna Freud: Pearl King and Ricardo Steiner (eds), *The Freud–Klein Controversies, 1941–45* (London, 1991). Susan Isaacs was in the same camp as Melanie Klein, accepting the possibility of studying phantasy and of envy and hate of frightening proportion in the very young child: Philip Graham, *Susan Isaacs: A Life Freeing the Minds of Children* (London, 2009), Chapter 12, 'Battling for the Minds of Children', pp. 279–307. Anna Freud was in the camp that paid more attention to the impact of external factors; nevertheless, the evidence from her study of wartime children indicates that she was interested in and happy to interpret the behaviour and views of her young charges. There would also be tension between the Kleinians and child psychologist Margaret Lowenfeld, who was an advocate of using children's play and drawing, and in particular their construction of children's worlds through figures and sandboxes: *A Report of a Conference Held at the Institute of Child Psychology on the Theory and Technique of Direct Objective Therapy* (London, 1950).

3

Bowlbyism and the Post-War Settlement

The popularization of the attachment psychology of John Bowlby and fellow mid-century British psychologists, and its message about the psychological deprivation and long-term damage that resulted when young children were separated from and deprived of parental (particularly maternal) love and affection—what this chapter will describe as 'Bowlbyism'—has a key position in a story of freedom and the landscape of the child between the Second World War and the 1970s.[1] However, its significance was more complex than sometimes appreciated, for it pointed in two directions. On the one hand, it encouraged and justified a closing in of the landscape of the child: the most important thing for the child was the protection and love of home and family. On the other hand, it also emphasized the importance of play, freedom, and social relations within that setting. It also fostered a reform and liberalization of institutional care. As such, freedom was lost but also gained: lost in the sense that children were increasingly tied to the protection of home and had less access to the outside world; gained in that there was a new emphasis on freedom within the home and institution. Bowlbyism therefore offered a model that could salve anxieties about emotional security while at the same time recasting a managed freedom as an essential element in the fostering of a social democratic subjectivity. However, it was always difficult to satisfy expectations for both emotional security and freedom, particularly as the two could be in tension, and particularly as social and economic circumstances changed and destabilized the locus of attachment, an idealized model of the home and family. This is why a post-war emotional settlement facilitated by the logic of Bowlbyism and centred on the landscape of home faced mounting problems and criticism. This chapter charts the history of this settlement from its pre-war roots, to its post-war fruition, its popularization, and the challenges it encountered in the 1960s and 1970s.

The second aim of the chapter is to use this subject to add a new dimension to our understanding of the history of the social democratic settlement in post-war Britain. It takes inspiration here from Eli Zaretsky's argument that British psychoanalytic culture, in its emphasis on attachment, took a distinctive path in this

---

[1] Edward John Mostyn Bowlby (1907–90) was a British psychologist, psychiatrist, and psychoanalyst, particularly influential as a result of his mid-century writing on the importance of attachment for children. The chapter adopts the term 'Bowlbyism' to emphasize that it is less concerned with the work of Bowlby himself than in the broader influence and popularization of some of his key assumptions, and the ideological and social and economic structures that encouraged this. The term was first used in this way, with a particular focus on its impact on wartime nursery policy, in Denise Riley's seminal study *War in the Nursery: Theories of the Child and Mother* (London, 1983).

period and that this was closely related to the emergence of the welfare state.[2] It also develops a response to a recent symposium on the current state and future prospects of modern British history where James Vernon calls for new work on what he describes as the 'short life of British social democracy'.[3] In particular, in focusing on the place of Bowlbyism within the post-war settlement, the chapter serves to begin an exploration of the relationship of the landscape of the child to one of the central narratives of British social history in this period: the move from a more social democratic towards a more individualist society. And it provides an opportunity to turn understanding of this settlement from the formal domain of social policy, to a history of feelings and expectations regarding care, assumptions regarding emotional need, and popular and professional attitudes towards the role of the family and informal agencies of childcare in supplementing the role of the welfare state and in the process making it viable.

Historians have provided us with a nuanced history of the motivations behind the welfare state, and of its modifications in the face of political and economic restraints. But we know far less about its operations in practice and at an individual and cultural level: why and when it changed behaviour, how it was experienced and responded to, and the significance of its meanings. Vernon has himself offered an example of what this new, cultural history of social democracy might look like in the concluding section of his own history of hunger. Here, he draws upon one of the key texts for a history that looks to bring together broad social structure and individual experience: Carolyn Steedman's autobiographical account of growing up in post-war Britain, *Landscape for a Good Woman*.[4] It is Steedman's recognition of the symbolic and emotional importance of free post-war orange juice, milk, and school dinners that strikes a chord. 'I think I would be a very different person now', she writes, 'if orange juice and milk and dinners at school hadn't told me, in a covert way, that I had a right to exist, was worth something.' It is because of these feelings, the experience of the physical comfort of feeding, and the care and affection that it symbolized, that Steedman finds it hard to accept the full thrust of a revisionist literature that downplays the achievements of the welfare state.[5] Her recollection of how it felt to be a welfare state child takes us into the territory of a rather different sort of welfare-state and social-democratic history: a history of the emotional experience and personal meanings of living in such, social democratic, times.[6] As these times become more distant both chronologically and in terms of the shift in values and expectations of recent decades, it is important, as Vernon recognizes, for historians of the post-war era to take up and develop the subject opened up by Steedman.

---

[2] Eli Zaretsky, '"One Large Secure, Solid Background": Melanie Klein and the Origins of the British Welfare State', *History and Psychoanalysis*, 1:2 (1999), 136–51.

[3] James Vernon, 'The Local, the Imperial and the Global: Repositioning Twentieth-Century Britain and the Brief Life of its Social Democracy', *Twentieth Century British History*, 21 (2010), 404–18.

[4] James Vernon, *Hunger: A Modern History* (Cambridge, MA, 2007), pp. 236–71.

[5] Carolyn Steedman, *Landscape for a Good Woman* (New Brunswick, NJ, 1986), p. 122.

[6] Though it is also the case that the experience of the school meal could be one of discipline, alienation, and resistance, and that this emotional history runs alongside that of care and attachment.

The history of Bowlbyism provides us with an important but strangely neglected route into this history of the emotional and personal underpinnings of British post-war social democracy. Its connection with the history of state orange juice, milk, and school dinners is in fact an intriguingly intimate one. Steedman herself hints at this. 'What my mother lacked, I was given', she writes. This is an acknowledgement of the post-war eradication of hunger and the advent of basic social provision as an experienced right; and of the shift from going without before the war as well as during and immediately after in the age of rationing and austerity, to the satisfaction of material needs and even afflu-ence beyond it. But it also reminds us that the state here provided symbolic care and affection in a way that Bowlby's mothers were supposed to (even if they sometimes struggled to match expectations).[7] The child psychology of the era recognized the close connections between love and feeding. Indeed, Bowlby famously described the importance of attachment in the first years of life as akin to that of the vitamins which had come to be recognized as such an essential element in child growth, and which came in rich supply in the welfare-state free school milk and orange juice.[8] More generally psychologists made it clear that the giving and accepting of food were essential symbolic acts in the dynamics of care and affection. A book with the wonderful title of *Oliver Untwisted* had shown the way: updating the plea for more gruel to one of more love.[9] In the Second World War, psychoanalyst Wilfred Bion presented the cookery class as a tool for the forging of morale.[10] And in the aftermath of war, the woman who cooked for herself was presented as a potential psychological problem, the tin that heralded a future of packaged food a psychological screen.[11] Most pertinent of all, the inner emotional turmoil of the child refugee was made manifest in the way that they handled their food.[12] Against such a background, even the regular juxtaposition of recipes and psychological advice in the parenting litera-ture of the era becomes suggestive of a close link between the psychological and the material expression of attachment within a post-war emotional economy.[13] Both reflected, not just the conclusions of nutritional or psychological science,

---

[7] Steedman, *Landscape*, p. 122.

[8] Though this statement was more hidden away than one might expect given its notoriety: *Child Care and the Growth of Love* (London, 1971), p. 69. Eduardo Duniec and Mical Raz, 'Vitamins for the Soul: John Bowlby's Thesis of Maternal Deprivation, Biomedical Metaphor, and the Deficiency Model of Disease', *History of Psychiatry*, 22 (2011), 93–107.

[9] M. A. Payne, *Oliver Untwisted* (London, 1929).

[10] Mathew Thomson, *Psychological Subjects: Identity, Culture and Health in Twentieth-Century Britain* (Oxford, 2006), pp. 226–7.

[11] Hilde Lewinsky, 'Psychological Aspects of Cooking for Oneself', *British Journal of Medical Psychology*, 20 (1946), 376–83.

[12] Margot Hicklin, *War-Damaged Children: Some Aspects of Recovery* (Thornton Heath, Surrey, 1946).

[13] The juxtaposition of the domestic (including cookery) and psychological advice on child-rearing is apparent in a popular magazine such as *Parents*. John Bowlby and his wife, Ursula, were regular contributors (along with Doris Odlum and J. A. Hadfield). The recipe pages take us back to an era of British culinary ignominy, but also of note is how the material, in the comfort food of the pudding (subject of a regular competition) or the ubiquitous adverts for vitamins, fish oils, and bed-time drinks, paralleled the emotional nutrition in advice to solve the problems of childcare through love.

but also the needs of the givers and the appeal of protecting the child at this time of war-stoked anxieties about human nature and in the context of increased affluence to come.

In its influence on the family home, Bowlbyism can be seen as helping to bring a social and democratic model of relations into everyday lives. It looked to real life experiences and the environment, and crucially to social relationships, care, and affection as central in well-being and in the formation of subjectivity. In doing so, it offered an alternative to the more individualist interwar model in which discipline, self-help, and reliance were foundational principles of good childcare. It also moved away from a more introspective focus on the internal dynamics of the unconscious that, for instance, dominated British Kleinian psychoanalysis in this period.[14] As recent scholarship has demonstrated, Bowlby's work developed in a context of intense concern about the rise of political extremism, intolerance, and international aggression. Against this background, and recognizing the potential of psychology as a key tool in post-war reconstruction, Bowlby worked alongside Labour's Evan Durbin in emphasizing the importance of a liberal and loving style of childcare in fostering the mental health and the social relations necessary for a democratic society.[15] In a post-war society still often suspicious of the role of the state, and one in which traditional community structures were weakening, such a psychological message would be projected into homes up and down the country in popular, common-sense terms. In this form, Bowlbyism could help turn the family home into a site for living out the meaning of social democracy, extending the reach of the post-war settlement into civil society, and thereby acting as crucial glue in holding it together.[16]

The influence of Bowlbyism in the social life of the era has in fact attracted remarkably little serious historical investigation. This is even more surprising given assumptions about its significance in a post-war idealization of domesticity, a

---

[14] Interviewed in 1986, Bowlby emphasized the difference between his focus on the actuality of the mother–child relationship and Melanie Klein's focus on the unconscious as a route into analysis of this relationship. As the interview recognized, and as was highlighted in the controversy sparked by Jeffrey Mason's critique of Freud during this period, psychoanalysis could also be accused of backing away from an early recognition of incest as a cause of trauma and instead locating such problems in the realm of fantasy: Robert Young, Karl Figlio, and John Bowlby, 'An Interview with John Bowlby on the Origins and Reception of His Work', *Free Associations*, 6 (1986), 36–64.

[15] For the social orientation of British psychoanalysis in the context of war and its interest in social democracy: Thomson, *Psychological Subjects*, Chapter 7: 'Psychology and the Mid-Century Crisis', pp. 209–49. Bowlby articulated his views on the psychological basis of social democracy in: John Bowlby and Evan Durbin, *Personal Aggressiveness and War* (London, 1939); and John Bowlby, 'Psychology and Democracy', *Political Quarterly*, 17 (1946), 61–76. On Bowlby's links to young Labour intellectual Evan Durbin, see also: Jeremy Nuttall, 'Psychological Socialist: Militant Moderate: Evan Durbin and the Politics of Synthesis', *Labour History Review*, 68 (2003), 235–52; and Stephen Brooke, 'Evan Durbin: Reassessing a Labour "Revisionist" ', *Twentieth Century British History*, 7 (1996), 27–52. Jeremy Nuttall reflects more broadly on the interconnections between thinking about qualities of character and the modern British left in his *Psychological Socialism: The Labour Party and the Qualities of Mind and Character, 1931 to the Present* (Manchester, 2006).

[16] As British psychoanalyst Edward Glover put it, the challenge was to 'extend the cultural authority of the family and to curtail the spurious cultural authority assumed by the state' (*War, Sadism and Pacifism* (London, 1946), p. 223).

theme that has attracted considerable attention.[17] The most significant work to date has come from a feminist perspective, but this has focused on implications of attachment theory for the persistence of gender inequality.[18] We do benefit from one impressive analysis of the influence and popularization of Bowlbyism, but the scope is largely limited to the war and its immediate aftermath.[19] Bowlby himself has also been the subject of several biographical accounts.[20] And his theoretical writing has been the subject of considerable attention among psychologists. What we lack is study of the broader influence, reception, and response to such thinking.

Histories of post-war psychological advice and child-rearing in the United States are better developed than in the British case.[21] Some of this work has left Bowlby appearing as a rather marginal figure.[22] On the other hand, recent historical research looking specifically at the American reception of Bowlby's work has demonstrated considerable interest, particularly because of its resonance with mounting post-war concerns about the working woman.[23] Interviewed in 1977, Bowlby claimed that the popular version of his landmark WHO study, *Maternal Care and Mental Health*, had sold disappointingly in the United States. Perhaps, he speculated, this was because the Americans had their own child psychology gurus such as Erik Erikson and Arnold Gessell. Or perhaps it was an issue of timing. The book had been published in Britain in the wake of the Curtis Committee Report on childcare, and of the state accordingly assuming new responsibility for the care and safety of the nation's children, and it was particularly popular among social workers, who would be the foot soldiers of the new system of care, and was a core text in the

---

[17] This is a phenomenon which has been seen as a general response to the trauma of the Second World War: Mark Mazower, *Dark Continent: Europe's Twentieth Century* (London, 1997), p. 227. The exceptional, rather than normative, nature of the gender settlement in Britain in the late 1940s and 1950s, with early and high rates of marriage, low female employment, and home-centredness has been highlighted by Pat Thane: 'Family Life and "Normality" in Post-War British Culture', in Richard Bessel and Dirk Schumann (eds), *Life after Death: Approaches to a Cultural and Social History of Europe during the 1940s and 1950s* (Cambridge, 2003). Though Claire Langhamer has argued that there has been a tendency to exaggerate the extent to which such idealization of home was a new phenomenon, and suggests that such developments can already be located in the 1930s: 'The Meanings of Home in Post-War Britain', *Journal of Contemporary History*, 40 (2005), 341–62. Unfortunately this analysis of 'home' pays little attention to the issue of children. See also Judy Giles, 'A Home of One's Own: Women and Domesticity in England, 1918–1950', *Women's Studies International Forum*, 16 (1993), 239–53.

[18] Though offering some defence from a feminist perspective on the basis of Bowlby's valuing of women's work as mothers: Birmingham Feminist History Group, 'Feminism as Femininity in the 1950s', *Feminist Review*, 3 (1979). Equally, Denise Riley writing from a feminist perspective acknowledges that the critique of Bowlby from this perspective has sometimes been guilty of exaggerating his position on attachment: *War in the Nursery*. For a defence of Bowlby against feminist criticism, see Jeremy Holmes, *John Bowlby and Attachment Theory* (London, 1993), pp. 41–50.

[19] Riley, *War in the Nursery*.

[20] Suzan van Dijken, *John Bowlby: His Early Life: A Biographical Journey into the Roots of Attachment Theory* (London, 1998); Holmes, *John Bowlby and Attachment Theory*; Judith Issroff, *Donald Winnicott and John Bowlby: Personal and Professional Perspectives* (London, 2005).

[21] In the British case, we still rely on populist accounts such as Christina Hardyment's *Dream Babies: Child Care from Locke to Spock* (London, 1983).

[22] For instance: Anne Hulbert, *Raising America: Experts, Parents, and a Century of Advice about Children* (New York, 2003), pp. 205–6.

[23] Marga Vicedo, 'The Social Nature of the Mother's Tie to the Child: John Bowlby's Theory of Attachment in Post-War America', *British Journal for the History of Science*, 44 (2011), 401–26.

new training courses for this expanding profession.[24] The experience of evacuation in the Second World War is also likely to have left Britain readier than the United States in the immediate aftermath of war for a childcare philosophy that emphasized the dangers of separation and the need for attachment. By contrast, as Betty Friedan described in *The Feminine Mystique*, the wartime advance of women in the United States appears to have spawned alarm about the overprotective and dominating mother: the problem of too much rather than not enough care. Educated women, argued Friedan, found themselves frustrated in the role of the suburban housewife and channelled their energy into the science of motherhood. The overprotected child became a victim of the mother's own suppressed ambitions and craving for love. Nowhere, in Friedan's influential account, is there in fact any mention either of Bowlby or of attachment and deprivation.[25] When the *New York Times* wrote about Bowlby and fellow attachment theorists in 1965, it was by way of highlighting Britain's distinctive childcare culture.[26] As this indicates, there may well have been considerable and growing interest in Bowlby in the United States, but this would obscure a history of the different timing and nature of popularization on either side of the Atlantic. Just as Bowlbyism is probably less central in America, particularly in the immediate aftermath of the war, 'momism' is much harder to locate in Britain. In that the one looked to environment and social relationships, and the other to the individualist ethics of independent self-realization and breaking free from social bonds, it is tempting to see this as a further indication that the influence of Bowlbyism in postwar Britain was related to the life of a more social democratic culture.

In order to pursue the lines of enquiry set out above, the remainder of the chapter is organized into three sections. The first considers the roots of Bowlbyism and develops the case for its social democratic orientation. The second section charts the post-war popularization of Bowlbyism, the extent to which it shaped child care in middle-class but also working-class families, and its implications for child freedom in these settings. The third section considers the emergence of critiques of Bowlbyism from the 1950s to the 1970s, and the reasons for this faltering of confidence in the family and home as an ideal landscape of the child.

ROOTS AND EARLY DEVELOPMENT

As Denise Riley has put it, 'The course of Bowlby's work cannot, in itself, be held fully accountable for the phenomenon of "Bowlbyism".'[27] This is a central theme in the analysis that follows. Nevertheless, it is still necessary to say something

---

[24] John Bowlby interview with Milton Senn, *Beyond the Couch: The Online Journal of the American Association for Psychoanalysis in Clinical Social Work*, issue 2 (December, 2007).

[25] Betty Friedan, *The Feminine Mystique* (London, 1971; first edn 1963), pp. 189–98.

[26] Evelyn S. Ringold, 'Bringing up Baby in Britain', *New York Times* (13 June 1965). It seems that Bowlby attracted increasing attention in the 1970s in relation to debate over the rights and wrongs of day care for young children: Sheila Cole, 'The Search for the Truth about Day Care', *New York Times* (12 December 1971). In 1974, Bowlby was given space to set out his own ideas: 'A Guide to the Perplexed Parent', *New York Times* (2 March 1974).

[27] Riley, *War in the Nursery*, p. 109. See also Erica Burman, *Deconstructing Developmental Psychology* (Routledge, 2008), pp. 130–3.

about Bowlby and the origins of his ideas here at the start. A history of Bowlbyism could start with its landmark text, Bowlby's 1952 WHO report on *Maternal Care and Mental Health*. Bowlby had initially been asked to write a report on delinquency (his own main area of expertise), and only accepted when the focus shifted to the subject of the homeless child.[28] It was this broader remit that gave the report potential for major significance: the subject of the homeless child so readily turned into the subject of what made a good home for any child. The broader remit also meant that the report was necessarily to a large extent a work of synthesis, drawing on a large body of research undertaken in the 1930s and 1940s: in that sense it reflected the fact that a concern about attachment and separation already went well beyond the man himself. Bowlby's own research base was still the rather slim one of his pre-war study of delinquency. This on its own certainly did not provide justification for his claims about maternal attachment. He was also able to draw on a broader body of research on the psychological problems caused by the separation from family that resulted from care in institutions, much of it from the United States. However, his biographers, Jeremy Holmes and Suzan van Dijken, both suggest that we should also think about the relationship to his own pre-war experiences. In doing so, they offer a picture of Bowlby as someone less concerned with defending the nuclear family and someone instead with a broader vision of the importance of social relationships and freedom of expression as the basis for mental health. Yes, like many in the middle class, he felt a personal sense of being deprived of affection through the tendency to separate children from their parents for a childhood spent in the nursery and then the boarding school. But in his own life, he reacted against this by choosing not to cocoon his children in the bosom of the nuclear family or to confine them to the walls of the home. There was a communal style in the comings and goings of his own house, which he shared with other psychologists and which drew on an extended network of friends for the bringing-up of his children. Family holidays on the Isle of Skye provided the opportunity for his children to roam the countryside free from adult supervision.[29] His work in the progressive Bedales and Priory Gate schools, and his reading of educationalist Homer Lane, exposed him to the permissive approach to behaviour that was to be a central feature of his popular message after the war, and which challenged the traditional model of the family. And his writing on politics with young Labour intellectual Evan Durbin, with whom he shared a house, explored the role of a liberal approach to child-rearing in prevention of aggression and development of sociable and democratically orientated citizens.[30] This interest in the effect of social relations, real life experiences, and environment would subsequently set him at odds with others within the psychoanalytic movement who prioritized the analysis of the child's imaginative and emotional world.[31] And it is this that also identifies Bowlby so intimately with the mid-century social democratic settlement.

[28] Dijken, *John Bowlby: His Early Life*, pp. 144–50.
[29] Holmes, *John Bowlby and Attachment Theory*, pp. 25, 40–1.
[30] On the relationship between psychology and interwar progressive pedagogy: Thomson, *Psychological Subjects*, Chapter 4, 'Psychology and Education', pp. 119–39.
[31] Young, Figlio, and Bowlby, 'An Interview with John Bowlby'.

Riley's comment about the accountability for Bowlbyism—that 'Bowlby's work cannot, in itself, be held fully accountable for the phenomenon of "Bowlbyism" '—refers in particular to what is the central focus of her book: the failure to maintain the wartime policy of providing nursery care so that mothers would be free to enter the workforce.[32] She demonstrates that psychological evidence and argument were more peripheral than sometimes has been assumed in the post-war move away from nurseries. In fact, there was little systematic wartime research comparing home and nursery. And even the most significant research on the subject, Burlingham and Freud's study of children in their wartime Hampstead nurseries, acknowledged that the future use of nurseries was an issue that should depend on social and economic need rather than psychological principle. Instead, as Riley demonstrates, the closure of wartime nurseries was an issue of expediency and cost and resulted from the complex relations between government departments.[33] As this suggests, not only does Bowlbyism take us beyond the work and influence of one scientist, but it also refers to a set of policies and practices that might not in fact depend on this psychological theory.

It also needs to be emphasized that much of the initial impetus for Bowlbyism came from identification of the psychological problems of children who lived in institutions rather than the family home (indeed, there was scarcely no research on the latter). This was also the case when it came to Bowlby's own research, which related not to the problems of separation of evacuated children from parents, but rather his pre-war study of the lack of a home as a factor behind juvenile delinquency.[34] So, although Bowlbyism has come to be seen as pre-eminently a psychological argument for keeping mothers in the home, in its origins it was at least as much driven by a desire to reform institutional care. Any analysis of the relationship of Bowlbyism to the post-war social democracy needs to consider this. The British welfare state was to a considerable extent driven by a mood of moving beyond the Poor Law ethos of the past, and probably the most concrete achievement of Bowlbyism was to expose the damaging psychological results of existing systems of institutional care for children. One of the most celebrated examples of this was when Bowlby and his colleague James Robertson at the Tavistock Children's Unit exposed the trauma suffered by young children separated from their parents in hospitals. This was strikingly demonstrated in the film *Going to Hospital with Mother*, which led to a transformation in the policy of visiting young patients following a Ministry of Health report under Chairman Harry Platt.[35] But more

---

[32] Riley, *War in the Nursery*, p. 109.

[33] Riley, *War in the Nursery*, pp. 113–16; Anna Freud and Dorothy Burlingham, *Infants without Families: The Case for and against Residential Nurseries* (London, 1965), pp. 107–8.

[34] However, this pre-war research would not be published until 1944: John Bowlby, 'Forty-Four Juvenile Thieves: Their Characters and Home Life', *International Journal of Psychoanalysis*, 25 (1944), 107–27.

[35] James Robertson, *Young Children in Hospital* (1958). On the tensions with Bowlby: Frank C. P. van der Horst and René van der Veer, 'Separation and Divergence: The Untold Story of James Robertson's and John Bowlby's Dispute on Mother–Child Separation', *Journal of the History of the Behavioral Sciences*, 45 (2010), 236–52. On the history of this episode: Harry Hendrick, 'Children's Emotional Well-Being and Mental Health in Early Post-Second World War Britain: The Case of Unrestricted Hospital Visiting', in Marijke Gijswijt-Hofstra and Hilary Marland (eds), *Cultures of Child Health in Britain and the Netherlands in the Twentieth Century* (Amsterdam, 2003), pp. 213–42.

fundamentally, Bowlbyism was the dominant psychology behind the vision of the Curtis Report of 1946 and the resulting Children Act of 1948 and its new blue-print for institutional care, encouraging authorities to look to alternatives such as fostering, but also encouraging a shift in the scale of residential settings and the inculcation of a family and small home atmosphere.[36] Likewise, evacuation may have done much to heighten rhetoric about the psychological importance of home and the dangers of separation, but it also exposed groups of troubled children who needed specialist care in residential settings, which would take the best features of home—its size and emotional security—but ally it to specialist supervision.[37] In sum, if the wartime social-psychological settlement for children was one that centred on the good home and maternal care, it was also crucially one that looked to the state ensuring that a proxy for such care was a right of all children without a normal home.

POPULARIZATION AND INFLUENCE

The thesis that post-war Bowlbyism was significant in halting an advance in the emancipation of British women has become commonplace, so much so that this critique itself is as important as anything in defining Bowlbyism.[38] Specifically, it is maintained that (on the basis of their limited and flawed research) the work of Bowlby and fellow 'attachment' psychologists, in particular Donald Winnicott, took advantage of media such as the radio, the cheap paperback, and childcare literature to reach a mass audience, popularizing a new emphasis on the impor-tance of attachment between mother and child, and offering authority to the view that maternal deprivation resulted in long-term psychological damage to the child. The critique also argues that this theory was embraced by a state keen to steer women back to the home after their contribution as part of the wartime workforce (and reluctant to take on the costs of a systematic early-years childcare programme).[39] As such, women were discouraged from entering the workplace in child-rearing years, were put at a resulting disadvantage throughout their working lives, and were tied by a sense of psychological responsibility to home and childcare. The result was not only ongoing inequality, but often a sense of isolation, frustration, and even resulting mental ill health as this process went alongside broader social

[36] Indeed the remit of the Curtis Committee was to inquire into methods of caring for children without parents, and not to look towards a shift away from institutional care: *Report of the Care of Children Committee* (HMSO, 1946), p. 5.

[37] Issroff, *Donald Winnicott and John Bowlby*, pp. 196–7.

[38] It is not clear at what point the term 'Bowlbyism' was first used, though it was almost certainly deployed as a language of critique. The analysis in the remainder of this essay indicates the long history of such critique, though also the degree to which the critique became more hostile in the 1970s, as in Patricia Morgan, 'Exploding the Medical Myths of Maternal Deprivation', *The Times* (17 January 1975), and Morgan's *Child Care Sense and Fable* (London, 1975).

[39] Jane Lewis, 'The Failure to Expand Childcare Provision and to Develop a Comprehensive Child-care Policy in Britain during the 1960s and 1970s', *Twentieth Century British History* (Advance Access published 23 May 2012).

changes, including a move to the suburbs, which reduced levels of social support from networks of friends and families.

Research on post-war women and domesticity indicates that we need to revise some of the assumptions that have contributed to this critique of Bowlbyism. For instance, in an analysis of women's magazines from the post-war decades, Liz McCarty indicates that few believed in this period that a woman's place was not in the home, but few felt otherwise that it was only in the home. Crucially, there was space for embracing but then modifying the terms of domesticity to better serve the interests of women.[40] Advances in the standard of living led many women to see work in the home as satisfying, emancipating, and even therapeutic. The attractions may have been particularly strong for working-class women, whereas middle-class women who had previously benefited from paid domestic assistance often found the situation more frustrating. However, it was the generation who were reared within this envir-onment, rather than the post-war mothers, who would go on to identify Bowlbyism as the subject for feminist critique in the late 1960s and 1970s.[41]

McCarty's analysis does not extend to attitudes towards child-rearing. Here we can turn to the popular monthly magazine *Parents*, which reached out to the same sort of audience.[42] Bowlby was an occasional contributor, though there is no sense that he was seen as more significant than the other psychological and medical authorities who regularly advised on childcare. The focus and style of their advice turns out to be rather different than later critique has implied. The Bowlbys and their fellow psychological experts offered a simple and universal solution to virtu-ally any question of childcare: the medicine of providing as much love as possible. And although their presence as well known authorities must indicate a reliance on the advice of the expert to some extent, they did not stand behind the authority of this expertise to impose lessons. They expressed themselves in simple, direct fash-ion. They warned parents not to worry unduly about the practice or science of childcare, and at no point did they themselves throw theory or rigid rules at their readers. Being a loving parent and trusting to one's instincts was all that was needed: 'love 'em and leave 'em be', as Bowlby put it, an idiom that emphasized the sim-plicity of this principle.[43] It was a position that rested on the assumption that this was simply plain common sense, the natural thing to do. 'Stop worrying about

---

[40] Elizabeth Anne McCarty, 'Attitudes to Women and Domesticity in England, *c.* 1939–1955' (unpublished DPhil, Oxford, 1994), p. 16.

[41] McCarty, 'Attitudes to Women and Domesticity', pp. 17–20.

[42] An indication of the readership of this magazine comes in articles that tried to encourage readers to at least visit the state primary school to see that these places were not as awful as they had imagined: Joan Rice, 'Why Not Visit the State Primary?', *Parents*, 11:5 (May 1956), 48. In an earlier incarnation, the magazine had been titled *Childhood*. It was able to attract a rich array of advertisers of patent medi-cines and child-rearing paraphernalia and sold for a shilling. Bowlby also published in the popular forums of *Mother and Child* and the *Child-Family Digest*.

[43] John Bowlby: 'Do You Demand Military Discipline?', *Parents*, 10:6 (June 1955), 36. See also Bowlby's 'Should a Baby be Left to Cry?', *Parents*, 9:3 (March 1954), 32–5; 'Does He Wake at Night?', *Parents*, 12:2 (February 1957), 42. Ursula published a series of articles on psychological types such as 'The Shy Child' and 'The Show Off'. The advice to parents always went back to the importance of more love. They were joined by other prominent authorities on mental health, for instance: J. A. Hadfield, 'Mysteries of Adolescence', *Parents*, 9:8 (August 1954), 22–4.

baby…above all things—use your common sense. Relax' were the typical guide-lines.[44] Running alongside a socially conservative position on family life and the role of women was a strikingly liberal one when it came to the child. Love meant accepting the child: excusing behaviour, letting children play out their grievances. 'Boys will be boys', wrote Bowlby in an article on 'Little Savages'.[45] Parents needed to turn a blind eye to a certain amount of disobedience, and perhaps more radically still accept that parental demands and expectations were often unreasonable. Punishment was never very effective, and it certainly did not produce nicer people. Bowlby claimed never to have used it on his own children.[46] If there was an alternative vision, this was less prominent, and it came not from a feminist perspective but from the position that adult interests needed to be reasserted over those of their children. The regular advice offered up by romantic novelist Barbara Cartland in the 1950s provides us with the clearest example of this position. Cartland highlighted the perils of what she called 'one-sided love'. All the talk of the importance of showing one's love for the child was in danger of leaving marital love in the shadow, and fathers in particular could often feel left out. The new child-rearing, she warned, could cause serious problems for marriage. It could also damage the child. Overprotectiveness and 'cloying, possessive love' held back self-reliance, and was producing a new generation of problem adolescents. Making children little monarchs in the home may have seemed loving, but it ultimately left them bewildered and unhappy.[47]

Magazines like *Parents* were not the only route to a popular audience. Famously, psychologists also reached out via BBC radio broadcasts. Here, as noted in the previous chapter, Bowlby's fellow attachment theorist Donald Winnicott was particularly prominent.[48] Again, these talks did not impose a rigid approach. Winnicott was always keen to emphasize that mothers should not worry about getting things right. The worry was a big part of the problem. They should trust their instincts and enjoy the role of mother. It was a view that combined scepticism about the role of the expert while at the same time naturalizing its own powerful philosophy of maternal attachment: the proper care of the infant could 'only be done from the heart'. Permissiveness, in terms of dropping the rigid rules of how mother should behave but also in attitudes towards allowing the playing out of childhood naughtiness, went alongside the normalization of what was sometimes presented as an almost absolute maternal sacrifice. As Winnicott put it: 'The period in which one is called on to be a mother or father is certainly a time of self-sacrifice. The ordinary good mother knows without being told that during this time nothing

[44] R. S. Illingworth, 'Stop Worrying about Baby', *Parents*, 12:1 (January 1957), 40–2.

[45] John Bowlby, 'Little Savages', *Parents*, 11:10 (October 1956), 40–2.

[46] Bowlby, 'Do you Demand Military Discipline?', 36–8. On the opposition to corporal punishment in this period: Deborah Thom, 'The Healthy Citizen of Empire or Juvenile Delinquent?: Beating and Mental Health in the UK', in Marijke Gijswijt-Hofstra and Hilary Marland (eds), *Cultures of Child Health in Britain and the Netherlands in the Twentieth Century* (Amsterdam, 2003), pp. 189–212.

[47] Barbara Cartland, 'The Perils of One-Sided Love', *Parents*, 12:5 (May 1957), 36–8.

[48] See, for instance, the collection of radio talks and popular articles in Donald Winnicott, *The Child and the Family* (London, 1957); and *The Child and the Outside World* (London, 1957).

must interfere with the continuity of the relationship between the child and herself.'[49] It is in statements like this that one certainly can appreciate why Winnicott and Bowlby would come to be blamed for confining women with the guilt of maternal responsibility.

Bowlby's famous WHO report is said to have sold over 400,000 copies in its English popular edition alone, and naturally tends to be seen as crucial in the popularization of Bowlbyism.[50] Yet any reading of the book itself rapidly puts in question the idea that this was writing that reached out with a clear message to the average mother or father. It seems far more likely that the average Briton came into contact with Bowlbyism via the radio or magazines like *Parent*, in mediated, diluted form, presented as common sense rather than theory, and with a greater degree for flexibility than isolated statements from Winnicott and Bowlby might suggest.

In their sociological research on attitudes towards infant care published in 1963, John and Elizabeth Newson poured cold water on assumptions that parents duti-fully and perhaps neurotically followed the instructions of childcare literature. Interviews with working-class parents revealed a widespread feeling that the big-gest shift was that children were now normally brought up under better economic conditions than their parents, and that this meant more opportunities. The Newsons recognized that this was also a factor in the relaxation of discipline within the home. Mothers often emphasized a new warmth and companionship, and this could be related to the fruits of economic well-being: more leisure time, a forty-hour working week, better housing, and smaller families, meaning that there was more space in this housing. And if childcare advice was important, it was the pro-gressive childcare of the interwar years which now filtered down to the working classes as economic change made it more feasible.[51] More apparent than anything was an attitude of not wanting children to be deprived, like parents felt they had been, of the material goods now available through more widespread prosperity. As the Newsons observed, the 'country's toy boxes [were] crammed to capacity'. The house was transformed accordingly: tidiness and quiet sacrificed to play.[52] Such a shift did find the support of the childcare advice industry in writing on play, and in guidance on how to manage the radically expanded apparatus of play, but it was driven not by this culture of advice but by the desire to provide something that parents had lacked. The defence against deprivation, in short, manifested itself in material and not just emotional form, and in toys and not just state milk and orange juice.[53]

---

[49] Winnicott, 'Young Children and Other People' (1949), in Winnicott, *The Child and the Family*, pp. 94, 99.

[50] The figure of 400,000–450,000 is commonly cited. See, for instance, Holmes, *John Bowlby and Attachment Theory*, p. 27.

[51] John and Elizabeth Newson, *Infant Care in an Urban Community* (London, 1963), pp. 219–34.

[52] Only 12 per cent of mothers, according to the Newsons, now demanded a high degree of clean and quiet behaviour in the house: John and Elizabeth Newson, *4 Years Old in an Urban Community* (London, 1988), pp. 136–7, 163.

[53] However, there was also an attempt during this period to tame this new commercialism by a science of the role of toys in development: Beatrix Tudor-Hart, *Toys, Play and Discipline in Childhood* (London, 1955).

A second survey that casts light on post-war childcare was undertaken by a young female sociologist, Hannah Gavron. A young mother herself, Gavron would commit suicide at the age of twenty-nine in Primrose Hill, just a few doors away from the house where poet Sylvia Plath had killed herself only two years earlier in 1963, aged thirty. There was a striking irony in such a fate for a woman whose main research subject had been the loneliness and depression of the isolated, house-bound mother.[54] Her book *The Captive Wife*, published posthumously in 1966, was based on doctoral research undertaken at the Institute of Community Studies, but whereas the best known studies of this centre, undertaken by Peter Wilmott and Michael Young, had focused on the established members of traditional communities, Gavron set out to study the young mothers who were at the cutting edge of social change. What she discovered was not a weakening of the family (something that had been a concern in Wilmott and Young's work in relation to care of elderly family members), but children receiving far more parental care than their parents had, and parents with a strong consciousness of a major shift in style.

Gavron's study is particularly revealing on the relationship between class and parenting. Although a very high proportion of the middle-class wives had worked before marriage (all but 6 per cent), just 37 per cent returned to work after leaving to have children. Childcare advice appeared to be a major factor in this. 'I think, now I have a child', one mother reflected, 'it's very wrong for me to leave him. I used to think I'd go on working, but then I read articles and books about leaving little children and, well, I decided I would not.'[55] A striking 48 per cent saw even a small amount of separation as damaging. As Gavron put it: 'Certainly the general impression gained from the interviews was that despite the presence or absence of help with children most mothers felt psychologically tied to their young children, and felt themselves compelled to stay at home whatever their own personal desires.'[56] Yet, the vast majority of these middle-class women still looked to a return to employment once their children entered full-time education. And 33 per cent were already sending their children to nursery school, while only 12 per cent said they would never use nursery care for the under-fives. This was not just an issue of finding relief from the stresses of childcare; many of these mothers believed that nursery school provided an environment that would be a stimulus to the development of their young children; and belief in the importance of children being able to express themselves may have provided them with further justification and confidence. What was also apparent was that even if middle-class mothers were tied to childcare during the day, they were able to maintain fulfilling outside interests and often pursued these in the evenings. Compared to working-class mothers, there was much less isolation. Among the working class there was less conflict between

[54] Hannah Gavron, *The Captive Wife: Conflicts of Housebound Mothers* (London, 1970). On Gavron's suicide: Jeremy Gavron, 'Tell the Boys I Loved Her', *Guardian*, 4 April 2009. As with Plath, the drama of Gavron's history contributed to her emergence as something of a feminist icon. For instance, on the relation between Gavron's work and that of performance artist Bobby Baker: Elaine Aston, ' "Transforming" Women's Lives: Bobby Baker's Performances of "Daily Life" ', *New Theatre Quarterly*, 16 (2000), 17–25.
[55] Gavron, *Captive Wife*, p. 72.   [56] Gavron, *Captive Wife*, p. 78.

the roles of motherhood and career, yet it also seemed there could be more difficulties in coping with the situation of being a mother. Poor housing, lack of play facilities, lack of nursery schools, lack of babysitters, reduced contact with extended family, and reduced earnings all made childcare a strain. Mitigating this to some extent was the 'striking' help from fathers. But the challenge was considerable as working-class families, like middle-class families, saw themselves as having moved beyond the practices of older generations. Moreover, a significantly higher proportion of working-class mothers felt it was their responsibility to remain with their young children all the time: 40 per cent compared to 7 per cent in the middle class. Gavron was unsure whether this was due to genuine feelings or to the fact that there was so little potential assistance available. Whichever was the case, the situation had worrying consequences. Many working-class mothers found themselves cooped-up all day on their own with young children, who had less opportunity, whether through choice, danger of traffic, or the shift to high-rise accommodation, for relief through going out to play on their own and with others than had been the case in the past. A striking 77 per cent spoke about this problem of isolation.[57]

Gavron was highlighting a serious problem of the 'captive wife', but as with the other social surveys the blame fell less on psychological theorists, such as Bowlby, and more on the broader social changes of the period. For this reason, her research suggested that the working-class mother was placed under particular strain.[58] However, this was not an inevitable destiny. Early marriage, opportunity in an era of full employment, and a declining birth rate which meant less time was taken up by care of young children all contributed to a situation in which married women in fact played a more active role in the post-war workforce than sometimes assumed. Entry to the workforce was particularly marked in areas like London, where opportunities were strong and costs of living high. Here, research by Dolly Smith Wilson indicates that 42 per cent of women with children in fact had an outside job in the early 1960s. This flew in the face of the wisdom coming from psychologists such as Bowlby and Winnicott. In these situations, it seems that working women were able to adapt the thesis of maternal deprivation to posit the extra income as a necessity in preventing their offspring from being 'deprived' of the benefits of affluence.[59]

Finally, one of the arguments of this chapter has been that Bowlbyism was something that emerged out of, and was directed towards, care of children in institutions and not just the family. What then of its influence here in the post-war

---

[57] Gavron, *Captive Wife*, pp. 88–9. On the problem of life in high-rise flats, Gavron drew on Hilda Jennings, *Societies in the Making* (London, 1962) and Joan Maizels, *Two to Five in High Flats* (London, 1961). See also Pearl Jephcott, *Homes in High Flats: Some of the Human Problems Involved in Multi-Storey Housing* (Edinburgh, 1971). For an overview of the literature on the relation between high-rise living and mental health: Hugh Freeman, *Mental Health and Environment* (London, 1984), pp. 215–20.

[58] The currency of such ideas is evident in an episode of *Man Alive* aired on BBC2 on 4 January 1967, the first in a series on 'Marriage under Stress', on the issue of the strain placed on young married couples by the challenge of coping with children: 'Children Make a Difference'. The programme is accessible via the BBC online archive: <http://www.bbc.co.uk/archive/marriage/10512.shtml>. The narratives of these young couples highlight in particular the problem of isolation across class, lack of support from husbands, and the impact of childcare on happiness about sexual relations.

[59] Dolly Smith Wilson, 'A New Look at the Affluent Worker: The Good Working Mother in Post-War Britain', *Twentieth Century British History*, 17 (2006), 206–29.

decades? In her study of the English domestic environment in post-war Britain, Alison Ravetz has pointed out that '[a]fter 1948 institutional living was transformed in two particular respects: the domestication of its environments and the giving of more privacy to inmates.'[60] When it came to children, the exposure of the emotional deprivation suffered in children's homes during the Second World War and the ensuing Curtis Report added new urgency to the sentiment for greater homeliness. The resulting 1948 Children's Act made it the responsibility of local authorities to provide 'homes' for children lacking an 'ordinary family life'.[61] The new legislation provided the basis not for ending the institution, as might seem to be the case given the emphasis of commentary on the importance of the home, family, and avoidance of separation, but instead provided the institution to some extent with new life in the guise of a replacement home and family. Given ongoing concern about the real family homes of many children, numbers in care continued to rise to a peak of about 100,000 in the middle of the 1970s, around 35,000 in children's homes. With average overall stays just a year and half, around 50,000 passed through these homes each year in the 1970s. Fostering had risen to 48 per cent of the total of all children in care by 1964, but the idealization of home could make it difficult to find places that satisfied high expectations or which could cope with the social and behavioural problems of the children.[62] The sheer number in need of care made it impossible to cope with demand, and by 1974 the percentage in foster care had fallen back to 32 per cent, little different from the time of the Curtis Report.[63]

CRITICISM AND RETREAT

In 1962, the World Health Organisation commissioned a review of Bowlby's influential study of 1952.[64] The new report recognized the huge impact of the earlier publication, particularly when it came to improving the quality of institutional care for children, but acknowledged that his theoretical conclusions had been subject to considerable criticism and modification as a result of new research. It was now recognized that it was difficult to distinguish the effect of maternal deprivation in isolation from other factors. Even when maternal deprivation was a factor, one needed to distinguish between physical deprivation—resulting from the absence of the mother—and psychological (or 'masked') deprivation—when the mother was present but unable or unwilling to provide the necessary level of love. What this also meant was that family and home could not necessarily be seen as the solution to emotional deprivation. In fact, perfectly adequate care could be

[60] Alison Ravetz, *The Place of the Home: English Domestic Environments, 1964–2000* (London, 1995), p. 93.
[61] Ravetz, *The Place of the Home*, p. 83.
[62] Christian Wolmar, *Forgotten Children: The Secret Abuse Scandal in Children's Homes* (London, 2000), p. 74.
[63] Wolmar, *Forgotten Children*, pp. 40, 62.
[64] WHO, *Deprivation of Maternal Care: A Reassessment of its Effects* (Geneva, 1962).

provided in environments other than the family. The kibbutz movement, which had blossomed in the post-war decades, provided one obvious example. The effects of emotional deprivation were also cast into doubt. Looking back to Bowlby's own research on delinquency, which now appeared increasingly flimsy, it was pointed out that only in a quarter of the cases had institutional care in fact resulted in long-term damage. Moreover, recent research on 500 children at a reception centre for placing children in care, undertaken by Hilda Lewis, had struggled to demonstrate any clear relationship between separation and long-term disturbed behaviour.[65] And other research had highlighted that it was possible to overcome the effects of early emotional deprivation.[66] The most scathing criticism was left to two women: the American anthropologist Margaret Mead and the British social scientist Barbara Wootton. Mead berated psychologists such as Bowlby for their lack of attention to anthropological studies of child-rearing.[67] She pointed out that a model of maternal attachment centred on the home was only possible in a culture which had seen the end of domestic production and in which contraception radically limited the size of families. In other cultures, the issue of separation was more likely to be traumatic when it related to the person providing nursery care rather than the mother. In truth, there were many possible forms of childcare, and each would play a role in shaping the identity of children. There was nothing natural about the model of the isolated mother of the nuclear family, and in an era of social change like the present it could offer an environment that was potentially harmful. Yes, Bowlbyism had undoubtedly done much good when it came to humanizing the impersonal style of residential care. But Mead fundamentally objected to the 'reification into a set of universals of a set of ethnocentric observations on our own society'.[68] Wootton's problems were different but equally damning. They drew on remarks in her influential book of 1959, *Social Science and Social Pathology*. Wootton argued that there had been a tendency to extrapolate research based on the bad effects of some of the worst sort of institutions (as with Bowlby's own research on delinquency) to make claims about the danger of maternal separation more generally. To date, the research basis for theories of maternal deprivation was in her view wholly inadequate. Such research claimed to show that love was more likely to come from the family rather than the institution, but this was little more than common sense and was ultimately a social rather than a psychological fact. Proper research would need to take into account the backgrounds from which institutionalized children came. It would need to prove that the supposedly affectionless child of maternal separation was really the fount of delinquency. And in order to do so, it would need a large-scale survey of behavioural problems and social background

[65] Hilda Lewis, *Deprived Children: The Mersham Experiment: A Social and Clinical Study* (Oxford, 1954). Bowlby responded with a letter to the *British Medical Journal*, expressing concern that the study might encourage complacency regarding separation of children from their mothers in the earliest years.

[66] D. Stott, 'The Effects of Separation from the Mother in Early Life', *Lancet*, 1 (1956), 624.

[67] Margaret Mead, 'A Cultural Anthropologist's Approach to Maternal Deprivation', in WHO, *Deprivation of Maternal Care*, pp. 45–62.

[68] WHO, *Deprivation of Maternal Care*, p. 58.

within the broader population.[69] In the face of such criticism, a full and careful response followed from Bowlby's colleague Mary Ainsworth.[70] The picture that emerges is of a theory which was far from hegemonic, but also one which in accepting qualifications and greater complexity was far from the crude vehicle for keeping mothers at home of later caricature.

By the late 1960s, we see this faltering confidence in home as an ideal environment for the development of the child becoming more prevalent. The post-war idealization of maternal care was coming to be seen, not as the solution, but increasingly as part of the problem. It had left many young mothers isolated. The child's physical needs might now be far more readily satisfied in an increasingly affluent society, but the same could not be said for emotional and social needs. In a report published in 1968, Simon Yudkin recognized that Bowlby was still the essential starting point, and that it was vital for mental health that 'the infant and the young child should experience a warm, intimate and continuous relationship with his mother (or permanent mother substitute) in which both find satisfaction and enjoyment'.[71] However, Yudkin argued that Bowlby was much misunderstood. The last qualification—both child and parent finding 'satisfaction and enjoyment'— was crucial. So too was the fact that Bowlbyism allowed for a mother substitute. And like others, Yudkin felt that there was a danger of far too narrowly interpreting Bowlby's use of the term 'continuous relationship'. In the past, mothers had provided this care with the assistance of extended family and domestic servants. However, social change was also now radically altering the conditions under which mothers operated. They were now more socially isolated than ever before. This was partly an issue of choice and economic opportunity: the move away from family driven by a desire for freedom and independence on the one hand, and education and pre-marital employment on the other. And it was sometimes exacerbated by a new type of building, the high-rise flat, which attracted considerable attention in terms of its affects on mental health. The sense of isolation for home-bound mothers was particularly acute when it came to women who had experienced the independence given by new economic and educational opportunities. In such a situation, unhappy and isolated mothers struggled to provide the physical and psychological environment necessary for healthy child development. But many women were resisting the role of stay-at-home mothers: an estimated 750,000 mothers with children were in some form of paid employment, two-thirds of them full-time. This reality of the working mother, the desperate need of mothers who did stay at home for some kind of relief, but also a new bulge in the birth rate (rising from 3.9 million in 1955 to 4.8 million in 1965) all exposed the very limited provision of pre-school day care. With little other choice, many mothers were left to farm out children to unregulated childminders in often squalid and overcrowded

---

[69] Barbara Wootton, 'A Social Scientist's Approach to Maternal Deprivation', in WHO, *Deprivation of Maternal Care*, pp. 63–73.

[70] Mary Ainsworth, 'The Effects of Maternal Deprivation: A Review of Findings and Controversy in the Context of Research Strategy', in WHO, *Deprivation of Maternal Care*, pp. 97–165.

[71] Simon Yudkin, *0–5: A Report on the Care of Pre-School Children* (London, 1968), p. 3.

environments.[72] In the 1970s, the street-level social investigations of Brian Jackson would help to expose the considerable extent of such a hidden childminding culture.[73]

Picking up on the growing criticism in professional circles, but also emerging out of parental experience, by the 1960s one can trace mounting disquiet over Bowlbyism in a liberal forum such as the *Guardian*. 'The isolation of the mother and the pre-school child is a new phenomenon', wrote teacher and psychotherapist Caroline Nicholson. 'Both are denied the support, interchange, stimulation, and variety of experience which a large social group, including a large family with various generations represented, can provide.' Living in such isolation, notably in the high-rise flats that attracted increasing attention, lack of freedom to play, rather than lack of love, emerged as the central problem in child development. There was desperate need for alternatives, and Nicholson looked in particular to nursery provision and playgroups. Blame now began to fall on Bowlbyism, if not Bowlby himself. As Nicholson put it: 'Dr John Bowlby's work on maternal deprivation has been a great service, particularly perhaps in hospitals: but his findings have sometimes been misunderstood or misused.' Crucially, there was 'no necessary virtue in keeping mother and child (of say 2½ to 5) clamped together day in and day out'. No mother could provide for all the needs of a child in such circumstances. It was wholly unfair to present mothers who failed to live up to this ideal as disowning their responsibility. Fault instead needed to be directed at a state unwilling to fund alternatives, though women could also contribute to the problem, guilty at times of being seduced by the 'indispensability myth'.[74]

Drawing directly on the WHO reassessment, a 1963 *Guardian* article, in its 'Mainly for Women' section, continued this critical line on 'mother lack'. Again, Bowlby himself was less to blame than the way he had been used and popularized. What we see now, however, is Bowlbyism emerging as a key political arena for post-war feminism. The article attacked the 'sheep-like self-satisfaction of educated women who have sunk all their former interests in full-time maternity'. It aligned itself with Margaret Mead's view that the campaign against maternal deprivation was little more than a form of subtle anti-feminism. And it drew on the 1962 WHO report to argue that it was no longer tenable to argue that home and mother were necessarily enough for the child on their own. If home was the site for 'masked deprivation', it was the result not of the bad mother, but of isolation and lack of stimulation.[75] Likewise, drawing on Simon Yudkin's work, an article in the *Observer* in 1963 publicized claims that women could go out to work without any harm to children under two as long as there was an effective mother substitute; indeed it could be a positive benefit to both mother and child. The problem with Bowlby's work was that it been based on cases of permanent separation. This was wholly different to the case of the woman who simply left her child temporarily in capable

---

[72] Yudkin, *0–5*, pp. 1–18.
[73] Brian and Sonia Jackson, *Childminder: A Study in Action Research* (London, 1979).
[74] Caroline Nicholson, 'Left Hand—Right Hand', *Guardian* (27 April 1962).
[75] Lois Mitchinson, 'Mother Lack', *Guardian* (16 January 1963).

hands while she took up part-time work.[76] By 1965, the tone of debate had become more heated. Caroline Nicholson accepted that new editions of Bowlby's seminal work downplayed the idea that he was exclusively advocating mother–child attachment. But the problem was that he could still very easily be read in this way. It was this simplified message that remained the most influential. And it was this message that provided ballast for the Ministry of Education in its recent decision to avoid any expansion of nursery care. There were signs of a shift of the pendulum, but in Nicholson's exasperated view there was still a generation of women trapped by the Bowlbyite message of 365 days-a-year mothering.[77]

The mounting critique of Bowlbyism was not simply a case of middle-class feminists picking up on the revisionist research. It also drew on a grass-roots response of women beginning to establish their own way out of isolated motherhood. In 1961 one such mother, Mrs Belle Tutaev, wrote a letter to the *Guardian* about her own experience and called for mothers to react by grouping together to provide their own nursery facilities.[78] There was an excellent response, with some 150 letters, and this led to the formation of the Pre-School Playgroups Association in September 1961. The first group was in Marylebone in London, but by early 1962 there were thirty other groups across the country.[79] In 1967, the association was catering for some 20,000 under-fives and was in receipt of a grant from Department of Education.[80] By 1968, it was providing play facilities for a remarkable 83,000.[81] The playgroup movement was closely aligned to the Nursery School Campaign, which petitioned against government failure to implement proposals for nursery care under the 1944 Education Act.[82] If the nursery and playgroups movements were to a large extent driven by middle-class frustrations, the working-class family was turning to often unregulated childminding.[83] And in inner-city areas, one also sees pre-school provision emerging as a site for radical and community political agitation, exemplified by events in Notting Hill in London in the later 1960s and attempts to take over unused private gardens to provide play spaces for children.[84]

By the mid-1970s there had been a major shift in opinion. Even the Trades Union Congress now set itself up as a supporter of 'Toddlers' Lib' and free nursery

---

[76] Katherine Whitehorn, 'Danger—Women at Work', *Observer* (17 February 1963).

[77] Caroline Nicholson, '4 Views of Child Care', *Guardian* (30 April 1965). Nicholson was a psychotherapist and teacher.

[78] The 50th anniversary led to renewed attention towards these efforts, which were particularly interesting in relation to cuts being experienced by the voluntary sector but also the new Conservative government's emphasis on both the 'big society' and the value of pre-school care. An interview with Tutaev can be seen on the Pre-School Playgroups Association website: <https://www.pre-school.org.uk/about-us/history/1262/interview-with-alliance-founder-belle-tutaev>. For an account of the early years: Joan Conway, 'The Playgroups Movement, 1961–1987', in *Memories of the Playgroup Movement in Wales, 1961–1987*: <http://www.playgroupmemorieswales.org.uk>.

[79] Jean Soward, 'Nursery Crusade', *Guardian* (21 February 1962).

[80] Caroline Nicholson, 'Playgroup Pioneers', *Observer* (15 June 1967).

[81] 'Pre-School Playgroups Association', *Guardian* (16 May 1968).

[82] 'The Topsy-Turvy World of Under-Fives', *The Times* (19 October 1966).

[83] Brian and Sonia Jackson, *Childminder: A Study in Action Research* (London, 1979).

[84] Jan O'Malley, *The Politics of Community Action: A Decade of Struggle in Notting Hill* (Nottingham, 1977).

care for all.[85] Psychologist Michael Rutter's *Maternal Deprivation Reassessed*, published in a popular paperback in 1972, in its title alone seemed to indicate that science no longer upheld Bowlby's findings (though it actually was much closer to Bowlby than this title suggests). It continued a revisionism that went back several decades and which was now placing increasing emphasis on the importance of the breakdown and discord of the family as a factor in problems of attachment.[86] The fact that there could now be calls for 'mothering to come back into fashion' and articles complaining about the guilt of the stay-at-home mother is an indication of the sea change in sentiment.[87]

From the early 1970s, grass-root efforts in supplementing childcare were also beginning to gain a degree of state support (evident in the government grant to the playgroups movement). In the process, the language of deprivation shifted from simply a critique of the absence of mother and instead found itself describing the result of the limited type of care that home and mother on their own could sometimes offer to the child. Even Margaret Thatcher, Secretary of State for Education in the 1970 Conservative government, accepted that nursery education had a value in providing a stimulus for children that many were unlikely to receive at home.[88] She is better known for earning the nickname of the 'milk-snatcher' for the withdrawal of free school milk for seven to eleven year olds in 1970. In fact, there is a striking symmetry in the two developments: the decline of the nutritive symbol of state care for the child at just the same time as a collapse in faith in familial emotional nutrition, echoing their parallel emergence to prominence in the aftermath of the war; linked symbols for a confidence in an approach to child well-being that had been an integral part of the post-war settlement, and which by the 1970s was being fundamentally destabilized.

One new factor in the heightened political interest in childcare was an increasing concern about immigrant children, particularly those from a non-English-speaking background.[89] A longer running concern, revived as confidence faltered on the Right when it came to the ability of the welfare state to eradicate rather than cement poverty, was the idea that a culture associated with 'problem families'

---

[85] '"Toddlers' Lib" Advocates get Unanimous Backing', *The Times* (7 September 1972).

[86] For Rutter's later reflections on this period, see his interview at: <http://www.ucl.ac.uk/histmed/downloads/hist_neuroscience_transcripts/rutter.pdf>.

[87] Dr Tony Smith (Medical Correspondent), 'Time for Mothering to Come Back into Fashion', *The Times* (6 December 1977).

[88] In fact, the principle of universalism had already been broken with the withdrawal of free milk for older school children under Harold Wilson's Labour administration, and Thatcher resisted complete withdrawal. Margaret Thatcher's statements on nursery education are available via the online archive of the Thatcher Foundation: <http://www.margaretthatcher.org>. See, for instance, her speeches to the National Society for Mentally Handicapped Children, 16 April 1971 (Document 102105) and to the Nursery School Association, 19 May 1973 (Document 102281), as well as her written statement accompanying the Education White Paper, 6 December 1972 (Document 102233).

[89] This is given further attention in Chapter 7. See Thatcher's speech on Pre-School Provision, House of Commons, 12 May 1972 (Document 102200). See also her speech to the Nursery School Association Conference, 19 May 1973 (Document 102281); and her House of Commons speech on Urban Deprivation and Children, 1 November 1973 (Document 102311).

spawned a cycle of social deprivation.[90] In the early 1970s, this was particularly associated with the Conservative Secretary of State for Social Services, Keith Joseph, who from 1972 to 1973 used the Pre-School Playgroups Association and the National Children's Bureau Conferences for several pronouncements on the issue and channelled funds to help extend playgroups and to foster research via the National Child Development Study.[91] The most controversial party political issue was over the targeting of such aid. The previous Labour government's Urban Aid Programme offered a way to target such pre-school provision at socially deprived areas; as Labour's Clare Short pointed out, playgroups had blossomed most where there had been an input from middle-class parents, and thus voluntarism on its own was unlikely to offer a solution. The White Paper 'Education: A Framework for Expansion' looked to a future in which pre-school provision should be a right for any parent who wanted it and within ten years would be free for children at the ages of three and four. However, in the short term, targeted pre-school provision provided an attractive tool in addressing social deprivation, a way to reach out to the children in homes where the family was deemed insufficient for good care, but also offering a model to these parents themselves.[92]

Joseph's remarks in a speech in Birmingham in 1974 on permissiveness, where he advocated birth control to address the cycle of deprivation, have attracted far more attention than these earlier iterations. In fact, his controversial views on birth control had already been rehearsed in his earlier speeches on deprivation.[93] Thanks to the recent work of John Welshman, we now have a detailed picture of the thinking behind Joseph's pronouncement on a cycle of deprivation and of the research projects that he drew upon.[94] This did not include Bowlby's own work, but this is

[90] The 'problem family' discourse, which was particularly prominent in the aftermath of the Second World War, was deeply connected with Bowlbyism and the concerns that fuelled it and saw social work as a key tool in addressing the quality of family life. See, for instance, Tom Stephen (ed.), *Problem Families: An Experiment in Social Rehabilitation* (London, 1945). There was a feeling that the 1948 Children Act's focus on residential care and fostering had sidestepped the vital issue of protecting children in the family: Report of a Joint Committee of the British Medical Association and the Magistrate's Association, *Cruelty to and Neglect of Children* (London, 1956). For an overview of the problem family literature: John Welshman, 'In Search of the "Problem Family": Public Health and Social Work in England and Wales, 1940–1970', *Social History of Medicine*, 9 (1996), 448–65.

[91] 'Minister Launches Campaign to Save Children from "Cycle of Deprivation"', *The Times* (30 June 1972); 'Sir Keith Joseph Sets the Targets', *The Times* (30 June 1972); 'Ministry Orders Study on Needs of Deprived Children', *The Times* (29 August 1972); 'Bad Parents Should Lose Rights to Their Children, Expert on Home Care Says', *The Times* (23 September 1972). For a detailed account of the origins and impact of Joseph's pronouncements on a cycle of deprivation: John Welshman, *From Transmitted Deprivation to Social Exclusion: Policy, Poverty, and Parenting* (Bristol, 2007).

[92] However, it would prove difficult to extend provision: Margaret Bone, *Pre-school Children and the Need for Day-Care: A Survey Carried out on Behalf of the Department of Health and Social Security* (London, 1977). See also: *Services for Young Children with Working Mothers: Report by the Central Policy Review Staff* (London, 1978). For a survey of changes across the century: Jack Tizard, Peter Moss, and Jane Perry, *All Our Children: Pre-school Services in a Changing Society* (London, 1976), pp. 69–90.

[93] Joseph offered his defence in a letter to *The Times*, 22 October 1974, and this is also covered in 'Birth Control Remarks Naïve, Sir Keith Admits', *The Times* (21 October 1974).

[94] The importance of Joseph's earlier thinking on social deprivation is acknowledged in detailed examination by John Welshman. Welshman does recognize the significance of psychologists in this debate, but particularly in relation to concern about educational attainment: 'Ideology, Social Science, and Public Policy: The Debate over Transmitted Deprivation', *Twentieth Century British History*,

perhaps no surprise given its fading prominence and the criticism that it now encountered. Nevertheless, assumptions about the problem of emotional deprivation were present in much of the research on problem families and juvenile delinquency. And Joseph's model of a cycle of deprivation did intriguingly echo the model of emotional deprivation in one generation producing children who would be unable to offer the necessary love to their children in turn. Joseph was too well-read not have been aware of this, and he was certainly conscious of attachment psychology. He is reported to have been deeply moved when he watched Robertson's film on the emotional effects of separating hospitalized children from their families.[95] He would use Winnicott's language of 'good enough' parents.[96] And he was particularly interested in the work of Michael Rutter, who was in the midst of updating Bowlby's work, albeit with some important revisionist qualifications.[97] It was no coincidence that Joseph chose meetings on pre-school play and nursery care for many of his speeches on social deprivation. Like others, Joseph had lost faith in the unwritten assumption of the post-war settlement that families, on their own, could be relied upon when it came to the care of young children. Instead, family and home environment was coming to be seen as a cause of poverty, and one which all the efforts and cost of the welfare state had done little to solve. If anything, social change was making this problem worse, with the loss of the social support of extended families and communities that had remedied parental shortcomings in previous generations.

The loss of faith in the family was travelling across the political spectrum. This was another reason why Joseph was channelling so much energy into the issue. The Left, and their academic supporters, had their own solutions: structural change and positive discrimination would lever these families out of poverty and provide them with the necessary assistance to bring up their children.[98] Joseph looked instead to addressing the transmitted effects of upbringing. Here, encouraging the development of playgroups and nurseries in areas of need was part of the solution. Another was to look to social work. However, following a high point of confidence in the aftermath of the Seebohm Report of 1968, the 1970s was a period of increasing difficulties for the profession as expansion slowed in the context of recession and economic retrenchment and professional confidence ebbed.[99] The furore that resulted from Joseph's inclusion of birth control among possible solutions did not help his cause, nor the fact that the Conservatives lost the General Election of

---

16 (2005), 306–41. For detailed analysis of the research behind the cycle of deprivation thesis: Welshman, *From Transmitted Deprivation to Social Exclusion*, pp. 27–44.

[95] Christopher Reeves, 'Why Attachment? Whither Attachment?: John Bowlby's Legacy, Past and Future', *Beyond the Couch: The Online Journal of the American Association for Psychoanalysis in Clinical Social Work*, 2 (December 1997): <http://www.beyondthecouch.org/1207/reeves.htm>.

[96] Welshman, *From Transmitted Deprivation to Social Exclusion*, p. 55.

[97] Welshman, *From Transmitted Deprivation to Social Exclusion*, p. 65. Joseph later played a role in the knighthood of Rutter: Normand Carrey, 'Interview with Sir Michael Rutter', *Journal of the Canadian Academy of Child and Adolescent Psychiatry*, 19 (2010), 212–17.

[98] 'Deprived Children Dangers', *The Times* (13 June 1973).

[99] Mary Langan, 'The Rise and Fall of Social Work', in John Clarke (ed.), *A Crisis in Care: Challenges to Social Work* (Milton Keynes, 1993), pp. 48–58.

1974 to Labour. This left the broader structural solutions of the Left, on the one hand, and the Right's rhetoric of a need to return to traditional values, on the other, as the main battle-lines of debate over the family and childcare over the next decade.[100] It was only under New Labour's Sure Start programme launched in 1998 that there was a return to a social policy centring on such early intervention in child-rearing, though this time driven more by economic arguments about the long-term impact of a poor start in life.[101] By 2012, David Cameron's Conservative administration was once again exploring the territory opened up by Keith Joseph in the 1970s, with proposals of setting up parenting classes, and this time drawing on neuroscience to revivify the idea that early-years care was fundamentally important as a cause of later social problems.

The collapse of confidence in home and family also extended to the sphere of education. In 1967, the influential Plowden Report had concluded that home environment was central to educational attainment.[102] But this was also a reflection of a growing sense that the benefits of a landscape of home could no longer be taken for granted. The fact that an increasing proportion of these homes were immigrant homes added to concern. An apparently high rate of 'educational subnormality' in children of West Indian immigrants was particularly controversial territory.[103] Research was suggesting that a cultural difference in the way West Indian families brought up their children was a root cause of the problem. Crucially, West Indian mothers appeared not to conform to normative expectations about good parenting. One observer remarked on 'the curiously cold and unmotherly relationship between many West Indian mothers and their children' in Jamaica as well as in London. Children appeared to be left to their own devices, with a prevailing attitude of 'pay you no mind'. Informal childminding was the norm. There was an absence of cuddling, fussing, and intimacy. There was no tradition of mothers playing with their children (also worrying, in Asian families play seemed absent altogether). Childhood, as such, was short and inadequate for the demands of development. It was suggested that traditional African practices had been destroyed in the trauma of slavery, and that European ways had not yet come to replace them. This left a 'maternal deprivation' comparable to that found in the orphanages of the past. There were signs that the situation was improving among second-generation immigrants. Earlier marriage was encouraging a move to more conventional family units. State provision also played a role, as single mothers were provided with council housing and social security, enabling them to stay at home

---

[100] For a detailed account of the lack of political will to institute a broader early-years childcare policy: Lewis, 'Failure to Expand Childcare Provision'.

[101] John Welshman, 'From Head Start to Sure Start: Reflections on Policy Transfer', *Children and Society*, 24 (2010), 89–99.

[102] *Children and Their Primary Schools: A Report of the Central Advisory Council for Education* (London, 1967), pp. 22–5. As John Welshman points out, Plowden and the ensuing policy of Educational Priority Areas can be seen as Britain's version of the United States' Head Start. However, the British recognized weaknesses in the American policy and by the mid-1970s there was a much greater emphasis on structural causes: 'From Head Start to Sure Star'.

[103] Edwin de H. Lobo, *Children of Immigrants to Britain: Their Health and Social Problems* (London, 1978).

and care for young children. But the ongoing inadequacy of care within the family appeared to be demonstrated by the high proportion of immigrant children entering care, estimated at between 14 and 20 per cent of the total.[104]

Adding to the alarm about the home life of immigrant children, and extending concern to the growing Asian population, was the problem of developing English language skills.[105] Here was a clear indication that deprivation could lie not just in emotional neglect but also in culture.[106] Such concern encouraged a policy of assimilation and the prioritization of teaching English. A 1965 government circular on the 'The Education of Immigrants' went as far as to recommend dispersal of immigrant populations; however, it proved very difficult to overcome a system of effective school segregation that emerged as a result of housing and neighbourhood schools. The policy of bussing children to schools in other areas, which was so influential in the United States, was considered by local authorities including Birmingham and the Inner London Education Authority, but was rejected. By the 1970s, a consensus on assimilation as the way forward was breaking down. Instead, there was a shift of emphasis to consider the curriculum and practices of schools themselves.[107] Likewise, when it came to educational outcomes more generally, a new body of research began to challenge the socially determinist consensus with evidence that suggested that the quality of schooling was central.[108] In short, we see in these debates about education a double move away from confidence in home and family as a site for the cultivation of the child: first, we see the landscape of home coming into focus as a potentially major problem and handicap; but we then see an emerging critique and loss of confidence in doing anything about this and a retreat to a focus on better schooling as the solution.

Just as schooling would feel the effects of the faltering of confidence in an idealized model of home and family, so too would the field of residential care. If isolation was the potential problem with home and family, it also came to be recognized as the downside of residential care in small units that mimicked the family unit. Career prospects through working in these settings were limited while the challenges were considerable, and this had a deleterious effect on the quality of staff. Often poorly trained, isolated, and without proper support or relief, those working in such homes could suffer acute stress. This in turn led to high staff turnover, which made it even harder to aspire to a vision of family care. With an increasing proportion of immigrant children entering care, racial difference between carers and residents offered a further challenge to the family ideal. Despite the recognition that stability and therefore permanent residence were essential in alleviating the already damaging effects of separation from family, the reality was that these homes were often acting as temporary holding places, and this further handicapped

---

[104] Lobo, *Children of Immigrants*, pp. 36–7.   [105] Lobo, *Children of Immigrants*, pp. 66–73.
[106] Lobo, *Children of Immigrants*, pp. 58–9.
[107] Sally Tomlinson, *Ethnic Minorities in British Schools: Review of the Literature* (Aldershot, 1987).
[108] Michael Rutter, Barbara Maughan, Peter Mortimore, Janet Ouston, and Alan Smith, *Fifteen Thousand Hours: Secondary Schools and Their Effects on Children* (London, 1979).

the development of bonds of attachment.[109] Most disturbing of all, by the end of the 1970s, there was emerging evidence that within these closed settings the rhetoric of attachment and love had the potential to be distorted in acts of sexual abuse.[110]

CONCLUSION

In his analysis of Melanie Klein and the origins of the British welfare state, Eli Zaretsky has argued that in the first decades of the twentieth century, Freudian psychoanalysis had an historical trajectory of 'defamilialization' in its exposure of the disjuncture between the cultural and the intra-psychic world. It was also preoccupied with the role of the father. During this period, with popular suspicion of its intra-psychic focus and its focus on sex, it was a counter-cultural project and was largely marginal to the working class. 'In 1930s and 1940s Britain, however, its fate became entangled with the creation of a modern social-democratic welfare state, committed to securing the material bases of personal life for all.'[111] Key in this transition was the wartime shift of focus to the relationship between mother and child, away from sex, and towards love and attachment. Zaretsky associates this with the influence of Melanie Klein in particular; though there is a case for seeing Bowlby and Winnicott as just as central in terms of broader appeal, and as noted above Bowlby would see his focus on social relationships and environment as in fundamental tension with the still intra-psychic focus of Klein and her followers and would be marginalized from the post-war psychoanalytic community accordingly. What Zaretsky pays less attention to is the relationship of psychoanalysis to the welfare state after 1945, and this has been one of the subjects of this chapter. Zaretsky suggests that psychoanalysis would support a welfare state settlement that was at the same time economically progressive and culturally conservative. This analysis of Bowlbyism offers some support to Zaretsky's thesis. Undoubtedly, the broad currency of Bowlbyism helped justify and support a role for mothers as unpaid carers which was important to the economic basis of the welfare state. Yet, as this chapter has argued, this offers us only a partial appreciation of the ways in which the implications of Bowlbyism reached into the fabric and emotional expectations of the welfare-state settlement. Alongside its recommendations about maternal attachment, Bowlbyism directed a popular audience towards a liberal approach in childcare. This set up a tension that could undermine confidence in the family: the family environment had to provide necessary freedoms for development when in fact it found itself increasingly isolated due to broader social changes. For this reason, it became difficult to sustain absolute faith in a landscape of home

[109] For a detailed account of the problems experience in one such setting: *Community Work and Caring for Children: A Community Project in an Inner City Local Authority by a Group of Workers from the Harlesden Community Project* (Ilkley, 1970).

[110] Wolmar, *Forgotten Children*, Chapter 7, 'Sexual Politics and the Zeitgeist'. The decline in the scale of residential childcare after the mid-1970s must also be attributed to a crisis in local government finances: Wolmar, *Forgotten Children*, 68.

[111] Zaretsky, 'Melanie Klein and the Origins of the British Welfare State'.

and family by the 1970s. In retrospect, one of the central flaws of the Bowlbyism that emerged out of the Second World War was that it focused so exclusively on the bonds of love within the family and saw freedom as something that could be explored within these boundaries. This was a view that emerged out of the traumas of separation that so marked the experience of war. However, it overlooked the findings of progressive education. And it overestimated the ability of the family.

The decline of confidence in home, family, and its emotional security did not bring the post-war settlement to an end, but it stripped it of part of the social glue that had held it together in its classic phase from 1945 to the middle of the 1970s. Jane Lewis has argued that in the United Kingdom 'the problem of childcare was not considered to be an issue for state policy until the later 1990s; men and women were free to enter the labour market, but were expected to make their own arrangements regarding care for their children'. The end of the post-war family settlement had to wait for the demographic and economic shifts in the final decades of the century, changes which encouraged a fundamental shift in government attitudes to the labour market and thus to childcare and in particular led to the development of policies to facilitate the entry of mothers into the workforce.[112] In other parts of Europe, the state was much earlier in accepting a duty to support the family and provide care. The British welfare state had depended not just on the state and on a settlement between capital and labour, but on a gender settlement between men and women at a household level, inscribed in the idea of the family wage, and based on assumptions of full male employment and stable families.[113] If we accept this thesis, then Bowlbyism readily assumes the role of scientifically legitimizing cement for this settlement. Yet, Bowlbyism's relationship to the post-war settlement was more complex, deeper, and in some respects more socially radical than this argument about its role in taking the family out of the state policy implies. Bowlbyism also helped bring social democracy—manifest in its valuing of relationships and love, but also in its emphasis on the importance of leaving children free to play and disrupt—into the sphere of the family home. For this reason, it was also one of the most intimately experienced features of that settlement, paralleling the embodiment of the settlement in the material nourishment of school orange juice and milk. However, the valuing of social relations and free play meant that it was difficult to sustain a settlement focused on the isolated family. In that sense, there was always a need to supplement the love of family with sites for extended social democratic emotional formation such as the playgroup, the nursery, and then the school. In fact, the development of such provision can be seen in some respects, not as a reversal for Bowlbyism, but as necessary for its ultimate fulfilment.

The wartime settlement reflected an ideological overestimation of the capacities of the landscape of home and family that had much to do with the trauma of the conflict. Over subsequent decades, social change gradually undermined the idea of the family home as a haven and thus the basis for this settlement: immigration and

---

[112] Jane Lewis (ed.), *Children, Changing Families and the Welfare State* (Cheltenham, 2006), p. 14.
[113] Lewis (ed.), *Children, Changing Families and the Welfare State*, pp. 2–5.

post-war building challenged normative assumptions about home life, women entered the workforce, feminism reacted against the gender settlement, and the family and its bonds of marriage proved increasingly unstable. Bowlbyism found itself at the centre of the debates that ensued. Indeed, as this chapter has demonstrated, a serious critique of Bowlbyism can be traced back at least to the start of the 1960s. However, Bowlbyism always left more room for adaptation than sometimes assumed, and as such the thesis of a war-born cocooning of the child and fundamental narrowing of the landscape for the child needs some qualification. Bowlbyism was a response, not just to concerns about the family, but also to the inhumanity of much existing residential care. Yet in providing a model for reform, it in fact offered residential childcare a new lease on life. Bowlbyism also provided grounds for supplementing the family if this did not provide the ideal environment that had been envisaged. Initially, this provided grounds for intervening in the 'problem family'. By the 1960s, the immigrant family was emerging as a new focus. Even when it came to the middle-class family home, there were grounds for arguing that this environment could foster a damaging isolation and a form of cultural deprivation. In such instances, the challenge was now translated from one of deprivation to de-privation: finding ways in which to reconnect the isolated mother and child.[114]

As Lewis has argued, the state was largely able to resist action in this post-war era. But action did bubble up from below, in the nursery and playgroup movements, in radical community politics, and in second wave feminism. And in the 1970s, we see the Left looking to policies of positive discrimination and targeting of aid to areas most in need, which reflected increasing academic and political support for the view that the problem was structural rather than personal. We also see the Right mounting a counter-attack on the 'cycle of deprivation' that found its origins in the problem home and family which would need to be tackled through social intervention. In short, by the mid-1970s, we see a significant faltering of confidence in the landscape of the family home as the locus of childcare. This would soon be further fuelled by a new recognition of physical and then sexual abuse located in the family and then an emerging discourse of children's rights, subjects which are taken up in the final two chapters of this book.

---

[114] Gavron, *Captive Wife*, p. 149.

4

Television and a Virtual Landscape for the Child

Wartime anxiety about British children encouraged not just idealization of the home but also efforts to fit the outside world to the mind of the child through the creation of special, protected landscapes. This chapter focuses on one of these places—the virtual landscape opened up through television—later chapters touch on another—the physical landscape of the adventure playground. Television was an increasingly important part of the landscape of the child in this period, accessible for just a few families at the start of the period but extending its range rapidly to reach 40 per cent by 1955 and 89 per cent by 1963.[1] At the heart of this expansion was the vision that child development would be fostered through special programmes designed with the child in the mind, and even that television at some times of the day would be specially given over to the child viewer.

In the post-war era, the increasing provision of facilities like this specially designed for the child went alongside, and probably in the end compounded, fears that the broader public arena was a dangerous place for the unprotected child. Anxieties about social danger, whether in the form of sexual predators or traffic, as well as the development of childhood into a key arena for consumption, have further encouraged this process. Children now move between specialized sites of safe leisure dislocated from the urban environment, accompanied or at least ferried in cars by their parents.[2] The antecedents of such a phenomenon might be located in the emergence of organizations such as the Boys Brigade and the Boy Scouts in the late nineteenth and early twentieth centuries, which aimed to occupy, reform, and contain working-class youth, particularly male, working-class youth.[3] In the interwar

---

[1] David Oswell, *Television, Childhood and the Home: A History of the Making of the Child Television Audience in Britain* (Oxford, 2002), p. 87.

[2] For a picture of this situation in Berlin: Helga Zeiher, 'Shaping Daily Life in Urban Environments', in Pia Christensen and Margaret O'Brien (eds), *Children in the City: Home, Neighbourhood and Community* (London, 2003), pp. 66–81.

[3] Though they tended to be more successful in reaching out to those who were already well-disposed rather than boys who were still hanging out on street corners: J. Springhall, 'Building Character in the British Boy: The Attempt to Extend Christian Manliness to Working-Class Adolescents, 1880–1914', in J. A. Mangan and James Walvin (eds), *Manliness and Morality: Middle-Class Masculinity in Britain and America 1800–1940* (Manchester, 1991), pp. 52–74. On the anxiety about young working-class men in this period: Harry Hendrick, *Images of Youth: Age, Class, and the Male Youth Problem, 1880–1920* (Oxford, 1990). On scouting: Allen Warren, 'Popular Manliness: Baden-Powell, Scouting and the Development of Manly Character', in Mangan and Walvin (eds), *Manliness and Morality*, pp. 199–219.

period, the club was also a panacea. What was different about the post-war development was that the emphasis shifted from one of control and integration of the child in institutional structures with rules and discipline, to one of play, exploration, and individuality: a move to the cultivation of a managed freedom. The new sites of childhood also emerged within a context in which home had been validated as the best place for children, particularly through the experience of war, but was now coming to be recognized as not providing for all the psychological needs of the child. The adventure playground and children's television provided bridges and sites for development between the safety of home and the freedom and danger of the outside world. Several basic psychological assumptions lay behind the design of such spaces. Firstly, children grew, through a series of developmental stages, in relation to their environment. As such, they needed both special provision and protection. Secondly, and this had found ratification in war, all children had within them a 'latent streak of cruelty': they did need protection and guidance, but in part because of the danger that they themselves represented if development went wrong.[4] The tensions between these two basic assumptions, and between concern about protecting children and protecting society from children, would permeate the debate over the next half-century.

In the period from the Second World War to the 1970s, television emerged as a fundamentally important aspect of the landscape of the British child. In a period in which independent physical access to the outside world diminished for many children because of concerns about safety, the television screen had the potential to compensate through broadening horizons safely within the cocoon of the family home. It also offered an opportunity to project a vision of the outside world matched to the psychological abilities and needs of the child: a model environment for healthy growth. Its potential as a tool of the more interventionist, paternalist government of the post-war era and for extending the reach of such efforts into the domestic sphere was at its greatest when it came to the child, and this has probably not attracted the attention it deserves, perhaps because it was not directly provided by the state. However, television was also a sphere of consumption, particularly after the introduction of choice through the emergence of Independent Television in 1954. The tension between social engineering and the market (and between the paternalism of the BBC's vision of developmental children's programming and the desires and appetites of children themselves) offers a second key context for the ensuing debates over the landscape of the child.

Television's critics argued that its seductions were no compensation for a life of outside play that was social, active, and creative. The example of American television provided a warning. It had exploded from a medium reaching just fourteen thousand to one encompassing five million families between 1947 and 1950, and

---

[4] Mary Field, *Good Company: The Story of the Children's Entertainment Film Movement in Great Britain, 1943–1950* (London, 1952), p. 154. Indicative of a broader anxiety was the impact of William Golding's 1954 novel *Lord of the Flies,* which explored the cruelty of a group of evacuee boys stranded on an island. Golding suggested that the Second World War had opened his eyes to this: John Carey, *William Golding: The Man Who Wrote Lord of the Flies* (London, 2009), p. 82.

was described in Britain as ministering 'to a public passively, silently, nightly view-ing escapist fantasy'.[5] Critics feared that it would not prove possible to provide a fit environment for the child through television: for some, it was an inherently debased cultural medium; for others, it had potential, but this was always fighting a losing battle with the drive to increase viewing figures, which drove broadcasters down the line of the lowest common denominator. Even if children's television was a protected environment, there was still the problem that what children watched, and indeed how they watched, ultimately depended upon some sort of responsible parental guidance. There was a serious danger that the child would be exposed to, attracted by, and influenced by inappropriate adult programming.[6] At the heart of such anxiety, throughout the first decades of British television still in the shadow of war, but also right into the 1970s, were the issues of fear and violence.

The first section of this chapter examines attitudes towards a screen landscape for the child provided by cinema, a medium that already reached a huge number of children before the war and which continued to overshadow the significance of television in the 1940s and early 1950s but then declined, partly in response to the challenge of television. It highlights, in particular, a heightened concern about the psychological effects of cinema arising from the Second World War, and efforts to produce a new sort of child-centred film in response: developments that paralleled and informed the medium of television. It then moves on to explore the develop-ment of television as a medium for children. It considers in particular the vision behind early BBC children's programming and its aim of providing a special devel-opmental landscape for the child, but also the way this clashed with the role of television as a medium of entertainment. These issues are brought into focus by analysis of what was one of the largest psychological studies in the country up until that date, the Himmelweit investigation into children and television published in 1958. Finally, the chapter concludes by considering the degree to which the pater-nalistic vision of children's programming was being challenged and was breaking down by the 1970s.

CINEMA

Before the advent of television, Britain had already been through three decades of reflection on the relationship between the screen landscape of the cinema and the social, moral, and psychological health of the child. This had been an issue since at least 1917 and the *Report of the Cinema Commission*, following an investigation undertaken by the National Council for Public Morality.[7] Much of the initial

---

[5] Bernard A. Smith, 'American Television at the Crossroads', *BBC Quarterly*, 7:3 (Autumn 1952), 129–35: p. 135; Lloyd Morrisett, 'The Age of Television and the Television Age', *Peabody Journal of Education*, 48 (January 1971), 112.

[6] See the discussion in Nick Lee, 'The Extensions of Childhood: Technologies, Children, and Independence', in Ian Hutchby and Jo Moran Ellis (eds), *Children, Technology and Culture: The Impacts of Technologies in Children's Everyday Lives* (London, 2001), pp. 153–69.

[7] National Council of Public Morality, *Cinema Commison of Enquiry: The Cinema: Its Present Position and Future Possibilities* (London, 1917).

debate focused on the supposed moral ills associated with the new medium; though more in relation to the site of the dark cinema and the dangers, particularly sexual dangers, it presented, than with the effect of the moving pictures themselves. The site of the cinema remained a subject of concern. In the context of alarms over delinquency and socialization in the Second World War, J. Arthur Rank set up his cinema clubs to contain the unruly and unaccompanied young of the Saturday Morning cinema. His model was soon taken up by competitors, attracting children of around seven to ten years of age, with about one million members out of a total child population of seven million. However, this too provoked concern when the findings of J. P. Mayer's *Sociology of Film* were published in *The Times* and then discussed in Parliament. Mayer highlighted in particular the authoritarian overtones of the Odeon National Cinema Club promise (for instance, its song included the words 'We are thousands strong | So we can't be wrong'). And he argued that the atmosphere of the cinema was one dangerously suited to mass suggestion.[8] Such anxieties help to explain why the emergence of an alternative site for a screen landscape, within the safety of the home, had its attractions in this period.

Despite public concern about the content of cinema posing a threat to the child and potentially encouraging delinquency, psychologists were often rather less alarmist. The leading child psychologist of the interwar period concluded that there was little evidence of a direct link between the subject matter of cinema and delinquency.[9] The real danger of influence was more subtle, lying in cinema's 'wild emotionalism' and unrealistic view of life.[10] Allied to this, there was also an appreciation that such an effect might be all the more powerful because the medium was particularly conducive to the child mind. As early as the First World War, Dr C. W. Kimmins had asked 6,700 London children (92 per cent of whom already turned out to be cinemagoers) to write about their favourite films. Kimmins discovered that these children found the medium natural and easy to interpret, readily connecting together visual scenes into a narrrative. He speculated that children might in fact be better suited to following the medium than adults, its visual sense closer to their more primitive mental world. Flashbacks and close-ups aided comprehension and compensated for limited powers of memory. And film's natural orientation to the fantastic, through the distortions of reality possible in manipulations such as the speeding up or slowing down of film, seemed naturally suited, like the fairy story, to the mental world of the child. However, the conclusions that Kimmins drew from this were far from pessimistic. Given the appetite of children for the medium, but also the ease with which they understood, there was in fact a great opportunity to develop the aesthetic sense of the type of child who did not normally benefit from a cultural education.[11]

[8] Discussed in Terry Staples, *All Pals Together: The Story of Children's Cinema* (Edinburgh, 1997), pp. 103–18; 'Films for Children: Entertainment as an Aid to Education', *The Times* (5 January 1946); House of Commons Debates, 27 November 1946, columns 1656–90.
[9] This was the conclusion of psychologist Cyril Burt, *The Young Delinquent* (London, 1925), pp. 143–50.
[10] Burt, *Young Delinquent*, p. 148.
[11] C. W. Kimmins, *The Child's Attitude to Life: A Study of Children's Stories* (London, 1926), pp. 91–108.

It was not until the Second World War that there a concerted effort to take up this challenge. The films that children watched until then were mainly the same as those for adults. They started their habit early, on average just four to five years old.[12] However, it was hard to see the type of fare that attracted these children as disturbing or morally dangerous. Typical was the Western B Movie series *Hopalong Cassidy*, whose eponymous character has been described as 'an inflexible moralist, a medieval knight transposed to the western range'. On the other hand, neither was such subject matter uplifting, educative, or designed with the qualities and needs of the child in mind.[13] The problem was apparent to J. Arthur Rank when he reflected on the films watched in his wartime Saturday morning clubs, and he set about exploring the possibilities of producing his own films that might serve a more moral role. The war made production difficult, but the first film was produced in 1943 and a Children's Film Department was founded with Rank's support in 1944. It was also important to establish how children responded to the new films. Thus, the Children's Film Department experiment would be doubly significant: first, in the attempt to produce a new type of film suited to the particular needs of the child; second, because it was soon tied to new research on how children watched films, even going as far as filming them in the act of watching by using infrared photography. Key to the new films such as *Bush Christmas* (1947) was a child-centred philosophy of having characters and situations for children to identify with (children were often the central characters) and of being able to provide these child viewers with 'good company'.[14] The problem was that these Rank films were seen by only a minority of children. Nevertheless, the idea of making films specifically with the needs of children in mind was praised by the Wheare Committee, set up in response to the anxiety about children and film that had erupted in 1946. This led to the formation of the Children's Film Foundation, funded by a levy on the sale of tickets, which only closed in 1985.[15] The heyday of such films was in the 1950s, though even then their popularity was far behind that of American Westerns and cartoons.[16] In the longer term, such a philosophy was to find a greater opportunity in children's television.[17] Meanwhile, children's attendance at cinemas fell as television established its grip in the post-war era. It was widely accepted that the relative fortunes of the two were integrally linked. By the 1970s, the mayhem of children's cinema matinees was winding down, and the tradition had virtually vanished by the early 1980s.[18] It is too simplistic to see this as the replacement of social by private watching, for the watching of television still

---

[12] J. P. Mayer, *British Cinemas and Their Audiences* (London, 1948), p. 151.

[13] On Hopalong Cassidy: Staples, *All Pals Together*, p. 63.

[14] Field, *Good Company*.

[15] Staples, *All Pals Together*, pp. 152–6, 240; K. C. Wheare, *Report of the Departmental Committee on Cinema and Children* (London, 1950).

[16] Mary Field, 'Children's Taste in Cinema', *Quarterly of Film, Radio, and Television*, 11 (1956), 14–23; Rowana Agajanian, ' "Just for Kids?" Saturday Morning Cinema and Britain's Children's Film Foundation in the 1960s', *Historical Journal of Film, Radio and Television*, 18 (1988), 395–409.

[17] Indeed, in 1959 the figurehead of the Children's Film Foundation, Mary Field, moved to become director of children's programmes at Anglia Television: Staples, *All Pals Together*, p. 197.

[18] Staples, *All Pals Together*, p. 237.

took place within the social setting of the family, while the dark of the cinema presented its own form of privacy.[19] Nevertheless, the social as well as the environmental conditions for constituting a landscape of the child through the screen would see a fundamental shift because of this move from cinema to the television.

TELEVISION

The BBC had begun a limited television broadcasting service before the Second World War, and this included an even more limited provision for children. The early effort in this direction was unsurprising, given that *Children's Hour* was already one of the BBC's longest running radio programmes, dating back to 1922. Indeed, when television closed down because of the war it had been in the middle of showing a Mickey Mouse cartoon.[20] When it resumed, it still reached only 0.2 per cent of family homes.[21] Soon after the resumption, the social survey organization Mass-Observation undertook an investigation of attitudes towards the new medium. The majority of the 684 participants were middle class, as indeed were most of the people who were willing to pay for a television set, which was still a relatively expensive item. The social constituency would subsequently broaden, with the middle classes more likely to look down on the medium. Such ambivalence was already evident in the Mass-Observation responses. Half of the respondents had seen television, and a similar proportion wanted one in their own homes. However, there was a high level of suspicion. There was a feeling that there was already too much 'synthetic entertainment', and compared to the wireless, the new medium suffered from cutting down the possibility of doing something else at the same time: it demanded too much concentration and offered too little in return. When it came to advantages, the child was a key figure, with television seen as having a potential for education and for furthering family life. In the words of one twenty-nine-year-old housewife:

> We have had a working television set for nearly two years now and have derived great pleasure from it. The children love it too, and they've learned a lot even at their immature ages of three and four. How many children of three have been to the Antarctic and seen the seals and the penguins, or viewed the antics of a skiing school in Switzerland, or laughed at Laurel and Hardy's tumbles and horse-play etc. Yes, they love it; with sucking thumbs and goggle-eyes they remain glued from start to finish. Television is certainly a very great broadening and enlightening invention.[22]

---

[19] David Morley, *Family Television: Cultural Power and Domestic Leisure* (London, 1986), pp. 19–22.
[20] Anna Home, *In the Box of Delights: A History of Children's Television* (London, 1993), p. 15.
[21] Oswell, *Television, Childhood and the Home*, p. 87.
[22] Mass-Observation, File Report 3106, 'Panel on Television' (1949), p. 11.

Already this hints at public interest in the potential of the new medium to open child eyes to a landscape well beyond the home, a vision that was perhaps at its most idealistic in these post-war years. Yet we also have the picture of 'goggle eyes' glued to the screen, an image intriguingly embraced by this young mother but which would also jeopardize and limit the reputation of television as a good thing for developing minds and bodies.

A key figure in the early days of children's television was the producer Freda Lingstrom, who joined the BBC in 1940 at the age of forty-seven after an earlier career as an artist and writer. As a radio producer for the Schools Department, she had been responsible for a series of books under the title *Looking at Things* and an illustrated book, *The Seeing Eye*, which aimed to develop the child's abilities in relation to form, design, and colour in everyday life. In 1951 she became head of the new children's department in television, and she brought these interests in the child's view of the world to the production of short programmes for the under-fives, such as *Muffin the Mule*, *Andy Pandy*, and *The Flowerpot Men*. She was the dominant force in the early days of the children's department, known to others as 'mum', and a defender of the possibility that television could be a medium of the highest quality when it came to child development.[23] Writing in the early 1950s, Lingstrom reflected on the fact that within a hundred-mile radius of the capital there was now emerging the first-ever generation who had grown up with television as a normal part of everyday home life. From the earliest age, their eyes had followed its moving patterns of light. They had grown into consciousness in front of programmes: some designed for the child; the majority not, probably unsuitable, yet just as influential. The power of the medium over young, impressionable, minds was not to be underestimated: even 'in one second a trick of light', she suggested, 'may release in a child a new conception, grant him a moment of pure joy or send an arrow to his heart.'[24] Consciously and unconsciously, these minds were constantly absorbing such influences, some falling deep within but all significant in shaping a developing personality. It was such a philosophy, like that of Mary Field at the Children's Film Foundation, that meant that television for children emerged fully conscious of its potential to offer a new sort of landscape for the child, one for the first time fitted to psychological capacity and need.

The new medium was also reshaping the rhythm of child life. The home-centred nature of post-war family life was thereby reinforced: the rush *home* from school for 'children's hour'; a 'new kind of table-talk' between mother and child derived from their common experience as viewers; bedtime and teatime rearranged in relation to home-centred television viewing. Where once the outside world had been brought into the home by the visits of friends or by books and letters, it now came in more easily and with a vigour, clarity, and strength that was much greater than it had been through sound or word alone through the 'small square of light and

---

[23] Monica Sims, 'Lingstrom, Freda Violet (1893–1989)', *Oxford Dictionary of National Biography* (2004), available online at <http://www.oxforddnb.com/index/65/101065425/>.
[24] Freda Lingstrom, 'Children and Television', *BBC Quarterly*, 8 (1953), 96.

shade' in the family living room.[25] The child of the new medium was to come to know the outside world through seeing rather than being told about it.[26] In their research on the life of four year olds in Nottingham in the mid-1960s, John and Elizabeth Newson found that the television was increasingly emerging as a hub of the house, and indeed that its location was 'always a good indication of the family's true living room'.[27] Like the street, television could offer the child a zone of freedom from supervision, and as such its potential for capturing the enthusiasm of the child was far greater than that of the school.[28] The Newsons noted how even their four year olds followed the television with 'rapt attention', and were offered a 'window through which to view a whole world of people, phenomena, artefacts and events which an earlier generation of children could never have become aware of until a much later age'. And they pointed to its significance, not just in expanding horizons of knowledge, but also in the child's understanding of social relationships.[29]

In a period in which intellectuals still tended to look down upon the new medium, or at best to view it with a condescending attitude of 'amused tolerance' as a source of light entertainment, Lingstrom emphasized that it would be a huge mistake to dismiss its significance for children. Adults may have turned to television for light relief—a 'narcotic' for the jaded and disappointed at the end of the day—but children watched in a completely different way. When it came to children, television was hugely important. This presented opportunities, but also dangers. Lingstrom argued that up to the age of ten, children would watch anything, only later beginning to develop any discrimination (she suggested limiting them to no more than an hour a day).[30] They watched the screen with hunger, full attention, and an open and plastic mind. The adults who had responsibility for these children needed to take the subject and their resulting moral obligations just as seriously.[31]

Lingstrom was not alone in recognizing this. The dawn of children's television, coming as it did amidst the broader ambitions of post-war reconstruction, was an exciting time for envisioning the potential of the new medium. If the child mind absorbed all that came before it, the issue of what children watched emerged as hugely important for the long-term health of society. Naomi Capon argued that there was a responsibility to use television to cultivate the 'visual appreciation' of future generations. BBC radio, fuelled by the vision of its first Director General John Reith, had already shown the way through its mission of elevating standards

---

[25] Lingstrom, 'Children and Television', 96.

[26] Lingstrom, 'Children and Television', 96–7, 96–102.

[27] John Newson and Elizabeth Newson, *Four Years Old in an Urban Community* (London, 1968), p. 34. The television came to assume pride of place in the post-war living room, taking over from the hearth as a central focus especially after the introduction of central heating: Oswell, *Television, Childhood, and the Home*, pp. 88–9.

[28] Lingstrom, 'Children and Television', p. 100.

[29] Newson and Newson, *Four Years Old*, pp. 63–4.

[30] This was confirmed by the Newsons: *Four Years Old*, p. 63.

[31] Lingstrom, 'Children and Television', pp. 98–101.

in terms of music and the spoken work. There was now a chance to address Britain's lamentable standing in the world of visual taste, not just by putting on art programmes for children, but also by involving artists in the making of other programmes, in the use of sets, and at the most fundamental level though the use of light and composition in all programming.[32]

It was also accepted that the child's 'unconscious viewing'—their watching of programmes that they could not understand—was generally a bad thing.[33] The implication of such logic was that television needed to be specially designed for the child and should provide, as Lingstrom put it, 'a complete service in miniature', or in the words of the Mary Adams, Head of the Talks Department at the BBC, 'a microcosm of television forms'.[34] This was not a wholly new philosophy. The idea of special children's programming had emerged in pre-war radio. It was now translated to television, with one title for the whole of the children's schedule: at first *For the Children*, and then *Children's Hour*. Infants had earlier provision. The idea was that children would settle down to watch on their return from school. At the end came the so-called 'toddler's truce', a *cordon sanitaire* of television close-down to avoid any clash with the family teatime and to keep children well clear of the evening programming for adults.[35] In reality, the ambition of a 'complete service in miniature' would prove very difficult to contain within such limits.

The concept of children's hour would run up against another basic tenet of child psychology: the developmental assumptions that made it clear that the perspective and the needs of the infant were very different to those of the adolescent. The answer perhaps was to produce a variety of programmes within a slightly extended children's schedule. For the very young child, the key was to stimulate the senses and to encourage participation but not imitation (the latter, one of the key early fears in light of apparent unconscious imitation in response to screen personalities and screen behaviour in the United States). One early result was television's adaptation of the puppet show, epitomized by *Muffin the Mule* or *Andy Pandy*: centred on non-realistic figures, with care taken to 'eliminate sources of conflict between eye and ear', and with the added safety of coming to the child in the security of the home and with nothing alarming and nothing to contradict the routines of the family.[36] When it came to the adolescent, the emphasis shifted to the use of television as a safe conduit between home and the outside world. Adult programmes

---

[32] Naomi Capon, 'The Child and the Dragon', *BBC Quarterly*, 6:1 (Spring 1951), 18–26.

[33] David Buckingham, Hannah Davies, Ken Jones, and Peter Kelley, *Children's Television in Britain: History, Discourse and Policy* (London, 1999), p. 19.

[34] Lingstrom, 'Children and Television', p. 101; Mary Adams, 'Programmes for the Young Viewer', *BBC Quarterly*, 5:2 (Summer, 1950), 82; Buckingham et al., *Children's Television in Britain*, p. 17.

[35] Anna Home, *Into the Box of Delights: A History of Children's Television* (London, 1993), pp. 15–18. Radio's *Children's Hour* was particularly designed for the seven to thirteen year old, and had a strong educative mission, aiming to develop adult listeners and doing so with programmes that attracted adult as well as child listeners: WAC, R11/51/2, 'Children's Hour Policy', 30 July 1942. Its audience fell with the spread of television and became increasingly middle class: WAC R11/51/3, Memo RM/MS 4 August 1960. By the early 1960s, the audience had fallen to 250,000 and a new title of 'An Hour for the Family' was suggested: WAC R11/51/4.

[36] Adams, 'Programmes for the Young Viewer', 87.

might be accessible to these children. Indeed, because of a greater experience in viewing television, their 'technical criticism' could be superior to that of the adult. But such viewing was often not emotionally or morally appropriate. What was needed instead was a type of programme that took the older child out into the world and to an appreciation of its real scale—not through models of the world but through participation in the real thing—and then associated the home-bound child with projects of real engagement with this world, for instance in building a house, an aeroplane, or a boat.[37] However, such grand ambition was difficult to realize. The models did tend to be models, not the real thing, and adolescent children moved elsewhere.

The early hopes for television in relation to the child mind had one further fundamental flaw. If the child saw television through child's eyes, how could the adults who designed the programmes understand its impact and plan accordingly? Was the attempt to do so in fact one that reflected adult desire for a landscape for a good childhood far more than children's own sensibilities?[38] How, moreover, in an age in which the child still had a very limited voice of its own, could research that still relied on adult and parental views of the child's likes and dislikes act as a useful guide?[39] To make matters worse, there was very little reliable evidence on what children were actually watching.

One possibility in response to this challenge of measuring the effect of the medium on children was to call on outside psychological expertise. The very fact that programmers were themselves now arriving at such doubts is at least indicative of the way that child psychology and a sympathy for being child-centred was 'in the air' at this time. Yet, there is very little to suggest that such an interest was particularly well-developed or that psychologists were being relied upon to conduct research into the subject. Several psychologists did in fact write general pieces in the trade press of the period, in which they reminded the BBC that they were the experts who might be needed in any such exercise.[40] And psychologists were consulted in the early 1950s on the issue of children's viewing. But their views were never given much weight.[41]

There were no psychologists involved when Freda Lingstrom organized what was the first significant British investigation into children and television in 1951–2. The panel, instructed to view and comment upon a week of children's programmes, ranged from members of the public such as housewife Mrs Evelyn Tillyard—'who throws open her house to village children for all television programmes'—to Mary Field, who had pioneered the child-centred approach in producing films for the Children's Film Foundation.[42] The panellists were to pay particular attention to six

---

[37] Adams, 'Programmes for the Young Viewer', 88.

[38] This argument is developed in relation to children's literature in Jacqueline Rose, *The Case of Peter Pan or the Impossibility of Children's Fiction* (London, 1984).

[39] Capon, 'The Child and the Dragon', p. 28.

[40] Sir Cyril Burt, 'The Psychology of Listeners', *BBC Quarterly*, 4:1 (April 1948), 7–13; T. H. Pear, 'Psychology and the Listener', *BBC Quarterly*, 4:4 (Winter 1949–50), 154–9.

[41] Oswell, *Television, Childhood and the Home*, pp. 116–17.

[42] Field, *Good Company*.

issues: firstly, whether television should be regarded as an amusement only, or was a service opening the door to other interests; secondly, the balance of output; thirdly, the suitability for each age group; fourthly, the needs of minorities, and particularly whether those with special disabilities or aptitudes were being served; fifthly, the effect on home life; and finally, what aspects of television were frightening for the child.[43] The research struggled to arrive at concrete conclusions. It was poorly organized and lacked rigour, with the findings largely anecdotal and little consistency in the methodology. The one key issue that did arise was the extent to which television involved a new kind of passive watching. No doubt this was encouraged by the presence of Mary Field, who already had an interest through her studies of how children watched the cinema.[44] The other panellists agreed with Field that this was a key issue as far as television was concerned. Lady Pakenham described the state of the watching child as a 'kind of coma' and warned that television was exacting a 'compulsive reaction' among urban children. Yet the panellists also acknowledged the potentially positive effects of television. It seemed that passive watching still allowed ideas to sink in, even if they did not emerge into consciousness until much later: 'it doesn't matter if they do forget it for a month or two's time; it is something which is incorporated in their development'. Television might not raise the intelligence of those watching, but as long as it 'stirred their brains' just a little they would be taking something in. On the vexed question of fear and violence, the panellists were not even willing to go with their hunches.[45] It must have been clear to those involved that outside expertise was necessary if such psychological questions were to be addressed more rigorously. A year later and facing mounting public concern over the effect on children of depictions of cruelty and violence, the BBC found such an opportunity in the proposal for an independent Nuffield-funded psychological study of the effect of television on the British child.[46]

THE HIMMELWEIT REPORT

The Nuffield-funded research project, begun in 1954, was headed by a young social psychologist from the London School of Economics, Hilde Himmelweit.[47] The report that followed in 1958—*Television and the Child*—often goes under her name. Its full title described it as an 'Empirical Study of the Effect of Television on

---

[43] WAC T16/46: Commissioned Report on Children's Television, 1951–2.

[44] See, for instance, her 'Unfinished Project', *Sight and Sound*, 18 (1949), p. 8. This had been picked up by the *Picture Post*, which ran an article using cut-down versions of some of Mary Field's photographs of children watching film to produce an exaggerated picture of fear: Staples, *All Pals Together*, pp. 157–73. She would go on to publish her Carnegie Trust research as *Children and Films: A Study of Boys and Girls in the Cinema* (Dunfermline, 1954).

[45] WAC T16/46, 'Report of the Meeting of the Children's Television Panel', 15 August 1952.

[46] WAC T16/303: Nuffield Foundation Enquiry, 1953–9.

[47] On Himmelweit: Marie Jahoda, 'Himmelweit, Hildegard Therese (1918–1989)', *Oxford Dictionary of National Biography* (2004, 2009), available online at <http://www.oxforddnb.com/index/39/101039974/>.

the Young', the choice of 'the young', rather than 'children', indicative of a tension in the report about where to draw the lines of childhood and any resulting regulation of content when it came to television. Not only was it the most substantial piece of psychological research of its day on the subject of television and the child, involving eleven separate studies and several thousand children, but it was also one of the most expensive British pieces of social scientific research ever at the time. When it came to children's viewing, there was nothing to match it in the British context over the following decades.[48] It offers us a uniquely detailed and complex picture of the role of television in relation to the landscape of the child in post-war Britain. Although its significance is acknowledged in the existing secondary literature, this chapter offers the first detailed examination of its findings.

When the investigation began in 1954, there were about three million British homes with a television. The research therefore captured the viewing habits of the British child on the cusp of the television age. It was also able to study some populations, such as in the Norwich area, before and after the advent of television and so to gauge effect in a way that would soon be impossible. Likewise, it could offer a picture before and after the first broadcasts from ITV.

The research took place in the context of heated public debate about whether television was a good or bad thing when it came to children. Keen to distance itself from the polemics, the final report painted its picture in greys. The effect of television was

> not as black as it is painted, but neither is it the great harbinger of culture and enlightenment which its enthusiasts would tend to claim for it. If television is a window on the world, it gives a view not very different from that provided in books, comics, films, and radio programmes. Similarly, its capacity for broadening a child's horizons is not spectacularly different from that of any other mass media.[49]

Not just the polemics of critics and supporters, but also the idea of television as a uniquely powerful medium, appeared on the face of it to have been put in their place. Indeed, so anodyne and equivocal was the language of the report's conclusions that, much to the frustration of Himmelweit, and after an initial flurry of interest, her report had the effect of quelling not just debate, criticism, and enthusiasm, but also of obscuring the implications that lay hidden within. For the academic psychologists, it was impossible to say whether television was a good or a bad thing. This was simply the wrong question. It was like asking whether an injection was good or bad: it depended on which child and which circumstances. But of course this was the very question that the public wanted answering. Because the report sat on the fence, others were able to make what they wanted of its evidence.

[48] Hilde Himmelweit, 'The Impact of Television—Need for Industry to Act Now', *The Times* (31 March 1962).
[49] Hilde Himmelweit, A. N. Oppenheim, and Pamela Vince, *Television and the Child: An Empirical Study of the Effect of Television on the Young* (London, 1958), p. 40.

In fact, hidden behind its balanced and modest conclusions, Himmelweit's research did emerge with a series of findings that were of considerable potential significance. The first of these was that children, contrary to the intentions of the broadcasters, had not been contained within the special environment of children's television. They were regular viewers of adult programming. The evidence on the matter was incontrovertible, presenting a fundamental challenge to the philosophy of children's programming that had emerged since the war. Three out of four children in the ten-to-eleven age range watched television until nine o'clock at night on a regular basis. Among thirteen and fourteen year olds, the same proportion watched until ten o'clock.[50] Younger children were also regular viewers of adult programming. The fact was that many homes had only one living room, and with the television constantly playing, children were often able to watch right up to their bedtime. In addition to this, there were also early signs that even when it came to teatime viewing children were more attracted by the programmes on ITV than those on the BBC. They were opting out of the developmental vision of Lingstrom in preference for a diet of American Westerns and adventure films served up by the new commercial rivals. On ITV, over 50 per cent of children's programming already consisted of adventure stories, not just American imports but also some home-grown products such as the highly successful *Robin Hood*. Even on the BBC, which was rapidly shifting in response to the commercial challenge and had consequently dropped the 'toddler's truce' in 1957, 50 per cent of the drama for children was now Westerns.[51] The report estimated that children with both channels could watch up to twenty-five of these shows every week, with sixteen of them likely to contain significant amounts of violence and aggression.[52]

The Himmelweit report found that the most popular adult programme among children, across class, was the detective series *Fabian of Scotland Yard*, and other evening detective stories were similarly popular.[53] Children also liked comedies and panel games. In fact, the research suggested that, by and large, children liked the same programmes as adults. With choice now becoming available through a second channel, it seemed likely that there would be a general narrowing of viewing in line with such taste and a rejection of more serious and challenging programming.[54] In other words, there was every sign that the forces of popular taste and commercialization would sustain what was in some ways a worrying picture of viewing uncovered in the research.

Such findings had the potential to stoke the fires of alarm surrounding children and television. In particular, they had the potential to reinforce fears that the violence of detective stories as well as Westerns was a factor in encouraging juvenile

[50] Himmelweit et al., *Television and the Child*, p. 53.
[51] Himmelweit et al., *Television and the Child*, pp. 170–2; Buckingham et al., *Children's Television in Britain*, p. 21.
[52] Himmelweit et al., *Television and the Child*, p. 177.
[53] Himmelweit et al., *Television and the Child*, p. 115.
[54] Himmelweit et al., *Television and the Child*, pp. 126–7.

delinquency.[55] However, when it came to the Western in particular—a staple, as already noted, of ITV's teatime programming—Himmelweit was keen to calm anxieties. True, the gun was central in these narratives. But counting up gunshots revealed little about the impact of such viewing.[56] Here, the researchers adopted a qualitative approach to understanding the impact of such content, using diaries and interviews, and engaging with mothers and teachers but also a selection of children in attempting to understand the emotional effects of viewing.[57] What they found with programmes like the Westerns *Gun Law*, *Hopalong Cassidy*, *Roy Rogers*, and *The Lone Ranger* was that children were rarely disturbed by the violence. This was because it was almost always situated within the context of a clear-cut struggle in which good triumphed over evil. As the report put it, the violence was: 'abstract, stylised, and made readily acceptable because the hero never hesitates to apply it and none of its moral consequences are ever dwelt on. Despite moments of tension, violence is disguised to look remote and inconsequential—in fact, a game.'[58] This is not to say that the Western emerged with a completely clean bill of health, particularly since it was so readily available for viewing by the youngest children. The report may have cut the ground from under the theory that such programmes actually *caused* delinquency as a result of emotional disturbance, but it left room for speculation about whether they might have *encouraged* delinquency through the idea that conflict could be solved through violence. More crucially, however, it also left little doubt that the programmes had few if any positive virtues for child development. A diet of such programmes offered a very limited palette in terms of models to identify with, and had little educational or intellectual justification.[59]

When it came to detective stories, such as the home-grown *Fabian of Scotland Yard* (BBC), and American shows such as *Dragnet* (ITV), Himmelweit suggested that the potential for damage was greater. Such shows were far more realistic than the Westerns. Their handling of morality was also less black and white. In a programme like the horror, suspense series *Inner Sanctum* (ITV), there was no clear moral division between villains and heroes, and criminals were often depicted as being driven not by greed or evil but by underlying neuroses. The violence was also very different in style to that of the Western, with greater realism, a tendency to dwell longer on the emotional nature of such events through personalization, and the use of close-ups.[60]

Yet even in the case of the crime drama there was still some doubt about the extent of serious danger to the child. As with the Western, children appeared to

---

[55] Though it is also worth noting that research in Coventry sponsored by Birmingham University claimed that television was having a positive effect on rates of delinquency, keeping children out of trouble but also stimulating them culturally: 'Influence of Television: Survey of Impact on Children', *The Times* (30 September 1952).

[56] Himmelweit et al., *Television and the Child*, p. 57.

[57] Himmelweit et al., *Television and the Child*, pp. 72–5, 179–91.

[58] Himmelweit et al., *Television and the Child*, p. 184.

[59] Himmelweit et al., *Television and the Child*, pp. 56–7.

[60] Himmelweit et al., *Television and the Child*, pp. 185–90.

become less frightened as they learned the general formula of the stories, and they were generally able to resolve any remaining tensions through play. In fact, Himmelweit identified neither the imported American Westerns nor the crime stories as the most disturbing type of programme seen by the children. Instead, she argued that the most upsetting material came in the dramatization of classics of English literature such as *David Copperfield* or *Jane Eyre*. Children, it appeared, were far more likely to be frightened and made anxious by things they identified with. Adults might be shocked by violence; children could be more disturbed by unexpected displays of anger or disapproval from adults.[61]

In sum, the report ultimately found no justification for the public alarm linking Westerns and detective shows with juvenile delinquency. Children had no great difficulty in recognizing even what to the adult mind appeared quite disturbing scenes of violence as part of a story. Comparison with control groups not exposed to this material suggested that the children fed on a diet of *Fabian* and *Robin Hood*, or even American shows such as *Inner Sanctum*, were no more likely to be violent or aggressive. Watching these programmes could give expression to violence, but this depended upon a predisposition. However, once again it needs to be emphasized that this clean bill of health on the main charge came with a serious coda: the programmes may have caused little serious harm, but neither did they have any value compared to what might have been on offer; and there was certainly no support for the idea that the shows could provide a healthy outlet. As such, there was enough evidence to support a recommendation to reduce the number of these programmes at times when children were watching television, and to research into alternatives that had the same attractions but which presented themes and characterizations that were 'morally and socially more worthwhile'.[62]

As this suggests, what has been lost sight of in the focus on the report's findings on violent programmes was that it had important things to say about the power of television as a force for shaping the values and the horizons of the child. The relationship was a subtle but still an important one. It was rarely the result of a single programme, and it rarely led to the imposition of model values; rather its effect was cumulative. To a certain extent, moreover, it depended on the existing values of the child, since this dictated 'selective perception'. And there was evidence to suggest that among thirteen and fourteen year olds, the influence was likely to be greater on the secondary-modern rather than the grammar-school student, particularly those below average intelligence (who were watching more television, watching for longer hours, and indeed watching the least educational programmes). But what the report was also pointing to was that the influence of television was mediated by class. Here, its effects were complex. The type of programme watched, and indeed the degree of watching, could reinforce existing divisions. However, it could also challenge the way the child had been brought up to see the world. Television brought the child a landscape of how the adult world operated that was not necessarily available in the home

---

[61] Himmelweit et al., *Television and the Child*, pp. 57, 192–210.
[62] Himmelweit et al., *Television and the Child*, p. 220.

or local community. It also influenced the way that children thought about jobs and success. It tended to stress the importance of initiative, good looks, brains, confidence, and material comfort. In doing so, it offered a visual education in class difference from a predominantly upper-middle-class perspective. The report also recognized, however, that the more serious adult plays watched by many older children could challenge values, and that this could produce considerable anxiety about their ability to deal with adult life. Here, there was particular concern about the influence on adolescent girls, since they were so often the tragic figures in such stories, while there were few alternative positive models on offer and no female equivalent to the heroes of the cowboy or detective story.[63] Hidden within the report then was the message that television, beyond the fun of the Western, and particularly through the powerful medium of drama, could have a very serious influence on children who perhaps otherwise had a rather limited moral and aesthetic education. Indeed, a report that was generally so cautious acknowledged that 'Television's powers are very considerable in shaping children's outlook as well as taste'.[64]

Finally, the investigation is also revealing on the extent to which watching television was contributing to the child's post-war retreat from the social space of the street to the home. Clearly, the fact that children in homes with television were watching for two hours or more every day meant that other activities were making way for this.[65] But the research indicated that the amount of outside play lost as a result amounted to an average of only about a quarter of an hour per day, and that there was little evidence to support the idea that television made children more passive when not watching. For many, television was a time-filler, something to do when bored and when nothing better was available. If outdoor activities did suffer, it tended to be those of a more spontaneous type such as cycling around, kicking about a ball, and looking for something to do. Television in that sense was perhaps acting to keep children off the streets and out of trouble.[66] On the other hand, the report was also sceptical about claims that television watching brought the family together. This may have been the case with the very young, but otherwise the sense of unity could be spurious: 'both parents and children frequently persuade themselves that viewing "unites" the family; the mother especially finds it useful in keeping husband and child under her eye, in staving off children's independence, and in keeping the younger child quiet.'[67] Again, this finding, which challenged an assumption that suited broadcasters, public moralists, and parents alike that television like radio before it had the virtue of cementing the family, appears to have attracted little broader attention.[68]

---

[63] Himmelweit et al., *Television and the Child*, pp. 258–9.
[64] Himmelweit et al., *Television and the Child*, p. 261.
[65] Himmelweit et al., *Television and the Child*, p. 98.
[66] Himmelweit et al., *Television and the Child*, pp. 151, 351, 363–5.
[67] Himmelweit et al., *Television and the Child*, pp. 383–4.
[68] A survey on radio listening conducted for the BBC had argued that it increased the attractiveness of the home for the child and that it increased family unity through listening together: Hilda Jennings and Winfred Gill, *Broadcasting in Everyday Life: A Survey of the Social Effects of the Coming of Broadcasting* (London, 1939), pp. 21–8.

In sum, Himmelweit may have chosen to avoid fuelling the anxiety about television, but behind her caveats and conclusions there was evidence that could be taken as more worrying: the new medium did shape values, and hence the generally low quality of the content mattered; outside play had been cut down, particularly that of the most independent type; and television was being used by some parents to contain children. Moreover, right at the end of the report comes a dramatic point that had been hinted at throughout in remarks about children of low intelligence, low expectations, and an inclination to look to others for entertainment, but which now takes shape in the coining of the term the 'television addict' and the claim that this was a condition affecting a third of the child population: in other words, a problem of major proportions.[69]

RESPONSE TO HIMMELWEIT

Lawrence Black has pointed to the way in which psychology contributed to a pathologization of television viewing in the 1950s and 1960s, with children a particular concern: part of a politics of cultural control which drew in the Left well before the more notorious critique from the moral Right spearheaded by Mary Whitehouse and her National Viewers' and Listeners' Association.[70] In fact, the Himmelweit Report had been rather more modest in its criticisms than such a line of argument would suggest. The response to the report also indicates the limited influence of psychology, as well as the hesitancy about ceding cultural control to those outside the industry itself. Commentators were divided about Himmelweit's report. This was partly a result of its cautious and equivocal tone, and the complexity and nuance of the findings. As an editorial in *The Times* put it: in the face of the 'solid and unspectacular conclusions' of the study, the 'theories of enthusiasts and alarmists go down like ninepins'. This astute review also recognized that one of the messages of the research was that there had been too much hot air on the issue of violence and its effect when the real issue was that television had the power to have a cumulative influence on the values of the child and that addressing this would mean interfering with adult programming.[71] Nevertheless, led by groups such as the Council for Children's Welfare, the anxiety about the effects of violence continued to surface, particularly among parents.[72] The issue also attracted interest within the mental health services. In 1958, research on young people in an institution for mental defectives offered support to the thesis that watching children's television increased levels of interpersonal violence.[73] And in 1962 the National

---

[69] Himmelweit et al., *Television and the Child*, pp. 385–96.
[70] Lawrence Black, 'Whose Finger on the Button? British Television and the Politics of Cultural Control', *Historical Journal of Film, Radio, and Television*, 25 (2005), 547–75.
[71] 'Standing Up to Television', *The Times* (12 December 1958).
[72] 'What Children Should See—Ill Effects of Violence', *The Times* (11 December 1957); 'Parents Attack Television', *The Times* (30 September 1957).
[73] G. De M. Rudolf, 'The Effect of Children's Television on Behaviour', *Mental Health*, 17:2 (Spring 1958), 55–60.

Association for Mental Health held a conference that considered the impact of television on violence.[74] However, any conclusions on this issue were of little significance unless there was also acceptance of greater regulation by government or experts over what went on within the private sphere of the home. From an early stage in her own research, having encountered criticism about intruding on family relations through the type of questions she was posing, Himmelweit had been made aware that any such action would be difficult and controversial.[75]

The broadcasters were particularly keen to avoid outside interference through government or psychological experts, and they resisted Himmelweit's steer to establish a stronger regulatory framework in relation to the under-nines. Instead, the BBC set up its own study group on the subject, and subsequently the BBC came together with the ITA to provide a joint response.[76] In doing so, the broadcasters resorted to the populist line of argument that parents, not specialists, knew best about what families should do in their evenings at home.[77] There was similar resistance to suggestions that programming should change. The BBC study group was happy with its current provision for the six-to-nine-year-old group. It pointed out that Himmelweit's proposal of improving the educational quality of programming seemed to contradict the claim elsewhere in her report that children would avoid programmes that set out to instruct. And it took the line that any problem lay not in children's programming but in parents allowing children to watch unsuitable programmes later in the evening. If more research was necessary, this could be handled through an extension of the existing apparatus of audience research rather than needing to rely on experts in child development. There was also resistance to Himmelweit's suggestion that the adolescent viewer needed special attention. Owen Reed, Head of Children's Programmes at the BBC, spoke of the 'case against splitting' and defended the sustainability of the children's programming philosophy of linking together a series of programmes for children of different ages: providing a kind of 'rope-ladder' in which a 'child's reach should outstrip its grasps'. Reed pointed to the poor quality of children's television in America as an example of the problems with departing from this mission. He conceded, however, that it might be time for a new title and that in order to provide for the different age groups it might be necessary to extend the range of current provision for children.[78]

Independent television was particularly vulnerable to public attack on their staple of Westerns and adventure stories.[79] So, as public debate mounted with the prospect of publication of Himmelweit's findings, Sir Robert Fraser,

---

[74] 'Violence and the Mental Health Services', *Mental Health* (April 1962), 4–16; T. A. Ratcliffe, 'Aggression—Good or Bad', *Mental Health* (April 1962), 17–18.
[75] WAC T16/303: Nuffield Foundation Enquiry, 1953–9.
[76] WAC, R34/1155/1, Joint BBC/ITA Committee on 'Television and the Child'. The BBC/ITA report was published as *Children and Television Programmes* (London, 1960).
[77] WAC, R34/1155/5, 'Draft Foreword to the Report of the Joint Committee on Television and the Child', 9 June 1960, pp. 2–3.
[78] WAC, T16/304: Nuffield Foundation Enquiry—BBC Study Group 1958–9.
[79] 'Parents Attack Television', *The Times* (27 November 1957).

Director-General of ITA, set out a pre-emptive public defence. Yes, it was important that the programmes that children watched contained no element of sadism. Yet the alarm about children being terrified had been blown out of all proportion. Children were perfectly able to distinguish between what was simply a story and what was real life. The cowboy's use of the gun was part of his fictional world, and the child had no trouble accepting this. At the same time, these stories had genuine virtues when it came to the emotional development of the child. They helped cultivate a sense of 'sympathetic pain' on the one hand, and an emotional response toward cruelty on the other. They also provided heroes to identity with, who may have toted guns but who nevertheless represented values associated with the struggle between the forces of good and evil.[80] The ITA also publicized the findings of its own survey of parental views which suggested an overwhelming level of satisfaction with its current provision. Parents may have harboured some concern about the impact of television on the physical life of their children, but in terms of the intellectual and emotional impact they had few worries and indeed welcomed the input. Ninety-two per cent felt that their children were better informed and more knowledgeable because of television. The majority felt that it had improved their social conduct. More often than not, they watched with their children and found television a tool for bonding within the family. And a quarter added that it had made it easier to bring up their children as they liked: a somewhat ambiguous description, but one that suggests the appeal of television as an aid to parenting, and probably a liberal and modern style of parenting that placed power in their hands rather than worked via tradition.[81] It appears from this survey at least, and the broader evidence tends to support this, that television for children suited many parents and that its content did not unduly concern them. The more vocal who complained were a minority.

The press was divided when it came to what was recognized as a clear rebuttal of the Himmelweit recommendation for greater regulation from the television authorities.[82] The *Herald* was sympathetic, criticizing 'do-gooders' for thinking that they could know better than parents when it came to what was good or bad for their children, and the provincial press also tended to accept the argument that parents were the best placed to decide on such issues. But there was a feeling in some quarters that the BBC and ITA were attempting to sideline some very serious issues about the effect of viewing on the child. The *Daily Mail* criticized the joint BBC/ITA response for being out of touch with reality. The left-wing weekly *Tribune* went even further, attacking 'smug television bosses' for not introducing proper controls.[83]

---

[80] Sir Robert Fraser, 'What Children Should See', *The Times* (7 December 1957).

[81] 'Television is Good for the Children—Parents Approve Programmes', *The Times* (25 September 1958).

[82] 'Television Report Attacked—Dissension over way to Protect Young', *The Times* (22 July 1960).

[83] WAC, R44/1/1,057/1, Survey of the press response to the 'Children and Television Programmes' report, 10 August 1960.

Himmelweit was clearly frustrated by the lack of action and appears to have regretted not making her case for regulation more forcefully.[84] Her relationship with the broadcasters was also exacerbated by their tendency to dismiss her, and psychologists more generally, as merely concerned with censorship and with no sensitivity to the creative process and its needs for freedom of expression. She maintained that her aim had always been to open up the issue, not to close it down.[85] She had a point. The party with the greater interest in closing down debate had always been the television authorities themselves. In the end, they had managed to use the episode to do just this. Long-term research continued, now under the Home Office, which established the Television Research Committee, with financial support from the ITA, in 1963.[86] But in the meantime, broadcasters could turn to Himmelweit to dampen alarm about violence, fear, and delinquency. Even a body like the Council for Children's Welfare, to the fore in the earlier debate on violence, had come to accept that this issue had been overstated. This did not absolve ITV in particular from the charge of a 'depressing lack of vision'. But this broader issue—one that Himmelweit herself had signalled as more crucial—was less suited to mobilizing opinion. The debate over content was always liable to be highjacked by conservative groups organized to defend family and Christian values (in the late 1960s and the 1970s, the lead would be taken by Mary Whitehouse's National Viewers' and Listeners' Association), and this made it harder to convince a liberal constituency.[87]

The BBC was likewise able to resist the call for an external advisory body, first by the argument about the need to maintain parental control, and secondly by introducing systems of internal regulation as it extended its audience research to cover children (surveying up to 500 a week). However, this was offering a very different type of service. It helped in understanding what children watched and liked, but it sidestepped the issue of what was good for them. The ITA adopted a Children's Advisory Committee, but its Chairman would point out that there was no evidence that normal children would suffer any injury from a diet of Westerns.[88]

The Himmelweit Report therefore had little effect in holding back children's television from moving towards seeing its role as just as much one of entertainment as of instruction and development. An investigation that had the potential to

---

[84] 'The Impact of Television—Need for Industry to Act Now', *The Times* (31 March 1962).

[85] WAC, T166/689, letters from Hilde Himmelweit to Mr McGivern (Deputy Director of Television Broadcasting), not dated, and Kenneth Adam (Controller of Programmes, Television), 8 November 1960.

[86] J. D. Halloran, R. L. Brown, and D. C. Chaney, *Television and Delinquency* (Leicester, 1970), pp. 7–12.

[87] Mildred Masheder (General Secretary of the Council for Children's Welfare), 'The Impact of Television—Relating Violence to Quality', *The Times* (9 April 1962). One of the concerns of such groups was that television threatened the strength of the family through, for instance, watching at meal times. A guide from the Catholic Church proposed a limit of two hours viewing per day for children: 'TV Viewing Code for Children—Roman Catholic Body's Seven Point Guide', *The Times* (8 August 1960). Whitehouse's campaign was sparked off by 'What Kind of Loving', a BBC programme dealing with young people and sex in March 1963, though it also came to focus on violence: Mary Whitehouse, *A Most Dangerous Woman* (Tring, 1982).

[88] Sir John Wolfenden, 'TV Western Films Defended', *The Times* (2 April 1962).

rein in programming, not just for children but also for adults, in fact gave it new licence. As the BBC Head of Children's Programmes, Owen Reed, emphasized, an improving mission would only be possible if television was popular.[89] In fact, Himmelweit's investigation, taking in just the first six months of ITV, had under-estimated the full effect of the advent of commercial television. By the time she returned to the subject in the early 1960s she noted the replacement of the rather tame and juvenile Westerns such as the *Lone Ranger* by a new more adult genre, with programmes like *Bonanza* and *Rawhide*. Her new research was designed to emphasize that television was creating taste and not just reflecting it, and that children towards the lower end of the social spectrum were particularly vulnerable. Her frustration with the broadcasters was difficult to contain: 'The image of the one-way traffic, with the public the master, the industry the servant is a travesty of the situation and negation of the industry's social responsibilities.'[90]

As Head of Children's Programming, Reed was under threat from a new genera-tion at the BBC who were keen to turn around its declining popularity in the face of the commercial challenge, and who regarded the children's department as too middle class and too culturally conservative. Looking back on the period, the Director-General, Stuart Hood, recalled it as a period in which a nineteenth-century concept of childhood was breaking down. It was time for the BBC to change in line with this. First, drama production—the jewel in the crown—was taken away from the Children's Department. Then, in 1964, the Children's Department lost its separate identity. Instead, children's programming became the responsibility of a new Family Programmes Department. Himmelweit, after all, had shown that there was no fundamental division between what the child and the family watched. This could also be a way of better addressing a group such as adolescents, which she had highlighted as a neglected area, as well as mothers, whose social isolation was emerging as an increasing concern. Indicative of this reorientation, Doreen Stephens, who had been working in Women's Programmes, was now put in charge of children's television and talked of a need to break with a style of programming which had been 'self-consciously middle-class and inclined to condescension' and which had skirted around difficult subjects. Children, particularly adolescents, had been overprotected, shoe-horned into the nursery of children's programming. The new model of good development emphasized the importance of engaging with children and offering freedom to make their own decisions.[91]

Publication of the Pilkington Committee report in 1962, which endorsed the value of the BBC and led to a favourable renewal of its charter, had the effect of easing pressure to put popularity above the public service mission. In doing so, it also put pressure on ITV to produce more quality programmes for children, and this led to the creation of separate children's departments in its regional compa-nies.[92] The Pilkington report also resulted in a second channel for the BBC, and

[89] Owen Reed, 'Adding Zest to the Tea-Time Ritual', *The Times* (20 November 1961).
[90] Hilde Himmelweit, 'Television Revisited', *New Society* (1 November 1962), 17.
[91] Buckingham et al., *Children's Television in Britain*, pp. 26–30; Home, *In the Box of Delights*, p. 36.
[92] Buckingham et al., *Children's Television in Britain*, p. 32.

this eased the pressure of scheduling that had held back provision of programmes for the different age groups. At the same time, family programming was not turning out to be a great success. This was symbolized by the response to a production of *Oliver Twist* in 1962 which contained a particularly disturbing scene of Bill Sykes' murder of Nancy. The protests that followed seemed to highlight the danger in taking away responsibility for children's drama from those trained to understand the needs of the child.[93] Against this background, in 1967 the BBC reversed its earlier decision and reintroduced a Children's Department.[94] Despite the short-term failure, this experiment with an alternative model points to a tension between protection and freedom evident since the birth of children's television. This tension would become even more acute in the 1970s.

THE EXPLODING TV[95]

By the 1970s, there was an acceptance that television was an integral part of children's lives. Perhaps because it had become less safe for children to be let loose outside—an issue that will be considered in the next chapter—there was surprisingly little debate or alarm about the effect of television on mobility and passivity. Children may have spent more time than previously in a room with a television that was switched on, but research suggested that they were still only focusing on it for about two hours a day on average, particularly when they were tired after school (the same figure as that given by Himmelweit).[96] The new discipline of media studies generally acted to downplay anxieties, presenting television, not as a retreat from life, but as a central part of experience, with a potential in its own right to expand the landscape of the child. It was not like cinema, where viewers lost their identity and a sense of place in the anonymity of the dark or through identification with stars. Television located the child firmly in the home and in the family, and through serials it introduced the child to characters who appeared again and again. The very size of the screen in comparison to the cinema made these talking heads seem real and simulated face-to-face human interaction. Television showed the child—a child whose sphere of social interaction was probably less extensive than it had been at the dawn of the television age—what life was like and how to act in social situations that they had no experience of. Rather than cutting the child off from society, it both integrated the child in the social setting of the family, and brought participation in a world of interconnection into the heart of the family home.[97]

[93] Home, *In the Box of Delights*, p. 36.

[94] Buckingham et al., *Children's Television in Britain*, pp. 31–2.

[95] In the 1970s, the term the 'exploding school' referred to attempts to break down the barrier between school and outside world. This is discussed in Chapter 7. Although the term was not used in relation to television, the suggestion in using this term is that these were parallel phenomena.

[96] Michael J. A. Howe, *Television and Children* (London, 1977), pp. 15–18.

[97] Grant Noble, *Children in Front of the Small Screen* (London, 1975); Morley, *Family Television*.

Concern about the potential effects of watching violence had not disappeared. Indeed, social change and an apparent decline in deference among the young, as well as a greater permissiveness in terms of what could be shown on television, particularly now in terms of sexual behaviour, lay behind the growing public support for the National Viewers and Listeners Association. The issue was kept to the fore by increasing government concern in the United States in the late 1960s, spurred on partly by the work of psychiatrist Frederick Wertham, which depicted television as a 'school for violence'. However, investigation of the links between television and delinquency in Britain, undertaken by the Home Office and the BBC, was still reluctant to conclude that there was a direct relationship, particularly given that it was now virtually impossible to find any control group of non-viewers so as to study the effect of television in isolation.[98] Parents, meanwhile, continued to express general concern—and they perhaps had good reason, given that research found about four violent incidents per hour on British television between four and eleven o'clock—but this had little correlation with their own practice in what they were happy to let their children watch.[99] There was also growing concern about the impact of advertising and about the way that psychology now seemed to be turning, from policing and managing the effects of the medium on the child mind, to selling its expertise on how to manipulate the emerging child consumer. The social research of psychologists John and Elizabeth Newson on the home life of four year olds speculated 'upon the effect of the endless succession of sweetly idealized television "mummies" who so devotedly minister to their children's needs during every television break'. Their conclusion—'no doubt the depth psychologists of the advertising agencies have this particular factor well under control'—was not one likely to reassure.[100]

In the early 1970s, the debate about the use of television as a tool for the good of children crystallized around the American programme *Sesame Street*. Provision

---

[98] Chris Dunkley, 'Barriers to the Real Assessment of the Effects of Television Violence', *The Times* (29 January 1972); Caroline Moorehead, 'Violence on TV: How Does It Really Affect Children?', *The Times* (12 September 1975); 'No Clear Evidence That Screen Violence Leads to Similar Acts by Audience', *The Times* (8 September 1977); Halloran et al., *Television and Delinquency*. The link remained contentious up to the end of the century, with the case of James Bulger murdered by two boys who had watched the 'video-nasty' *Child's Play 3* provoking a wave of public alarm in 1993. The discipline of media studies continued to cast doubt on the link, now highlighting the need to consider how children themselves defined and communicated their emotional responses. Research also highlighted the lack of hard evidence for desensitization or for association with killers (rather than victims). It also suggested that children had a strong capacity to develop coping strategies when presented by disturbing material. It agreed with the earlier research that what frightened the child could be rather different from the material that most concerned adults, and again it highlighted the way that parents and children often displaced the concern about the effects of such material onto others. This was one of the reasons why attempts to restrict the viewing of children proved ineffective. Finally, such research now called for a greater appreciation of the interlinking of positive with negative emotional responses: David Buckingham and Mark Allerton, *Fear, Fright and Distress: A Review of Research on Children's 'Negative' Emotional Response to Television—Prepared for the Broadcasting Standards Council* (London, 1996); David Buckingham, *Moving Images: Understanding Children's Emotional Responses to Television* (Manchester, 1996).

[99] Howe, *Television and Children*, pp. 24–7.

[100] Newson and Newson, *Four Years Old*, p. 65.

for children on American television had generally been viewed with a great deal of criticism in Britain. America had less of a tradition of sectioning off an area of television as specifically designed with the child's needs in mind, or indeed of making programmes shaped by an agenda of child development. Pressure to improve the situation had increased after the report of the Surgeon General in the wake of a National Commission on the Causes and Prevention of Violence.[101] The children's programme *Sesame Street* emerged out of this context and was met with acclaim. Opinion in Britain, however, was sharply divided, and this came to a head in debate over whether the BBC should purchase rights to the programme. For some critics, it was regarded as completely unsuitable, and this was a view shared within the Children's Department of the BBC. The fact that it would have been very expensive was an easy excuse for rejection by the BBC, but the reasons for resistance went considerably deeper. *Sesame Street* was attacked for translating the brainwashing techniques of advertising, such as fast edits and repetition of messages, into the arena of pedagogy. The use of bite-sized pieces of information, the segmentation of the programme, and the hectic pace may have made it easy to digest and attractive to those with poor concentration, and as such *Sesame Street* could stake a claim to being peculiarly and democratically accessible to young child minds, but the critics argued that it did not develop real understanding of the world, it lacked integration, and it was too detached from the real-life situation of British children.[102] One might say it worked too much on the conscious and immediate level, and neglected those unconscious, casual, and more subtle lessons that had always been a part of the British tradition and the landscape it projected. Thus, Monica Sims, head of the Children's Department at the BBC in this period, controversially described *Sesame Street* as 'authoritarian'. The British approach in children's television had always been to provide a space for the child to explore and discover through the development of the senses, but also increasingly to question and be creative. The BBC's *Play School*, with its agenda of learning through play, offered a fundamentally different vision of how television could help in the development of the preschool child. The *Sesame Street* approach was too directive and too concerned with right and wrong when it came to answers as well as behavioural norms.[103] Those in favour highlighted instead the technical brilliance of the production and its benefits in terms of academic preparation for the preschool child.[104] They also highlighted the slum setting and the programme's more multicultural, multiracial palette, neither of which justified the criticisms of conservatism. Indeed, it was the tradition of the BBC that might be criticized as far more middle class, and in a context of increasing concern about social inequality and deprivation the BBC was vulnerable on this charge. *Sesame Street* might have been offering an American urban landscape—and the critics did focus on the issue of the unfamiliarity of place

---

[101] Halloran et al., *Television and Delinquency*, p. 10.

[102] Buckingham et al., *Children's Television in Britain*, p. 35.

[103] Chris Dunkley, 'Sesame Street', *The Times* (30 March 1971); 'Sesame Street Rejected as Authoritarian', *The Times* (7 September 1971); letter from Pendarel Kent, *The Times* (29 December 1971).

[104] Letter from Lady B. Q. Urquhart, *The Times* (14 September 1971).

and language—but it was perhaps still closer to the truth of what lay beyond the safety of the middle-class home than the standard fare of BBC children's program-ming. Indeed, it would find support on such grounds from one of the most radical forums of the period, the new journal *Children's Rights*, though also intriguingly from some on the Right including future Conservative Chancellor Nigel Lawson.[105] In the short term, the BBC stuck to its guns. In the long term, in terms of both the fast-paced technique and the move beyond a more traditional and middle-class British landscape for the child, *Sesame Street* would nevertheless herald the start of a significant shift in the style of the virtual landscape projected in British children's television.

CONCLUSION

It is tempting to see the introduction in 1978 of the controversial and, in the con-text of the time, grittily realistic serial about children in a comprehensive school, *Grange Hill*, as part of the shift in style in children's programming of the 1970s: in particular marking a move from a world in which children were no longer passive subjects for improvement but were given the voice to resist and talk back, a reflec-tion of the new child rights movement of the era. In fact, it can also be seen as tied to the tradition of child-centred drama, albeit now with a working-class inflection, and as fitting into the vision of a ladder of development, somewhere between *Play School* and *Play for Today*.[106] For all the change that undoubtedly had taken place by this time, not least when it came to the adolescent audience, the continuities up to the 1970s are more striking. They are highlighted moreover in comparative perspective. They stand in contrast to the American television of the era. And they contrast with the retreat from television watching, the decline in children's pro-gramming, and the explosion of greater choice in virtual entertainment that would all later follow. British post-war children's television had offered a specialized land-scape for child development, designed both with a vision of how the child saw the world in mind and with an interest in guiding the child through a series of devel-opmental stages. This had helped it in evading blame for fundamental changes in the lifestyle of the child including delinquency and a decline in outdoor play. Throughout the period, it had its critics, not just social conservatives worried about declining standards of behaviour, but also those who saw it as condescending, paternalistic, and middle class. Nevertheless, it was generally successful in present-ing itself as a social good. For children growing up in post-war Britain, television as a result became an important part of everyday life. It located them in the home, but it offered them a virtual landscape that connected the home and the world. It offered, albeit in paternalistic form, protection but also new freedom.

---

[105] Nigel Lawson, 'The Minor Miracle of Sesame Street', *The Times* (22 December 1971). An interview with inner-city children in *Children's Rights* found them favourable towards the new programme and not aware that it was set in America: 'Sesame Street', *Children's Rights*, 1 (1971), 16–17.
[106] Buckingham et al., *Children's Television in Britain*, pp. 37–8.

By the late 1950s, it was clear that watching television was going to take up a significant part of every child's waking life. The minority of children with a television in their home were spending on average two hours a day on this new activity. By the 1970s, virtually all British children were. As such, the virtual terrain of television has to be seen as a significant part of the landscape of the child during this period. It was important for the shape of children's television in Britain that it emerged in the wake of the Second World War. The war fuelled anxieties and aspirations with regard to the psychological health and development of the child. It also established a platform for ambitious, paternalist cultural intervention to create the good society. In this context, there was considerable excitement but also concern about children and television. Over the post-war decades the perspectives and interests of government, broadcasters, producers, psychologists, moralists, parents, but also children, as viewers in a medium acutely aware of the need for popularity, interacted to shape this new landscape. Inevitably, the result was neither as paternalistic as some hoped for and others feared, nor though did it reflect mere populism. Indeed, set in comparative perspective, the persistence of a philosophy of children's television acting as a developmental tool is striking: a tool to open the eyes of the child, albeit indirectly and through the engagement of entertainment, to the child's own position within a broader social, cultural, and geographical landscape. The claim that children's television had such a value was significant in defending it against critics. Here, concern about whether television was encouraging passivity was more muted than we might now expect from a perspective of twenty-first-century alarm over sedentary, screen-bound children and lost freedom. Perhaps this was because the home- and family-centred nature of television had attractions both for moralists and for those informed by post-war psychology. The evidence suggests that it also suited parents, who were increasingly concerned about keeping their children safely off the streets and who found television convenient. Instead, at the centre of criticism was a feeling that the window on the world provided by television could be a sometimes dangerous one. Children, it was clear from as early as the 1950s, roamed freely over the imaginary boundary between children's and adult television. However, controlling what children watched would have meant controlling and limiting adult appetites. This was not going to happen. Thus, we arrive at the conclusion that the landscape designed for the child through post-war television was a significantly different phenomenon to the landscape that the child actually inhabited. This was a core tension throughout the period. In practice, the broadcasters recognized the problem as they whittled away at the target child of children's TV until at times they appeared to be talking about children in as narrow a range as six to eight years old. This meant that the critics were in a sense right: the content of television as a whole needed consideration. If children's television could be an environment for the cultivation of the child, then surely given patterns of viewing the environment beyond was equally important in shaping values. This was the hidden bombshell in the Himmelweit Report. Children's television provided a screen, in fact, for evading the issue. Of course, children's television did spark some alarms about lost freedom, but in the period up to the 1970s the relative lack of anxiety is more striking, and it can be argued that children's television for a time rather successfully marked out an influential new space that provided a form of protected freedom in the spirit of the post-war settlement. Loss of confidence in the paternalism of this solution, and then an explosion of new technology, would be key factors in undermining this settlement and in an escalation of anxiety about the relationship between virtual landscapes and the loss and containment of childhood freedom in the decades to come.

5

Out and About: Traffic, Play, and Safety

In the second stage of their longitudinal study of children and their social worlds in post-war Britain, the first in the mid-1960s taking as its subject four year olds in Nottingham, and the second now at the start of the 1970s turning to seven year olds in the same city, the focus of psychologists John and Elizabeth Newson was home life.[1] This is unsurprising. It reflected, after all, the central spatial preoccupation of developmental psychologists in the post-war era. It also reflected the Newsons' first-hand experience of the pressure of being good parents in the post-war era. At the heart of their study was one of the central normative assumptions of the post-war settlement: that being cut off from the 'frame of reference' that was the family home would have a 'disorienting and disturbing effect' on the child.[2] The focus on home and family also reflected the fact that the source for this study was a series of some seven-hundred interviews with parents, rather than interview with or direct observation of the children themselves. There was little opportunity, then, even if there had been interest, to study children's own experience of an outside world beyond home and family. Nevertheless, this research on seven year olds, and even the earlier work on four year olds, is still illuminating for our understanding of the degree to which British children had freedom to play and explore beyond the family home at the start of the 1970s: to get 'out and about', as the Newsons put it. Even if this was not its primary purpose, and even if it must be read with the preconceptions of the researchers and parents in mind, it provides an invaluable snapshot of the degree to which young children could move around the urban environment on their own at the start of the 1970s. And in recording both a turn towards increasing protection and restriction, and a much greater degree of mobility than that recorded in research on children later in the century, the reports add to the case that the 1970s was in some ways a turning point in a story of lost childhood freedom.

The Newsons' research symbolizes a transition from a psychological towards a more sociological approach to understanding issues of child development. The husband and wife psychologists adopted what has been described as an ecological orientation, which is what makes their work so illuminating for the purposes of mapping the landscape of the child. Rather than focusing on internal psychological dynamics, they set out to map the roles of social relations and social space in the

---

[1] John Newson and Elizabeth Newson, *Four Years Old in an Urban Community* (London, 1968); John Newson and Elizabeth Newson, *Seven Years Old in the Home Environment* (London, 1976).
[2] Newson and Newson, *Seven Years Old*, p. 68.

forging of subjectivity. For this reason, the research tended to be too sociological (in its interest in class in particular) for fellow psychologists, even if it was also still too psychological for the sociologists.[3] The ecological orientation, the timing and location of the research in one of the provincial universities (in Nottingham), but also the popular appeal of the work situate it as part of what Mike Savage has described as the post-1962 'sociological moment' in the development of British social science.[4] However, the Newsons' studies also point to the limitations of this landscape orientation when understanding was still based on interview with the parents, rather than discussion with the children themselves. This was reflective of the paternalism of the post-war settlement when it came to the landscape of the child, and it was this that also lay behind the dominant solutions of relying on a combination of parental responsibility, organized play, and road safety consciousness in addressing the increasing challenge of enabling children to get out and about and to grow and develop through play in the face of an inexorable increase in the volume of road traffic. It was an approach that ultimately left children increasingly marginalized from the urban landscape, and this was only fully challenged as a landscape perspective was radicalized in the 1970s by turning to the views of children themselves.

The Newsons provide us with a picture of increasingly protective parents, caught between two worlds, and as a result increasingly preoccupied and worried about the question of childhood freedom. Some seemed to be struggling with the fact that their children had lost all independence, too shy or reluctant to stay even a single night away from home. Others were worried about the tendency of their children to roam beyond the home and to talk to strangers. The Newsons summed up the problem:

> In fact, as soon as the child walks unaccompanied down a city street, his mother is faced by one of the central dilemmas of bringing up a child in modern urban society. She wants him to be outgoing and receptive, both socially and intellectually, and these characteristics can be encouraged without any check when he is at home and when he is in school—that is when he is under adult supervision. It is *between* home and school that the difficulty arises, and here mothers become consciously ambivalent about the friendliness or independence which in other ways they value.[5]

The two dangers that they were particularly worried about in the absence of adult supervision were traffic and 'strangers'—the latter a euphemism for sexual molestation (sexual danger within the home or as a result of friends and family, by contrast, was rarely if ever acknowledged). Both have become central in our own anxieties about lost childhood freedom. This chapter explores the development of the first of these fears, and the more crucial in terms of limiting the landscape of the child. The next chapter takes up the story of fears about sexual danger.

---

[3] For reflection on their careers, work, and methodology: John Newson and Elizabeth Newson, 'Psychology as a Listening Ear', in G. Bunn, A. D. Lovie, and G. D. Richards (eds), *Psychology in Britain: Historical Essays and Personal Reflections* (Leicester, 2001), pp. 411–21.

[4] Mike Savage, *Identities and Social Change in Britain since 1940: The Politics of Method* (Oxford, 2010).

[5] Newson and Newson, *Seven Years Old*, p. 70.

THE NEWSON EVIDENCE

As far as the Newsons were concerned, young children faced four main potential dangers in the urban environment: getting lost, non-traffic accidents, traffic accidents, and sexual molestation. They suggested that the first was not a significant anxiety when it came to parents of seven year olds, since they could trust their children to wander only within defined limits (this in itself is an indicator of the degree to which attitudes towards safety were still relatively relaxed, particularly given the distances independently traversed by these children).[6] The second— the non-traffic accident—was difficult to generalize about since it depended on the specific locality, and therefore the Newsons chose to pass over it in their analysis. It could relate to a river, a rock face, or even the heavy equipment of a playground. The Newsons concluded that parents did their best to make any such special dangers clear to their children. The final two dangers had the most serious repercussions in terms of limiting the child's freedom to get out and about. Parents could warn children to stay away from a dangerous stretch of water, but the danger of traffic or sexual molestation was ever-present whenever children were out on their own.

Significantly, the Newsons in fact made little attempt to account for the parental fear of traffic. Like the parents they interviewed, the researchers seemed resigned to the problem. The planners' visions of a separation between pedestrians and cars was deemed to have little immediate prospect of realization.[7] There was also a degree of pessimism when it came to educating the child in road safety, the report noting that the child who complied fully with the 'wait until the road is clear' advice would never get across. In the end, the child had to learn through experience. Often mothers found out that their children were crossing busy roads by catching them unaware in the act of doing so. Seeing their lack of care and impulsiveness did nothing to allay anxiety. Yet it was through such a route that 40 per cent of the respondents said that they now trusted their children to cross busy roads on their own, and the Newsons remarked that the remainder would soon have to let their children take the same kind of independent risks if they were to learn.

Although parents of the seven year olds were keen to make it clear that they were well aware of the potential dangers facing their children when they strayed from the home, and were suitably concerned, the Newsons' research in fact demonstrates that these children still had much more freedom than they would by the end of the century. Particularly striking is the response to the question of whether seven year olds played or roamed around in the street. Seventy-four per cent of parents said they did. Within this figure, there was significant variation across class: a response of 65 per cent at the top of the social scale, compared to 83 per cent at

---

[6] The parent of a four year old saw it as protective to allow children to roam independently no more than 100 yards from the front door: Newson and Newson, *Four Years Old*, p. 51.

[7] Though there were areas that continued to be held up as a model, such as the new town of Stevenage: Stina Sandels, *Children in Traffic* (London, 1975), p. 148.

the bottom. This was despite the fact that the working-class streets tended to be the most dangerous as measured by actual accidents (they tended to be narrower than middle-class suburban roads and carried a higher volume of heavy traffic associated with local proximity of factories and warehouses). Working-class mothers recognized the danger and expressed concern, but only in exceptional cases did they bar their children from playing in the street. In one of these instances, the mother reported criticism for 'molly-coddling', even though the child in question was only three. In another, there were disagreements between the parents when the husband called for a child, previously hit by a car, to go back out in order to gain confidence. Middle-class mothers may have been more worried, but they had less cause in that their suburban residential roads tended to be safer. A middle-class mother who lived on one of the more dangerous roads frequented by working-class children forbade her own children from playing on it.[8]

The Newsons' earlier study of four year olds points to the importance of housing as a factor in the class differences in keeping children within the safety of the home. Nottingham, like many of Britain's industrial cities that had mushroomed in the nineteenth century, was now made up of three types of housing: the old red-brick terraces of central areas of the city; the new working-class council estates; and the more middle-class suburbs of detached and semi-detached housing. The key problem with the terraces was that they lacked gardens which could provide a safe space for outdoor child play, and this meant that mothers often found themselves cooped up all day with children in cramped kitchens. The back area of these terraces did offer a communal space for play, but the Newsons pointed to the problems of protecting young children from 'bullying children and frightening dogs'. There was no sign here of romanticism or nostalgia when it came to the street. Instead, the design of the terraces and the difficulty of keeping children from straying down side passages on to the road emerged as a central problem of childcare. The new council houses, like middle-class suburban housing, presented their own challenges when it came to child-rearing. In particular, the research highlighted the loneliness experienced by many of the mothers in these less socially integrated areas. On the other hand, the suburban parents did have the option of being able to let children go out to play in the security of the back garden, and the Newsons recognized how much easier this made the task of the young middle-class mother: the garden provided a necessary environment for play and development, but it also meant that these mothers could leave their children and have some time to themselves.[9]

When it came to seven year olds, the Newsons were less preoccupied by the presence of a garden space. Instead, they asked questions designed to cast light on how far the children could move about in the streets on their own, whether they were allowed to cross busy streets, whether there was a boundary to the distance they could travel or a time by which they had to return, and whether they had to gain permission first. The responses indicated that the vast majority of seven-year-old children made their own way home from school (78 per cent), and only in the top

[8] Newson and Newson, *Seven Years Old*, pp. 75–7.
[9] Newson and Newson, *Four Years Old*, pp. 33, 37–8.

social classes was this trend significantly different (66 per cent). It is likely that the class differential reflects both a greater likelihood of there being an available car and driver towards the top of the social scale and a tendency to travel further because of living in less-densely populated areas and opting out of the local school. However, the Newsons suggested that this was not on its own enough to account for the difference and that a more protective attitude within the middle-class home also played a part. The fact that there was a marked overall disparity between boys (just 15 per cent fetched from school) and girls (30 per cent) lent further support to this thesis.[10]

Though the majority of children may have been free to make their own way home from school, nearly all of the parents (92 per cent) were keen to make it clear to the interviewers that they had strict expectations about the children coming straight home and reporting to them before going off anywhere else.[11] The evidence suggests that this could be a site of tension but that children tended to comply. The researchers suggested that this was because of tiredness and hunger at the end of the day; and for this reason, similar rules about permission, time, and geographic boundaries were harder to police at weekends and in holidays.[12] Unfortunately, the Newsons did not attempt to calibrate the degree (in terms of distance and duration) to which the children could actually roam, recognizing that interpretation of any such figures would need to take into account variation in local conditions such as traffic density.[13] They did, however, offer a range of parental opinion on the question. At one extreme was the report from a bricklayer's wife, who lived on a back street just off a 'medium-busy' road and never let her son out for more than five minutes, and only then, when she was cleaning outside and could keep an eye on him. At the other end of the spectrum was a caretaker's wife, this time living right on a 'medium-busy' road that ran through a council estate, who was happy to see her seven-year-old son going all the way across town on his own as long as she knew where he was going.[14]

In 12 per cent of cases parents admitted that they were unable to keep track of where their children were, as they would have liked to. The wife of a rigger's mate reported of her son: 'He plays on the street. Always missing. We've got to look for him every night'. Asked whether this was a problem, she responded: 'Yes, because he can go miles away without ever telling you where he's going—he will often.'[15] Such a situation was more common among the working class, but the interviews suggested that this was partly because the middle-class parents had better resources

[10] Newson and Newson, *Seven Years Old*, pp. 77–9.

[11] Newson and Newson, *Seven Years Old*, pp. 79–81.

[12] Newson and Newson, *Seven Years Old*, p. 82.

[13] On this theme: C. I. Howarth, D. A. Routledge, and R. Repetto-Wright, 'An Analysis of Road Accidents Involving Child Pedestrians', *Ergonomics*, 17 (1974), 319–30; C. I. Howarth, D. A. Routledge, and R. Repetto-Wright, 'The Exposure of Young Children to Accident Risks as Pedestrians', *Ergonomics*, 17 (1974), 457–80; C. I. Howarth, D. A. Routledge, and R. Repetto-Wright, 'A Comparison of Interviews and Observations to Obtain Measures of Children's Exposure to Risk as Pedestrians', *Ergonomics*, 17 (1974), 623–38.

[14] Newson and Newson, *Seven Years Old*, pp. 84–5.

[15] Newson and Newson, *Seven Years Old*, p. 85.

to deal with it. Less tied down to looking after other children, and more likely to have access to a car and a telephone, they found it easier to fetch and keep in touch with the child. A more striking differential was the overall figure of 18 per cent of boys compared to just 6 per cent of girls. The researchers explained this in terms of different interests: the boys' inclination to be more adventurous about outside play. But it also reflected gendered expectations. This is evident even in the reported cases, with parents invariably most concerned when girls wandered off, in contrast to the element of pride about independence that often accompanied accounts of their sons.[16]

How, then, do we sum up the findings of the Newsons when it comes to the picture of the child's relation to the world beyond the home in the early 1970s? This of course was not their main concern. Their central preoccupation was the changing pattern of childcare in post-war British society and the degree to which a more permissive but still protective and loving attitude was permeating down the social scale. However, like the child psychologists discussed in relation to Bowlbyism, they also had a keen ecological interest in the development of a social subjectivity as an inherent and essential element of this culture of childcare. They therefore mapped a social subjectivity that in the child's early years developed most crucially in relation to parents, and which opened up via the living space at the hub of the house, the television, the garden, and ultimately the outside street.[17] In doing so, they offered a picture of a reasonably happy and healthy equilibrium between parental control and the developing needs of the child for a zone of greater freedom still closely tied to the security of home.[18] There is little sense that they saw any loss of childhood freedom or opportunity for broader social exchange as a fundamental threat or problem, and little sense that they regarded their findings as worrying in this regard.

Viewed from the perspective of twenty-first-century Britain, which has become more conscious and anxious about the restricted freedom of the young child within such an urban environment, the Newsons' findings appear rather different. The independent mobility of the urban seven year olds, from this distance, is at times striking. The survey appears to offer us a picture of the landscape of the urban child at a turning point. It was already a world of increasing concern about the urban environment as a dangerous one for the child, but not one in which these dangers were perhaps yet serious enough or in which there was the will or the means to sacrifice the benefits to both parent and child of a still considerable degree of independent mobility when it came to young children; neither was there any sign yet of major anxiety about lack of freedom. We also see that the car (and the telephone) could open up, as well as close down space: for instance, enabling children to be fetched across town. As such, the impact of new technology on the culture of time and space was more complex than we might assume.[19] However, the anxiety about

---

[16] Newson and Newson, *Seven Years Old*, p. 87.

[17] They contrasted their approach in this regard to that of psychoanalytic work: Newson and Newson, *Four Years Old*, pp. 17–18, 34.

[18] Newson and Newson, *Seven Years Old*, pp. 88–9.

[19] For reflections on the impact of earlier new technology on time and space: Stephen Kern, *The Culture of Time and Space, 1880–1918* (London, 1983).

traffic (and to a lesser extent molestation), and the situation for girls (where anxieties about safety were higher), and in the middle class (where the means for protection and the existence of alternatives to the street were greater) were all indicative for future development.

TRAFFIC, ROAD SAFETY, AND CHILDHOOD MOBILITY

By the end of the century, a decline in independent child mobility had emerged as a major social concern.[20] The school car journey was a symbol of the problem. Public opinion saw it—the popular stereotype was the mother in her four-wheel drive—as a symptom of over-anxious and overprotective parenting and as turning affluence into a new sort of deprivation as children lost their independence and fitness. In turn, the volume of traffic resulting from this culture was seen as making parents even move reluctant to allow children to travel independently by foot or bicycle. Indeed, the idea that parents should allow seven year olds to travel home without chaperonage was now increasingly out of the question for many parents, policed less by law than by new informal social codes of responsibility. National Travel Survey data indicated that only 10 per cent of eleven year olds travelled alone at the end of the century, compared to 21 per cent in 1985/6, and close to 80 per cent in the Newsons' research. The change in behaviour appears even more dramatic in the research of Mayer Hillman, who would emerge in the 1970s as the pioneer in highlighting the effect of traffic on independent mobility of British children. By 1990, as Hillman pointed out, only half of the population of nine year olds was allowed to cross roads on its own, only a third was allowed to go on non-school journeys alone, and only one in ten was allowed to travel on the bus alone. Twenty years earlier, virtually all nine year olds would have been doing such things independently.[21] The shift in the nature of the school journey finds further support in oral history research which shows that 40 per cent of those born between 1932 and 1941 had travelled alone at age ten to eleven (albeit a notably lower figure than in the Newsons' findings, even though dealing with older children), compared to just 9 per cent of those born between 1990 and 1991. The same research indicated that there had even been a significant fall among seventeen to eighteen year olds, from 80 per cent to just a third.[22]

---

[20] It also came to be recognized that the road death toll was now a major problem even in low and middle income countries, and it was predicted to become the fifth leading cause of death across the world by 2030. However, it was the link of an associated decline in mobility due to obesity and disease that would lead to the conclusion that 'Making towns and cities safer for pedestrians and cyclists... might not be as cutting edge as stem-cell research but will save more lives this decade' (Editorial, *The Lancet*, 377 (7 May 2011), 1543).

[21] Mayer Hillman, John Adams, and John Whitelegg, *One False Move: A Study of Children's Independent Mobility* (London, 1990), p. 106.

[22] Colin Pooley, Jean Turnbull, and Mags Adams, 'The Journey to School in Britain since the 1940s: Continuity and Change', *Area*, 37 (2005), 43–53.

The decline can be partly explained by the fact that the average distance of the school journey rose because of the trend towards selection on criteria other than locality. But this is insufficient to account for the rise in chaperonage (which was a factor even among those children walking to school).[23] Research on the declining numbers of children walking to school by 1998 indicated that fear of traffic was now a ubiquitous factor—evident in 90 per cent of parents surveyed—though it had become so much part of the landscape that it was now overshadowed by fear of abduction (however unlikely) as a factor in parental explanations for what determined the mode of travel.[24] Just as crucial, however, was the other side of the traffic equation: the rising level of car ownership (particularly towards the end of the century among women, with many families coming to have a second car), which led to a culture in which parents habitually transported children on even relatively short journeys.[25] Here, the rise of car travel to school was indicative of what geographers have described as a new 'hyperactive' mobility, in which increasingly time-pressed parents relied on the car in juggling jobs, childcare, leisure activities, and shopping.[26] The irony was that the likelihood of accidents involving child pedestrians and cyclists was also falling to its lowest point since the early days of the car: by 1990, the decrease in the rate of child road accidents per vehicle on the road since 1922 was a staggering 98 per cent. Of course, this did not mean that roads were becoming safe, or even safer. Rather, the accident rate had fallen so dramatically because children had largely been forced off the streets by the volume of traffic and by a culture of safety which placed the onus on the pedestrian.[27]

Already in the first decades of the century there had been considerable concern about the danger presented by motorized vehicular traffic to the child, while concern about non-motorized traffic went back to at least the 1870s (with proposals for pedestrian refuges, education, and even playgrounds to ameliorate the situation).[28] As early as the First World War, there were attempts to address this problem through the development of a culture of road safety consciousness among children, and through instituting practices and codes of safety.[29] The car exacerbated an already dangerous situation. Even before the advent of the motorized vehicle, the death rate per vehicle through horse-drawn traffic accidents was similar

[23] Among children walking to school, chaperonage rose by a third between the mid-1980s and mid-1990s: Caroline Woodroffe, Ian Roberts, and Carolyn DiGuiseppi, *The School Run: Blessing or Blight?* (London, 1998), p. 12.

[24] C. DiGuiseppi, I. Roberts, and D. Allen, 'Determinants of Car Travel on Daily Journeys to School', *British Medical Journal* (1998), 1426–8.

[25] Woodroffe et al., *The School Run*, pp. 3–6.

[26] Colin Pooley, 'Mobility in the Twentieth Century: Substituting Commuting for Mobility?', in David Gilbert, David Matless, and Brian Short (eds), *Geographies of British Mobility* (Oxford, 2003), pp. 8–99; Nigel Thrift, 'A Hyperactive World', in R. Johnston, P. Taylor, and M. Watts (eds), *Geographies of Global Change: Remapping the World in the Late Twentieth Century* (Oxford, 1995), pp. 18–35.

[27] Hillman et al., *One False Move*.

[28] Muhamad M. Ishaque and Robert B. Noland, 'Making Roads Safe for Pedestrians or Keeping Them Out of the Way?', *Journal of Transport History*, 27:1 (2006), 119.

[29] Joe Moran, 'Crossing the Road in Britain, 1931–1976', *Historical Journal*, 49 (2006), 477–96; Sean O'Connell, *The Car in British Society: Class, Gender, and Motoring, 1896–1939* (Manchester, 1998), pp. 112–49.

to the rate today.[30] The first motorized vehicles appeared on British roads in the mid-1890s. Initially, a man on foot had to walk in front and the speed limit was four miles per hour. The vehicles were expensive, and there were only 16,000 on the roads by 1905.[31] Thereafter, falling cost encouraged a rapid rise in numbers: from 143,877 in 1910, to 650,148 in 1920, to 2,273,661 by 1930.[32] Rising speeds, lack of familiarity with the danger and with codes of safety, and the fact that the roads also still carried horse-drawn vehicles all contributed to a high accident rate.

By the First World War, children were being identified as particularly at risk. In 1917, the recently founded London 'Safety First' Council, which in 1941 would become the Royal Society for the Prevention of Accidents (RoSPA), launched the first of many campaigns to educate children about road safety.[33] By 1928, its regular children's essay competition was reaching 250,000, and it reached even more through films shown in cinemas. Nevertheless, the number of road fatalities among British children continued to rise in the 1920s: from 1,232 in 1926 to 1,685 by 1930.[34] It was particularly high among boys (a 2:1 sex ratio in 1930). Indeed, children were more at risk than any other age group, with the peak danger for pedestrians between the ages of three and seven, and for cyclists between fourteen and sixteen.[35] The government responded by instituting an Interdepartmental Committee on Road Safety among School Children, which reported in 1936 with the recommendation that road safety be taught in schools.[36] From this period onwards, fatalities among children in fact began to fall.[37] There were two exceptions to this pattern. There was a small rise during the first years of the Second World War, which has been associated with the special difficulties of the blackout and evacuation of the war. Secondly, there was a rise in the 1950s and 1960s, in the context of a very rapid growth in the number of cars on the road in an increasingly affluent society: 680 child pedestrian fatalities in 1959, rising to 900 in 1965; and accidents involving injury to child pedestrians rising from 24,203 in 1957 to 37,331 in 1966.[38] Thereafter, levels fell again. By 1992, fatalities for child pedestrians were just 180, and for child cyclists 48. By 2002, the figures were 79 and 22, respectively.[39] Either roads were becoming much safer from the 1970s onwards, or a turning

---

[30] Ishaque and Noland, 'Making Roads Safe for Pedestrians', 117.

[31] William Plowden, *The Motor Car and Politics, 1896–1970* (London, 1971), pp. 14, 25.

[32] Plowden, *The Motor Car and Politics*, Appendix B: 'Motor Cars in Use 1914–69', pp. 456–7.

[33] For the history of RoSPA and road safety: <http://www.rospa.com/about/history/>.

[34] Royal Society for the Prevention of Accidents, *Road Accident Statistics* (London, 1966), p. 3.

[35] RoSPA, *Road Accident Statistics*, p. 9.

[36] Board of Education and Ministry of Transport, *Report of the Inter-Departmental Committee on Road Safety among School Children* (London, 1936), p. 8.

[37] Bill Luckin, 'War on the Roads: Traffic Accidents and Social Tension in Britain, 1939–1945', in Roger Cooter and Bill Luckin (eds), *Accidents in History: Injuries, Fatalities and Social Relations* (Amsterdam, 1997), pp. 234–54.

[38] RoSPA, *Road Accident Statistics*, Table 2, p. 4.

[39] <http://www.statistics.gov.uk> (Road Accident Casualties 1992–2002). The total level of fatalities (involving those of all ages in cars as well as pedestrians and cyclists) also fell, despite the huge increase in traffic from 8,302 in 1971, to 3,501 in 1998: <http://www.statistics.gov.uk> (Accidental Deaths UK—Road Accidents). Before this time, the overall rate had remained more level, already at more than 7,000 fatalities per year by the early 1930s: Luckin, 'War on the Roads', p. 236; Plowden, *The Motor Car and Politics*, pp. 456–7.

point had been reached in which the danger of the road and the culture of safety had largely pushed child pedestrians and cyclists off the street altogether.[40]

PLANNING FOR PLAY

Although the history of concern over the safety of children in relation to roads and traffic predates the Second World War, the wartime focus on the child heightened anxiety. Just as television emerged out of this context as offering a safe, specialized landscape for child development, so did new solutions to the provision of safe outdoor play. If an idealized home and family was at the centre of the post-war landscape settlement, the challenge of engineering a solution to outdoor play was an essential supplement. A focus on special spaces for play offered an easier solution than tackling the environment as a whole. Even so, in the longer term, the primacy of home and family, and the reluctance to take action that would fundamentally challenge the freedom of the car, meant that it would prove easier still to focus on strategies of safety consciousness.

Analysis of the surge in road accidents under the blackout of the Second World War has highlighted the muted nature of the victim's voice: stoicism a feature of the wartime emotional climate.[41] However, it was more difficult to ignore accidents when it came to children, who were such a focus for war-born anxieties and protectiveness. For all the alarms about the threat of bombing, almost as many children were killed and injured through the ongoing menace of traffic: 5,000 dead between 1938 and 1944, about half of them under the age of five, and a further 15,000 injured.[42] So when it came to the child victims of the wartime road, stoicism to some extent broke down, or at least it turned into activism for a better future. Here, the context helped turn such figures—which were in fact lower than they had been at the start of the 1930s—into a platform for reform. For instance, the issue was taken up by the Five Million Club, so-called because of the number of British children without a park or a playground in easy distance. And play became an increasingly political issue, with local authorities open to criticism for preferring places like bowling greens that brought in revenue at a time when children had nowhere else but the bombsite.[43]

A meeting of the National Safety Congress, in the year following the war and with the hoped-for programme of playground construction nowhere in sight, explored the playground street as an alternative: putting streets out of bounds to wheeled traffic (apart from residents) during the day.[44] This was permissible under legislation passed in 1938, and it followed the introduction of a local scheme in Salford and the success of the policy in New York. However, they were deemed

---

[40] Hillman et al., *One False Move*, pp. 1–2.   [41] Luckin, 'War on the Roads', p. 244.
[42] 'Playgrounds for Children', *The Times* (8 February 1944).
[43] 'Playgrounds for Children', *The Times* (8 February 1944).
[44] 'Selected Streets as Playgrounds', *The Times* (24 May 1946).

only a second best alternative until the creation of proper playgrounds. Like pedestrian barriers, it was a way of keeping children from running out in front of traffic, as much as keeping the traffic away from the children. After the war, there was continued worry that such streets would lead to a dangerous confusion in the child mind, and that it could be a deleterious step for road safety in general. Although the 1945 Interim Report of the Committee on Road Safety praised the idea of the play street, it recommended it only as an interim measure before post-war provision of new open spaces.[45] Indeed, all mention of such use of the street was absent in the Final Report in 1947.[46] Social worker Pearl Jephcott, while acknowledging the need for something to compensate for 'the home that gives no scope for play or hobbies' in her survey of the 'troubled area' of Notting Hill in the early 1960s, described how parents and schools were very wary of the dangers surrounding the four play streets in the area, one of them just off the busy Portobello Road.[47] In fact, a considerable number of play streets would emerge in the post-war decades, with an estimate of 750 across the nation by 1963. But, thereafter, they would face the problem that streets became increasingly full of parked cars—the average London residential street is estimated as having just 5 parked cars in the 1950s, but 70 by 1970. By the 1980s, the policy was largely forgotten, though it has had a recent renaissance from those looking to reverse the trend of the evacuation of children from city streets.[48]

Ultimately, even the play street was only a partial solution to squaring the circle of facilitating a free flow of traffic while providing children with safe outside play. Indeed, the very idea of the play street was an acknowledgement that normal streets were not appropriate places for children. Instead, the playground emerged as the preferred way forward.[49] For Labour's post-war Home Secretary, Herbert Morrison, the solution was to use the 1947 Town and Country Planning Act to assist local authorities to buy up green spaces on which children could play. Speaking to the National Playing Fields Association, he recalled his own experience of how inconvenient it had been to play on the streets when he was growing up. For Morrison, this was a simple issue of ending deprivation through state intervention: 'Streets are not designed for children. Neither are children designed for streets. I want better streets. I want better children. That is why I want more light, more air, and more grass.'[50] In sum, streets and children did not mix; the street was not only a dangerous place and a site for the production of the bad child, but the street itself would be better without the problem of the child. Prime Minister Clement Attlee was similarly happy to back the fitness and moral-fibre vision of the National

---

[45] Ministry of War Transport, *Interim Report of the Committee on Road Safety, December 1944* (London, 1945), p. 25.

[46] Ministry of Transport, *Final Report of the Committee on Road Safety, May 1947* (London, 1953), p. 23.

[47] Pearl Jephcott, *A Troubled Area: Notes on Notting Hill* (London, 1964), p. 108.

[48] Through organizations such as London Play: <http://www.londonplay.org.uk/document.php?document_id=1198>.

[49] Report of a speech by Herbert Morrison: 'Streets not Made for Children', *The Times*, 21 October 1948. A subsequent editorial suggested that there had been considerable enjoyment in 'Inconvenient Games', *The Times*, 28 October 1948.

[50] 'Streets not Made for Children', *The Times* (21 October 1948).

Playing Fields Association: 'Well spent leisure is necessary to balance hard work'. This was a vision of solving the problem, not by transposing the freedom of the street to the playground, but by channelling energies into organized sport and play in clearly demarcated, healthy, green spaces.[51] Concern about traffic may have been a factor here, but so too was the longstanding struggle to police the behaviour of working-class street children which had been a major concern of the juvenile courts in the interwar period and which continued to be so in the 1940s and 1950s.[52]

By the early 1950s, with growing interest in the street game as part of a fading culture, there was an increasing tendency to downplay Morrison's 'inconvenience' and to look back more nostalgically; and perhaps this helps to account for the vogue for the play street.[53] However, social change meant that there was no going back. Television now drew children inside, material comfort and education brought new expectations and tastes in terms of games, and road safety campaigns left parents and children increasingly wary of the street.[54] Life in the new landscape of high-rise flats seemed to symbolize the problem. Very evidently the idea that home and garden could provide sufficient opportunities for play broke down in this setting. The working-class children who lived in these flats showed a clear preference for playing outside, but they lacked the traditional culture that had spawned the world of the street game, while the networks of roads that surrounded these high-rise blocs were regarded as dangerous and as offering nothing to exercise the imagination.[55]

From the late 1940s, through into the 1970s, the planned landscape of the playground developed as one response to the problem, offering a way of addressing new understanding of the needs of the child despite the tension between these needs and the changing physical environment of the city. Its most radical form was the adventure playground. The idea was deeply rooted in the experience of the Second World War. It had first arrived in Britain via Lady Allen of Hurtwood's visit to the 'junk playground' of Emdrup set up in Nazi-occupied Denmark. But its central inspiration was the cathartic idea of transforming the wartime destruction of the urban landscape into a symbol of freedom. Indeed, it remained closely associated with wartime bombsites well beyond 1945; one report on plans for a playground in Glasgow described it as a process of creating a bombsite in the city.[56]

---

[51] 'Streets not Made for Children', *The Times* (21 October 1948); 'Growing Demand for Playing Fields—Influence on Greater Production', *The Times* (31 May 1949).

[52] Louise Jackson and Angela Bartie, 'Children of the City: Juvenile Justice, Property and Place in England and Scotland, 1945–60', *Economic History Review*, 64 (2011), 106–7. On the interwar period: S. Humphries, *Hooligans or Rebels: An Oral History of Working-Class Childhood and Youth 1889–1939* (Oxford, 1981), pp. 121–49.

[53] Iona and Peter Opie were pioneers in this area in the 1950s. In their *Children's Games in Street and Playground* (Oxford, 1969) they depicted the street as a natural environment for the child and for children's play, which was not the same thing as far as they were concerned as organized games and sport. For more on post-war nostalgia for the street child see Chapter 1.

[54] 'The East End at Play', *The Times* (26 January 1951).

[55] L. E. White, 'The Outdoor Play of Children Living in Flats', in Leo Kuper (ed.), *Living in Towns* (London, 1953), pp. 237–64.

[56] 'Junk Playgrounds for Glasgow Children', *Edinburgh Evening News* (25 July 1956).

However, there was frustration among supporters that many empty bombed-out spaces still lay vacant or boarded up. Moreover, the adventure playgrounds which did emerge often raised objections for their apparent lack of safety and seeming encouragement of reckless behaviour, and they struggled for local acceptance as a result; even if the key role played by adventure playground supervisors meant that they were in fact better policed than traditional playgrounds, and indeed they were often promoted as a way to divert vandalism.[57] At its heart, the adventure playground was part of the war-born vision of providing children not just with space, but a space that provided real challenges like those that the free citizen of a democracy would have to face. Indeed, Roy Kozlovsky has suggested that they performed a role for play akin to the psychological clinics and the spread of a new psychological common sense described by Nikolas Rose: extending the role of liberal government into the shaping of individual subjects—here internalized via a new way in play.[58] However, as press coverage indicates, such ambitions were often at odds with the chaotic reality on the ground. There was also considerable resistance to the new vision. Manchester City Council's Director of Parks argued that children in fact preferred the old playgrounds, with their swings and slides and found little satisfaction in sliding down the muddy slopes of a play area that lacked such equipment.[59] Others worried about the compensation claims that might face local councils if the adventure playgrounds really did offer the more adventurous and risky environment that they seemed to promise.[60]

Within an increasingly safety conscious culture by the early 1970s, there was even concern that the traditional playground of swings and slides was perhaps too dangerous a place for children. An investigation into the subject asked seventeen hospitals around the country to report on playground accidents during a four-week period and received information on 158 incidents, including 49 involving swings, 32 linked to slides, and 18 to roundabouts. The Design Council undertook further research, this time based on thirteen hospitals in a one-week period, and was notified about 207 accidents, with swings again the leading culprit. Leicester Infirmary estimated that it admitted eight to ten children per day in summer, and Manchester Hospital put the figure at ten to twelve (including two to three with fractured skulls every week). Such research reflected the fact that there were no

---

[57] For local objections in the mid-1950s: MSS.121/AP/10/2. For instance: 'Just Like a Jungle Cry Local Residents. But Two More are on the Way', *News Chronicle* (30 January 1956); 'No to Adventure Playground Idea', *Shields Gazette* (9 February 1956); 'Wreckers of Town's Parklands are Wasting the Money You Pay for Beauty', *Wolverhampton Chronicle* (23 March 1956). Roy Kozlovsky, 'Adventure Playgrounds and Postwar Reconstruction', in Marta Gutman and Ning de Conink-Smith (eds), *History, Space and the Material Culture of Children* (New Brunswick, N.J., 2008), pp. 171–90. For insight on the tension between play and policing of behaviour: Marie Paneth, *Branch Street: A Sociological Study* (London, 1944).

[58] Roy Kozlovsky, 'Urban Play: Intimate Space and Post-War Subjectivity', in Vittoria Di Palma, Diana Periton, and Marina Lathouri (eds), *Intimate Metropolis* (Abingdon, 2009), pp. 195–216; Nikolas Rose, *Governing the Soul: The Shaping of the Private Self* (London, 1990).

[59] Letter from R. C. MacMillan, 'Changes in Playgrounds—What Children Really Want', *The Times* (12 July 1957); response from Lady Allen, *The Times* (19 July 1957).

[60] Letter from Harold Marshall (Chairman of Clydesdale Adventure Playground), *The Times* (11 May 1954).

official statistics on the issue in Britain. In Holland, where figures were kept, there were around twenty recorded deaths every year. The problem was that the very essence and attraction of playground equipment was that it offered a physical challenge; almost inevitably, this involved risk of accident. Of course, better standards of design could help reduce the chance of injury; and by this time the British Standards Institute had eighteen separate standards for different types of playground equipment. Whether such standards were strictly followed was another matter. Indeed, after investigation of the 600 Greater London Council playgrounds prompted by the collapse of several roundabouts in 1971, half were recognized as having equipment that needed to be put out for repair or replacement. But it was also coming to be realized that even good design could not rule out accidents. An understanding of child psychology taught that it was in the very nature of children to seek out danger and to explore and adapt their landscape. In that sense, misuse of playground equipment, and resulting danger, was likely to remain endemic and inevitable.[61] Moreover, even in an area with an adventure playground, children could still be found playing on the street just down the road.[62] If play was the necessary route for children to explore the idea of reality, as post-war psychology argued, this psychology also pointed out that these children in truth really needed not playgrounds, even adventure playgrounds, but 'real situations, people, and experiences'.[63]

SAFETY CONSCIOUSNESS

Given the limitations of a strategy centred on the creation of urban play spaces, efforts to offer the post-war child a landscape beyond the home also focused on making road safety consciousness an essential part of every child's upbringing. RoSPA played a leading role in such efforts. Government initially turned to RoSPA in the context of wartime anxiety about safety, and this support increased in the post-war decades. The RoSPA philosophy of emphasizing codes of conduct and attitudes of mind, rather than attacking the car as the source of the problem, was politically attractive. By contrast, what Bill Luckin has described as the 'radical neo-Luddite', more anti-car Pedestrians' Association was far less influential than it had been before the war. Part of the story here was a democratization of driving. The road accident had been a more obviously political issue in the days when drivers had invariably been of a higher class than the people they were knocking down. The post-war emphasis on road safety was also a reflection of a more general vogue, boosted by the wartime experience of psychology in the armed services and industry, to consider the

---

[61] 'Dangers for Children at Play', *The Times* (6 June 1973).
[62] 'A London Junk Playground', *The Times* (24 December 1952).
[63] Clare Britton, 'Children Who Cannot Play', in New Education Fellowship, *Play and Mental Health* (London, 1945), pp. 12–17. Republished in Joel Kanter (ed.), *Face to Face with Children: The Life and Work of Clare Winnicott* (London, 2004).

role of the 'human factor' in organizing systems, and to see solutions as lying in psychological readjustment.[64]

The strategy of imposing safety consciousness did have its critics. When 'safety first' lessons were considered by the 1936 Interdepartmental Committee on Road Safety among School Children, some witnesses expressed misgivings that taking away the thrill of danger might undermine the development of courage necessary in the development of healthy boys.[65] The Chairman of the Pedestrians' Association condemned the 'inherent viciousness' of 'safety first' education for creating a culture of fear in the minds of the child—setting out to 'make the child the subconscious guardian of his own safety'—while absolving drivers of responsibility. Describing safety consciousness as a breeding ground for anti-social attitudes, he also suggested that it was an approach that belonged in a fascist rather than a democratic society (and pointed out that it had been Italy and Germany which had led the way in placing the onus of responsibility on the pedestrian through road safety).[66]

The kerb drill promoted by the Ministry of Information in the Second World War certainly did have a distinctly militarist tone: at the kerb HALT; eyes right; eyes left—then if the road is clear; quick march.[67] Joe Moran suggests that wartime interventionism in everyday life made such propaganda more acceptable, even if attempts to compel pedestrians to use specified crossings (the pre-war Belisha crossings marked by amber globes on striped poles, and then zebra crossings from the late 1940s) or to fine them for jaywalking were less successful.[68] By 1943, with a fall in child road deaths from the peak of 1941 to the lowest figure for ten years, the propaganda campaign appeared to be a success.[69] After the war, the Ministry of Transport continued the appeal to parents and to mothers in particular. However, in the late 1940s and early 1950s, the safety message had shifted from the kerb drill to getting young children off the streets altogether. This was in line with broader post-war efforts to tackle the traffic problem primarily through a strategy of making it easier for cars to move through cities.[70] In one publicity image, a mother is pictured approaching her front door with the shopping and her little daughter in tow. Just beyond the garden gate, we see a busy road. The 'traffic jimp' says to the mother: 'Forgotten the bread? Send Mary!' Below the image, a caption instructs: 'Even if you're tired. Even if you're busy, don't listen when the traffic jimp suggests sending a young child to face traffic alone.'[71] In another, alongside the picture—again of a

---

[64] Luckin, 'War on the Road', p. 236. On the interwar tensions between the National Safety First Association and the Pedestrians' Association: O'Connell, *The Car in British Society*, pp. 123–46.

[65] Referred to in Gerald Cummins, 'The History of Road Safety': <http://www.driveandstayalive.com/info%20section/history/history.htm>.

[66] J. S. Dean, *Murder Most Foul: A Study of the Road Deaths Problem* (London, 1947), pp. 59–60. See the discussion in Moran, 'Crossing the Road', 484.

[67] For instance: 'Is Your Child Educated', *The Times* (18 September 1944).

[68] Moran, 'Crossing the Road', 479–84.

[69] 'Road Deaths in April—Lowest Total for Ten Years—Children's Kerb Drill', *The Times* (4 June 1943).

[70] Colin Pooley and Jean Turnbull, 'Coping with Congestion: Response to Urban Traffic Problems in British Cities, *c.* 1920–1960', *Journal of Historical Geography*, 31:1 (2005), 78–93.

[71] 'Don't Listen to the Traffic Jimp', *The Times* (15 January 1949).

young girl, even though boys had a higher fatality rate—the message read: 'Happy future...or NONE? Facts a parent <u>must</u> face.' And below: 'Never let your children face traffic alone.'[72] The message was stark, and far more restrictive than it had been even during the Second World War: not just real road safety, but also responsible parenting meant ensuring that young children did not go out alone.

The shifting onus of responsibility from children to their parents was in line with the broader post-war focus on the importance of mothering and provision of a secure, loving home. Within this context, concern about child safety extended from its original site of the road to consideration of the various dangers such as fireplaces and electrical equipment within the family home itself (indeed, by 1949 there were in fact more children killed in accidents in the home than on the roads, though this had a lower profile in public consciousness).[73]

The shift to parents also reflected recognition that the principles of the kerb drill hardly equipped children to deal with the complex dangers of traffic and even then proved difficult for the youngest children to follow. In that sense, psychology could undermine as well as reinforce confidence in road safety.[74] When it came to older children, psychology again unearthed problems with existing road safety advice. Research on road safety films for the Petroleum Films Board, undertaken by psychologists at the Tavistock Clinic, highlighted that effective propaganda would have to take into account the child's perspective. This meant listening to the responses of children, incorporating their views, and recognizing that what appealed to the child and the adult could be two very different things. Children liked the films where there were characters and situations which they could identify with. They disliked being preached at and talked down to, and they tended to distrust adults who did so in the films. The psychologists concluded that 'Playing in the Road' was the most effective of these films because it provided the opportunity to open up a discussion of the problems associated with traffic, allowing children to think through the issues themselves rather than having to accept a list of instructions. What was also apparent was that children could be critical of the motorists. In 'Playing in the Street', for instance, they wondered why they, rather than the drivers, were the ones who should be 'looking out' on a street that was wide, straight, and relatively traffic free; what was wrong about sharing?[75]

However, listening to how children saw and felt about their environment, and then doing something about this when this might clash with adult interests, was the most challenging of the ways forward. It was far easier to accept the other lesson of psychology: that embracing the child's perspective meant being sceptical about the efficacy of any kerb drill, a position that validated the view that the real solution was to clear children off the street altogether. Scepticism regarding the

---

[72] 'Happy Future...or NONE?', *The Times* (28 January 1950).
[73] C. A. Boucher, 'Accidents in the Home', *Monthly Bulletin of the Ministry of Health* (May 1949), p. 20.
[74] Luckin, 'War on the Road', p. 236.
[75] Petroleum Films Bureau, *Film Production for Child Audiences—A Psychological Study* (London, 1952).

kerb-drill style of approach mounted in the 1960s, as child fatalities took an upward turn from 680 in 1959 to 900 in 1965, and as the sheer volume of traffic on the roads entered a wholly different realm—around four million vehicles in use at the end of the 1940s, but nearly fifteen million by 1969.[76] RoSPA made overtures towards being more child-centred as it launched a series of clubs for children, first the Teddy Club, followed by the Tufty Club in 1961. The latter had two million members by 1972.[77] But such propaganda was also a way of reaching out to the parents of young children. Indeed, mothers were an increasing focus for road safety efforts. They were also at the heart of a new government investigation at the end of the 1960s.[78] This investigation was particularly concerned by its findings that many parents still allowed their children to play on the street—31 per cent of the two-to-four-year-old group, and 40 per cent of the five to eights.[79] It offers particularly striking insight on the freedom of the very youngest children, with a quarter of the two year olds in the survey allowed to cross roads on their own and 11 per cent able to ride tricycles or bicycles on the street.[80] Also significant was the finding that social class had little effect: that in the late 1960s, albeit usually in less heavily trafficked areas, the middle classes were as happy as the working classes to allow their children independent access to the street.[81] However, the assumption throughout was that the presence of these children on the street was a problem, rather than in any respect a good thing. Questions to mothers attempted to find out why they allowed their children this freedom and what type of road safety advice they handed on. Though many mothers were worried about the danger of traffic and many knew of children who had been in accidents, the safety advice they passed on turned out to be very basic.[82] Further implicit criticism of parenting came in the psychological research of Lindy Burton, which shifted attention from the danger itself to the psychological reasons for some children being more vulnerable to road accidents than others. Here, the accident was recast as a response to 'maternal stresses, rejection, excessive dominance, and unsettling environmental experiences', and as 'an attempt at gaining sympathy, or an effort to punish unloving parents'.[83] Within this context, it is intriguing to see signs that some mothers were now taking the initiative, rather in the way that they were also doing in relation to playgroups. For instance, two Hendon housewives found themselves in the news for setting up their own organization to promote teaching of effective road safety in schools.[84] And as the final chapter will discuss, the politics of traffic would emerge as a focal point for women in the community activism of the 1970s.

[76] RoSPA, *Road Accident Statistics*, p. 3.   [77] Moran, 'Crossing the Road', 486–7.
[78] Judy Sadler (Enquiry for the Road Research Laboratory), *Children and Road Safety: A Survey amongst Mothers, 1969* (London, 1972).
[79] Sadler, *Children and Road Safety*, pp. 11–12.
[80] Sadler, *Children and Road Safety*, pp. 32, 75.
[81] Sadler, *Children and Road Safety*, p. 1.
[82] Sadler, *Children and Road Safety*, pp. 60–70.
[83] Lindy Burton, *Vulnerable Children: Three Studies of Children in Conflict: Accident Involved Children, Sexually Assaulted Children and Children with Asthma* (London, 1968), pp. 77, 83.
[84] Moira Keenan, 'Road Safety—Whose Problem?', *The Times* (18 March 1970).

Representing the interests of drivers, the Automobile Association was happy to focus some blame on parents. It accepted that there was a problem with kerb drill. Research showing that only 43 per cent of young children could tell their left from their right made something of a mockery of relying on the look right and left instructions. Instead, the AA argued that the problem lay in the very presence of accompanied children. It condemned the fact that a quarter of the parents saw no harm in allowing their children to play in local streets, and it pointed out that half of all accidents involving children happened within twenty yards of home. Although most parents now made sure that young children were accompanied by adults or older children on the school journey, the fact was that most accidents took place after they had arrived back home between 4 and 6 pm.[85] In other words, the real problem was one of parental lack of supervision.

'Parrot-like' kerb drill now found itself pilloried as a potential 'death ritual': not just ineffective because of its rigidity, but dangerous because its incantation gave the illusion of guaranteed security.[86] It was at odds with an increasing emphasis within educational circles on understanding rather than rote learning, and with a shift towards appreciating that the world looked very different from the perspective of the child. New academic research concluded that children were biologically and psychologically incapable of managing the demands of the modern traffic environment.[87] Children struggled to understand that traffic rules needed to be interpreted according to the highly varied and constantly shifting circumstances of the modern road environment. Psychologically, it was very hard for children to divide their attention, to appreciate changing situations, or to maintain concentration on such a complex challenge. Sheer physical size also made it far harder for children to see on the streets and in turn to be seen. And there was also the dreadful paradox that they had a biological urge for rapid and impulsive movement that was repressed in the constrained environment of the small modern home but which therefore found inevitable expression in the dangerous context of the street.[88]

By 1971 the old kerb drill had made way for the Green Cross Code. In partial recognition of the problem of understanding, the code was to be taught only once children reached the age of seven. And it adopted instructions that depended less on concepts like left and right, and aimed for language and ideas that would make sense to children: 'find a safe place to cross, then stop; stand on a pavement near the kerb; look and listen for traffic; if traffic is coming, let it pass; look all around again; when there is no traffic near, walk straight across the road, looking and listening for traffic while you cross'.[89] There was also a growing interest in understanding what this meant for the children involved. One of the outcomes of this reorientation was a published collection of essays on road safety written by London children in the early 1970s. This material certainly suggests that children did take

---

[85] 'AA Blames Parents for Accidents', *The Times* (6 January 1970).
[86] 'Parrot-like Kerb Drill "Can Kill"', *The Times* (6 March 1970).
[87] Sandels, *Children in Traffic*, p. 147. This research was first published in 1968.
[88] Sandels, *Children in Traffic*, pp. 130–4.
[89] '£500,000 to Change Children's Kerb Drill', *The Times* (29 April 1971).

on board the message of the importance of not forgetting the Green Cross Code. However, it also points to the ways in which fantasy and imagination complicated interpretation. And it highlights the emotional legacy. Among other things, it suggests that within this culture of safety consciousness children could come to internalize the potential accident as something that was their fault. Adults now had the challenge of thinking their way through the perspective and feelings of the seven-year-old mind of a child like Rachel that are difficult to ignore beneath her efforts at regurgitating the road safety mantra: 'there was a ghost boy and he was playing football by the ghost road. Suddenly he ran across the road. A car was coming, but luckily the car went through him because he was a ghost. So remember, don't run across the road because a car cannot drive through you.'[90]

Within a short time, the new Green Cross Code found itself under criticism. It was too complicated, children could not remember it in full, and only 18 per cent were able to find a safe place to cross.[91] In reality, there was no longer confidence in making children and cars compatible partners to share the streets. A point was close to being reached at which educating children to cope with traffic seemed to run the risk of being more dangerous than not doing so at all. On the one hand, this encouraged the view that town planning and road safety had to look to the separation of pedestrians and cars: that it was an issue of engineering safety through barriers, underpasses, pedestrian town centres, and an increasing number of roads unimpeded by pedestrians in order to lessen congestion.[92] On the other hand, and the recent literature on the history of road safety has tended to overlook this aspect of the story, responsibility was further thrown onto the shoulders of the parents, who placed new restrictions on the independent mobility of their own children. Together the two developments accelerated the departure of the child from the street, with perceived rather than real risk driving the problem.[93] This departure, rather than progress in road safety education or the technology of the crossing, was the crucial issue in the substantial fall in child accident and fatality rate over the next decades. By the 1990s, with a host of side effects, including implications for physical and mental health beginning to attract attention, the victory for well-being seemed less clear-cut.[94]

CONCLUSION

Anxieties about the safety of British children posed by road traffic have a relatively long history. They can be traced back to the first decades of the century. But they blossomed in particular in the context of the Second World War, leading to a post-war

---

[90] Camden Road Safety Campaign, *A Selection of Entries from the Camden Junior Schoolchildren's Short Story Competition* (London, 1974), foreword from Councillor Richard Arthur.

[91] 'Kerb Drill "Too Complicated"', *The Times* (10 July 1974).

[92] Ishaque and Noland, 'Making Roads Safe for Pedestrians'; 128–34; Moran, 'Crossing the Road', 489.

[93] John Adams, *Risk* (London, 1995), pp. 11–13.

[94] Mayer Hillman (ed.), *Children, Transport and the Quality of Life* (London, 1993); Woodroffe et al., *The School Run*.

exploration of the two responses of a planned environment for play centred on special play spaces, and the promotion of safety consciousness. In this history, an initial ambition with regard to planning for play faltered and remained limited in scale. However, a focus on safety consciousness also encountered criticism. Here, a desire to take into account the perspective of the child could in fact hold back efforts: the psychological challenge of dealing with traffic coming to be seen as beyond the capacities of young children. Parental responsibility consequently emerged as just as important a target for propaganda but also psychological research. There is a sense of the resulting guilt in the parental attitudes to child mobility at the start of the 1970s, captured in the Newsons' research. And the Newsons' evidence on differences across class and gender indicates that parental protectiveness was increasing. However, this material is now even more striking for what it reveals about the relative freedom of young children compared to the situation several decades later. In that sense, the efforts at planning for play and understanding the child's capacity to safely navigate the dangers of the city emerge, for all their limitations, as part of an age of optimism in planning a landscape for the child in the post-war decades: related in character to the broader post-war landscape settlement, a settlement that looked to the resources of the welfare state, to public intervention, to education, paternalism, and the inculcation of responsibility, and to managed freedom. The final chapters of this book will attempt to explain why this settlement began to break down.

Although this chapter has acknowledged the profound impact of the car in reshaping the child's experience of the city, it has also noted that there was not a direct correlation between an increase in the volume of traffic and a closing down of the child's access to urban space. The relationship between the two was mediated by cultural attitudes. Moreover, children subverted adult instructions on safety, and on where and how they should play, and thus there was an ongoing tension between creating landscapes for the child and the situation of children within this landscape. This is one of the reasons children still had a considerable degree of freedom despite mounting parental and broader social anxiety. Nevertheless, by the start of the 1970s the danger of traffic was largely accepted as part of the landscape of the child. Thereafter children were less likely to be killed on the roads, but not because roads became significantly safer, rather because children were increasingly kept away. By 1970, even if the most substantial decline in independent mobility was still to come, it was already clear that one of the major transitions in the post-war landscape of the child was to be this closing down of independent access to urban space.

6

Sexual Danger and the Age of the Paedophile

The last chapter considered the degree to which an increase in road traffic, and the fears and concerns about safety that this induced, contributed to a closing down of the landscape of the British child and a loss of childhood freedom in the post-war period. This chapter provides us with a picture of the role of sexual danger in this process. Because it has been more overlooked to date, but also because of its importance in relation to the story of lost freedom, the chapter will concentrate on the threat of child molestation outside the home. However, in the concluding section it will also briefly discuss sexual abuse in the two other landscape settings of the home and residential institutions, and the explosion of alarm in these two other settings only in the period after the 1970s. Analysis of concerns about sexual danger will tend to confirm the view that the period up until the early 1970s was one of growing appreciation of the dangers that children might encounter in the outside world, yet also one in which levels of resulting anxiety were more muted than in our own times. As with the analysis of children and traffic, it appears that a growing awareness of the importance of taking into account the child's own perspective did not necessarily lead to greater concern about the danger. Indeed, in professional circles one encounters what now appears a remarkable willingness to downplay the threat of sexual abuse.[1] Though in the period before the 1970s the fear of sexual danger was less important than that of traffic in making the world beyond home less accessible for children, it would subsequently become revealing in ways that the subject of children and traffic is not. This is partly an issue of timing: the danger of traffic had become an accepted part of everyday life by 1970; that of sexual danger was still to a large extent hidden from view, clouded in euphemism, and yet to explode into public and political consciousness. It is also because the subject of sexual danger provides a route for exploring the degree to which anxieties about safety moved from activity outside the home to what went on within the home itself as well as within institutions set up to provide care for child.

By the end of the twentieth century, the paedophile and the problem of child sexual abuse had become central features of the landscape of the child.[2] Public and

---

[1] In contrast, on the explosion of anxiety in the late twentieth century: Frank Furedi, *Culture of Fear: Risk-Taking and the Morality of Low Expectation* (London, 1997); Deborah Lupton, *Risk* (London, 1999), pp. 8–9.

[2] On the explosion of media concern from the 1980s and of the language of 'paedophilia': John Silverman and David Wilson, *Innocence Betrayed: Paedophilia, the Media and Society* (Cambridge, 2002); K. Soothill, B. Francis, and E. Ackerley, 'Paedophilia and Paedophiles', *New Law Journal* (1998), 882–3.

parental fear about the threat of sexual molestation by strangers was broadly accepted as one of the key factors behind a closing down of a physical landscape beyond the home.[3] And surveys based on self-reporting now suggested that a large proportion of the population had experienced abuse. A MORI poll for Channel 4 in 1984 produced the headline that one in ten British adults claimed to have been sexually abused before the age of sixteen.[4] Just three decades earlier, at the start of the 1970s, the situation had been radically different. This chapter asks two questions. Firstly, why was there comparatively little concern about paedophilia and child sexual abuse before the 1970s? Secondly, why did this situation change? In addressing the first question, the chapter will suggest that there is in fact more evidence than we have hitherto recognized across the century as a whole, and that the issue in need of explanation is what held back earlier alarm. In addressing the second question, the focus will be the key period of transition in the 1970s. Here, the chapter will consider in some detail a set of attitudes and a series of events that now appear remarkable in their contrast to the present. In particular, paedophilia came to the fore of public consciousness in response to efforts to legitimize the identity and role of the 'child-lover'. The chapter explains how this was possible. In doing so, it contributes to the view developed elsewhere in this book that the 1970s can be seen as an important turning point for debates about childhood freedom and for a post-war settlement in relation to the landscape of the child.

It has been pointed out that there is a strange gap in history between the child-saving efforts of the late nineteenth century, epitomized by the efforts of the National Society for the Prevention of Cruelty to Children (NSPCC) to rescue the working-class child from physical brutality or neglect, and the 'rediscovery' of abuse in the final decades of the century.[5] This chapter sets out to help fill but also

---

[3] In July 2000, in the aftermath of the high-profile cases of children Sarah Payne, Jessica Chapman, and Holly Wells, a MORI poll suggested that 47 per cent of the British population were afraid that their children were at risk of sexual assault, with 78 per cent viewing this risk as being greater than it had been in the past. A second MORI poll in September 2002 indicated that 71 per cent of parents reported increasing levels of concern about the safety of their children, with 61 per cent stating that they were now less likely to leave their child unsupervised. An increase in policing in the 1990s—including the creation of the Sex Offenders Register in 1997—appeared to have done nothing to dim anxieties, and perhaps to have fuelled it: Anneke Meyer, *The Child at Risk: Paedophilia, Media Responses and Public Opinion* (Manchester, 2007), pp. 6–8.
[4] Stuart Bell, *When Salem Came to Boro: The True Story of the Cleveland Child Abuse Crisis* (London, 1988), p. 50 (though less notice was taken of the fact that the definition of abuse within this survey was a very wide one including 'talking about things in an erotic way'). Other research based on self-reporting estimated that 12 per cent of women and 8 per cent of men, or in total 4.5 million adults, had experienced abuse in their childhoods: Don Grubin, *Sex Offending against Children: Understanding the Risk* (Police Research Series Paper 99, 1998). See also Jan Silverman and David Wilson, *Innocence Betrayed: Paedophilia, the Media and Society* (Cambridge, 2002), pp. 20–2; Anthony Baker and Sylvia Duncan, 'Child Sexual Abuse: A Study of Prevalence in Great Britain', *Child Abuse and Neglect*, 9 (1985), 457–67.
[5] The problem is noted in one recent account, which attempts to delineate a connection via comparative analysis of late-nineteenth- and late-twentieth-century child protection. However, this account in fact offers little detail on what came between the two, either in terms of practice or in terms of the real or perceived nature of abuse: Harry Ferguson, *Protecting Children in Time* (Basingstoke, 2004). The story remains one mainly of the 'rediscovery' of abuse from the 1960s onward. For an overview: Harry Hendrick, *Child Welfare: England 1872–1989* (London, 1994), pp. 242–57.

explain that gap. In particular, it casts light on a background issue of the danger from strangers that has in fact attracted relatively little attention. For instance, in his survey of the 'making and molding' of child abuse, Ian Hacking offers a convincing and compelling account of the social construction of the family abuse that dominates our own fears, but he rapidly passes over what he describes as 'a sort of constant: flashing, molestation in parks, children picked up in cars by strangers and assaulted'. This is something, Hacking suggests, that has no recent history, not because it does not happen, but because it has always been there in the background. 'I know of no reason', he writes, 'to think that this sort of behaviour has changed in a hundred years.'[6] One of the aims of this chapter is to begin to establish an historical trajectory for this type of child abuse: to suggest that the flasher and the park-molester may not have been unique to a particular period, but that in terms of cultural significance they, like the figure of the paedophile, did have their time. This would have important consequences in reshaping the landscape of the child in post-war Britain.[7]

Before the 1970s, the terms 'paedophile' and 'paedophilia' were virtually non-existent in Britain. Now they are such an integral part of our daily language that even young children throw the abbreviated terms 'paed' and paedo' at one another in playground abuse. Before the 1970s, the only place one would find these terms was in specialist psychiatric literature. By the first decade of the century, it had been used by Havelock Ellis and Krafft-Ebing in their classificatory systems of psycho-sexual pathology.[8] The forensic psychiatrist Norwood East also listed paedophilia in an overview of sexual crime in 1948, but only as among a set of esoteric sexual conditions such as necrophilia, voyeurism, and bestiality which did not in themselves lead to criminal behaviour. He noted that it could be related to factors that delayed the development of normal sexual and social relationships, such as mental deficiency, retarded emotional development, or senile impotency, though he added that 'Interference with girls under age is hardly to be considered as abnormal if the girl is sexually mature, consenting and conceals her true age.'[9] In other words, it was an accident of development, perhaps even an easy mistake. Growing psychiatric recognition and concern is hinted at in its inclusion in the first edition of the DSM—the *Diagnostic and Statistical Manual of Mental Disorders*—in 1952. But even in psychiatry, a survey in 1964 pointed out that there was not even one major study of the subject to date.[10] There is even less evidence to suggest that the terminology gained broader public usage before the 1970s.

---

[6] Ian Hacking, 'The Making and Molding of Child Abuse', *Critical Inquiry*, 17 (1991), 274.

[7] In the American context, this issue is addressed in Philip Jenkins, *Changing Concepts of the Child Molester in Modern America* (London, 1998).

[8] The *Oxford English Dictionary* cites the first usage (of 'paidophilia') as that of Ellis in the fifth volume of his *Studies in the Psychology of Sex* in 1906; however, the Viennese psychiatrist Richard von Krafft-Ebing had already included 'paedophilia erotica' in his *Psychopathia Sexualis* of 1886.

[9] Sir William Norwood East, 'Sexual Crime', *Journal of Criminal Science*, 1 (1948), 67, 79.

[10] J. W. Mohr, R. E. Turner, and M. B. Jerry, *Pedophilia and Exhibitionism* (Toronto, 1964), p. vi. East, in fact, contributed an article on exhibitionism as early as 1924 and commented further in his 1946 survey, suggesting that the level was inflated by the overlap with paedophilia: Mohr et al., *Pedophilia and Exhibitionism*, pp. 113–14; W. N. East, 'Observations on Exhibitionism', *Lancet*, 23 (1924), 370–5.

To highlight the absence of a language of paedophilia is not to say that there was no recognition of the problem of sexual molestation of children. Indeed, because children had greater freedom to move around beyond the home without adult chaperonage, they were probably more likely before 1970 than afterwards to encounter adult sexual advances in public spaces such as the street, parks, and cinemas. However, prior to the 1970s, there had been a tendency to avoid discussion or to adopt a euphemistic language. The scale of the problem had been masked by the fact that responsible adults were often reluctant to take legal action. Moreover, in medical and psychiatric circles, a growing post-Freudian acceptance of the sexuality of the child as well as recognition that the child viewed such issues differently to the adult acted to underplay the damage caused by such adult–child sexual encounters. The shift in language in the 1970s would reflect a step-change in public consciousness and anxiety. It was made possible by the fact that Britain was becoming a more sexually permissive society by the early 1970s. This made public talk about such matters easier. But a more permissive attitude centred on expression of adult sexuality also led to debate about its limits (and this was sharply exposed by the issues of child sexuality and child protection). The emergence of a common language and consciousness of paedophilia was a product of both tendencies.[11]

Looking back from our side of this historical divide and from within its climate of heightened sensitivity, there has been a tendency to suspect that paedophilia and child sexual abuse in fact existed on a similarly large scale in the past but was simply hidden from view. For psycho-historian Lloyd de Mause, writing in the 1970s on the cusp of the divide, child sex abuse was in fact a nightmare from which we were only *now* beginning to awaken: in other words, it had always been there, it was just hidden in the past, and current revelations were a positive sign of a society waking up to the problem.[12] To a certain extent, the analysis of behaviour before the emergence of paedophilia as a prominent category offers support to this thesis from a new direction. Nevertheless, in terms of consciousness there is an important distinction between the two eras, and this matters as this consciousness in turn has had a series of results. On this side of the divide, our culture has promoted two images of childhood that are in fundamental tension. On the one hand, the media and advertising bombard us with images of the child-like figure as a desirable sexual ideal, and place pressure on children to enter a world of adult sexuality. On the other hand, in the midst of moral upheaval, there is a stronger desire than ever to cling on to an ideal of childhood innocence. Our own resulting unease about this tension, argues James Kincaid, is a significant factor in our obsession with child sexual danger—manifest in the figure of the omnipresent paedophile. The paradox, he argues, is that the idealized image of innocence is in turn a key component in what makes the child so desirable. Unable to recognize or deal with children for what they are, rather than what we desire them to be, and unable in particular to

---

[11] Jeffrey Weeks, *Sex, Politics and Society: The Regulation of Sexuality since 1800* (London, 1989), Chapter 13, 'The Permissive Moment'.
[12] Lloyd de Mause, *The History of Childhood* (London, 1976), p. 1.

face up to childhood sexuality, our culture is caught in a vicious circle.[13] Kinkaid presents a controversial and uncomfortable argument, particularly when it comes to his suggestions regarding the ubiquitous nature of adult desire for the child. What he also forces us to ask, as historian on this side of the child-sexual-abuse divide, is whether an approach such as De Mause's risks interpolating not only our own anxieties about childhood, but also our idealization of innocence, into our reading of the past. Kinkaid's analysis indicates, at the very least, the importance of a history not just of the child as victim but of child sexuality itself.[14] In taking on this challenge, the discussion of children and sexual danger in the twentieth century that follows suggests that a shift away from a model of innocence was in fact more evident than we have sometimes appreciated throughout much of the century. By the 1970s this came to the fore in challenging a model in which children were merely the passive recipients of the right to protection—'in the name of the child'—from others. The confusion and tensions that resulted was an important element in the shift to the age of the paedophile.

CHILD SEXUAL MOLESTATION BEFORE THE AGE OF THE PAEDOPHILE

The period from the late nineteenth century to the 1970s, in fact, saw increasing consciousness of adult sexual contact with children, even if this did not precipitate the type of moral crisis and fundamental rethinking of the landscape of the child that was to follow. A central reason for the growing consciousness, but also the relative lack of alarm, was one and the same: the transition from a moral and religious to a psychological understanding of sexual matters. Recognition of the psychological profile of the victims as well as the perpetrators encouraged the handling of the issue as one of medicine rather than law. In the earlier part of the period, mental deficiency was often seen as a contributory factor. In due course, the emergence of psycho-sexual systems of psychiatry turned such behaviour into the subject for research and classification. And most crucially, a post-Freudian growing appreciation of the sexuality of the child fundamentally complicated attitudes to the danger of such contact, encouraging the view that children were often not

---

[13] James Kinkaid, *Erotic Innocence: The Culture of Child Molesting* (London, 1998).

[14] Writing from a queer theory perspective, Steven Angelides has suggested that the discovery of child sexual abuse since the 1970s has led to a misguided attempt to erase childhood sexuality: 'Feminism, Child Sexual Abuse, and the Erasure of Child Sexuality', *GLQ: A Journal of Lesbian and Gay Studies*, 10 (2004), 141–77. New work has adopted this orientation: Danielle Egan and Gail Hawkes, *Theorizing the Sexual Child in Modernity* (London, 2010). In fact, as Anne Higonnet has demonstrated in her history of child photography, the story of the child as sexual victim is only one part of our recent history. She sees signs of the emergence of a new way of representing childhood that is more in tune with what, after all, have been some radical shifts in the nature of the family and in understanding of sexuality in the late twentieth century: *Pictures of Innocence: The History and Crisis of Ideal Childhood* (London, 1998), pp. 210–11. On the high rate of abuse by children of other children: Pat Cawson, Corinne Wattam, Sue Brooker, and Graham Kelly, *Child Maltreatment in the United Kingdom: A Study of the Prevalence of Child Abuse and Neglect* (London, 2000).

wholly innocent in such relationships and were not necessarily damaged by an early exploration of sexuality. In a climate of Bowlbyism, the view that the central need of the child was one of love could also sometimes be used to downplay the damage that resulted from intergenerational sex. And appreciation of the complexity of the child's psychological world and of the different way in which the child saw the world compared to the adult encouraged a belief that dealing with such issues as crimes, and thereby exposing children to cross-examination in the legal system, both was more damaging than simply leaving them to move on and placed them in an inappropriate environment in which their actions and views had to be judged by adult standards. In short, a growing appreciation of the child mind up until the 1970s contributed to a greater awareness of a world of sexuality which involved children but held back rather than fuelled anxiety about sexual danger.

Already in the nineteenth century, child-saving had emerged as one of the most significant areas of charitable social work. A combination of the philanthropic impulse, poverty and urban squalor, and increasingly romanticized middle-class views of childhood fuelled the efforts of groups such as the NSPCC to rescue poor children from streets and abusive homes.[15] However, as Louise Jackson has demonstrated, recognition of and discussion of sexual abuse remained rare within such a child-saving culture. The number of prosecutions involving such acts was tiny. If sexual abuse was recognized, it was invariably obscured in language of euphemism. In many cases, rather than pursuing perpetrators, the response was to institutionalize the girls involved to protect them but also to prevent them from spreading the corruption.[16] Concerns over protection did lead in 1885 to the raising of the age of sexual consent to sixteen; but the law dealt unsympathetically with girls on the cusp of this age and often excused men on the grounds that the girls looked older. Not until 1908 was there in fact a law prohibiting incest.[17]

By the 1920s, there had been a significant shift in tone.[18] This was evident in an increasing willingness to protect children through the law, a trend which went back to the raising of the age of consent on intercourse to sixteen in 1885 and the 1908 legislation on incest, and which continued in 1922 with the age of consent being raised from thirteen to sixteen in assessing other forms of indecent assault. The greater alertness to questions of child sexuality can be explained only partly by acceptance of Freud, with the British remaining cautious about his emphasis on sex.[19] Equally important was a more pragmatic concern about sexual hygiene, a

---

[15] George Behlmer, *Child Abuse and Moral Reform in England, 1870–1908* (Stanford, 1982).

[16] Louise Jackson, *Child Sexual Abuse in Victorian England* (London, 2000), pp. 35, 55, 68–9.

[17] V. Bailey and S. Blackburn, 'The Punishment of Incest Act 1908: A Case Study of Law Creation', *Criminal Law Review* (1979), 708–18.

[18] Jackson, *Child Sexual Abuse*, 152–5.

[19] For an overview of the history of childhood sexuality: S. Fishman, 'The History of Childhood Sexuality', *Journal of Contemporary History*, 17 (1982), 269–83; George Rousseau (ed.), *Children and Sexuality from the Greeks to the Great War* (Basingstoke, 2007). On the role of Freud in discovery of the sexuality of the child: S. Kern, 'Freud and the Discovery of Child Sexuality', *History of Childhood Quarterly*, 1 (1973), 117–41; Lutz Sauerteig, 'Loss of Innocence: Albert Moll, Sigmund Freud and the Invention of Childhood Sexuality around 1900', in A. H. Maehle and L. Sauerteig (eds), *Sexology, Medical Ethics and Occultism: Albert Moll in Context*: special issue of *Medical History*, 56 (2012), 156–83.

shift from ignoring or denying child sexuality to seeing it as something that needed
to be channelled in a healthy direction as part of normal childhood development.[20]
The role of women advancing into roles in social work, local government, and
medicine was significant here.[21] Crucial at the time, and for a surprising time afterwards, was the new legislation on mental deficiency in 1913, which provided a
mechanism for translating what had previously been regarded as sexual immorality
into a marker of feeble-mindedness. For instance, we find the government Report
on Sexual Offences against the Person of 1924–5 acknowledging underage sexual
activity as a significant factor in what appeared to be a rise in minor sexual offences,
however largely dismissing it as an effect of what was believed to be the major and
growing problem of mental deficiency.[22] A parallel investigation in Scotland shared
the view that mental deficiency was a key part of the problem, but it placed more
emphasis on environmental causes. Overcrowding, it suggested, was almost certainly a factor in a hidden problem of incest within the home. Such overcrowding,
in turn, contributed to the problem of keeping children in after dark, and this
exposed them to sexual dangers outside the home. Indeed, the issue was probably
underestimated: it was difficult to arrive at accurate figures, in part because of
secrecy, but also because children could be active partners. 'In many cases', the
report suggested, 'parents remain ignorant of the offence, because the victim is
afraid to tell of what she knows she ought not to have done, or because an incipient
sex instinct has been stimulated and the child is gratified, and has no wish to tell.'
This particular point was directed at girls. Elsewhere, the report noted that almost
17 per cent of cases involved underage boys as the perpetrators. However, it also
suggested that the recorded level of offences hid the scale of real activity:

> Even if they are aware of the offence, many parents, both for their children's sake and
> for their own, are apt to shrink from the publicity which is given to a painful episode
> by investigation and trial, and for that reason refrain from reporting. Others regard
> such happenings as part of the normal risks of life, and are not disposed to report an
> offence provided that the child has suffered no physical hurt.[23]

---

[20] Danielle E. Egan and Gail Hawkes, 'Childhood Sexuality, Normalization and the Social Hygiene
Movement in the Anglophone West, 1900–1935', *Social History of Medicine*, 23 (2010), 56–78.

[21] See, for instance, Louise Jackson, 'Women Professionals and the Regulation of Violence in
Interwar Britain', in Shani De Cruze (ed.), *Everyday Violence in Britain, 1850–1950* (Harlow, 2000),
pp. 119–35.

[22] *Report of the Departmental Committee on Sexual Offences against Young Persons* (London, 1926).
There is now an extensive literature dealing with the relation between the new diagnosis of mental
deficiency, under the 1913 Mental Deficiency Act, and the sexuality of 'feeble-minded' girls, for
instance: Pamela Cox, 'Girls, Deficiency and Delinquency', in David Wright and Anne Digby (eds),
From Idiocy to Mental Deficiency: Historical Perspectives on People with Learning Disabilities (London,
1996), pp. 184–206; Mark Jackson, *The Borderland of Imbecility: Medicine, Society and the Fabrication
of the Feeble Mind in Late Victorian and Edwardian England* (Manchester, 2000); and Mathew Thomson,
The Problem of Mental Deficiency: Eugenics, Democracy and Social Policy in Britain, 1870–1959 (Oxford,
1998). On the hygienist shift towards appreciation of childhood sexuality (to be contrasted to an
embrace of the child's agency—the sexuality of the child): Gail. L. Hawkes and R. Danielle Egan,
'Developing the Sexual Child', *Journal of Historical Sociology*, 21:4 (2008), 443–65.

[23] *Report of the Departmental Committee on Sexual Offences against Children and Young Persons in
Scotland* (London, 1926), p. 13.

This mix of attitudes was characteristic: on the one hand, increased awareness from medical and social experts, though a tendency to turn this behaviour into signs of broader medical and social pathology; on the other hand, among professionals, a growing willingness to acknowledge the involvement of children in sex which complicated diagnosis, and among parents a tendency to dismiss it to some extent as an inevitable feature of the environment, a normal part of growing up, and something that fuss would make only worse.

Nevertheless, a combination of the extension of the age of consent and increasing opportunities for detection, not least as a result of the growing net of welfare and police services, meant that levels of sexual offences did rise. In 1950 the criminologist Leon Radzinowicz initiated an investigation of sexual offences in fourteen areas of England and Wales. Radzinowicz concluded that an increase in sexual offences was partly a reflection of the fact that indictable offences as a whole had risen by 60 per cent between 1937 and 1954, and could partly be attributed to broader causes such as more effective policing. However, the rise in sexual offences had been much sharper than other crimes: up by 252 per cent, from 1.6 to 3.5 per cent of the total; 4,448 cases in 1937, compared to 15,636 in 1954.[24] Although these figures applied to all ages, 82 per cent of the victims were under sixteen: about 12,000 in 1954.[25]

Closer analysis of these figures complicates this picture. Radzinowicz suggested that in a significant number of these cases the children appeared to have been acting consensually. In only 43 per cent of cases were the boys recorded as objecting. The figure for girls was significantly higher, at 62 per cent, but was still low enough to suggest that the law may have been blurring the line between assumed consensual sexual activity and abuse.[26] The research also pointed to the relatively minor nature of many of these offences. Of cases involving girls, the most common offence was placing hands under clothing or on private parts of the body (53.7 per cent). When it came to boys, offences involving masturbation were the most common (47.7 per cent).[27]

Only in 30 per cent of cases was the perpetrator well known to the victim, though under-reporting was particularly likely in such cases. In the remainder of cases involving strangers or casual acquaintances, Radzinowicz offers an insight into the location of the child within the post-war landscape via his suggestions of the main sources of contact: strangers might come up to children playing or standing around in the street or park; they might sit beside them in the cinema; they might offer them a ride in their car or on their motorcycle or cycle. The picture is of encounters that arose because children were still relatively free to move independently within the urban environment. Data on the place of offence offer further support to this landscape of sexual offence: 39.6 per cent in open spaces such

[24] L. Radzinowicz, *Sexual Offences: A Report of the Cambridge Department of Criminal Science* (London, 1957), pp. 3–4.

[25] Radzinowicz, *Sexual Offences*, p. 85.   [26] Radzinowicz, *Sexual Offences*, p. 103.

[27] Radzinowicz, *Sexual Offences*, p. 97.

as parks and fields; 13.3 per cent in the street; and just 18.4 per cent in houses.[28] So does the fact that the majority of cases occurred in daylight hours.[29]

Indecent exposure was a particular problem. Half of all indecent exposure offences against women involved girls under sixteen. Again, the fact that children could play on their own in streets and parks was a crucial context: 47 per cent of these cases occurred in streets and 30 per cent in parks or other open spaces.[30] Indeed, there is a case for arguing that if the period after the mid-1970s was the age of the paedophile, then the period from the 1950s to the 1970s was the age of indecent exposure. The figure of the 'flasher' was a frequent reference point of popular culture: recognizable in the stereotype of the dirty old man in his mackintosh coat, and subsequently an object of family humour through the comedy of the likes of Benny Hill and Dick Emery. In an age in which anxieties of bodily exposure now instead focus on the virtual, pornographic landscape of the Internet and new social media, this figure of the flasher has faded from prominence. However, research in the early 1970s looking back on data since 1948 calculated that indecent exposure had in fact been the second commonest sex offence in the period. As with other minor sexual offences, the period in fact saw a steady rise in convictions for indecent exposure, reaching a level of 2,839 per year by 1970. Intriguingly, as with some other sexual offences, this research also suggested that the young were not simply prime victims of indecent exposure but that the problem was in part a reflection of the illegal expression of childhood sexuality itself, with the rise in convictions during the period particularly marked when it came to adolescents.[31]

One of the reasons why sexual offences involving children did not escalate into a public crisis was that the complexity of the law, and the lack of specific offences for attacks on children, obscured the problem. There was no crime or legal category of paedophilia or child sex abuse. Instead, a complex range of legislation came into play, and this tended to lump children together with adults, making it hard to differentiate them in any statistical analysis. The offence of sexual intercourse with girls came under the legislation dealing with rape; that dealing with boys, the law on buggery. Action on indecent assault came under the 1861 Offences against the Person Act. Loopholes in the law undermined chances of prosecution. For instance, up to the age of twenty-three, those charged under indecent assault could be acquitted on the basis that they had cause to believe a girl to be over sixteen. The use of the defence that an assailant would benefit from mental treatment also frustrated the police.[32] In the late 1950s magistrate Basil Henriques reported on a discrepancy between the number of cases of unlawful sexual interference with girls known to police and magistrates and the number

[28] Radzinowicz, *Sexual Offences*, pp. 100–1.   [29] Radzinowicz, *Sexual Offences*, p. 101.

[30] Radzinowicz, *Sexual Offences*, p. 106

[31] Graham Rooth, 'Changes in the Conviction Rate for Indecent Exposure', *British Journal of Psychiatry*, 121 (1972), 89–94; Graham Rooth, 'Exhibitionism, Sexual Violence and Paedophilia', *British Journal of Psychiatry*, 122 (1973), 705–10.

[32] J. Hughes, 'The Increase in Sexual and Indecency Offences', *Police Journal*, 1:29 (January–March 1956), 54–8.

which went on to legal proceedings: just 684 out of 2,586 in 1958. This was partly a reflection of the problems of proof, but it also reflected reluctance among parents to put their children through a court case.[33]

The approach of tackling such issues via surveillance, control, and legal sanction—a strategy centred on the police and the NSPCC—clearly had some serious limitations.[34] From the 1960s, the emphasis would shift to strategies of situating such problems instead within a broader social setting—a strategy centred on the expanding field of social work. However, given that the integrity of the family was regarded as so important to social stability, there was a reluctance to act in any way that challenged this. As such, the social, like the legal approach, would continue to hide the scale of abuse. Psychological views of the issue were also increasingly influential, leading many to question the efficacy of looking to the law as the primary route of action. Psychiatrists, psychologists, and psychiatric social workers challenged the black and white logic of corruption and innocence. They also emphasized that the most serious cases involving rape and murder, which attracted by far the most public attention, were extremely rare. Far more common was the type of case—'familiar to child guidance clinics'—where (in the view of one commentator) no serious or damaging offence had occurred. His examples are particularly illuminating of the shift in attitudes, and of the way in which a psychiatric perspective was shifting the focus from tackling the criminal act to addressing the psychology of children and their parents. In one, a man would pick up a girl in a car, and after a while, realizing that she was not interested in sex, he would put her down. When her parents found out they would show great alarm and would treat her for 'shock' by putting her to bed in a darkened room, keeping her off school, and consulting the doctor. In the end, the child would begin to think that something terrible had happened. The over-anxious parents had thereby helped turn a minor incident into a serious psychological issue for the child. In a second example, a girl who lacked affection at home looked for it outside. For instance, she might visit a shopkeeper on a regular basis because he gave her sweets, and this could lead one day to an invitation into his backroom and some kind of minor indecent act—touching, peeping, or cuddling. When the parents found out, they would compensate for their own guilt about the problem of emotional neglect—the issue that really underpinned the child's actions—and react by turning with anger on the accused, and the situation would rapidly escalate. It was hard to keep this a secret and the girl would soon become an object of fascination among her friends at school. Some children would revel in this. Others would suffer. Either way, it was not a situation conducive to mental health. If the child was sent away, it would give the impression that she was being punished. If the case went to court, there was the problem that she would be carefully rehearsed so as not to let down the reputation of her family, and this was bad for justice. Cross-examination (sometimes by the assailant)

---

[33] Basil Henriques, 'Sexual Assaults on Children', *British Medical Journal*, 2 (16 December 1961), 1629–31.

[34] Louise Jackson, *Women Police: Gender, Welfare and Surveillance in the Twentieth Century* (Manchester, 2006).

also led to the public unearthing of painful memories, and this could be terrifying for the victim and was likely to exacerbate psychological damage.[35]

As well as questioning whether it was good for the mental health of the victim to prosecute such minor offences, psychiatric experts argued that the children were rarely complete innocents in such cases and indeed often knew a great deal about the subject. They might not participate in a full emotional sense, but they could still take a lead role in precipitating the sexual act. There were cases of blackmail, for instance, in which children, particularly when there was more than one involved, demanded payment in return for repetition of an indecent act, or they would tell. Or there were cases like that of a girl aged fifteen who suffered psychological damage from the gaoling of the twenty-three year old with whom she had a sexual relationship.[36] Those who did participate in sex, it was claimed, often did so 'to satisfy unconscious personality needs'.[37] The influential Kinsey report, which revolutionized views of sexuality in the United States, offered further support to those who felt that the danger of sexual assaults needed to be downplayed. As Kinsey put it, 'In most instances the reported fright was nearer the level that children will show when they see insects, spiders or other objects against which they have been already conditioned.'[38]

A recasting of the figure of the victim was also at the heart of psychologist Lindy Burton's thesis regarding the 'vulnerable child'. In this study, Burton looked at the psychological profile of children involved as victims in sexual assault (as well as victims of traffic accidents and asthmatics). Her findings confirmed a hypothesis that these children tended to have a 'vulnerable' psychological profile, with an unusual need for affection. The 'affection hungry child', she argued, would look for 'attachment' even if this meant befriending someone on the lookout for sexual victims. Burton also suggested that the sexual assault could be emotionally satisfying for the child and lead to a longer-term appetite which was difficult to relinquish. As a consequence, it was not unusual for such children to become perpetrators in later life.[39]

Another line of argument was to highlight the psycho-sexual problems of adolescence within the context of recent rapid social change. Psychiatrist Graham Rooth pointed out that data indicated a rise in minor sex crimes, such as indecent exposure, in which adolescents were the perpetrators (for instance, annual convictions under the age of twenty-one rising from an average of 311 in the period 1948–57, to 754 in 1970; whereas offences for men above this age rose only from

---

[35] T. C. N. Gibbens and Joyce Price, *Child Victims of Sex Offences* (London, 1963), pp. 3–4.

[36] Gibbens and Price, *Child Victims of Sex Offences*, pp. 5–8.

[37] Lindy Burton, *Vulnerable Children: Three Studies of Children in Conflict: Accident Involved Children, Sexually Assaulted Children and Children with Asthma* (London, 1968), pp. 161–9.

[38] Burton, *Vulnerable Children*, p. 106. On the British reception of and response to Kinsey more generally: Liz Stanley, *Sex Surveyed 1949–1994: From Mass-Observation's 'Little Kinsey' to the National Survey and the Hite Reports* (London, 1995); Adrian Bingham, 'The "K-Bomb": Social Surveys, the Popular Press and British Sexual Culture in the 1940s and 1950s', *Journal of British Studies*, 50 (2011), 156–79.

[39] Burton, *Vulnerable Children*, 162.

1,887 to 2,085). Given that there was a high correlation between perpetrators of such minor offences and more serious sexual crimes, he suggested that sex crime in general was 'dominated by the same immature goals of genital display, inspection and manipulation', which were a characteristic aspect of normal childhood, and which were given free rein in some permissive and primitive societies but which were now often repressed in a Western context. In other words, if one wanted to tackle the problem of sex crime, one needed to start first with the general problem of the fundamental and mounting tensions between adolescent sexuality, social change, and traditional social values.[40] Within this climate, even the moralists were inclined to question the innocence of the adolescent. Responding to the latest increase in the number of cases of indecent assault, the Chair of the Federation of Committees for the Moral Welfare of Children argued that the affluent society needed to instil greater discipline in children. As he observed: 'When a boy can get material goods on hire-purchase it is hard to make him understand that he cannot get a girl as easily.'[41]

An emerging social scientific understanding of homosexuality also complicated understanding of child molestation in this period. In one of these studies, published in 1960, Gordon Westwood interviewed 127 homosexuals about their sexual experiences. Westwood classified three of the men as 'paedophiliacs', on the basis that they were attracted only to boys, showed no sign of shame, and had a 'psychopathic disregard' for the consequences. One was a youth leader, another was a school teacher, and the third (who had served prison sentences) had been a scout master. However, he also found that a larger proportion of those interviewed (7 per cent) admitted to some experience of sexual activity with boys. Given that these men did express feelings of shame, and given that they also experienced homosexual relations with other adults, Westwood did not classify them as 'paedophiliacs'. Their activity with minors was often a one-off or an experiment and was likely to extend no further than mutual masturbation. Some of the men claimed that the boys were the ones who had made the initial sexual approach. An even larger proportion of men within the sample (24 per cent) said that they would entertain thoughts of engaging in homosexual relations with boys under the age of 17. What such research began to suggest was that some element of adult–adolescent sexual encounter might be a normal part of homosexual culture; a very different phenomenon to the problem of the psychopathic paedophile. Advocates of tolerance could also point to evidence of the effect of such encounters on the children. For instance, an enquiry into borstal boys found that a third remembered an adult making a pass at them. However, the fact that the percentage was the same for heterosexual boys as for those with homosexual tendencies was seen as reassuring evidence that this experience did not have a damaging effect. Psychologists also tended to lend support to the idea that casual and infrequent homosexual activity

---

[40] Rooth, 'Changes in the Conviction Rate for Indecent Exposure', 89–94; Rooth, 'Exhibitionism, Sexual Violence and Paedophilia', 708–9.
[41] 'Sexual Assaults on Children', *The Times* (28 November 1961).

between boys and men was unlikely to have a long-term effect upon the former unless a predisposition was already there. In short, genuine homosexual 'paedophilia' was rare, while much of what went on under the name of sexual molestation was relatively harmless in the long term and to a degree consensual.[42]

There are signs that this type of view did filter into the media. In 1965, for instance, the *Daily Mirror* sent one its journalists off to the cinema to test the psychologists' view that it was the boys not the men who were often taking the lead in acts of seduction. Indeed, once he sat down in the dark, he found the hands of fifteen-year-old David moving up his leg. As the journalist rather starkly put it, David 'was the corrupter'. On the other hand, this went alongside the sympathetic report of an interview with David, the suggestion that it didn't do much harm, and that the real cause of such acts was a flawed relationship with the parents.[43] Such tolerance was also evident in Tony Parker's pioneering oral history *The Twisting Lane*, based on taped interviews with sex offenders and published in 1969. The book included the stories of several men who had sexual relations with children. But they were included alongside a range of other offenders, rather than as a distinct category. And in line with prevailing liberal sympathy for treatment over punishment, Parker offered a picture of how ineffective the law could be. In offering these people a voice, Parker invited understanding and recognition of humanity. In one of his cases, the offender even turns victim, tormented by local children who knew about his inclinations and who exploited the situation.[44] Parker went on to write the screenplay for the television play *Chariot of Fire* (1970), which offered a sympathetic portrayal of child molester 'Stanley Wood'.[45] Likewise, a television play based on Quentin Crisp's *The Naked Civil Servant* (1975) would echo Parker in its depiction of young boys attempting to extort money through the threat of reporting abuse. As Philip Jenkins has suggested, these characterizations provide us with reminders of what can be seen as the final moments in a liberal era of attitudes towards child molestation.[46]

---

[42] Gordon Westwood, *A Minority: A Report on the Life of the Male Homosexual in Great Britain* (London, 1960), pp. 159–65. The 1957 Wolfenden Report on Homosexuality had used the term 'paedophiliac' in a similar sense, distinguishing two types of homosexual, with paedophilia relating to men attracted only to 'boys who had not yet reached the age of puberty'. However, this was the one reference to the subject. Elsewhere, the report addressed at greater length the question of homosexuality among adolescents and below its proposed age of consent of 21: *Report of the Committee on Homosexual Offences and Prostitution* (London, 1957), p. 26.

[43] 'The Boy Who Sat by in the Cinema', *Daily Mirror* (15 April 1965).

[44] Tony Parker, *The Twisting Lane: Some Sex Offenders* (London, 1969).

[45] On Parker's career: Keith Soothill, 'Opening Doors and Windows for Tony Parker', in *Papers for the British Society of Criminology Conference, Leicester, July 2000* (October, 2001): <http://www.britsoccrim.org/volume4/002.pdf>.

[46] His focus is the United States, but he also includes some analysis of Britain. His liberal era extended 1958–76. He sees it being preceded by an 'age of the sex psychopath'; however, this is less readily translated to the British context and relies heavily on racial and cold-war anxieties that were particularly acute in the United States. Jenkins also notes several earlier British films that offered a liberal line, including *Victim* (1961); *Never Take Sweets from a Stranger* (1960); and *Serious Charge* (1959) (*Moral Panic: Changing Concepts of the Child Molester in Modern America* (New Haven and London, 1998), pp. 107–9).

One of the factors that began to change this situation was the increasingly high profile of sexual crimes within the media. Already in the mid-1950s, a report in the *Police Journal* described grave sexual offences against boys and girls as a constant theme in Sunday editions of the press.[47] Discussion of the subject also reached into the field of advice literature. Writing in the magazine *Parents* in 1958 Barbara Cartland, whose attention had been drawn to the subject through her work as a county councillor, warned parents about the fact that figures on the level of 'defilement' of girls had risen sharply over the past twenty-five years—from an average of 361 to 1,491 by 1955—and that this represented 'a mere fraction of the foulness that menaces children today'. For Cartland, this was further reason to uphold the maxim that 'a mother's place is at home'. They needed to protect their children, and they, not schools or sex educationalists, were also the best placed to advise their children on sexual questions so as to help prevent them falling into such difficulties.[48]

Cases involving murder attracted particular attention. Most notoriously, in the mid-1960s the Moors murders captured the national imagination. The case centred on a young couple: Ian Brady, born in Glasgow in 1938, and Myra Hindley, born in Manchester in 1942. In 1966, they were convicted of the murder of five children aged between ten and seventeen, with at least four of these cases also involving sexual assault. Brady and Hindley both grew up in the shadow of war. Hindley's father had been a paratrooper. When her younger sister was born, she had to move to live with her grandmother. Brady never knew his father and was brought up by a friend of his mother. As a child, he developed an obsession with the Nazis. This would become a key part of his relationship with Hindley. The couple moved in with each other in Hindley's grandmother's house in the new overspill estate of Hattersley on the eastern edge of Manchester, and this was the base for their sadistic murders, with the victims buried on nearby Saddleworth Moor. Children were said to welcome life on the estate because of the freedom of the moor. However, the case put such freedom, but also the lack of community on the estate, in rather different light: post-war planning exposing these children to hitherto undreamt of dangers. More damaging still was the sense that the isolation and lack of any cultural centre left the young so alienated that they might follow in Hindley and Brady's perverted footsteps in the search for excitement. When the case came to trial, Brady and Hindley both objected to the involvement of psychiatrists.[49] Nevertheless, the case raised the question of how a society was rearing young people who would develop such disturbed views and desires. It was this question of the loss of innocence and perversion of youth, and not just the fact

---

[47] Hughes, 'The Increase in Sexual and Indecency Offences', 54. On the important role of the popular press in opening up public discussion on sexual matters: Adrian Bingham, *Family Newspapers? Sex, Private Life and the British Popular Press 1918–1978* (Oxford, 2009).

[48] Barbara Cartland, 'Guarding against the Sex Assailant', *Parents*, 13 (June 1958), 40–2.

[49] John Deane Potter, *The Monsters of the Moors: The Full Account of the Brady–Hindley Case* (London, 1966); Jonathan Goodman, *The Moors Murders: The Trial of Myra Hindley and Ian Brady* (London, 1973).

(in reality the remote possibility) that any child might fall victim, which made the case so disturbing.

In their study of childcare in Nottingham, John and Elizabeth Newson recognized the role of the media in stoking anxiety about protecting children from strangers, and such news was perhaps more accessible for children with the spread of television.[50] A builder's wife reported that her daughter was 'a bit scared when she hears on TV about those little girls having been picked up—or such as the Moors murders—and we try, like, not to let her take too much notice of them'.[51] Parents were worried that such news might upset their children and make them fearful about going out, yet they were also worried when daughters and sons were too trusting of and friendly towards strangers. 'You know,' said a bus driver's wife, 'you read in the papers of such awful things happening about children, you know, being run off with and everything; well every night I say to her "Has anybody spoke to you or anything like that?" and she says "No", and I says "Well, don't you ever speak to anybody".'[52] Such anxiety extended to boys, though it tended to be less acute. A labourer's wife worried that her son would 'probably go with them if anyone offered to take him. I mean, even a stranger he'd go with—I've tried to drill it into him not to talk to men or anything, but he don't seem to take any notice of you.'[53] The Newsons also pointed to the importance of local networks of news, rumour, and warning. Indeed, the local press could be even more influential than national media because of the way it would report even minor incidents, and because it linked the danger to the local landscape. Word of mouth also played a role in spreading fear of attacks on local children. And teachers and visiting members of the police force reinforced the message through talks within school. A scaffolder's wife reported that her daughter

> always comes straight home—they all do, I've always drilled that into them. She seems to have got the message. 'Cause the oldest girl, she went to Colwick Woods once, and a man got hold of her, but she had the sense to bite his hand—he put his hand over her mouth and she bit it; and he let her go, you see. But it frightened her and frightened the others too, because they knew about it.[54]

The Newsons noted that euphemism masked the exact nature of the danger. Children were told not to talk to, take sweets from, or accept rides from strangers who might 'take them away', 'hurt' or 'harm' them. The Newsons, likewise, avoided any explicit detail. And neither parents nor investigators used the terms 'paedophile' or 'paedophilia'. Such evidence suggests that by the 1970s parents did consider sexual molestation to be one of the main dangers facing their children when outside the home, though they were rarely explicit about the particular nature of the sexual threat. It also indicates that efforts were made to extend this concern to the children themselves in the hope of modifying social contact with unknown adults.

---

[50] John Newson and Elizabeth Newson, *Seven Years Old in the Home Environment* (London, 1976), p. 93.
[51] Newson and Newson, *Seven Years Old*, p. 94.   [52] Newson and Newson, *Seven Years Old*, p. 94.
[53] Newson and Newson, *Seven Years Old*, pp. 94–5.
[54] Newson and Newson, *Seven Years Old*, p. 90.

Though some children became anxious as a result, and sometimes this emerged as a new concern, others remained too relaxed about the potential danger for the comfort of the responsible adults. The Newsons' finding that girls had less freedom to roam beyond the home than boys may well reflect such anxieties. However, as with anxiety over traffic, social fears about 'strangers' would escalate as the actual threat—at least in terms of the declining independent mobility of children during the same period—in fact fell. For all the parental concern evident in the Newson research, what is now most striking is how *much* freedom and independent mobility these children were nevertheless granted at the start of the 1970s.

This insight into media and parental attitudes indicates a gulf between popular and expert opinion by the start of the 1970s. Among the psycho-social professionals we find a picture of acknowledged low-level sexual danger facing the child in the outside world, even a recognition that some types of offence may have been on the increase, yet a remarkably relaxed attitude, in part because of a shift away from a model of innocence towards recognition of childhood sexuality, and in part because professional standing was based on special understanding and a preference for psycho-social over legal strategies for handling the situation. Among families and within the media, on the other hand, there is some indication of increased concern about such outside dangers. The tensions caused by this gulf in attitudes would be an important factor in the explosion of controversy over paedophilia in the decade ahead.

THE EMERGENCE OF THE PAEDOPHILE

The 1970s would be the crucial period in transforming this background concern about sexual danger facing children in the outside world into one that became a major public issue and that extended from the stranger to the hitherto largely hidden dangers of systematic sexual abuse within the family and residential care. The second half of this chapter will consider this transition. Here, the story of the emergence of the figure of the paedophile is one that jars fundamentally with our image just three decades later. In reminding us of this history, the chapter offers further indication that the 1970s saw an important shift in the landscape of postwar British childhood. The liberal moral tendencies set out in the first half of the chapter, which had led professionals to downplay the dangers of certain sexual offences, were co-opted by those who now, in a parody of gay and feminist liberation, wanted to claim the identity of the 'paedophile' as a way to differentiate the child lover from the child molester. The fact that there was a time when such a group could believe that a strategy of self-promotion might gain public support and sympathy now seems remarkable. And for a brief moment, the paedophile case would attract support from professionals, academics, other pressure groups, and even a liberal public. However, it also clashed with those other tendencies that have been highlighted as increasingly significant by the 1970s: a permissiveness that provided opportunities for the media to bring such issues out more explicitly in public, a press keen for such sensationalist subject matter and for the perfect villain in the figure of the predatory paedophile, and a culture of childcare in which the pressures of protection had spread across class and in which the tensions of maintaining the ideal family in the face of social change made this outside danger an attractive alternative target of blame.

In September 1977, the University College of Swansea hosted a conference on the subject of 'Love and Attraction'. For an academic conference—it was organized under the auspices of the British Psychological Society—it attracted a remarkable degree of attention in the national press. The reason for the furore was that alongside psychiatrists, psychologists, and sociologists, the conference looked likely to provide a platform for a group who called themselves the Paedophile Information Exchange (PIE). In retrospect, what is equally significant is the degree to which some of the views of this organization in fact, for a brief period, attracted broader sympathy.[55]

In the report on the conference, Kenneth Plummer, a pioneer in marking out a new field of the sociology of sex in British academia, reflected on PIE's involvement and on why the paedophile issue had attracted academic and liberal interest. As Plummer saw it, PIE's involvement was not out of place in a forum such as this. Just as discussion a decade earlier had played a role in countering views of homosexuality as a sickness, so paedophiles had a right to put their own views forward. It would be wrong not to listen to the sort of reasoned argument and evidence that was now emerging on the issue. Such research was indicating that public understanding of the nature of these individuals was very far from the reality. The stereotype of the dirty old man certainly did not match the membership of PIE, which was predominantly much younger and which included a high proportion of professionals. The research also suggested that preference for sexual relations with very young children was in fact rare; much more common was attraction towards adolescents.[56] If there was a case for reconsidering the stereotype of the child molester, there was also a case for questioning assumptions about child sexuality itself. There was certainly a fundamental problem with the popular view that children were not sexual.[57] Research from Holland, based on people who had been involved in such relationships as children, indicated that they often reflected back on such relationships as a positive experience, a source of love, affection, and security, and sometimes sustained long-term resulting friendships. This research also found little evidence of long-term trauma or of influence on later sexual orientation, suggesting instead that it was the prurient attitude of society that invariably had the most negative effect on the children involved.[58] This last point was also supported in

---

[55] Mark Cook and Glenn Wilson (eds), *Love and Attraction: An International Conference* (Oxford, 1979).

[56] Here, Plummer could also draw on sociological study of PIE membership: Glenn D. Wilson and David N. Cox, *The Child-Lovers: A Study of Paedophiles in Society* (London, 1983).

[57] Ken Plummer, 'Images of Paedophilia', in Cook and Wilson (eds), *Love and Attraction*, pp. 537–40. On the benefits, Plummer pointed to F. Bernard, 'An Enquiry among a Group of Paedophiles', *Journal of Sex Research*, 11 (1975), 242–55; J. Z. Eglinton, *Greek Love* (New York, 1964); and P. Rossman, *Sexual Experience between Men and Boys* (New York, 1976).

[58] Fritz Bernard, 'Pedophilia: The Consequences for the Child', in Cook and Wilson (eds), *Love and Attraction*, pp. 499–501. Bernard also published on this in *Journal of Sex Research*: 'An Enquiry among a Group of Paedophiles', 11 (1975), 242–55.

another paper based on analysis of ninety-one boys referred for counselling after sexual relations with adults.[59] Finally, some speakers now approached the subject from the perspective of the 'sexual rights of children'. Here, the line of argument was that active child sexuality was natural, and was normal in liberated environments; repression was the abnormal situation and the more dangerous one. Children, in other words, were being protected from the wrong thing, and the best way forward was to provide them with a right to express their natural sexuality.[60]

As we have seen, such opinion did not come completely out of the blue. It built on the platform already established through the increasingly liberal attitudes of psycho-social expertise in the 1950s and 1960s. In particular, many of these experts had come to question whether the existing legal route was the most appropriate way of handling the matter. And in a post-Freudian world there had been a growing appreciation of child sexuality. However, these issues now spilled over into a broader public debate about the boundaries of sexuality. The ensuing furore needs to be set within this context. The legalization of homosexuality and the questioning of the age of sexual consent in relation to both homosexual and heterosexual sex were particularly important in this regard.[61]

A growing number of psychiatric, medical, and legal experts had for some time been uncomfortable about using the law as a way to police sex across the boundary of the age of consent. By the early 1970s, this was leading to calls for lowering the legal age of consent. Evidence suggested that teenagers were becoming more sexually active anyway: just 6 per cent of fifteen-year-old boys and 2 per cent of girls of this age were estimated to be sexually active in the mid-1960s, compared to 26 per cent of boys and 12 per cent of girls by the mid-1970s.[62] From the perspective of public health, and faced by the reality of widespread underage sex, pregnancy, and sexual disease, the British Medical Association and the Family Planning Association both expressed concern with the current law.[63] There was also the argument that the age of sexual maturity had biologically changed since the age of consent had been raised to sixteen nearly a century earlier.[64] But it was not just medical professionals who began to question the age of consent. D. J. West, Professor of

---

[59] Michael Ingram, 'The Participating Victim: A Study of Sexual Offences against Pre-Pubertal Boys', in Cook and Wilson (eds), *Love and Attraction*, 511–17.

[60] Larry L. Constantine, 'The Sexual Rights of Children: Implications of a Radical Perspective', in Cook and Wilson (eds), *Love and Attraction*, 503–8.

[61] The boundaries of sexuality, and the question of the sexuality of the child, were also to a degree coming to be challenged through sex education. Until the late 1960s, sex education had been relatively uncontroversial and an issue of sexual hygiene. The early 1970s saw an explosion of the debate, driven in large part by conservative concern about permissiveness: J. Hampshire, 'The Politics of School Sex Education Policy in England and Wales from the 1940s to the 1960s', *Social History of Medicine*, 18 (2005), 87–105. For a longer term perspective: Lutz Sauterteig and Roger Davidson, *Shaping Sexual Knowledge: A Cultural History of Sex Education in 20th Century Europe* (New York, 2008).

[62] 'A Problem that Will Not Go Away', *The Times* (24 October 1978).

[63] 'Age of Consent Irrelevant for Many Girls', *The Times* (8 May 1971).

[64] It was estimated at fourteen years on average. There has been a subsequent further fall to an estimate of 12 years and ten months: Matthew Waites, 'The Age of Consent and Sexual Consent', in Mark Cowling and Paul Reynolds (eds), *Making Sense of Sexual Consent* (Aldershot, 2004), p. 82.

Criminology at Cambridge University, urged abolition.[65] Even, on the progressive wing of Christianity, the Quakers supported a lowering and equalization of the age of consent for heterosexual and homosexual sex to fourteen.[66] Whereas previously age of consent had in truth been based on calculations about the necessary age of protection (with little evidence of efforts to adjudicate on the age at which children could decide for themselves), the 1970s saw this coalition of forces argue that it needed to be rethought in terms of the perspective and psychological maturity of the child.[67] There is, in fact, some indication that interpretation of the law may have become laxer within this context. This would be one way of explaining why prosecutions for unlawful sexual intercourse with girls in the age group 13–16 fell from 5,000 per year in the later 1960s, to 3,681 in 1977.[68] And this shift of logic may have been at play behind the decision of a Sheffield judge to acquit a man who had sex with several fifteen-year-old girls on the grounds that nowadays girls of this age had the sexual maturity to make their own decisions in such a situation.[69]

Although it was this debate about the heterosexual age of consent that helped open the door for a broader debate about adult–child sexual relations, it was the fact that the homosexual movement felt particularly aggrieved about inequality in this area that was crucial in the emergence of a campaign centred on the rights of the paedophile. Given that the age of consent for (male) homosexuality in England and Wales, following legalization in 1967, was still so markedly out of line with that for heterosexual intercourse—twenty-one compared to sixteen—the Gay Liberation movement was at the fore in joining the debate over the age of consent.[70] It was out of this context that the first groups also began to organize in defence of 'paedophile' rights. And as conservative moral hostility shifted focus from homosexuality to paedophilia, there was an inclination to see paedophilia as the next front in campaigning against prejudice and in support of sexual liberation.[71] For a brief period, this helped attract sympathy, not just from sections of the broader homosexual movement, but also from liberals and progressives.

The two main British paedophile organizations of the period, Paedophile Action for Liberation (PAL) and the Paedophile Information Exchange, both emerged out

[65] 'Abolition of Age of Consent Urged by Criminologist', *The Times* (7 July 1973).
[66] 'Quakers Call for Lower Age of Consent', *The Times* (17 April 1972).
[67] Waites, 'The Age of Consent and Sexual Consent', p. 78.
[68] Richard Card, 'Paedophilia and the Law', in Brian Taylor (ed.), *Perspectives on Paedophilia* (London, 1981), pp. 6–8.
[69] 'Reduce Age of Consent to 14, Barrister Says', *The Times* (25 March 1978).
[70] 'Report Calls for Age of Consent to be 14', *The Times* (6 September 1974). The legalization of 1967 covered just England and Wales. Scotland followed only in 1980, and Northern Ireland in 1982. Despite the Home Office recommendation to lower the age of consent for homosexual sex to 18 (1979), it remained at 21 until 1994, when attempts to equalize the age at 16 failed, leading to a compromise on homosexual sex at 18. At the end of the century, new pressure came from cases reaching the European Court of Human Rights. Overcoming resistance from the House of Lords by invoking the Parliament Act, the age of consent was equalized at 16 in 2000. Examining the relationship between anxieties regarding homosexuality and paedophilia: Kevin Ohi, 'Molestation 101: Child Abuse, Homophobia, and the Boys of St Vincent', *GLQ: A Journal of Lesbian and Gay Studies*, 6 (2000), 195–248.
[71] Lucy Robinson, *Gay Men and the Left in Post-War Britain: How the Personal Got Political* (Manchester, 2007), pp. 129–30.

of this context in 1974/5: PAL developed as a breakaway group from the South London Gay Liberation Front, and PIE set up initially as a special interest group within the Scottish Minorities Group, before relocating to London in 1975. It was not long before PAL found itself the subject of an exposé in the tabloid newspaper the *Sunday People*. Its members were described as 'the vilest men in Britain'. However, rather than retreating into hiding, PIE took the decision to channel its energies into tackling public opinion head on. For a couple of years, it seemed like this strategy was showing signs of success. Its Chair Keith Hose represented PIE at the annual conferences of MIND (the leading mental health charity) and the Campaign for Homosexual Equality. Such invitations suggested a degree of legitimacy, and the potential to follow in the footsteps of the case for legalization of homosexuality nearly a decade previously. The fact that such optimism was possible now seems extraordinary.

If one aim of PIE was to develop a media profile which could challenge and change expert and public opinion, the other was to provide support, advice, and contacts for fellow paedophiles. The two ultimately turned out to be incompatible. The central mechanism for this attempt to bring isolated paedophiles together into a community and movement was the publication of a magazine. This started life as the PIE *Newsletter*. Under editor Warren Middleton it took on the title of *Understanding Paedophilia*, reflecting an agenda of legitimization through inclusion of supportive studies by psychologists and other academically orientated researchers. This made way for *Magpie*, which included more material directed at members, including film and book reviews, non-nude images of children, humour, and letters. This use of magazines, contact advertisements, and letter writing aimed to help break down a sense of isolation among individuals and to develop a sense of collective identity. By 1977, the year of the Swansea conference, PIE had about 250 members.[72]

At the same time as this development of an organized paedophile rights movement, radical attitudes about child sexuality, sex education, and child rights were also seeping into the counter-cultural fringes of local government, education, and social work.[73] Within this climate, the new paedophile movement and their arguments would attract interest and at times a surprising degree of sympathy. Several notorious episodes have come to symbolize this radical flirtation with child sexual liberation. One was the scandal caused by attempts to provide children with access to translations of a radical Danish advice book, *The Little Red School-Book*, which among others things spoke openly to children about their sexuality. Another was the famous *Oz* obscenity trial, which centred on an edition of the magazine

---

[72] Robinson, *Gay Men and the Left*, p. 130; Tom O'Carroll, *Paedophilia: The Radical Case* (London, 1980).

[73] This was not merely a British phenomenon. See for instance Julian Bourg, *From Revolution to Ethics: May 1968 and Contemporary French Thought* (Montreal, 2007), pp. 204–18. On sex education in the period: James Hampshire and Jane Lewis, '"The Ravages of Permissiveness": Sex Education and the Permissive Society', *Twentieth Century British History*, 15 (2004), 290–312. And on its broader history: Roger Davidson and Lutz Sauerteig (eds.), *Shaping Sexual Knowledge: A Cultural History of Sex Education in Twentieth-Century Europe* (New York, 2009).

produced by school children containing sexually explicit material. In both instances, the publications were prosecuted for conspiring to corrupt public morals through involvement of children in discussion on sex.[74] But even after *The Little Red School-Book* had been revised so that it was fit for publication, the new edition of 1971 still spoke to children in strikingly open sexual terms. And when it came to adult sexual interest in children, the *School-Book* aimed to dissipate rather than stoke up fear, encouraging children to be understanding rather than to demonize. These weren't 'dirty old men', they were rarely dangerous, they were 'just men who have nobody to sleep with'; more often than not, they just wanted to expose themselves.[75] In short, even before the emergence of the paedophile, we see progressive opinion not only looking to liberation of child sexuality but also downplaying alarmism about the danger of child molestation. Attacks on such publications from the moral right just strengthened the idea that liberation of child sexuality was something that radicals should support.

For others, sympathy for the paedophile arguments on child sexual freedom appears to have been connected to their activism in providing children with adventure playgrounds and in critiquing the way children were becoming passive and trapped victims of the urban environment. Father Michael Ingram, who would emerge as a leading paedophile spokesman in 1977, had earlier worked with children in London providing opportunities for free play—where they could 'light fires, climb trees, fight, swear, be destructive and in general uncork themselves'. He had also spoken on children, overcrowding, and the problem of lost freedom at the Vancouver United Nations Conference on Habitat in 1976.[76] Support also came from a child's rights perspective from Roger Moody, a pioneer of libertarian adventure playgrounds.[77]

Radical social work was another field that flirted with paedophile arguments in the mid-1970s. This was evident in a notoriously sympathetic article in the journal *Community Care* in 1977.[78] However the most significant support came from Peter Righton, Director of Education at the National Institute for Social Work, and a consultant for the National Children's Bureau. Righton's views are particularly interesting in providing us with insight, not only into the way in which the paedophile could be presented as a more harmless character than the child molester, but more radically still into the way in which child love could be presented as a therapeutic good. Coming from someone with such an influential role in social work education, these views are worth setting out in some detail. First, argued Righton,

---

[74] John Sutherland, *Offensive Literature: Decensorship in Britain, 1960–1982* (Totowa, 1983), pp. 111–18; Gerry Dawson [David Widgery], 'The Politics of Pornography', *Socialist Worker* (24 July 1971).

[75] Søren Hansen and Jesper Jensen, *The Little Red School-Book*, trans, Berit Thornberry (London, 1971), p. 103.

[76] Michael Ingram, *The Owl and the Pussycat: My Autobiography* (Cambridge, 1997), pp. 87–93.

[77] Roger Moody, 'Man/Boy Love on the Left', in Daniel Tsang (ed.), *The Age Taboo: Gay Male Sexuality, Power and Consent* (London, 1981). He also contributed to Warren Middleton (ed.), *The Betrayal of Youth: Radical Perspectives on Childhood Sexuality, Intergenerational Sex, and the Oppression of Children and Young People* (London, 1986).

[78] Mary Manning, 'Should We Pity the Paedophile?', *Community Care* (19 October 1977).

there was the problem that the law on age of consent did not reflect social realities. When paedophilia involved teenagers it was in fact a condition that by his estimate covered, not a tiny minority, but at least 1 per cent of the population. Secondly, the stereotype of the psychopathic, vicious child molester, as far as Righton was concerned, was in the majority of cases far from the reality. Many paedophiles never acted on their attractions. Many confined themselves to cuddling and caressing. And many were not the first to initiate physical contact. Paedophiles were child-lovers, a position that placed them in opposition to anyone who wanted to harm children; child molesters were often not genuine paedophiles at all. Thirdly, if paedophilia was so tied up with emotional feelings for the child, it was unsurprisingly likely to be a particular issue within the family; and it was less likely to be an issue that centred on strangers. In other words, the focus of emerging anxiety was misdirected. Finally, referring to his own work in counselling children, Righton argued that the boys he had interviewed who had experienced sex with adults had largely enjoyed it, though many felt guilty about this. The latter in his view was the real dilemma: the potential for emotional damage as a result of social attitudes. However, this danger needed to be counterbalanced by a recognition that deprived children were often in desperate need of love from adults. It was this last logic that appears to have been an additional factor in some social workers moving from being merely sympathetic towards the paedophile arguments to becoming more directly supportive or involved themselves.[79]

Coverage of the issue in the *Guardian* newspaper indicates that a degree of initial sympathy even extended into the liberal mainstream of the mid-1970s. For a brief period, paedophilia became something of a touchstone issue in challenging and testing the boundaries of liberal tolerance when it came to sexual liberation. Liberals faced a series of dilemmas: was paedophilia just another word for child molestation, or was it something that needed understanding; how should they respond to the call for paedophiles, like other sexual minorities, to be recognized as having a right to express their opinions and a right to expression of their sexuality if it did no harm to others; and what was to be made of the proposition that adults needed to rethink their attitudes towards childhood sexual innocence and to recognize that most damaging of all was the parental disapproval, the guilt, and the immersion of children in traumatic court cases that resulted from the current stance on sexual relations between adults and consenting children?[80] So when John Torode attacked PIE as nothing more than a front for child molesters, in his *Guardian* 'London Letter' column in 1975, he encountered a torrent of criticism.[81]

---

[79] Peter Righton, 'The Adult', in Brian Taylor (ed.), *Perspectives on Paedophilia* (London, 1981), pp. 24–38. Righton also wrote on the issue in *Social Work Today* in 1977: Christian Wolmar, *Forgotten Children: The Secret Abuse Scandal in Children's Homes* (London, 2000), pp. 137–49. The link to sexual abuse in children's homes is discussed in the final part of this chapter.

[80] 'Paedophilia: Where Tirades Don't Help', *Guardian* (15 September 1975).

[81] Warren Middleton (Vice-Chair PIE), 'PIE: Right to Exist?', *Guardian* (6 September 1975); 'London Letter', *Guardian* (28 August 1975, 5 September 1975, 10 September 1975, 13 September 1975, 18 February 1977).

By 1976, the National Council for Civil Liberties (NCCL) had also become embroiled in the debate. In 1976, Tom O'Carroll of PIE addressed the NCCL conference, deploring the use of chemical castration for paedophiles. And although the NCCL eventually rejected PIE affiliation, its evidence to the Criminal Law Revision Committee nevertheless recommended a lowering of the age of hetero-sexual and homosexual consent to fourteen (and to the lower age of ten when it involved consenting partners under the age of fourteen—with a further leeway of two years on either side of these ages). It had come to the conclusion that the only reason for making sex illegal was if it harmed others. And it had come to accept the argument that there was often less lasting damage for children in paedophilia than there was in the current situation in which they were thrown into the jaws of the legal system and the press.[82]

Despite this support, by 1977, the year of the Swansea conference, the decision of PIE to engage in a high-profile campaign was beginning to backfire spectacu-larly. The age of consent debate led PIE into making a politically disastrous state-ment in support of lowering the age of consent to four years (below which consent was accepted as unfeasible). The statement was read as confirming people's worst fears that this talk of sexual liberation was just a front for opening the floodgates on perverted desires for sex with the very youngest of children. Under the title 'For adults only', the *Daily Mirror* described PIE's proposals as 'totally repulsive'; it was a tolerant newspaper, but this tolerance had its limits, and this was it (though it was happy to run such pronouncements alongside pictures of a seventeen-year-old girl like 'Feb' baring her breasts to its readers).[83] Venues began to refuse to stage events involving PIE. And the proposed attendance of leading paedophiles at Swansea sparked heated debate in the run-up to the meeting. One of these speak-ers, Dr Edward Brongersma, a Dutch MP, did speak at the Campaign for Homo-sexual Equality conference in Nottingham in August and received a standing ovation.[84] However, PIE had to cancel a planned meeting in a London hotel

---

[82] 'NCCL Wants Incest Made Legal', *Guardian* (9 March 1976); 'Make Age of Consent 14', *The Times* (6 March 1976).

[83] 'For Adults Only', *Daily Mirror* (24 August 1977). The image of 'Feb' ran alongside another item on PIE: 'Child Sex Group Goes On' (26 August 1977).

[84] In 1976, the Dutch National Centre for Public Mental Health report on Paedophilia and Society had recommended the abolition of all sections of the Penal Code dealing with non-violent sexual conduct with children. Leader of the campaign for legalization, MP Edward Brongersma, questioned the evidence on long-term harm and suggested that the hidden scale of such behaviour indicated that the current stance of legal prohibition was not proving effective: Edward Brongersma, 'The Meaning of "Indecency" with Respect to Moral Offences involving Children', *British Journal of Criminology*, 20 (1980), 20–32. Brongersma was a lawyer by background and was a member of the Dutch Senate for the Labour Party 1945–50 and 1963–77. He had been arrested in 1950 for having sexual relations with a seventeen year old, when the age of consent was twenty-one, and spent eleven months in prison. As a result, he became an advocate of more liberal legislation and played a role in abolition of Article 248a of the Dutch Civil Code, which led to the lowering of the age of consent for homosexual sex from twenty-one to sixteen. He subsequently supported a further lowering. He resigned from the Senate in 1977 and devoted his energies to the work of a foundation bearing his name which collected books and papers on the subject of paedophilia. He also worked on a study of *Loving Boys*, published in 1987 and 1990. Controversy followed his death in 1998 when pornographic images of children were discovered in his collection. This material was removed by the authorities and the archive was deposited at the International Institute for Social History in Amsterdam.

because of protests from the staff.[85] Tom O'Carroll, the new Chair of PIE, now began to attract increasing press attention, and he was placed by his employers on extended leave from his position as Press Officer at the Open University. Within this context, critics of the proposal to lower the age of consent began to claim that the liberals who supported this, including the Labour Home Secretary Roy Jenkins, had been seduced by arguments that were, in fact, emerging out of the paedophile movement.[86]

The press was soon running regular bulletins on who was going to attend the Swansea conference, surely a first for a meeting of the British Psychological Society. It was caricatured as a 'talk-in on sex', a misjudged cross between academic conference and counter-cultural happening or therapy session, epitomizing the way in which radical academic and liberal opinion seemed to have lost its bearings in its exploration of sexuality and its support for freedom of expression.[87] Events did not disappoint. The conference provided a farce in sexual and academic politics worthy of the campus novels of the decade, an ideal target for moral outrage, mockery, and salacious revelation. O'Carroll was forcibly removed from the conference after the National Union of Public Employees, representing the labour behind the conference industry and a broader mass of working-class opinion, threatened strike action. But this made some even more alert than before to the fact that there was also an issue of academic and intellectual freedom at stake here. Delegates expressed revulsion for O'Carroll's views, but often found themselves standing up for his courage. 'He is somewhere between Jesus Christ and Jack the Ripper', as one of them put it.[88] While O'Carroll was, albeit messily, extricated from attendance, others whose words would shock when broadcast to a broader audience were not. This included Catholic priest and child counsellor Father Michael Ingram, who acknowledged that in his survey of ninety-one cases of child molesting involving boys under fourteen he had only contacted the police in two instances, and who claimed that the good that this love could do for the child could far outweigh any harm. His remarks would unsurprisingly attract considerable attention and would lead to public pillory and a painful descent.[89] Though O'Carroll was prevented from speaking, his controversial role in the conference did not end there. Following being thrown out of the conference, he was assaulted in a pub by the wife of the organizer, who threw beer over him and called him a 'dirty pervert'. The ongoing drama provided wonderful material for the media, putting not just the paedophile movement on show but also casting ridicule on radical academia.[90]

---

[85] 'Paedophile Talks Backed by Homosexuals', *The Times* (30 August 1977).

[86] Ronald Butt, 'Who Really Wants a Change in the Age of Consent?', *The Times* (22 January 1976).

[87] 'No Love Lost as Talk-in on Sex Begins', *Guardian* (6 September 1977).

[88] 'PIE Man Thrown off Campus', *Guardian* (8 September 1977).

[89] In later life, Ingram would publish an extraordinary memoir. He struggled with his mental health, and this was exacerbated by the resurfacing of accusations about his own involvement in abuse. He died following severe injuries after driving his car into a wall: 'Priest's Child Sex Views Repudiated', *Guardian* (9 September 1977); Ingram, *The Owl and the Pussycat*. Ingram's findings were also published as 'A Study of 92 Cases of Sexual Contact between Adult and Child', *British Journal of Sexual Medicine*, 6:44 (1979), 22; and 6:45 (1979), 24.

[90] 'Paedophile Group Leader had Beer Poured over Him', *The Times* (8 December 1977).

The shift in public opinion was evident in a new tone of reporting in the previously open-minded *Guardian*. Not only was this a case of a turn in liberal opinion, but it also echoed a more grass-roots anger typified by a Bournemouth woman who had started a local petition on the subject.[91] The political and moral Right also now came to recognize the issue of paedophilia as one that could provide a focus for a broader critique of permissiveness having gone too far.[92] The far-right political party, the National Front, took a lead in disrupting public meetings of PIE.[93] Margaret Thatcher, the new leader of the Conservative party, lent support to a campaign, fuelled by the spectre of 'kiddie porn' in the United States, and led by Mary Whitehouse, chair of the National Viewers' and Listeners' Association, to introduce legislation banning the use of children under the age of consent in the preparation of pornographic material.[94] And Conservative MP Cyril Townsend introduced a private members bill on the issue, which led to the Protection of Children Act, 1978. Subsequent amendments would extend the reach of this legislation to include computer images as well as photographs and to outlaw the downloading and printing as well as the creation of such images. The legislation was pushed through at striking speed, despite the paucity of evidence and without waiting for the results of a broader government-sponsored review of the law on obscenity (under the left-leaning moral philosopher Bernard Williams, this review would eventually produce a report in 1979 recommending abandoning obscenity and indecency as legal terms, which was shelved by the incoming Conservative government). Townsend linked the need for the legislation with what he claimed was a mounting problem of unlawful sexual offences against children, and it is clear from the debate in the House of Commons that the high profile of the PIE episode had done much to stoke alarm in this regard.[95]

PIE now found itself in an increasingly precarious position. It was infiltrated by journalists from the *News of the World* and exposed in the tabloids. It was unable to find a printer willing to publish its journal *Magpie*. *Gay News* withdrew advertising for PIE following the refusal of the newsagents W. H. Smith to stock any magazine that publicized the group. O'Carroll lost his job at the Open University. And the police raided the homes of O'Carroll and other prominent members of PIE. O'Carroll and four others were charged with printing contact advertisements in *Magpie* which were designed to promote indecent acts between adults and children. Others were charged with the lesser offence of sending indecent material to one another via the mail. And in 1981, O'Carroll was convicted and sentenced to two years' imprisonment.[96]

---

[91] Tom Crabtree, 'Adults Only', *Guardian* (19 May 1977).
[92] More generally on Thatcherism and the politics of sexual morality: M. Durham, *Sex and Politics: The Family and Morality in the Thatcher Years* (Basingstoke, 1991).
[93] 'Paedophiles Jeered and Pelted by Angry Crowd', *The Times* (20 September 1977).
[94] 'Mrs Thatcher Urges Action over Child Pornography', *The Times* (6 September 1977).
[95] Protection of Children Bill, *House of Commons Debates*, vol. 943, Cols 1826–1922, 10 February 1978.
[96] Robinson, *Gay Men and the Left*, pp. 133–6.

Despite the law closing in on the paedophile movement, there was a continuing airing of the paedophile position in the early 1980s. This included O'Carroll's *Paedophilia: The Radical Case*, published in 1980, which included the name of several leading academics in the acknowledgements.[97] The early 1980s also saw publication of sociological research on PIE members undertaken in 1977–8, which sympathetically suggested that 'the sexual preferences of the paedophiles are not so far removed from those of the normal man as they might as first appear'.[98] A third study from the early 1980s dropped the language of paedophilia from its title, turning its subject instead into one of the 'betrayal of youth' and the 'social oppression of children and young people'. In vain, this book suggested that rather than outright opposition to incestuous and other adult–child sexual relations, the real issue needed to be whether the child had rights and power within that relationship. Here, it attempted to side with a radical challenge to the family. Children should have the right to choose their own guardians. It could also now point out, as new evidence was increasingly making clear, that the vast majority of abuse, in fact, took place within the supposedly safe environment of the family. And it could suggest that the family had been destabilized in practical terms but also ideologically by the women's movement, and that it was anxiety about this collapse of the family that lay behind the current hysteria regarding child abuse that was so often (and in their view wrongly) directed at the paedophile.[99]

However, by the mid-1980s, just a decade on from the formation of the paedophile movement, the space that had briefly made public debate about its arguments possible had disappeared. The issue was now one cast firmly in black and white. Conservative Home Secretary Leon Brittan condemned PIE and offered a reassurance that legal routes to control the group were being fully explored. He presented the group, not as the marginal purveyors of some misguided intellectual argument, but as the tip of the iceberg of a much broader phenomenon. Pointing to a recent 'brutal attack' on a boy in Brighton, he argued that 'it was important to emphasize to parents the necessity of keeping a close eye on children, especially in the evenings, and to the public at large to notify the police of any suspicious activity'.[100] In 1984, threatened by further prosecution under new legislation dealing with child pornography, O'Carroll fled the country and PIE folded. In the early 1970s, few had known what paedophilia meant. PIE and its sympathizers had seen this as an opportunity to open a new frontier in the battle for sexual liberation. From the start, it was clear that this was a battle too far when it came to the media, conservative politicians, and the general public. Instead of transforming attitudes on intergenerational sex and child sexuality, the paedophile movement had provided an object for public pillory that helped to justify the fixing of boundaries and the strengthening of the law to defend them. By the mid-1980s, it provided a

[97] O'Carroll, *Paedophilia: The Radical Case*.

[98] Glen D. Wilson and David N. Cox, *The Child-Lovers: A Study of Paedophiles in Society* (London, 1983), p. 124.

[99] Middleton (ed.), *The Betrayal of Youth*.

[100] 'Minister Condemns Paedophile Views', *The Times* (2 September 1983).

target for a set of fears that went far beyond its own marginal activity.[101] It was such fear, as much as any shift in risk, which set the landscape of the child before the 1970s apart from that which came after.

THE RISE OF CHILD SEXUAL ABUSE IN THE LANDSCAPES OF HOME AND INSTITUTION

The irony is that the explosion of concern about paedophilia from the 1970s had little to do with the real evidence on the level of child sexual abuse. In fact, this period was beginning to see a remarkable shift in understanding of the threat. Research began to indicate that the major risk of abuse came from within the family itself. Initially, this came largely in the form of evidence on physical abuse. By the end of the 1970s, research began to highlight that this abuse often took a sexual form, though full acceptance of the sexual dimensions of abuse took until the mid-1980s.[102] Therefore children became more homebound on grounds of safety, just as there was a developing consciousness, particularly among the experts, that the home itself was not necessarily a haven from abuse. Indeed, by the end of the 1970s, research was suggesting that the very fact of being tied to a home with few outside social contacts could be both a sign and a symptom of abuse.[103]

The roots of the shift towards sexual abuse being recognized as something likely to originate within the home were very different to those that lay behind the emergence of paedophilia. They are to be found in medical reports on battered babies, emerging first in the United States at the start of the 1960s, then taken up by radiologists and paediatricians in Britain, followed by the NSPCC, social workers, and others working in the multidisciplinary field of child welfare by the mid-1970s.[104]

---

[101] For insight on contemporary fear: Meyer, *The Child at Risk*; Rachel Pain, 'Paranoid Parenting? Rematerializing Risk and Fear for Children', *Social and Cultural Geography*, 7 (2006), 221–43. The idea that a 'risk society' has emerged in late modernity is particularly associated with the sociologist Ulrich Beck: *Risk Society: Towards a New Modernity* (London, 1992).

[102] The history of child abuse (though not specifically sexual abuse) is much better covered than that of the paedophile: Ferguson, *Protecting Children in Time*; Nigel Parton, *The Politics of Abuse* (Basingstoke, 1985); Hendrick, *Child Welfare*, pp. 242–57; Margaret Jay and Sally Doganis, *Battered: The Abuse of Children* (London, 1987); Nigel Parton, 'The Natural History of Child Abuse: A Study in Social Problem Definition', *British Journal of Social Work*, 9:4 (1979), 431–51; Nigel Parton, 'Child Abuse, Social Anxiety and Welfare', *British Journal of Social Work*, 11 (1981), 391–414. Only in the 1980s did the public become more aware that abuse was often sexual. See, for instance: Jay and Doganis, *Battered*, p. 7.

[103] Jack Chapman, 'Ill-Treatment of Children: The Social and Legal Context in England and Wales', in Henry Kempe, Alfred White Franklin, and Christine Cooper (eds), *The Abused Child in the Family and in the Community: Selected Papers from the Second International Congress on Child Abuse and Neglect, London, England*, vol. 1 (Oxford, 1980), p. 53.

[104] The battered baby had its roots in post-war radiography and in particular an influential article on the 'Battered-Child Syndrome' in the *Journal of the American Medical Association* by C. Henry Kempe: 181 (1962), 17–24, and a subsequent editorial in the *Journal*: 181 (1962), 42. For the emergence of a public consciousness in Britain, spearheaded by the NSPCC, by the late 1960s: 'The Case of Battered Babies', *The Times* (9 June 1966); 'You See a Clean Pinny: The Bruises are Underneath', *The Times* (8 January 1969); 'Call for Law to Aid Battered Babies', *The Times* (12 September 1969); Edwina Baher et al., *At Risk: An Account of the Work of the Battered Child Research Department, NSPCC* (London, 1976).

Particularly after the Maria Colwell case of 1973, there is a clear sense of a shift in the balance of protection, from a post-war focus on protecting the integrity of the family as necessary for the well-being of the child, towards a new willingness to accept that well-being could often demand removal of the child from a pathological family environment.[105] This reflected a mood of taking more seriously the rights, interests, and voice of the individual child. But the turn against the family (or more accurately some families) also drew on a powerful current of medical, social work, and even political suspicion towards the 'problem family' as a source of intergenerational abuse and neglect. This concern was exacerbated by the perceived breakdown of the family evident in rising divorce rates. It could also still have a remarkably strong eugenic dimension, as evident in recommendations for the targeting of birth control and sterilization. It is intriguing in this regard that one of the main reports on child abuse was prepared by Keith Joseph's 'Tunbridge Wells Study Group' in 1975; Joseph had become notorious for adopting what to some seemed a new eugenics in relation to problems of welfare during this period.[106] So, the emergence of child abuse by the mid-1970s has been seen as being driven by a conjuncture between a process of medicalization and a system of new signs to be picked up by social workers, on the one hand, and of ideological misgivings towards welfare provision and permissiveness whipped up into a moral crisis, on the other.[107]

In 1979, Henry Kempe, the American paediatrician who had coined the term 'battered child' back in 1962, and who was now writing in the 'International Year of the Child' as decreed by the United Nations, pointed to six stages in the development of dealing with child abuse: first, denial; second, the lurid case; third, the infant who physically failed to thrive; fourth, the recognition of emotional abuse and neglect; fifth, sexual abuse; and finally, guaranteeing that all children were wanted. However, Britain was still at stages three and four. The debate about child abuse in 1970s Britain was still almost exclusively about physical abuse. Public attention was still focused on the threat from outside the home. If sexual abuse within the family came to the attention of GPs it was still common to keep this confidential in the belief that it was something best sorted out in private and that removal of the child would usually not be in the best interests of the child.[108]

In the 1980s, sexual abuse within the family would go on to attract increasing attention, becoming a major concern among professionals such as social workers

---

[105] Born in 1965, Colwell had initially been placed in foster care but returned to live with her mother and died following beatings by her step-father and despite concern about her condition being communicated to various agencies. The main study of the history of abuse in the period has concluded that the level of public awareness was still relatively low in the 1960s and early 1970s, and the Maria Colwell case escalated the issue and precipitated a major public inquiry: Parton, *The Politics of Abuse*, pp. 63, 97.

[106] Alfred White Franklin (ed.), *Concerning Child Abuse: Papers Presented by the Tunbridge Wells Study Group on Non-Accidental Injury to Children* (Edinburgh, 1975).

[107] Parton, 'Child Abuse, Social Anxiety and Welfare' and 'The Natural History of Child Abuse'.

[108] Paula Case, *Compensating Child Abuse in England and Wales* (Cambridge, 2007), p. 26. There was even the suggestion by some that intrafamilial sexual relations might be part of normal sexual development: A. Yates, *Sex without Shame* (New York, 1978).

in the field of child safety. Here, a new constituency in drawing attention to the issue was feminists, who linked sexual abuse of children to the broader problem of male violence within the family.[109] However, it would remain a far less palatable social fear, and a less obvious or easy target for attack, than the paedophile. There was a struggle to reconcile detecting and protecting the sexually abused child with an ongoing entrenched view that the stability of the family was crucial to childhood well-being. This left policy veering between being too eager to see signs of abuse and to remove children from families, as in the notorious Cleveland episode in 1987, and then being perceived in response as too reticent, leaving children in danger.[110] As argued earlier, the shift can be seen as related to the weakening by the 1970s of a post-war social settlement based on the dual roles of the family and the welfare state. Social and ideological change eroded confidence in the family as an essential bulwark to this settlement. But a decline in confidence in the welfare state would also limit the viability of intervention to protect the child. The profession of social work in particular found itself trapped in the middle of these contradictions, a target for attack and blame alongside the paedophile. Nevertheless, a significant shift in public consciousness had taken place by the mid-1980s. Even if the paedophile remained at the forefront of moral panic, the words of a newspaper article from the time pointed to a new common sense: the reality was now 'less the man in the dirty mac lurking at the gates than the familiar step on the stair which makes the blood run cold'.[111]

Consciousness of sexual abuse in the third landscape of the institution came latest of all. If the panic about paedophilia can be dated to the press and then political campaigns against PIE and child pornography in the mid-1970s, and that surrounding abuse in the family to the mid-1980s, the first exposure of systematic abuse within residential homes for children did not surface until 1989, with a focus on sexual abuse not to the fore until well into the 1990s.[112] Here, the radical thinking about child sexuality within social work in the late 1970s had fostered a sexual culture within some childcare homes that was radically at odds with conventional morality.[113] As society became increasingly sensitive towards child sexual abuse from the 1980s, it was inevitable that such practices would be exposed. Once the children's home became the subject for investigation, and fuelled by an emerging

---

[109] For instance, the Child Abuse Studies Unit was set up at the Polytechnic of North London in 1987 following a conference on the subject: Mary MacLeod and Esther Saraga, *Child Sexual Abuse: Towards a Feminist Professional Practice* (London, 1987). For reflections on this relationship in the United States: Angelides, 'Feminism, Child Sexual Abuse, and the Erasure of Child Sexuality', 141–77; Beryl Satter, 'The Sexual Abuse Paradigm in Historical Perspective: Passivity and Emotion in Mid-Twentieth-Century America', *Journal of the History of Sexuality*, 12 (2003), 424–64.

[110] Bell, *When Salem Came to the Boro*.

[111] Clare Dyer and Michael Levin, 'Revealed: the Sad Secrets of Abused Children', *The Times* (30 November 1984); D. J. West, *Sexual Crimes and Confrontations: A Study of Victims and Offenders* (Aldershot, 1987), p. 55.

[112] The case related to Castle Hill, a privately owned home. A decade earlier there was another case at Kinkora in Northern Ireland, but this attracted little attention in England: Wolmar, *Forgotten Children*, p. 3.

[113] Wolmar, *Forgotten Children*, pp. 29–30.

industry of legal compensation, complaints of institutionalized abuse would snowball. Many of the worst abuses related to what had formerly been approved schools, where a harsh disciplinary culture was swept away in the 1970s by a generation of young, radicalized social workers. These social workers brought with them a radical sexual politics, and this was able to flourish in closed institutional settings and within the context of the devolution of management responsibility in an era of local government upheaval.[114] The scandals that resulted lifted a veil of silence about these practices, and also about a culture of longstanding physical, emotional, and even sexual abuse that had characterized institutional care for many years. Yet the scale of the scandals led some to suggest that this was the latest face of an ongoing moral panic about the safety of children, with perceptions, fears, and responses again in danger of becoming disproportionate.[115]

In fact, despite a growing apparatus for detecting child sexual abuse in institutions, in the family, from strangers, and from the expanding virtual world of the Internet, figures not just on sexual offences but for the number of children officially at risk remained tiny compared to estimates of the danger and to reported levels of experience. Child sexual abuse was a central feature of life because it had become such a powerful social fear and because it was an issue of widespread reported experience and memory. Perceptions of abuse were taken seriously in a way that had simply not been the case before the 1970s. In that sense, the culture of fear about sexual danger was in part a result of efforts to appreciate the child's perspective that had roots in the child rights reorientation of the 1970s; it also, however, reflected a powerful set of beliefs about what was sexually appropriate for the child which had emerged intact and even reinforced after the turmoil and questioning of the 1970s.

CONCLUSION

It is clear from this analysis that concern about protecting children from sexual danger increased from the mid-1970s and has become a more important factor in a story of lost childhood freedom. The emergence of the figure of the paedophile was crucial in this process. It took longer for concern to extend to sexual abuse within the family home and in institutional childcare settings. Consciousness that children faced sexual danger from strangers was by no means new in the 1970s, but before that time certain factors had mitigated alarm. This included a pre-permissive tendency to avoid open discussion of sexual matters, which deterred parents from addressing the problem and ensured that the issue had a lower profile in the media than it would later assume. It also reflected the fact that doctors, psychiatrists, and social workers had doubts over tackling such issues via the law, and that they were

---

[114] Wolmar, *Forgotten Children*, pp. 137–52.

[115] See for instance Richard Webster, *The Great Children's Home Panic* (Oxford, 1998). A new organization—Falsely Accused Carers and Teachers—represented those who claimed to have been falsely accused as a result: <http://www.factuk.org/about-us/fact-the-first-decade/>.

moving towards the position that children were sexual actors in their own right. The explosion of concern about the sexual danger of strangers was brought to the fore by the profile of such issues increasing within the media, but also by the emergence into the public arena of interrelated debates about the age of consent and homosexual and then paedophile rights. A coalition of radical academics, liberals interested in rights, and welfare workers excited by new talk of children's liberation briefly provided the climate for paedophile activists to launch their ill-fated campaign for legitimacy. The main result was to highlight the danger as never before and to give it a name and a focus that has become a central feature of the landscape of modern British childhood. On the other hand, this has gone alongside a radical post-permissive liberalization of attitudes towards other areas of sexuality, and an increasing presence of sexuality in the media and popular culture within which childhood is embedded. Therefore, although children emerged as subjects with a firmer right to sexual protection, surrounded by increasingly extensive safeguards, this was a right that, judged by rates of under-age pregnancy and sexual disease and the high rate of sexual abuse of children on children, has proved very difficult to realize effectively and was arguably in some respects misdirected, not least because within an increasingly sexualized culture they were placed in the position of challenging protection in expressing sexuality.

7

Radicalization and Crisis of the Post-War Landscape Settlement

Colin Ward's influential book, *The Child in the City*, published in 1978, offered two powerful messages about the landscape of the child in post-war Britain. On the one hand, it highlighted a fundamentally changed and changing environment, transformed by the car, urban planning, and post-war reconstruction, and it pointed to new anxieties about the resulting mental health problems among children and to the problem now increasingly, not of lack of attachment, but of an isolation born from a culture of attachment. On the other hand, it emphasized the capacity of children to overcome the limitations imposed by such an environment and still to find in the city essential opportunities for physical and imaginative exploration. Therefore, despite its pessimistic picture of environmental deprivation, optimism about the potential of the child for subverting such a situation shone through.[1]

Looking back on his study after a further two decades of social and political change, Ward later recognized that British children of the 1970s still in fact had a striking degree of freedom. This was brought into stark contrast by a recent media frenzy sparked by the case of a young child who had been given the name of 'rat boy' in the press.[2] 'Somehow', Ward concluded, 'adult choices have created a world in which we only trust the indoor child, safely at home with all that consumer software. The outdoor child is automatically suspect.'[3] Collaborating with students in a study of the landscape of the child at the end of the century, he accepted that it was 'hard to escape the conclusion that the turn of the century urban child is an *indoor* child'.[4] The students' own studies of life in Liverpool confirmed this. As one

---

[1] Colin Ward, *The Child in the City* (London, 1978), p. 210.

[2] Ward's 'rat boy' is likely to be the case discussed in the *Independent* on 7 October 1993: a fourteen year old who had escaped from custody 37 times and had committed 55 offences since the age of ten, and who had gained his nickname through living in a warren of tunnels in a council housing complex. However, it was not until 2002 that there was an explosion of concern about 'feral' children. Here one of the sparks was the murder of Damilola Taylor. This was part of the background for the new policy of Anti-Social Behaviour Orders, commonly known as ASBOS: Jo-Ann Goodwin, 'The Savages—It's the Week Britain Realised We Have Produced a Breed of Amoral and Feral Children', *Daily Mail* (23 March 2002; which compared the new phenomenon to the 'Third World street child'); and 'The Time for Sentimentality is Over: Let Us Tame these Feral Children', *Independent* (29 April 2002).

[3] Colin Ward, 'Opportunities for Childhoods in Late Twentieth Century Britain', in B. Mayall (ed.), *Children's Childhoods Observed and Experienced* (London, 1994), p. 152.

[4] Mark Harris et al. (eds), *The Child in the City: A Case Study in Experimental Anthropology* (Manchester, 2000).

reported: 'outside of shopping centres of the city, children are very rarely found—and almost never without the presence of an adult. Play spaces are usually empty and areas that children might once have made their own play spaces are deserted.' The ingenuity that Ward had found among the children of the city had not disappeared, but it was now expressed through indoor play and often under adult supervision. Parents were afraid to let their children out on the streets on their own. Children were also afraid. And often this fear was greatest in relation to the 'feral' outside children who did remain.[5]

Ward's *Child in the City* has attracted interest as a precursor for an end-of-century paradigm shift in appreciation and understanding of the landscape of the child: and a shift to seeing the child as subject rather than object, active in responding to, in adapting to, and in giving meaning to environmental circumstances, rather than a passive and inevitable victim.[6] This book has argued that aspects of such an orientation can, in fact, be found well before Ward's seminal account of the situation faced by children in the 1970s. For although the Second World War had provoked anxieties which encouraged paternalism and protectiveness, it also opened eyes to the importance of understanding the child's feelings. Over the next decades, the two tendencies were sometimes in tension, but by and large there was an aspiration to design a landscape for the child that did take into consideration the idea that children had their own landscape perspective. Whether children really were listened to, or were properly understood, is another matter altogether. Indeed, the model of the child's perspective that dominated throughout the period was one that, in emphasizing the difference of children, the developmental nature of their understanding of the world, and the importance of certain social relations, would later come to be seen as fundamentally in tension with a position of empowering and properly listening to the child. This chapter now locates Ward's *Child in the City* in relation to a series of broader developments in the 1970s, reframing it less as a uniquely prescient text, more as one that was situated within a particular set of historical circumstances; and not simply as a beginning, but in some ways as a radical culmination to a way of thinking about and responding to the landscape of the child that can be traced back to the Second World War and which reached a point of radicalization, crisis, and to a degree collapse, in the 1970s. The fact that Ward now appears to be something of a unique pioneer has much to do with changes that would follow the 1970s.

---

[5] Ward's comments are reported in Harris et al. (eds), *The Child in the City*, p. 20. The postgraduate course at Manchester University expected students to undertake their own field work inspired by and along the lines of *The Child in the City*, and Ward attended a final workshop to discuss the research and contributed to a resulting publication. Following Ward's death in 2010, his contribution in this field was marked by a conference on 'Colin Ward, Education, Childhood and Environmentalism' held at the University of Cambridge, 11 March 2011. His papers have been deposited at the International Institute of Social History in Amsterdam.

[6] A key text in heralding such a paradigm shift was Alison James and Alan Prout (eds), *Constructing and Reconstructing Childhood: Contemporary Issues in the Sociological Study of Childhood* (London, 1990). Identifying Ward's book as an inspiration, see, for instance: Pia Christensen and Margaret O'Brien (eds), *Children in the City: Home, Neighbourhood and Community* (London, 2003), p. 1.

The chapter takes us back to the period portrayed in Ward's seminal study, to its mounting concerns about lost freedom for the child, but also to its often radical visions of a way forward. In focusing on the 1970s, it touches on an era of social history that has to date attracted relatively little attention from historians of modern Britain. The chapter deploys the subject of the child to help open up an appreciation of the radical and ambitious grass-roots politics of the era, its conjuncture with social science, and its focus in particular on the relationship between experience and space. The latter now attracts growing attention from followers of 'psycho-geography'. In fact, this movement towards psycho-geography was itself in part born out of the conditions described in this chapter, part of the broader conjuncture between radical politics, new social science, and the environmentalist challenge of creating a landscape of man in the face of post-war urban development. In that sense, this chapter offers insight into the roots of a psycho-geographical reorientation within the social sciences and the role of the story of the landscape of the child, and of the politics of play, therein. It also provides us with a case study of a period in which the lessons of social science were becoming popularized in such a way that they were not just played out and often radically interpreted by young teachers, social workers, and criminologists, but they were now increasingly part of the landscape itself, integral to the way that the participants of study—here the children—described, understood, and reacted to their situation.

In order to develop these lines of analysis, the chapter deploys four case studies (in many respects, the explosion of debate on child sexuality considered in the previous chapter provides another). Focusing on the late 1960s and 1970s, it looks in turn at the histories of environmental education, the children's liberation movement, the politics of play, and radical criminology and vandalism. These four themes overlap to provide a narrative of radical efforts to recast the landscape of the child in the period. Together they cast particular light on debates in the sphere of education. The chapter also includes a preliminary section that discusses the broader context for the post-war move towards environmental and landscape thinking in relation to social questions such as child well-being and social deprivation. A final section turns to the collapse and aftermath of the radical experiments discussed in the chapter.

HUMAN ENVIRONMENTALISM

The end of the 1960s and start of the 1970s saw what has been described as an environmental revolution.[7] However, in the Britain of the early 1970s, environmental concern was just as likely to centre instead on man's struggle to adapt in relation to a rapidly changing man-made, and in particular urban, environment.[8]

---

[7] Keith Wheeler, 'The Genesis of Environmental Education', in George C. Martin and Keith Wheeler (eds), *Insights into Environmental Education* (Edinburgh, 1975), p. 13.

[8] On the development of concern about the environment in relation to traffic: Simon Gunn, 'The Buchanan Report, Environment and the Problem of Traffic in 1960s Britain', *Twentieth Century British History*, 22 (2011), 521–42.

This other sort of environmentalism did attract some significant international consideration at the time. It featured at the United Nation's Stockholm Conference on the Human Environment of 1972, and in 1976 the United Nations organized a conference in Vancouver specifically on Human Settlements and Habitat. Yet, this moment of human environmentalism soon passed, pushed off the agenda by the increasingly pressing crisis in natural ecology. A second United Nations Habitat Conference, held in Istanbul, had to await a further two decades. The questions of human adaptation to urban life, which had already been pressing at the start of the 1970s in the highly urbanized context of Britain, were by this time ones faced by half of the world population.[9] In a series of international reports in the 1990s, the child's experience of city life therefore came to be recognized as a key element in sustainable development, and the child's right to play even within the environment of the modern city was entrenched in the United Nation's Convention of the Rights of the Child.[10] This seemed new, but in many respects this international voice—which was now projected into a British debate about toxic childhood which took off in the 1990s—was a reprisal and extension of concern first developed in Britain in the early 1970s.[11]

Post-war British concern about the human environment had links to broader efforts to use planning to manage a rural landscape under threat from commercial development.[12] But this now took on a psychological dimension. In a world in which man's control over the environment meant that distance had collapsed and in which the scale of construction and industrial development dwarfed an associational life that had existed for thousands of years, there seemed a danger of 'dissociation'. This was also reflected in concern about a breakdown of community, which became the dominant theme in post-war British social science. Not only was man losing a relationship of attachment to the world he had built, but the danger was that he would retreat as a result into the satisfactions of individual materialism within the space of his own home. In this context, the idealization of home, and of attachment within the family, that had offered a solution to war-born insecurities now found itself under question. Was the real danger facing modern man one of isolation, and the challenge one of reintegration in a social

---

[9] Wade Rowland, *The Plot to Save the World: The Life and Times of the Stockholm Conference on the Human Environment* (Toronto, 1973); John McCormick, *The Global Environmental Movement* (London, 1995).

[10] Roger Hart, *Children's Participation: From Tokenism to Citizenship* (Florence, 1992); Roger Hart, *Children's Participation: The Theory and Practice of Involving Young Citizens in Community Development and Environmental Care* (New York, 1997); Sheridan Bartlett, Roger Hart, David Satterthwite, Ximena de la Barra, and Alfredo Missait, *Cities for Children: Children's Rights, Poverty and Urban Management* (New York, 1999); and Roger Hart and Alfhild Petren, 'The Child's Right to Play', in Alfhild Petren and James Himes (eds), *Children's Rights: Turning Principles into Practice* (Stockholm, 2000).

[11] E. Adams, J. Bishop and J. Kean, 'Children, Environment and Education: Personal Views of Urban Environmental Education in Britain', *Children's Environments*, 9:1 (1992), 49–67. Roger Hart, the author of the UNICEF reports and by this time professor of environmental psychology at City University New York, had worked in environmental education in 1970s Britain. He drew on developments such as the Notting Dale Urban Studies Centre in 1970s London as a model in his later writing.

[12] D. Matless, *Landscape and Englishness* (London, 1998).

world? In such circumstances, landscape was crucial, argued Geoffrey and Susan Jellicoe, because it could counter such isolation, offering a 'middle-distance' to give meaning to life in a way that religion and art once had.[13]

The child, and the experience of trying to look at the world through the eyes of the child, provided the perfect figure for launching the new philosophy of landscape and an environmentalism that saw its first principle as one of human subjectivity and scale.[14] By the 1960s, we see architects, town planners, and even politicians taking note. Town-planners began experiments in looking at children's mental maps of the city. Doctors began to talk about the study of environmental psychiatry, and were especially concerned about the mental health of children living in high-rise flats.[15] A new discipline of environmental psychology looked to turn the child's-eye maxim into the basis for a domain of expertise.[16] And academic

[13] Geoffrey Jellico and Susan Jellicoe, *The Landscape of Man: Shaping the Environment from Prehistory to the Present Day* (London, 1975), in particular the epilogue, 'Towards the Landscape of Humanism', pp. 373–4.

[14] Lady Allen of Hurtwood and Susan Jellicoe, *Gardens: The Things We See (7)* (London, 1953), p. 5; Marjory Allen and Mary Nicholson, *Memoirs of an Uneducated Lady* (London, 1975), p. 99.

[15] Lord Taylor and Sidney Chave, *Mental Health and Environment* (London, 1964); E. Hare and G. Shaw, *Mental Health on a New Housing Estate* (London, 1965); D. Fanning, 'Neurosis in Flat-Dwellers', *British Medical Journal* (1967), 382–6; Michael Rutter, 'Why are London Children So Disturbed?', *Proceedings of the Royal Society of Medicine*, 66 (1973). For reflections on the emergence of epidemiological psychiatry: Michael Shepherd, *The Psychosocial Matrix of Psychiatry* (London, 1983), pp. 29–84. On the difficulty in drawing conclusions from the data: Michael Shepherd, 'Childhood Behaviour, Mental Health, and Medical Services', in *Psychosocial Matrix*, pp. 159–74; M. Shepherd, A. N. Oppenheim, and S. Mitchell, *Childhood Behaviour and Mental Health* (London, 1970). The same authors earlier published their results in several articles: 'The Definition and Outcome of Deviant Behaviour in Childhood', *Proceedings of the Royal Society of Medicine*, 59 (1966), 379; 'Childhood Behaviour Disorders and the Child-Guidance Clinic: An Epidemiological Study', *Journal of Child Psychology and Psychiatry*, 7 (1966), 39; 'A Comparative Study of Children's Behaviour at Home and School', *British Journal of Educational Psychology*, 36 (1966), 248; 'The Child Who Dislikes Going to School', *British Journal of Educational Psychology*, 37 (1967), 32. Specifically, on the problem of life in flats: J. L. Gilloran, 'Social Health and Problems Associated with "High Living" ', *Medical Officer*, 120 (1968), 117–18; D. M. Fanning, 'Families in Flats', *British Medical Journal*, 4 (1967), 382–6; W. F. R. Stewart, *Children in Flats: A Family Study* (NSPCC, 1970). Pearl Jephcott, *Homes in High Flats: Some of the Human Problems Involved in Multi-Storey Housing* (Edinburgh, 1971), pp. 80–101. Psychiatric concern came to centre on the dual problem of the effect of such an environment on mothers as well as on their children: on the one hand, the impact of isolation and lack of support experienced by the mothers on their mental health and thereby on their capacity to care for their young children; and on the other hand, the lack of stimulus in such an environment having a negative impact on the mental health of the child, and this in turn placing further stress on the mothers. N. Richman, 'Effects of Housing on Preschool Children and Their Mothers', *Developmental Medicine and Child Neurology*, 10 (1974), 1–9; B. Ineichen and D. Hooper, 'Wives' Mental Health and Children's Behaviour Problems in Contrasting Residential Areas', *Social Science and Medicine*, 8 (1974), 369–74; B. Ineichen and D. Hooper, 'Adjustment to Moving: A Follow-Up Study of the Mental Health of Young Families in New Housing', *Social Science and Medicine*, 13 (1979), 163–8; B. Ineichen, 'High Rise Living and Mental Stress', *Biology and Human Affairs*, 44 (1979), 81–5; D. R. Hannay, 'Mental Health and High Flats', *Journal of Chronic Diseases*, 34 (1981), 431–2. This research continued throughout the 1970s and into the early 1980s: Hugh Freeman, *Mental Health and the Environment* (London, 1984), p. 220.

[16] David Canter, *The Psychology of Space* (London, 1977). For instance: F. Berbaldez, D. Gallardo, and R. Abello, 'Children's Landscape Preferences: From Rejection to Attractions', *Journal of Environmental Psychology (JEP)*, 7 (1987), 169–76; J. M. Brown, J. Henderson, and M. P. Armstrong, 'Children's Perceptions of Nuclear Power Stations as Revealed through their Drawings', *JEP*, 7 (1987), 189–99; E. A. Holman and D. Stokols, 'The Environmental Psychology of Child Sexual Abuse', *JEP*, 14 (1994), 237–52. In total, some 94 articles after 1981 dealt with children.

disciplines such as geography, psychology, and urban sociology came together with professions such as planning and architecture in dialogue around the intersection between mind and place.[17] In the visions of environmental psychology and planning, the neat draughtsmanship of the urban plan was to make way for the sketches of lived experience and memory: the images of space that people held in their heads, and which shaped the way they perceived, used, and felt about their environments. The city was to be seen in a new way, and this was to guide a human-centred, psychological form of planning in which the figure of the child was central.[18] From the late 1960s, this was also a perspective that became fashionable in radical circles, where further inspiration came from the French situationists, and this is why play emerged as a key political battlefield in efforts to transform the urban landscape.[19]

There is a cartoon image from 1976 in *New Society*—a journal that was key in the popularization of social science—that captures what had happened to the idea of urban space over the past decade.[20] It addresses the idea of 'neighbourhood', and through a series of frames it indicates that within a social scientific culture that had come to see space as an issue of perspective, the romanticized notion of the organic neighbourhood—foundational in the community studies that had dominated post-war British sociology—was now increasingly difficult to sustain. At first, this seems a paradoxical outcome. For the idea that environment was a matter of emotion and individual understanding does in some ways help to explain how regions became neighbourhoods, and this had been important in a reinvigorated emphasis on community in the early 1970s.[21] But taking the lessons of social science further,

---

[17] Jeff Bishop, Eileen Adams, and Joan Keen, 'Children, Environment and Education: Personal Views of Urban Environmental Education in Britain', *Children's Environments*, 9:1 (1992).

[18] The approach began to attract large-scale attention in the aftermath of geographer Kevin Lynch's influential *The Image of the City*, which used sketch maps based on interviews to understand the underlying structures of how city space was perceived, made sense of, and experienced. Such work suggested that the extent to which a city was 'imageable' might be key to its success: Kevin Lynch, *The Image of the City* (Cambridge MA, 1960). Lynch later extended this study in relation to children in his comparative study *Growing up in Cities: Studies of the Spatial Environment of Adolescence in Cracow, Melbourne, Mexico City, Salta, Toluca, and Warsawa* (Cambridge, MA, 1977). Reflecting on the roles of geography and psychology in the development of this new field: Douglas Pocock and Ray Hudson, *Images of the Urban Environment* (London, 1978), pp. 3–17. As with many areas examined in this chapter, the 1990s would see a rediscovery of this work which would inspire a follow-up study. It has been suggested that Lynch's findings foundered because of reluctance to take children's views seriously in the late 1970s, and this is contrasted unfavourably to attitudes by the 1990s: Louise Chawla, 'Growing Up in Cities: A Report on Research under War', *Environment and Urbanization*, 9 (1997), 247–51.

[19] French situationist Raoul Vaneigem's 'Banalités de Base' (1962–3) was translated as *Totality for the Kids* (1967). The interest in the psychological of space is evident in the Interzone Edition of *International Times*, 30 (1968). The history of these developments emerges from the psychogeographical writings of Tom Vague, much of which is accessible online: <http://www.housmans.com/booklists/TomVague.php>.

[20] On the popularization of social science and the role of *New Society*: Mike Savage, *Identities and Social Change in Britain since 1940: The Politics of Method* (Oxford, 2010), pp. 112–19.

[21] The momentum behind turning the city into a series of neighbourhoods is evident in an earlier article in the journal: Michael Hall, 'Parish Councils for Cities?', *New Society* (29 January 1970), 178–9.

and given the recognition that a social scientific frame of mind was now being incorporated into the way that people made their own sense of space, the idea of neighbourhood was becoming harder to sustain: it was increasingly clear that it rested in reality on multiple points of perspective, and since the various constituencies were increasingly conscious of this, and conscious of the social science of perspective, it had tensions and political divisions at its very heart. So the *New Society* cartoon shows us the gulf between the planner's view of a neighbourhood and those of the sociologist, the politician, the speculator, the housewife, and the child: each envisaged the neighbourhood in a strikingly different way, and in ways that revealed a politics of perspective. The planner saw a network of buildings and streets: a neighbourhood of 'amenity areas', 'support zones', and 'communication spines'. The sociologist saw people rather than streets: a neighbourhood of 'subgroups', 'social leaders', and 'pair relationships'. The speculator saw the opportunities of turning the neighbourhood into a landscape of office blocks, car parks, and supermarkets. The image of the housewife's and the child's views are particularly significant for us. The housewife looked out at the word though the bars of the window, secure but separated from the outside world. The child saw the neighbourhood as an impenetrable maze, and stood with a catapult half-hidden behind his back, a symbol of resistance against this fact.[22]

What made the reorientation in the sciences and practices of place more than a debate within academia is that it coincided both with a collapse of confidence in top-down, post-war, urban planning as a solution to social problems and with a new climate in favour of democratization. For all the efforts of the post-war planners, the human environment began to take the blame for what seemed to many an increasingly sick society.[23] The fault, it now began to be argued, lay not in planning per se, but in the fact that the planners had failed to look at the issue from the perspective of those who would live in these cities. Post-war housing demand, fuelled by a baby boom and rapid urban commercial development, had destabilized the controlled planning that had been a feature of the late 1940s and early 1950s and had led local authorities to contract out responsibility to developers.[24] This was also a period that saw the retreat of traditional middle-class control of urban government. Such factors weakened the connection between local government and community as power passed into the hands of professionals and private developers. The need for a shift towards greater participation in the planning process was recognized by the Town and Country Planning Act of 1968 and the (Skeffington) People and Planning Report of 1969.[25] A similar process was seen in the field of social work, where there was growing emphasis on the importance of community work, rather than case work: social workers and local government to work

---

[22] Charles Mercer, 'What Neighbourhood?', *New Society* (22 January 1976), 154–9.

[23] Canter, *Psychology of Space*, p. 6.

[24] Peter Mandler, 'John Summerson, 1904–1992: The Architectural Critic and the Quest of the Modern', in Susan Pedersen and Peter Mandler (eds), *After the Victorians: Private Conscience and Public Duty in Modern Britain* (London, 1994), pp. 240–1.

[25] Peter Shapely, 'Planning, Housing and Participation in Britain, 1968–1976', *Planning Perspectives*, 26:1 (2011), 75–90.

with deprived communities in helping them create community solutions to local problems.[26] The new approach to planning and development was also evident in the founding of the Centre for Environmental Studies in 1967, which aimed to advance education and research on planning and design of the physical environment, and in the creation of a programme of Community Development Projects focused on socially deprived areas of the country.[27] These schemes aimed to facilitate research on the origins of deprivation and to encourage local innovation and coordination. They reflected a loss of confidence in centralized state planning and in the ability of the post-war welfare state to eradicate deprivation, and instead an ambition to rethink these challenges in relation to local contexts and the role of local communities. Rising concern about immigration and its social effects in inner city areas was also a factor. From 1968 to 1975, it has been estimated that some 3,750 local projects were approved under the scheme, costing nearly £35m, including a large number providing educational and community facilities for young people.[28]

In summary, post-war British social science, social policy, and social politics were all seeing something of a landscape turn by the start of the 1970s. At the heart of this turn was appreciation that the subjects of study and welfare had their own perspective, and that the limitations and failings of policy had much to do with a failure to take on board this fact. Children were at the heart of this shift. They were a symbol for this problem of perspective. And they would emerge as the most accessible population in developing the implications of the landscape turn. The central sections of this chapter will now turn to this story through four linked case studies.

ENVIRONMENTAL EDUCATION

The importance of the subject of the child in this landscape turn is perhaps most evident in the environment education movement, within which Colin Ward was a central figure. In a British context, the term 'environmental education' began to be used from the early 1960s in relation to discussions about integrating issues of conservation into education, and this led to the formation of the Society for Environmental Education. The Schools Council also became involved, setting up Project Environment to explore the relevance of what was termed 'rural studies', and a Council for Environmental Education was established to offer direction. In this initial iteration, environmental education was rural and biological

---

[26] Drawing on the American example, the influential Younghusband Report (1959) had drawn the distinction between group work and community work: David Thomas, *The Making of Community Work* (London, 1983); M. K. Smith, 'Community Work', in *The Encyclopedia of Informal Education*: <http://www.infed.org/community/b-comwrk.htm>.

[27] Martin Loney, *Community against Government: The British Community Development Project 1968–78* (London, 1983).

[28] Timothy Whitton, 'The Impact of the Community Development Projects on Assessing Urban Deprivation', in Monic Charlot (ed.), *Britain's Inner Cities* (Paris, 1994), p. 13.

in orientation.[29] This move to rural field studies, and the use of 'field centres', was related to several broader currents within post-war progressive education: it was in line with a new style of school architecture and classroom design which responded to the broader ambivalence about closed institutions as offering a fit landscape for the child and which aimed to allow freer contact with the outside world; it was encouraged in the post-war training colleges; and it was facilitated by the abolition of the eleven-plus examination in many schools, which freed them to concentrate more on child development. But there was no sense yet of the subversive orientation that was to come.[30]

At the end of the 1960s and in the early 1970s, environmental education took a striking shift in direction: towards the urban environment, towards a more political orientation, and towards a radical pedagogy of trying to see the world from the child's perspective. The new direction was encouraged and facilitated by the 1969 Skeffington People and Planning Report. One of the outcomes of this report, and of its recommendation to take more seriously the role of participation but also education in planning, was the setting up of an education unit at the Town and Country Planning Association in 1970. The appointment of Education Officer went to Colin Ward, who had a background working in an architect's office (though he was not a trained architect) and as a lecturer in liberal studies at Wandsworth Technical College, but who had also since the Second World War been a leading figure and writer in the British anarchist movement. Alongside his deputy Anthony Fyson, who read geography at Oxford and had been a town planner with Westminster City Council as well as a teacher, Ward would use this platform and the publication of a new journal, the *Bulletin of Environmental Education*, to transform environmental education and develop it as a tool in efforts to rescue the landscape of the child.

There was considerable excitement about this new development of human environmentalism. For some in the early 1970s, the attempt to bring to life a debate about the local urban environment seemed more likely to capture the imaginations of British children than the rather doom-laden picture emerging out of ecology.[31] Indeed, Maurice Ash, Chairman of the Town and Country Planning Association, was reported in 1972 as describing environmental education as 'dynamite': about to explode assumptions in the arena of planning as well as education. Debate about the better design of the urban environment was of course not new, but it had tended to become the preserve of the privileged few and locally had often come to focus on defending the pleasant areas where these privileged people lived against the encroachment of roads and modern development: it had become trapped in conservationism. This was the case, for instance, in the Barnsbury area of London where protection of the environment had notoriously been used as justification for diverting traffic from a middle-class to a working-class residential area. Via environmental

[29] Anne Armstrong, *Planning and Environmental Education: Centre for Environmental Studies*, Occasional Paper 7 (London, 1979), pp. 9–14.
[30] Wheeler, 'The Genesis of Environmental Education', p. 5.
[31] 'Monitor: A Challenge for Youth', *Guardian* (26 April 1972).

education, children were to be the vanguard in a new approach to planning. They would be educated in the politics of their environment, encouraged to grapple with controversies—like the Barnsbury case—and thereby developed as the future citizens of a society that would regard participation in planning as a vital social responsibility.[32] Even the socially conservative *Times* recognized that there was now a real need to educate children about issues of environmentalism and ecology that looked likely to become ever more important.[33]

The *Bulletin of Environmental Education* responded to this moment of possibility and to the appetite for education by providing a stream of ideas, reports on local experiments, and resources to guide teachers, planners, and administrators in developing environmental education. As a forum for news and debate but also a vehicle for practical plans about how to integrate environmental education in the classroom, in local study centres, or in planning departments, the *Bulletin* soon established itself at the centre of a multidisciplinary social movement. The vibrant nature of the journal in the 1970s reflected a broad excitement about environmental education as a vehicle for change. It was also a response to the fact that efforts to institutionalize environmental education in the traditional manner—as an academic subject in its own right—soon proved unrealistic, and energies were instead directed towards demonstrating multiple uses and applications and the value of an environmental perspective in virtually every subject across the curriculum. It was particularly easy to argue the case for the importance of environmental education in relation to the study of geography, but practical suggestions were also developed for its role in the study of history, English, and art. Energies focused, in particular, on the integration of environmental education at the secondary school level. It was not that primary education was seen as unimportant, more that the place of learning about one's environment, and a pedagogy of doing rather than being told, was already recognized as deeply embedded when it came to post-Plowden Report progressive education for the youngest age groups. The focus on secondary schools was also a reflection of a desperate effort to find ways to keep these older children engaged, a challenge that was exacerbated by the raising of the school leaving age to sixteen in 1972. Alongside this impact on education, the movement could also claim some notable successes in integrating the perspective of the child in the planning process. Examples of school work inspired by environmental education that had implications for planning included projects on the building of the M4 and on the child's view of the cityscape in an area of Birmingham.[34] There were also proposals for city colleges that would use the savings on the cost of school buildings for a high teacher–student ratio to supervise community-based education for children who were too difficult to teach in the school environment.[35]

---

[32] Judy Hillman, 'A Task for Children', *Guardian* (2 June 1972).
[33] Tony Aldous, 'Stammerers in Popular Ecotalk', *The Times* (17 August 1971).
[34] Wiltshire Schools M4 Motorway Project, *Birth of a Road: A Study in Environmental Education Based on the Wiltshire Schools M4 Motorway Project* (London, 1973); David Spencer and John Lloyd, *A Child's Eye View of Small Heath Birmingham: Perception Studies for Environmental Education* (Birmingham Centre for Urban and Regional Studies, 1974).
[35] Ward, *Child in the City*, pp. 177–85.

Although the school system was the most obvious focus for environmental education, the message, in fact, went well beyond formal schooling. Most notably, it inspired the urban study centres that sprung up across the country and which provided a base for community activities. These often centred on children but were not confined to them, and they took the environmental education philosophy as the basis for a new approach to involving local citizens of all types in taking control of their communities. Examples included Centreprise in Hackney and the Notting Dale Urban Studies Centre in West London.[36] Along the lines of the Interpretation Centres in the American National Parks, such urban studies centres could provide a venue for children from the local community to learn about and engage with local issues, but they would also act as a venue for groups of visiting children to find out about the city. In other words, the new field studies looked to reverse the idea that had been so powerful since the Romantics of children needing the innocence of nature to fully flourish and instead pointed to the importance of children engaging with the conflicts of urban life: it would send them, not out to nature, but into the city.[37] Indeed, if children needed to learn about the countryside, it was important to recognize that the image of unspoilt, virgin nature was no more than a romantic myth, that countryside farming was now an industrial process, and that (just as was now happening in the developing world) the city child's ancestors had fled the harsh realities of the countryside for the attractions of the town. So, rather than reinforcing such mythology, a series of experiments brought the country to the city via setting up projects such as city farms which would challenge stereotypes in both directions, and which rather than fostering rural nostalgia were to integrate aspects of rural life in an urban context.[38]

Ward's thinking on environmental education was influenced by the writing of the American anarchist Paul Goodman, in particular his *Growing up Absurd* (1961), as well as the 'deschooling' writing of Ivan Illich.[39] As early as 1965, Ward had written an article arguing for repeal of compulsory education in the magazine *Anarchy*.[40] He also looked to the United States for models of practice, and he was influenced by schemes such as the Parkway Education Program in Philadelphia and others in Chicago and Montreal. In such experiments, the traditional school building was often abandoned, teaching took place in the community, and the search for facilities became an integral part of the education: the art galleries, the zoo, and the workplaces of the city serving as the new classrooms and laboratories of education. In Britain, the raising of the school leaving age from fifteen to sixteen in 1972 and rising youth unemployment were exposing the inadequacy of schools in engaging the interests of pupils. Ward believed that the solution lay in breaking

---

[36] Ward, *Child in the City*, pp. 198–9.   [37] Ward, *Child in the City*, pp. 199–202.

[38] Ward, *Child in the City*, pp. 188–97.

[39] The following account draws on Colin Ward and Anthony Fyson, *Streetwork: The Exploding School* (London, 1973). On Ward's influences: Colin Ward, *Influences: Voices of Creative Dissent* (Bideford, 1991).

[40] Leila Berg, 'Towards Self-Government', in Paul Adams et al. (eds), *Children's Rights* (London, 1972), p. 44.

down the institutional and physical boundaries of the school. He also recognized that the urban environment itself was in desperate need of a new engagement with this section of the population. Children had become cut off from the streets of the city by an approach to the city space that had given little if any consideration to the perspective of the child. Responding to the opportunity opened up by the Skeffington Report's call for a link between education and town planning, Ward advocated involving children in a critical engagement with the politics of planning. This would also help invigorate the curriculum and make subjects like history and geography interesting for the alienated student. In looking to develop an environmental education that located children in relation to time as well as space, Ward was keen to distance environmental education from what critics would come to lampoon as nostalgia-driven 'heritage culture', but it clearly shared some of the energy that fuelled a grass-roots energy for local preservation, town trails, and local history.[41] Perhaps most obviously, however, environmental education challenged what many critics saw as the stale fare on offer in the subject of geography.

In 1973, Ward and Fyson elaborated on their vision for environmental education in a book that trumpeted their radical orientation in its title of *Streetwork: The Exploding School*. The first of these terms echoed the avant-garde efforts and community orientation of 'street theatre'. The second reflected a sense of frustration at the protective shell of school architecture and rules.[42] The authors were aware that teachers and schools faced real difficulties in this regard. The discipline of the timetable, safety concerns and regulations, and insurance liability all militated against efforts to get children out into the environment. Concern was such that the Schools Council ended up publishing its *Out and About: A Teacher's Guide to Safety on Educational Visits* (1972), with advice, for instance, on how to walk through the streets in crocodile formation. As far as the *Streetwork* authors were concerned, the tragedy was that walking in such a regimented way was 'also the most effective way to prevent the journey having any educational utility'.[43] Yet, at the same time, Ward and Fyson realized that teachers who did follow their recommendation of encouraging students to recognize the political dimensions of environmental issues could easily end up in trouble, as some already had.[44] Drawing heavily on material and examples already published in the *Bulletin of Environmental Education*, they set out a series of practical solutions. In doing so, they outlined the route towards a fundamental change in the ambition and scope of secondary education. As Ward put it:

> My concept of Environmental Education revolves around community contact, community problems, and the notion that the pupil must leave school not only knowing

---

[41] Critiques of 'heritage culture' came to the fore in the 1980s in the context of Thatcherism: Robert Hewison, *The Heritage Industry: Britain in a Climate of Decline* (London, 1987); Patrick Wright, *On Living in an Old Country* (London, 1985). Pointing to the democratic dimensions of interest in heritage via collecting, preservation, and local history: Raphael Samuel, *Theatres of Memory* (London, 1996).
[42] Colin Ward and Anthony Fyson, *Streetwork: The Exploding School* (London, 1973), p. 16.
[43] Ward and Fyson, *Streetwork*, pp. 19–20.   [44] Ward and Fyson, *Streetwork*, p. 22.

'how things are' in his environment, but also what he as a citizen can do about them. If streetwork outside the school is undertaken where I would argue it most often should be—that is in the district and community in which the pupil lives and learns— then it can form the very bridge between 'school life' and 'real life' for which teachers and parents alike are constantly searching. Fieldwork will no longer mean an occasional visit to the countryside, but constant involvement in the problems of the locality.[45]

Fyson published a second practical guide under the title of *Change the Streets* in Oxford University Press's educational 'Standpoints' series, this time directed at children themselves. Once again, the 'street' was figured as the central symbol and landscape for the battle over the environment. His opening address to the child reader strikingly captures the political intent of the movement:

These are the streets we use all our lives, and what happens to them makes a difference to us. For this reason, perhaps we should show more interest in the kind of streets we have. You may not feel very concerned about such things but you can be sure that even if you pay no attention to what is happening in your district, others will. And they are likely to be people who will shape the environment in which you live for their own purposes and goals. These may not be yours. *Don't let them get away with it.*[46]

Children were told that they needed to understand that home was so much more than a house; crucially, children had the right to feel at home in the city. The rich may have been able to find all they needed to find in the city, and through the mobility of the car they could mix the excitements and opportunities of the city with the peace of the countryside. But the working-class child, through the processes of slum clearance, the building of high-rise housing, the effects of traffic, and the inadequacy of outside play space, had invariably lost this broader 'home'. They would need to fight to get it back, whether through community groups, occupying the streets through parties, closing streets to traffic, making the urban landscape liveable through street furniture and planting, or reclaiming the street through study and writing.[47]

Environmental education was also a product of increasing concern about the limits of the welfare state settlement in eradicating social deprivation. Here, the research of Basil Bernstein was indicating that middle-class mothers tended to place more emphasis on the use of language in socializing children, and that this was crucial in giving their children an advantage in an education system where this type of language use was central. If this situation was to change, the central assumptions of the education system needed to be challenged.[48] An environmentalism that shifted the focus of education to the world around the child and which worked with the child's senses and interests was one way forward. And this was made

[45] Ward and Fyson, *Streetwork*, p. 88.
[46] Anthony Fyson, *Change the Streets* (Oxford, 1976), p. 2.
[47] Fyson, *Change the Streets*, pp. 34–54.
[48] Basil Bernstein, 'Education Cannot Compensate for Society', *New Society* (26 February 1970), 344–7.

possible under the government's Community Development Project, which provided funding to help establish urban study centres in socially deprived areas.

Ward reiterated concern about class and social deprivation in an article in 1978, with reference not to Bernstein but to the Newsons' research on the advantage to middle-class children of being talked to more by parents and of being subject to higher parental expectations. As discussed in the earlier chapter on the decline of confidence in the family home, this type of thinking was a factor in increasing support for compensatory nursery schools by the early 1970s. But Ward now extended this line of argument to include the compensation that could be provided by the full apparatus of environmental education: town trails, urban studies centres, the use of role play and improvised drama, the investigation of what he described as the autobiography of place, or even a reinvention of tradition with the use of carnivals and beating the bounds of the local area. All these could be found in London by the late 1970s, and all could be seen as 'valid and valuable attempts to make the inner city child at home in his own city, to make him master instead of the victim of his environment'. Working-class children, who had once owned the city, roaming freely and learning through interaction with the challenging environment, were now, argued Ward, in danger of becoming 'lost in their own city'. Increasingly they lived in a very narrow geographical zone. Poverty, the dangers of the environment, and fear, on the one hand, and the handicaps of an upbringing which saddled these children with limited linguistic skills, on the other, left these children isolated, unfamiliar with public transport, ill-equipped to take advantage of the compensatory technology of the telephone or the information available via public libraries, and poorly prepared to engage with strangers, to perform in public arenas such as the café, and to undertake the advance planning necessary to negotiate the complexities of modern urban life. They were developing into victims of 'experiential starvation'.[49]

By the 1970s, deprivation was also coming to be recognized as a racial issue. Before the war, middle-class parents from the outskirts of London had been keen to find places for their children in the excellent schools of the inner city. The destruction of the city in the war and then its high-rise rebuilding helped to change this situation. Outward migration increased, leaving the poor and the unstable behind. Immigrants from Britain's former colonies were among those who filled the vacated space.[50] Though immigrants tended to be allocated housing in the most deprived areas of the city, there was a view that this would hopefully be a 'zone of transition'. And there was the hope that immigrant children from West Indian, Pakistani, Bangladeshi, Indian, and East African backgrounds would benefit from strong familial and cultural bonds in easing adjustment to an alien landscape. Such strong roots were also seen as potentially helpful in coping with the education system and in fostering longer term social and economic success. Indeed,

---

[49] Ward's use of this term drew on Kevin Lynch. His comments were in relation to his new book *The Child in the City*; however, they offer a rather bleaker diagnosis than the book itself: Anne Karpf, 'Lost in Their Own City', *Guardian* (28 February 1978).

[50] Ward, *Child in the City*, p. 166.

research on mental health of children revealed a lower rate of maladjustment among the children of Indian parents, who had limited English and who had been poor peasants in Gujerat and the Punjab, than among English children in the same deprived areas. The temptation was to explain this in terms of the strong family, discipline, and community bonds in the immigrant community.[51] However, already in the early 1970s, it was being recognized that other immigrant children could come to resent and rebel against the restricting bonds of traditional culture. And it was suggested that this might help to account for the apparently higher rates of mental health problems among children in the West Indian population. High rates of unemployment in this section of the population also appeared to be a factor, leaving young people increasingly disenchanted with the education system and liable to get in trouble in school that could be a trigger to diagnosis within the mental health system. There was a feeling that a clue to this problem might be found in the disturbing findings of American psychological research on self-contempt among black children: their identification with dolls and pictures of white children, and their rejection of black images. Again, Asian children did not seem to be struggling with this issue to the same degree.[52] In the early 1970s, the assertion of black pride appeared as a possible solution. Yet, some commentators felt that this in turn was becoming a problem, seeming to foster contempt for parents who were uncomplainingly mired in menial jobs, and thus appearing to be another agent of social disintegration.[53] An apparent absence of play in West Indian culture also attracted blame. West Indian children, it was claimed, spent too much time doing nothing or just watching television. A leader of the adventure playground movement bleakly suggested that establishing one of these centres for West Indian children presupposed that they played 'whereas in fact they do not; nor is play part of their culture, upbringing, or education'.[54] Such evidence and assumption presented profound challenges for confidence in the existing approach to education and childcare. The concern about the immigrant child was an important factor, as the earlier chapter on this subject discussed, in abandoning the post-war faith in the home and family and moving instead towards support of more extensive nursery provision.[55]

[51] A. M. Kallarackal and Martin Herbert, 'The Happiness of Indian Immigrant Children', *New Society* (26 February 1976).

[52] Bernard Coard, *How the West Indian Child Is Made Educationally Sub-normal in the British School System* (London, 1971). From Grenada, Coard studied for an MA at Sussex University before becoming a Youth and Community Development Officer in South-East London and then teaching for several years at ESN schools. Subsequently, Coard returned to Grenada where he was involved in the communist revolution. When the Americans invaded in 1983 he was given a life sentence. His work has recently attracted renewed attention, striking a chord with ongoing concern about the educational performance of young black people in London: Polly Curtis, 'Opportunity Locked', *Guardian* (1 February 2005).

[53] Graham Lomas, *The Inner City* (London, 1975).

[54] Joe Benjamin, *Grounds for Play* (London, 1974) quoted in Ward, *Child in the City*, p. 171.

[55] Department of Education and Science, *Education: A Framework for Expansion* (London, 1972); and the appropriately titled *A Right to be Children: Designing for the Education of the Under-Fives* (London, 1976). Another government policy statement in 1972 called for 50 per cent of 3 year olds and 90 per cent of 4 year olds to have nursery provision (15 per cent full-time): Ward, *Child in the City*, p. 174.

In the early 1970s, issues of race, class, and social deprivation, but also the evidence and language of social scientific research, were turning education into a political battlefield in inner city areas. In London, there were accusations that the education system was inherently racist. The Inner London Education Authority provided evidence of a disproportionate number of immigrant children in schools for the educationally subnormal. In 1967, five of these schools had over 30 per cent immigrant children, and by 1968 one had 60 per cent. Across all the authority's educationally subnormal (ESN) schools, 28 per cent of the pupils were from immigrant families, compared to 15 per cent in ordinary schools. Once again, the figure was especially alarming when it came to West Indian children who made up three-quarters of the immigrant children in the ESN schools compared to only a half in mainstream education. By 1970, the figures were even worse: 17 per cent of the children in ILEA schools were from immigrant backgrounds, compared to 34 per cent in ESN schools, and 80 per cent of these were West Indian. The Grenadian Bernard Coard, who worked in a series of London ESN schools and youth clubs in this period, published an influential report drawing on such statistics as well as data on what happened to children who were deemed to have been wrongly placed in an ESN environment. He argued that West Indian children of average or even above average intelligence were much more likely than other children of similar intelligence to be misdiagnosed as educationally subnormal. Indeed, the schools often recognized this, but immigrant children were less likely to be moved back into the mainstream.[56] Worse still, the education process was in Coard's view too often a fundamentally alienating one and as such directly contributed to the problem: 'the black child's true identity is denied daily in the classroom. In so far as he is given an identity, it is a false one. He is made to feel inferior in every way. In addition to being told he is dirty and ugly and "sexually unreliable", he is told by a variety of means that he is intellectually inferior.'[57] In the context of such problems, the alternative pedagogy of environmental education had increasing appeal.

In summary, by the mid-1970s a new movement of environmental education had established itself as offering a solution, not just to an apparent alienation of many young people from the traditional subject base of academic disciplines, but also as a solution to a broader problem of children in danger becoming 'lost in their own city'. It offered practical solutions that appear to have had widespread appeal and influence in modifying teaching. However, in its radical roots, its direct appeal to children, and in its at-times combative and confrontational language, it also hinted at a more radical reorientation. The next section of this chapter turns to consider a series of experiments that did take the implications of such thinking to the next level. Here, the politics of class, race, and social deprivation made education a magnet for young radicals; indeed, the problems of the landscape of the

[56] Bernard Coard, *How the West Indian Child is Made Educationally Subnormal in the British School System* (London, 1974), pp. 5–9.
[57] Coard, *How the West Indian Child is Made Educationally Subnormal*, p. 28. See also Hazel V. Carby, 'Schooling in Babylon', in the Centre for Contemporary Cultural Studies, *The Empire Strikes Back: Race and Racism in 70s Britain* (London, 1982), pp. 183–211.

child and of lost childhood freedom emerge as key elements in the broader radical politics of the era.

CHILDREN'S RIGHTS AND RADICAL EDUCATION

In her personal memoir of the *Sixties*, Jenny Diski has described her involvement in establishing one of the resulting radical educational experiments, the Freightliners Free School in Camden. The school was set up in 1971, initially over a weekend in her flat, as a way to prevent a group of children 'who hung out in the streets and adventure playground nearby' from being taken into care for persistent truanting.[58] Diski was in training to be a teacher, and had recently had an article published in a new journal with the title *Children's Rights*. A curriculum and staffing was rustled up over the weekend, and it was to include the Editor of *Children's Rights*, her future husband Roger Marks (though he would soon resign from the journal, disillusioned that its editorial committee were so preoccupied by childhood sexual rights, which as we have seen was another direction in which the radical energy for freeing childhood was moving in these years). Typically, the school day was to start later than normal (at 10.30) to give the children time to wake up, though Diski had to battle with her radical school committee for even this early a starting time. Camden Council nevertheless approved of the plans and gave the group a grant of £20,000 for the year on the condition that they used the abandoned 'freightliner' site behind King's Cross Station and set up a series of other community services alongside the school, which was to include a city farm.

What emerges from Diski's account is that by the early 1970s the issue of childhood freedom was providing an important focus for those who wanted to translate the dreams of sixties radicalism into practical achievement, and one crucially that even the white middle-class radical could speak for. As she recalls:

> If ever any group was unrepresented, powerless and without a concerted voice in society, it was children. The Children's Rights movement allowed anyone to project. Even if we had never been a woman, black or working-class, we had all been children, and recalled that outraged helplessness at the adult world being arbitrary and unfair towards us.[59]

The new politics of children's freedom was a natural next step for a generation mobilized around the student politics of the late 1960s. For young teachers like Diski, the 'comprehensive system had stopped looking like an experiment in the liberation of working-class children and seemed already to be achieving little more than providing a minimally educated workforce for an industrial economy'.[60] The new generation looked to ideas like the free school and environmental education as ways to liberate children who seemed to be the victims of this system. And as Diski later recognized, the young teachers and radicals idealistically,

---

[58] Jenny Diski, *The Sixties* (London, 2009), pp. 97–118.
[59] Diski, *The Sixties*, p. 103.   [60] Diski, *The Sixties*, p. 108.

at times paternalistically, and with a certain lack of realism, saw themselves and their own liberation in the children who were often only a few years younger. Rejecting discipline, and often acting more as social workers than teachers, they had the satisfaction of seeming to connect with students who had often been abandoned as unteachable. For Diski, Ivan Illich's *Deschooling Society* had been an inspiration, though she later came to recognize that Illich in fact went much further in rejection of schooling and in his adherence to individualism than she and others believed in at the time. Her vision of small local groups of teachers and learners and of engagement with the local community in fact appears closer to that of environmental education: a tool for transforming state education, rather than rejecting it altogether; and a tool for enhancing social identity, rather than abandoning it for individualism. Diski is particularly illuminating on the way in which the orientation towards a child-centred approach said as much about the romance of lost childhood freedom among this young generation of teachers, as it did about the real needs of the children. The irony was that this most protected generation— the children of the 'golden-age' of the family and maternal attachment, and of a welfare state social security which had provided them with the free further education and the dole to support their radical lifestyles—looked to a style of education that offered children freedom but also deprived them of much of the security that had provided the basis for their own liberation.

Radical thinking about childhood freedom is strikingly evident in the *Children's Rights* magazine to which Diski had contributed in the early 1970s. However, the debate within this forum is also indicative of the volatile nature of the movement and of the inherent contradictions and tensions in its ideas. Diski's future husband Roger Marks was one of three original editors alongside Julian Hall and Andrée Harrison. By the third edition, Hall was on his own. Whether Harrison stepped down, like Marks, because of concern about too much focus on sexual rights of the child is unclear. The first editions had certainly shown sympathy for a greater openness about childhood sexuality. One statement from psychiatrist Robert Ollendorff, a member of the editorial advisory board, gave the impression, perhaps wrongly, that this was a position strongly endorsed by all those behind the magazine. 'All the people involved in Children's Rights, book or magazine,' wrote Ollendorff, 'will carry on the Freudian and Reichian formulation by stating that the integration of sexuality in the life of persons of any age is one of the major objects of our fight for the rights of children.'[61] The magazine also touched on controversial territory when it offered advice on gay rights within schools. Even, breastfeeding was advocated in terms of sexuality: 'a great erotic exchange', satisfying the 'lust' of the child, and depending upon the arousal of the mother—and thus her erect nipples—for success.[62] However, in truth, the emphasis of *Children's Rights* did lie elsewhere.

[61] *Children's Rights*, 1 (1971), 14.
[62] Leila Berg, 'Into the Dangerous World', *Children's Rights*, 3 (1971), 1–4.

At the very centre of debate within the journal were the politics of children's rights within the institutional setting of the school. The first edition opened with a piece by Bernard Coard on racism in British education. Then Michael Duane, the headmaster who had tried unsuccessfully to introduce radical progressive methods at Risinghill comprehensive school in the mid-1960s, led a discussion on Illich's *Deschooling Society* and Keith Paton's *The Great Brain Robbery* (the latter a British underground contribution on the subject). Interestingly, in Duane's view, much of what Illich was saying about the failings of modern education was, in fact, there already in British studies of the subject. He pointed in particular to J. W. B. Douglas's work on the relationship between home environment and success or lack of success at school and to Basil Bernstein's recent work on social class and linguistic ability.[63] The problem was that the mainstream system hid its failings and gave little opportunity for alternative voices—as Duane had discovered at Risinghill. The result was a pressure-cooker situation, which in his view was about to explode: 'a mood of resentment and revolt, not only among the younger generation of teachers but among the younger generation of social workers'. Duane addressed these groups, teachers in particular, calling, not for a deschooling of society (or at least he felt that this term had wrongly come to be understood as an absolute rejection of education), but for a 'disestablishment of education': a route of radicalizing the existing system, and of encouraging more of the 'free schools' which were appearing in this period.

Along with Duane, a group of illustrious commentators offered support and credibility as editorial advisers for *Children's Rights*. This included two leading American authorities, Paul Adams and John Holt. Adams was a psychiatrist, a Quaker, and a socialist, and had made his name as a writer in educational and psychiatric journals. Holt was the influential author of *How Children Fail* and *The Underachieving School*, where he attacked mainstream education, and he was an advocate of the idea that real learning was what went on outside of school altogether. The remaining advisers represented the way that this American debate was not simply being transplanted to Britain—Holt had suggested that there was a tendency for what happens in America to always happen in Britain seven to eight years later—but in fact also drew on its own deep national roots. As a schoolchild and anti-fascist in the 1930s, and then as a young teacher during the Spanish civil war, Leila Berg had already been involved in a struggle to extend political activism within the sphere of education. After the war, she had gone on to a mission of writing children's books—notably her *Little Nippers* series—which radically broke with middle-class convention in engaging with the lives of the most deprived children, based on her philosophy (paralleling the ethos of environmental education) that children only learnt to read if they felt that they were accepted. She also wrote a successful account of Duane's Risinghill experiment, and she was in the process of writing a new book, *Look at Kids*, which would provide one of the most intriguing

---

[63] J. W. B. Douglas, *The Home and the School* (London, 1964); Basil Bernstein, *Theoretical Studies towards A Sociology Of Language* (London, 1971).

statements on the importance of looking at landscape from the perspective of the child.[64] Another adviser was Nan Berger, a member of the National Council for Civil Liberties (NCCL), and author of the NCCL's *The Rights of Children and Young Persons* (1967). Finally, a link to the longer British tradition of radical education came in the figure of A. S. Neill, the now famous headmaster of Summerhill school, which had been founded in 1921.[65] Advertised in *Children's Rights*, the deeper roots of the movement were also being explored by the new radical group of historians, History Workshop, which held one of its early conferences on the theme of 'Children's Liberation'. The conference included a paper by radical teacher Chris Searle and a paper on 'The Theories of Basil Bernstein', but also historical papers by Dave Marson on 'Children's Strikes in 1911', Raphael Samuel on 'Struggle against School in Nineteenth Century London', Anna Davin on 'London Work Girls', and Peter Burke on 'The Origins of the Idea of Childhood'.[66]

The children's rights movement had also published a book to coincide with the launch of the new magazine. Here, a series of contributions from the editorial advisers offered expert analysis of the history of efforts in the area and of the legal, psychiatric, and educational dimensions of the question.[67] By contrast, the magazine rapidly moved in a very different direction: adopting the cut-and-paste and cartoon-adorned style of the radical underground journals of the era, establishing itself through advice, letters pages, and listings of local initiatives as a forum for practical activism, and developing a far more confrontational rhetoric. Crucially, it also began to address not just radical teachers but children themselves. The shift in direction was evident in a 'Communique' from the 'Children's Angry Brigade'. Presented in suitably angry capitals and bold font, it was little less than a call to arms, in the voice of and directed at school children themselves:

CHILDREN'S ANGRY BRIGADE COMMUNIQUE NO. 1

WARNING FROM CA BRIGADE

EDUCATION CAN DAMAGE YOUR MIND

WE ARE TIRED OF BEING A REPRESSED GENERATION. OUR GENERA-TION IS REPRESSED BY CENSORSHIP LAWS, AGE REGULATIONS, SCHOOL ? (PRISONS), AND SADLY OUR OWN PARENTS. NO LONGER SHALL WE ACCEPT THIS REPRESSION. WE ARE ANGRY. THE ONLY HOPE FOR A FUTURE SOCIETY LIES IN US. THE PRESENT SYSTEM OF INDOCTRINATION WILL FAIL TO MAKE WAY FOR THE NEW EDUCA-TION. THE REPRINTING OF AN UNCENSORED 'LITTLE RED SCHOOL

---

[64] Leila Berg, *Look at Kids* (London, 1972); Patricia Holland, *Picturing Childhood: The Myth of the Child in Popular Imagery* (London, 2004), 98–103.

[65] Jonathan Croall, *Neill of Summerhill—The Permanent Rebel* (London, 1983).

[66] History Workshop had its first meeting in 1967 at Ruskin College in Oxford. The 'Children's Liberation' meeting was advertised as 'History Workshop 6' on the back cover of *Children's Rights*, 3 (1971). This was well before the launch of *History Workshop Journal* in 1976. The first issue of the journal noted in a preface the early interest in children, with three of the twelve pamphlets published before 1976 on the subject of children and two on education. This included Dave Marson and Billy Cohnlle, 'Fall in and Follow Me, a Play about the Children's Strikes of 1911'.

[67] Paul Adams, Leila Berg, Nan Berger, Michael Duane, A. S. Neill, and Robert Ollendorff, *Children's Rights* (London, 1971).

BOOK' FOR FREE DISTRIBUTION WAS OUR FIRST ACT. WE SHALL NOT
LIMIT OURSELVES TO NON-VIOLENT ACTS IF THE SCHOOL SITUATION
PERSISTS. ANGRY PEOPLE ARE VERY DANGEROUS TO ANY SYSTEM. NO
LONGER DO WE ACCEPT BLIND ORDERS FROM OUR ADVERSARIES.
NEVER DO WE GROW UP LIKE THEM. ALL SABOTAGE IS EFFECTIVE IN
HIERARCHICAL SYSTEMS LIKE SCHOOLS—UNSCREW LOCKS, SMASH
TANNOYS, PAINT BLACKBOARDS RED, GRIND ALL THE CHALK TO
DUST—YOU'RE ANGRY—YOU KNOW WHAT TO DO.

The attempt to act as a direct line to children themselves, and the willingness to encourage strategies of sabotage, rapidly came to dominate. Children were encouraged to recognize that there was nothing wrong with not going to school and were advised to present truancy as a mode of protest.[68] And efforts began to focus on distribution of the magazine within schools. Viv Berger, a schoolboy, who was one of those involved in production of the controversial 'School Kids' issue of *Oz* magazine, now became an influential voice and advocate of 'Pupil Power' in *Children's Rights*, and was soon added to the list of editorial advisers.[69] Letters from children came to predominate in the lively correspondence pages. And notices began to appear publicizing a series of magazines, such as *(Hackney) Miscarriage* and the Oxford-based *Brain Damage,* produced by school children themselves.

However, the move in this direction unearthed a series of tensions and contradictions. *Children's Rights* had developed out of a longer tradition in progressive education and reflected the thinking of radical teachers and educationalists, and to some extent the radical parent. However, the new stance on child rights suggested that the role of teachers and parents was inherently malign; indeed, that it was time to challenge the very categories of the teacher and the parent. As Keith Paton put it, children's rights needed to 'evaporate' teachers' rights over children. It was also time to dissolve the category of the parent. Liberated children could lead the way, showing their parents the route to a true self-realization beyond the confined strictures of parenthood.[70]

There were soon signs of misgivings about the tone and direction of the deschooling rhetoric. For instance, the thirteen-year-old daughter of a progressive teacher wrote in to say that she was disturbed by the calls for 'power to the kids' and by the encouragement of vandalism.[71] However, the issue came to a head with publication of the 'Children's Bust Book' edition of the magazine. Clearly, the complaints had begun even before publication: copies of the issue were accompanied by a disclaimer from the Editor that the edition was entirely his responsibility and that he had received objections from some members of the editorial advisory board

[68] 'Truancy', *Children's Rights*, 1 (1971), 13.
[69] Viv Berger, 'Pupil Power', *Children's Rights*, 2 (1971), 27–8. The 'School Kids' issue of *Oz* was published on 28 May 1970. Viv Berger was 15 at the time of the Oz trial in 1971. He reflected back on this in the *Independent* (19 December 2007). It is possible that he was related to Nan Berger. Music journalist Charles Shaar Murray was another of the Oz kids: 'I Was an Oz School Kid', *Guardian* (2 August 2001).
[70] Keith Paton, 'Children's Rights or Learners' Rights?', *Children's Rights*, 3 (1971), 29–31.
[71] Letter from Jennifer Hyams, 'What are we aiming for', *Children's Rights*, 4 (April–May 1972), 9.

including Leila Berg and Michael Duane. The seven-page 'Bust Book' offered advice to children on the process of arrest and on what they could do to defend themselves against the police on the street. The anti-authoritarian tone is indicated in advice against cooperation in court: 'They only have as much power as you let them have. To smash it, you have to fight back. Attack everything they say about or against you. Keep fighting right from the time you get nicked.' This was advice from a perspective that saw the law as illegitimate. It was also advice that appeared keen to inflame resistance, rather than simply to protect the rights of the child. A 'Bust Book' part two was intended for the next edition of the magazine, offering advice on how to abscond arrest, but it never appeared.[72] Instead, the next and final edition of *Children's Rights* saw an abrupt halt to the call to arms. It announced the sacking of the editor, Julian Hall. A new format, without the glossy front covers, reflected the financial problems that appear to have followed the Bust Book edition.[73] And letters from Leila Berg, John Holt, Michael Duane, and A. S. Neill set out objections to the Bust Book, condemning it as irresponsible and inflammatory. Neill also questioned the approach of directly addressing children, suggesting that the real need was to change parental attitudes.[74] Reprimanded for its childishness, the energy, which had sustained this intriguing explosion of a child-rights politics, now began to collapse.[75]

A journal like *Children's Rights* and its surrounding culture of school students spurred on to rebellion provides us with an example of the way in which liberation of the child became a mantra of radical education in the early 1970s. This did build on earlier roots, but it was spurred on by a young generation who saw the child's loss of freedom as a natural next frontier in their own struggle for liberation. Though this culture did cross over with environmental education, it took an increasingly radical turn, particularly once it moved from being a project of realizing the vision of educational progressives to one of turning over increasing control to children themselves. The resulting tensions meant that these projects were difficult to sustain. Their significance nevertheless is in pushing the implications of taking into consideration the child's perspective to a new level, and as a consequence pushing this way of thinking towards a breaking point.

THE POLITICS OF PLAY

In 1973, Colin Ward reflected on the difficulty in realizing the post-Skeffington ambition for a new participative planning process. Clearly, the ambition appealed to his anarchist sensibilities. But he was well aware that for all the rhetoric about consultation, the reality was often a process of simply talking to the public about

---

[72] 'Children's Bust Book—Part I', *Children's Rights*, 5 (May–June 1972), 14–21.
[73] Publisher's Letter (Michael Duane), *Children's Rights*, 6 (July–August 1972), 4.
[74] 'Bust-Book Feedback', *Children's Rights*, 6 (July–August 1972), 8–9.
[75] Though for an indication of the interest in radical thinking among new teachers in this period: Michael Smith, 'The Alternative Press and Teacher Education: A Review', *British Journal of Teacher Education*, 1 (1975), 55–62.

what had already been done in their name. Looking to the work of American sociologist Richard Sennett and his book on identity and city life, *The Uses of Disorder*,
Ward wondered whether it was time to question the value of planning altogether.[76]
Play, and in particular the adventure playground, provided in Ward's view an 'anarchist parable' of a different way forward. Here, the traditional playground of swings
and tarmac now came to represent all that was wrong, and inherently authoritarian, about top-down planning. These were spaces based on the flawed premise that
design could provide the necessary environment for free play. For all the apparent
playfulness of a new modernism, this remained a fundamental problem. Nevertheless, for Ward, the adventure playground still offered some hope. Here, the contra-
design principle of starting afresh each year could help ensure that these sites were
always a reflection of the creativity of the child rather than the planner.

However, there was an inevitable tendency even for these radical spaces to
become more institutionalized and less spontaneous over time. Adventure playground pioneer Joe Benjamin had become less optimistic by the 1970s. For Benjamin,
the creation of any special play space, even the adventure playground, raised the
fundamental dilemma of whether such policies in fact exacerbated and facilitated
a tendency of modern life to segregate child and adult life. Yes, it was difficult not
to look with some satisfaction at the increase in number of adventure playgrounds
over the past twenty-five years—with now around 20 permanent sites in London
alone, 70 across the country, and an estimated 1,700 holiday schemes—but in the
process the project had unfortunately lost its 'sense of purpose'. The dynamism of
the adventure playground lay in the way that the idea had sprung not just from
adult philanthropy and social work but crucially from the way that children had
taken the issue into their own hands through their occupation of bombsites. But
over time these spaces had often been turned into extensions of the traditional
playground:

> The swings and slides of the engineer have been replaced by those of the scrap
> merchant: the tubular steel frame of the equipment manufacturer by the GPO tele-
> graph pole or the British Railway sleeper; the chain by the rope, the wood swing seat
> by an old tyre. What is worse, they are leader inspired and built with a permanence in
> mind which is rejected by the children and, perhaps arguably, is a contributing factor
> to the vandalism they suffer.[77]

Real play was in inherent contradiction with such institutionalization. It demanded
independence. The urban landscape had to be reclaimed by the child, not parcelled
off in specialized and inevitably sanitized child-friendly zones. Yes, the modern
urban environment might be a dangerous one. But rather than hiding the child

---

[76] Colin Ward, *Anarchy in Action* (London, 1973), p. 61. Sennett's *The Uses of Disorder: Personal Identity and City Life* (New York, 1970), like other statements of the radical urban environmentalism of the 1970s, now attracts new attention as a prescient statement and was republished in 2008.

[77] Joe Benjamin, *Grounds for Play: An Extension of In Search of Adventure* (London, 1974), p. 2. The earlier edition, under the title *In Search of Adventure*, had been first published in 1968. By 1974, Benjamin was working as an Administrative Adviser in Community Work at North East London Polytechnic.

away, or looking for a romanticized 'natural' environment, it was these unregulated spaces of the modern city that provided exactly what the modern child needed. 'The point is', argued Benjamin, 'that the streets, the local service station, the housing estate stairway—indeed, anything our community offers, is part of the natural environment of the child. Our problem is not to design streets, housing, a petrol station or shops that can lend themselves to play, but to educate society to accept children on a participatory basis.'[78] In short, Benjamin recognized the danger of the logic of the post-war landscape of the child: a future of specialized ghettoes and sanctuaries for modern childhood, designed by those who, in good faith, believed that children needed to live in environments adapted to the way the child saw the world. And despite recognizing some positive developments in the 1970s, such as environmental education, Benjamin lamented the way that play was in danger of becoming institutionalized, particularly in the middle classes, where children 'overburdened with up to two hours' homework each night, pressed to play games for the school at week-ends, and subject to constant parental pressures and "educational toys" are, as far as play is concerned, among the most deprived sections of the child community'.[79] The landscape of deprivation, in short, was being turned on its head.

By the early 1970s, local communities and social workers had taken on board the message that children and play were central to a new politics of helping communities take back control of their cities. The jobs pages of a journal such as *New Society* reflected this, with a flood of posts for local play workers.[80] The emerging importance of play in relation to community activism is highlighted in a series of studies on the Notting Hill area of London stretching across the period from the late 1950s to the early 1970s. The race riots of 1958 had initially drawn attention to social problems in the area. And here one of the early responses, led in fact by Lady Allen of Hurtwood, had been to set up a local adventure playground in 1960. Psychologist Marie Jahoda and social work leader Eileen Younghusband also became involved. They took a lead in setting up the North Kensington Family Study, seeing it as a case study in moving beyond a strategy of solving social problems by pulling down slums to one of looking at the human roots of deprivation and working with people instead. One outcome was the 1964 survey, *A Troubled Area*, undertaken by social worker Pearl Jephcott, a new type of study of the relationship between housing, immigration, community relations, and self-help in which Jephcott again identified the vital importance of compensating for the 'home that gives no scope for play or hobbies'.[81] Another was the setting up of the

---

[78] Benjamin, *Grounds for Play*, p. 3.   [79] Benjamin, *Grounds for Play*, p. 89.
[80] For instance, posts in provision of play advertised in January 1975 included a full-time Playleader for the Arbury Adventure Playground Association (2 January); a post in Playleadership and Community Development for Camden County Council (9 January); posts at the Save the Children Fund, the Handicapped Adventure Playground Association (Playleader and Assistant Playleader), and at the Triangle Adventure Playground (all 16 January); a Playleader post at the Queen Elizabeth Hospital for Children, and a Playground Organiser for Wolverhampton Borough Council (23 January); and posts for the Westminster Play Association and as an Adventure Playleader in Knowsley (30 January).
[81] Pearl Jephcott, *A Troubled Area: Notes on Notting Hill* (London, 1964), p. 108.

North Kensington Playgroups Committee, with aid from the Save the Children Fund. By 1964, there were three playgroups in the area run by local mothers: part of that response from below to the challenge of childcare discussed in the earlier chapter on Bowlbyism, but also reflective of the desire to move beyond an era of welfare and charity, to one of participation.[82] In the late 1960s, the politics of play in Notting Hill took a further turn. Play now became a symbol and a central language for an increasingly subversive, social effort to reclaim the city and its space. Counter-cultural radicals initially turned to the language of play in setting up the London 'Free School' in 1966, in fact more a venture in self-help and adult education. Then from 1967 they began setting up play schemes and closing down local streets so that children could play without the danger of traffic. The focus on play was sparked by several local children being run over by cars. More fundamentally, it was a perfect subject for playing out situationist theories about the subversion of space while at the same time grounding this in some of the everyday realities and needs of family life. And it was a subject that linked radical epistemology to real material concerns in the local area: the effects of the private housing market on space; and the violations of community interest in the planning of the roads and flyover that began to cut through the area. The links were made manifest in the setting up of a series of play sites. An adventure playground was opened right under the new elevated Westway flyover. Three local streets were turned into play-streets. But most spectacular of all were the efforts to take over the locked and largely unused private gardens in Powis Square, with children and adult protesters (including a group of situationists dressed up as pantomime animals) pulling down the gates and staging an occupation of the site. In response, the council came to an agreement with the owners to convert the gardens into a play space. However, this led to further confrontation as demonstrators attempted to block contractors sent in to turn the gardens into the sort of place that the planners and paternalists understood as a playground—a square of tarmac, surrounded by a fence—rather than the more subversive free space that had captured the radical imagination. Such pressure also led the local council to set up a Play Association in 1970. Play, which had previously been something provided only by voluntary groups or through self-help, consequently became a responsibility of local government in the area and attracted increasing funding: from an estimated £5 in 1967, to £40,000 by 1974.[83]

In summary, the politics of outside play had emerged by the late 1960s and early 1970s as a central battleground in grass-roots radical efforts to counter lost childhood freedom within the urban landscape. Children's play provided a practical focus but also a perfect symbol for a radical epistemology about the subversion of space. Efforts could be directed at the provision of playgroups and playgrounds, and there was some success in moving beyond voluntary effort to the securing of

---

[82] Roger Mitton and Elizabeth Morrison, *A Community Project in Notting Dale* (London, 1972).

[83] Jan O'Malley, *The Politics of Community Action: A Decade of Struggle in Notting Hill* (Nottingham, 1977); Tom Vague, *Notting Hill History Timeline*, Chapter 11, 'Open the Squares': <http://www.vaguerants.org.uk/wp-content/pageflip/upload/TL/timelinechap11.pdf>.

statutory funding. But the message was ultimately a more challenging one: the whole urban environment needed to be the playground for childhood; and the trend towards institutionalizing children that tended to result from this (and which included the provision of special play spaces) threatened to make the problem worse.

AN ENVIRONMENT FOR VANDALISM

In 1973, Ward edited a volume of essays on *Vandalism* which pushed debate about the landscape of the child into further controversial territory. This language of 'vandalism' had become prominent in the late 1960s and early 1970s.[84] Critics of social and moral decline drew on the term with increasing regularity to point to the paradox of an apparent increase in mindless violence among the young despite all the improvements in economic well-being over the past decades. It was particularly coming to be associated with anxieties about damage to the urban environment, and with the 'concrete jungle' that appeared to be emerging out of the visions of post-war planners. Though most obviously associated with concern about inner-city areas and the poor, it was also a concept that was extended out to include militant middle-class students. Radicals, on the other hand, attempted to recast vandalism as an extension of children's play, and as an outcome of expecting children to grow up in such an environment.

Ward's volume was heavily influenced by deviancy theory, and had contributions from a new generation of radical criminologists such as Stanley Cohen.[85] However, it also reflected the psychological turn in thinking about environment. It presented vandalism, not just as an issue of why and how society came to define its rules of acceptable behaviour and deviance, but also as a product of the way that children and young people perceived, understood, and experienced their environment. The volume did not deny the significance of destructive behaviour, though there was no attempt to measure this or to test the notion of such an increase in vandalism. It was more interested in the talk itself, and in the way that a new language and apparatus was emerging in response. Building on the insight that children had their own perspective, it challenged conventional thinking about the very nature of vandalism and its diagnosis and cure.

A starting premise for the volume was that the vandalism of young people paled in comparison to the vandalism of the developers and the affluent society, which had devastated a liveable landscape for the child. Addiction to the car, in particular, had 'destroyed the human habitat at the point of departure, at the destination and

---

[84] This is evident for instance on a new public campaign in 1969: 'Poster Plea on Vandalism', *The Times* (4 December 1969).

[85] A landmark in the new approach was Howard Becker's *The Outsiders* (New York, 1963). In Britain, the new criminology was marked by a series of publications in the early 1970s, for instance: Jock Young, Ian Taylor, and Paul Walton (eds), *The New Criminology* (London, 1973) and Stanley Cohen (ed.), *Images of Deviance* (London, 1971).

all along the route'.[86] Acts of vandalism needed to be understood as often necessary outlets for youthful energy in an environment which closed off other opportunities. Indeed, Cohen provocatively suggested that within this context, vandalism was 'just right': it was 'the ideal form of rule-breaking both in expressive (expressing certain values) and instrumental terms (solving certain problems). It is satisfying and provides just the right amount of risk.'[87]

Another of the contributors to the volume was the sociologist Laurie Taylor, who had recently published a book in collaboration with Cohen, and who had been part of the radical National Deviancy Symposium, which broke away from orthodox British criminology in the late 1960s.[88] Taylor drew on examples from experimental psychology to emphasize the need to move beyond, not just an essentialist view of delinquency, but also the view that delinquents were simply passive victims of their environment. He felt that an experiment in which psychologists had attempted to demonstrate that some people had more environmental sensitivity than others was particularly significant. In this experiment the psychologists had set out to measure the length of time that people could put up with conditions of sensory deprivation before pushing a panic button. What the experiment also uncovered was something in some ways even more interesting, and something particularly important for social science. It found that even under normal conditions (before the onset of sensory deprivation), people were already more inclined to hit the button if they believed they were part of an experiment. In other words, it was the meaning of any situation, rather than simply the actual conditions, which were the key to behaviour. This raised an important question in relation to a powerful sociological tradition, going back to the Chicago school of ecological sociology in the 1930s, which had assumed that conditions such as delinquency could be mapped against environmental determinants. And as Taylor pointed out, such a philosophy was now at the heart of many of the arguments about the failings of post-war planning, and was the logic, for instance, for seeing high-rise living as a determinant of a childhood gone wrong (though now, with blame focusing on too much planning, the logic of the 1930s—that causation lay in the chaos and lack of order in urban life—had been turned on its head). The problem was that such research invariably failed to ask what the environment meant to the delinquents themselves. So when children vandalized their council flats and carefully

[86] Colin Ward (ed.), *Vandalism* (London, 1973), p. 18.

[87] Stanley Cohen, 'Property and Destruction: Motives and Meaning', in Ward (ed.), *Vandalism*.

[88] For Jock Young's reflections on this breakaway: <http://www.malcolmread.co.uk/JockYoung/Critical.htm>. Young notes that the National Deviancy Conference meetings also provided an impetus for a broad range of radical thinking: 'The NDC was hectic, irreverent, transgressive and, above all, fun. It took no notice of disciplinary boundaries, it was as important an arena for the emerging field of cultural studies (Stuart Hall, Mike Featherstone, Paul Willis, Dick Hebdidge, all gave papers), antipsychiatry (Peter Sedgwick, Jeff Coulter), critical legal theory (Boaventura de Sousa Santos and Sol Picciotto), the sociology of sexualities (Ken Plummer, Mary McIntosh), as it was for the sociology of deviance.' By contrast, the central figure in the criminological establishment in this period, Professor Leon Radzinowicz, would dismiss the seriousness of the breakaway in his memoir *Adventures in Criminology* (London, 1999), pp. 229–30. For reflections on this period: Paul Walton and Jock Young (eds), *The New Criminology Revisited* (London, 1998).

laid public flowerbeds, the inclination was to conclude that they were reacting against a planned environment and against the loss of the freedom of the slums and the open bombsites of the past. Taylor argued that attention needed to shift to meaning from the perspective of the children themselves. And he suggested that in this particular instance a key factor in such behaviour may have been the fact that these children knew that the flats and the flowers belonged to someone else. In short, one had to understand the child's view of the environment, not just the material circumstances. Indeed, on its own, he argued, 'No amount of objective environmental manipulation' would dissipate vandalism; it was 'palpably absurd' to believe that one could solve the problem of the ghetto by simply opening a few adventure playgrounds.[89] The second implication of the psychological research was that in a world in which social science was increasingly a commonplace in the logic of everyday life, there was also a need to recognize how awareness of being a subject of study (the panic button phenomenon) and awareness of the nomenclature that social science used to order modern life were now inherent elements in experience and its meaning. So when criminologists and sociologists were studying the vandal, they were in fact studying an increasingly self-conscious 'vandal', shaped by and responding to society's efforts to define and control this identity.[90] Again, this had major implications when it came to understanding the meaning of their actions.

These challenges of looking at vandalism from the perspective of the young people involved led the new criminologists to break down the barriers between themselves and their subjects. This was typified by a study of boys in Liverpool in the early 1970s, which outlined the researchers' detailed efforts at crossing into the world of their subjects through sharing in the boys' boozing, joining in with their football, and adopting their dress and grooming.[91] The next step was to describe and interpret vandalism from this perspective. One of the essays in Ward's *Vandalism* volume adopted this approach. Its title—'Hey mister, this is what we really do …'—summed up the new spirit. Based on the study of a single day in an area of Bradford, the researchers were keen to emphasize the 'purposive and creative' forms that delinquency took. However, they were also keen to frame and validate acts of vandalism in a language of the political; and here they were surely in fact projecting their own sympathies. When a group of six year olds smashed a lock on a park, they described it, 'from the kid's point of view', as a 'real blow for Play Power'. They suggested that the very idea of the park, particularly when it was locked or supervised by the 'parkie', was 'totalitarian', unfavourably contrasting it to areas where children took play into their own hands by appropriating supermarket trolleys and creating climbing games with empty crates. They were keen, once again, to cast such behaviour as a form of subversion, rather than mere meaningless

---

[89] Laurie Taylor, 'The Meaning of the Environment', in Ward (ed.), *Vandalism*, p. 58.
[90] On the shift from an ecological approach to one that took into account a feedback effect but also the development of subcultures: Owen Gill, *Luke Street: Housing Policy, Conflict and the Creation of the Delinquent Area* (London, 1977).
[91] Howard Parker, *View from the Boys: A Sociology of Down-Town Adolescents* (London, 1974).

vandalism, and keen too to point to a class prejudice at the heart of the different handling of the issues of the hippy and the vandal in the media: 'If the Play Power of middle-class flower children can be seen as a purposive revolt against a consumer society, then the destruction of consumer technology to create objects of play must be seen as a necessarily illegal, but entirely purposive, attempt to use a technology the working-class kid cannot afford to ignore.'[92]

If the *Vandalism* volume indicates that radical criminology was among those fields that came together to challenge thinking about the landscape of the child at the start of the 1970s, the volume also offers intriguing insight into the potential responses among the architects whose role it was to design this landscape. This was a profession under increasing criticism. The media was encouraging the idea that the modern 'concrete jungle' was a root cause of delinquency and social break-down, and the colour supplements of the era provided the perfect medium for such exposure. The architects' award-winning designs seemed to be increasingly empty victories in the face of the new technology of the aerosol can and the felt-tip marker: unable to maintain their clean modernist aesthetic in the face of vandal-ism, but also visibly unable to claim a victory in planning the good life through the design of space. One of the responses was to turn to sociology. A survey of articles in the architectural press indicated that claims about good building design increas-ingly gestured in this direction. And reinforcing this reorientation, the Royal Insti-tute of British Architecture now integrated sociology within its own training programme.[93] Another response was to accept vandalism, not as an aberration, but as an inevitable part of the modern landscape, and to adapt architectural design accordingly. So we see architects offering detailed advice on which type of wall surfaces were best in coping with graffiti: which resisted marking, which were cleanable, which hardest to break, the rise of the ceramic mosaic wall partly to be explained by this. We find a new architecture of avoiding large open spaces, hidden nooks and crannies, and access to flat roofs, and a micro-level attention to conceal-ing vulnerable fixings and fittings, careful placement of prickly bushes, and the location of lavatories close to (otherwise fouled) lift areas. The post-war solution of designing special play areas to cater for the needs of children was by contrast seeing a loss of confidence. Architects needed to realize that playgrounds could never contain children; worse still, they attracted children from outside estates whose vandalism spilled over into the broader environment. It was better perhaps to accept that low level damage was an inevitable product of children's play and explo-ration. A strategy of upkeep and regular repair might be the best way forward.[94] If

---

[92] Ian Taylor and Paul Walton, 'Hey mister, this is what we really do …', in Ward (ed.), *Vandalism*, pp. 91–5. These debates find echoes in the response to riots in Britain in 2011, the controversy over whether there was any political dynamic to these actions or whether they simply reflected bad behav-iour, and the contrast in response to student demonstration over fees earlier in the year.

[93] Gail Armstrong and Mary Wilson, 'Delinquency and Some Aspects of Housing', in Ward (ed.), *Vandalism*, pp. 64–84.

[94] Alexander Miller, 'Vandalism and the Architect', in Ward (ed.), *Vandalism*, pp. 96–111. See also Farmer and Dark, 'The Architect's Dilemma—One Firm's Working Notes', pp. 112–16; and Alan Leather and Anthony Matthews, 'What the Architect Can Do: A Series of Design Guides', pp. 117–73.

this new vision can in some ways be seen as in line with the radical liberalism of early children's rights thinking, it also pointed towards a form of control that would in the longer term be a probably more important legacy for the landscape of the child. In its detail and its aspirations to micro-manage vandalism, this was an architecture that swapped the authoritarian power of the high-rise modernist statement for what was, in fact, a potentially far more pervasive governance of everyday space.[95]

Stanley Cohen recognized this extension of governance in the increasing range of strategies now deployed to cope with vandalism. Society was coming up with multiple solutions: guards and patrols, the micro-level design of modern architecture and the street furniture of the urban environment, education campaigns, experiments with close-circuit television, and even a reinforcement of the sanction of retribution. But this was all going to be hugely expensive. There was also very little evidence to suggest that it would work. The stark truth, argued Cohen, was that vandalism itself was the solution.[96] A case study of vandalism in Liverpool, where it was costing the city an estimated million pounds a year by the late 1960s, suggested that the approach of trying to deflect the problem by channelling resources into play facilities and setting up specific anti-vandalism schemes was generally doomed to failure.[97] In fact, turning vandalism into such a high profile social problem could come to be seen as having the effect of confirming it and making it even harder to eradicate.[98] Worst of all, defining particular areas as having a problem of vandalism risked alienating the very communities who were the best hope of doing something about this on the ground, while also promoting the identity of the vandal as a symbol for the disenchanted and a badge of alienated local pride.[99]

Until this point in the early 1970s, the design of a landscape for the child had been based on the assumption that provision of a good home life and of specialized landscapes for the cultivation of childhood beyond the home would help prevent delinquency. Indeed, the threat of delinquency had been an important factor in the energies which had been directed into efforts to build the new postwar landscape, its role in the origins of Bowlbyism a case in point. However, there had always been a tension within this vision: it was recognized that children needed freedom, and that naughtiness could be an expression of this basic drive and looked very different from the perspective of the child. In the initial

[95] Explored in detailed analysis of the pioneering Park Hill Estate in Sheffield: Matthew Hollow, 'Governmentality on the Park Hill Estate: The Rationality of Public Housing', *Urban History*, 37 (2010), 117–35.

[96] Stanley Cohen, 'Campaigning against Vandalism', in Ward (ed.), *Vandalism*, p. 257, 220–57.

[97] For broader indications of the concern on cost: 'The Price of Vandalism', *The Times* (23 February 1970).

[98] Similarly on the double-edged role of a discourse of race relations: Chris Waters, '"Dark Strangers in Our Midst": Discourses of Race and Nation in Britain, 1947–1963', *Journal of British Studies*, 36 (1997), 207–38.

[99] David Pullen, 'Community Involvement', in Ward (ed.), *Vandalism*, pp. 259–75.

post-war decades, this tension in the relationship between permissiveness and
delinquency was fairly comfortably contained. Now, radical voices were exploding the consensus. In the form of vandalism, delinquency was recast as inevitable
and even purposive, a natural and even healthy part of the young person's view
of the world. As such, it was time to move beyond efforts at redesigning the
environment to prevent and contain delinquency, and time to see it instead as
part of the fabric of modern life. Looking to the future, Ward suggested that
vandalism might become increasingly organized and even explicitly ideological
in its orientation. Linking vandalism to the modern phenomenon of adolescence, he saw no prospect of it dying away: the violence of the vandal as a form
of release for a generation frustrated by an absence of constructive outlets.[100]
This line of argument would become increasingly powerful in the 1970s, and it
would find a focus in relation to phenomena ranging from football hooliganism, to subcultural youth movements, Rastafarianism, and race riots.[101] Ward
saw no prospect of society properly addressing the issue: the illness, in reality,
for all the outcries, still more palatable than the solution. Perhaps the psycho-
analysts were right: perhaps it was a case of adult society seducing its young
delinquents into acting out its own deviant fantasies; the young performing the
role of scapegoats but also, in fact, shock-troops for their elders (a welcome
subject for vilification, but also a channel—at a distance—for exploring and
condemning their parents' own repressed attraction for breaking free of moral
shackles). Like others in the volume, Ward supported the case for giving the
working-class vandal the same licence for rebellion as that allowed to the
middle-class student radicals. Ultimately, he was tempted to agree with Guy
Debord, the French situationist in his 'Decline and Fall of the Spectacular
Commodity Economy' written in the aftermath of the riots in Watts, Los Ange-
les in 1965: vandalism could, in fact, be a sign of moral health and human
dignity. As such, the vandals of the British city of the 1970s were perhaps little
less than 'urban guerrillas involved in a struggle for the control of the environment'. And there were signs that children were even beginning to realize this,
Ward pointing to the way that kids were now deploying arguments about the
inadequacy of play facilities in accounting for their acts of vandalism. Modern
British society, in short, was seeing a new sort of land-use conflict, children pit-
ted against adults, armed not just with the weapon of unbounded play and
nuisance but now also with the language of social science.[102]

[100] Here he drew on Frank Musgrove's analysis, *Youth and the Social Order* (London, 1974).
[101] Such work was particularly associated with the Centre for Contemporary Cultural Studies at
the University of Birmingham, which had links with the earliest meetings of the National Deviancy
Conference and which also played a major role in investigation of questions of race following on
from studies of educational inequality. For other aspects of the Centre's history: Norma Schulman,
'Conditions of Their Own Making: An Intellectual History of the Centre for Contemporary Cultural Studies at the University of Birmingham', *Canadian Journal of Communication*, 18:1 (1993),
51–73.
[102] Ward, 'The Future of Vandalism', in Ward (ed.), *Vandalism*, pp. 276–311.

RETREAT AND AFTERMATH

By the time Colin Ward's *Child in the City* was published in 1978, the radical moment of which it was part was drawing to a close. A series of public scandals heralded a retreat of child liberation and environmentalist thinking within mainstream education. The rejection of traditional academic approaches, while finding some continuing support from radical local authorities, teachers, and social workers, could also upset parents and was soon attracting criticism in the media. At the Sir John Cass School in Stepney, teacher Chris Searle in environmentalist vein—he called it 'critical literacy'—encouraged his pupils to write about their own lives in a way that connected with broader political struggles. The controversial nature of this writing in a series of booklets under the title *Stepney Words* eventually led to Searle's dismissal.[103] More well known is the scandal over discipline and an undermining of academic standards which developed in response to efforts to introduce teaching designed to help disadvantaged children at the William Tyndale School in London.[104] Such cases fuelled a debate over the damaging effects of progressive pedagogy that had been building since publication of a series of counterblasts which came to be known as the *Black Papers*.[105]

The *Black Papers* backlash was one of the issues taken up by Conservative Party ideologue Keith Joseph, in his notorious Birmingham speech in 1974, where he attacked the effects of progressivism within education and social work.[106] He cast blame on the way in which liberals had come to condone 'antisocial' behaviour, either as a form of legitimate protest against an unjust society or in terms of liberation (and thus how the views of a volume like Ward's *Vandalism* or of radical inner-city teachers and social workers had become part of a new orthodoxy). This, and not just the premise of moving away from selection, was why comprehensive schools were in his view proving such a disaster. For Joseph, the crisis of behaviour reflected much that was wrong with the post-war settlement. This was a settlement which had seen politicians far too focused on economic solutions. The need now was for 'remoralization'. Prosperity and the welfare state on their own had failed to solve social problems, and at the centre of this failure was the child. Real incomes had risen beyond what anyone dreamed was possible a generation earlier, and so had education and welfare budgets, but for Joseph the paradox of affluence was that 'so also have delinquency, truancy, vandalism, hooliganism, illiteracy, and decline in educational standards'. Such a statement marked a loss of faith in the

---

[103] See the special issue on Chris Searle in *Race and Class*, 51:2 (2009). Searle reflected on his pedagogy in *None But Our Words: Critical Literacy in Classroom and Literacy* (Buckingham, 1997). Searle publicized the children's strike in response to the attack on 'Stepney Words' in *Children's Rights*, 3 (1971), 32–3.

[104] John Davis, 'The Inner London Education Authority and the William Tyndale School Affair, 1974–1978', *Oxford Review of Education*, 28 (2002), 275–98.

[105] C. B. Cox and A. E. Dyson (eds), *The Black Papers on Education* (London, 1971); Adrian Wooldridge, *Measuring the Mind: Education and Psychology in England, c. 1860–1990* (Cambridge, 1994), pp. 384–93.

[106] Speech of Sir Keith Joseph at the Grand Hotel, Edgbaston, Birmingham, 19 October 1974: <http://www.margaretthatcher.org/document/101830>. For a detailed account of the events surrounding the speech: Andrew Denham and Mark Garnett, *Keith Joseph* (Chesham, 2001), pp. 265–76.

morality of the post-war settlement, which had been spawned in the emphasis on love and tolerance within the home, and which had been taken forward by a new generation of professionals and social scientists who tried to take into account the child's view of the world.

Joseph presented himself, like pioneer of the uprising against permissiveness Mary Whitehouse, as speaking from the margins, battling against the permissive establishment. However, a broader shift of direction within education was signalled in 1976 when even Labour Prime Minister James Callaghan, in a speech at Ruskin College, announced his own determination to ensure that educational progressivism did not get out of hand. Indeed, he promised 'to slam the lid and screw it securely down'.[107] Teachers also expressed growing concern, particularly about a decline of discipline and rising levels of violence in schools, and this was exacerbated by drug use, which was emerging as a growing problem from the mid-1970s.[108] By the end of the decade, the attack upon a progressivism which had gone too far in its efforts to liberate the child had broad purchase.[109] This contributed to the groundswell of opinion that enabled a retreat from the post-war settlement after the election of Margaret Thatcher in 1979. In fact, it took some time for the Conservative critique of progressivism to be translated into policy in the sphere of education, delayed until after the election of 1983 and Joseph's appointment as Secretary of State for Education.[110] However, the energy of the progressive movement was already dissipating. Free school initiatives, which had blossomed in the early 1970s, struggled to survive due to problems of finance, their dependence on charismatic leadership, and then the shifts in educational policy later in the 1980s.[111] More fundamentally, a turn against child-centred progressivism, attempts to improve discipline, a shift of power away from the local authorities and teachers who were blamed for an errant progressivism, an increasing emphasis on auditing academic results, and then eventually the introduction of a national curriculum in 1988, all contributed to a retreat of environmental education and its vision of using school as a vehicle for challenging and transforming the increasingly confined position of children within their local communities.

The retreat of environmental education was also a reflection of a broader faltering in support of Community Developments Projects as a solution to social deprivation.[112] Those who worked in the projects often came to reject the assumption

[107] Brian Simon, *Education and the Social Order, 1940–1990* (London, 1991), pp. 446–51; M. Punch, *Progressive Retreat* (London, 1977).

[108] For instance: 'Teachers Concerned about Increase in School Violence', *The Times* (25 March 1975).

[109] 'Sir Keith Calls for "Remoralization" and Reassertion of Civilized Values', *The Times* (21 October 1974). For further signs of mounting concern over progressivism within comprehensives and a link to vandalism: 'Social Engineering for Children', *The Times* (6 June 1974); 'Education: A Sorry Tale of Two Conflicting Cultures in the Country's Classrooms', *The Times* (18 July 1974).

[110] For an account of the shifts of the 1980s: Adrian Wooldridge, *Measuring the Mind: Education and Psychology in England, c. 1860–1990* (Cambridge, 1994), pp. 398–408. On Joseph's role: Denham and Garnett, *Keith Joseph*, pp. 366–407.

[111] John Shotton, *No Master High or Low: Libertarian Education and Schooling in Britain, 1890–1990* (Bristol, 1993), 252.

[112] Glen O'Hara, *Governing Post-War Britain: The Paradoxes of Progress, 1951–1973* (Basingstoke, 2012), pp. 178–90.

that social problems could be solved through education and mobilization of local energies alone. Increasingly, they saw deprivation instead as an issue rooted in structural inequality and deindustrialization, and one to be addressed through oppositional political tactics rather than community volunteering.[113] A report by the Centre for Environmental Studies in 1977 dismissed the government's strategy as simply 'gilding the ghetto', more interested in managing the poor than in eradicating poverty.[114] From the government perspective, there was also a rapid dimming of enthusiasm, particularly after the oil crisis of 1974 put strain on funding. As early as 1973, there was a feeling that a scheme which had been set up to foster community cooperation in solving social problems had in fact often veered towards diagnosing issues instead in economic terms and too often looked to conflict rather than cooperation as the way forward.[115] By the mid-1970s, government was coming to see the Centre for Environmental Studies—the research unit that they had supported to chart progress of the schemes—as both too costly and too ideological.[116] And by the 1980s, the idea of addressing the problems of deprived areas by community group activity had made way for an era of managerial solutions and hope in the private sector as the source of a new form of social entrepreneurialism. Although inner-city problems were exacerbated by economic recession and unemployment, local authority funding for urban development fell after a cut in the rate support grant from central government. Under the Conservative administrations of the 1980s, the new focus was on tackling urban deprivation via urban development corporations. Here, the success in urban property renewal tended to benefit the wealthier sections of society, but the benefits for the poorest via a trickle-down effect have been seen as less impressive.[117]

If one cause of transition was that radicalism had overstretched itself and provoked a reaction, another was that a new generation of social scientists would come to recognize that post-war approaches to childhood had been characterized by several fundamental limitations. The first of these was the tendency to universalize the child of the post-war landscape settlement. The emerging recognition of how poverty and ethnicity complicated thinking in this area has already been noted. There was also a growing appreciation that the child of the landscape settlement had invariably been a male child.[118] This was the case in early concern about

---

[113] Loney, *Community against Government*.

[114] 'Initiatives on Poverty Have Failed', *The Times* (23 February 1977). The criticism of community action was reiterated in the work of a leading figure within the Centre for Environmental Studies, Cynthia Cockburn: *The Local State: Management of Cities and People* (London, 1977).

[115] 'Social Help from Conflict', *The Times* (26 March 1973).

[116] For the debate about withdrawal of funding: 'Grant Cut Closes Deprivation Unit', *The Times* (22 January 1976); 'Minister Reverses his Decision to Close Poverty Studies Unit', *The Times* (11 February 1976).

[117] Timothy Whitton, 'The Impact of the Community Development Projects on Assessing Urban Deprivation', in M. Charlot (ed.), *Britain's Inner Cities* (Paris, 1994), pp. 9–22; M. K. Smith, 'Community Work', in *The Encyclopedia of Informal Education*: <http://www.infed.org/community/b-comwrk.htm>; Monica O'Brien Castro, 'On the Privatization of Inner Cities: The British Conservative Government's Urban Policy from 1979-to the 1990s', Paper to Urban History Annual Conference, Reading 2006; Nicholas Deakin and John Edwards, *The Enterprise Culture and the Inner City* (London, 1993).

[118] There were exceptions, for instance: Pearl Jephcott, *Girls Growing Up* (London, 1942); Gloria Swanson, *Drunk with Glitter: Space, Consumption and Sexual Instability in Modern Urban Culture* (Abingdon, 2007), pp. 54–72.

children playing in streets, and it continued into the 1970s, with the focus on vandalism, subcultures, and resistance still largely a focus on male youth.[119] However, from the 1970s the feminist movement would begin to challenge such assumptions.[120] Ward's *Child in the City* acknowledged this problem in a brief chapter on the 'girl in the background'.[121] In fact, this girl remained firmly in the shadows in the rest of his book. Indeed, Ward acknowledged that his conventional use of 'he' for the generalized child was only partly because he could not bear to use the word 'it' and found 'he or she' too cumbersome; it also reflected the fact that in writing the book he had been made conscious that, in fact, he generally did mean 'he'. Ward argued that boys not only experienced the city differently to girls, but they had also historically experienced it more. To a large extent, the story of the child in the city—a story of the ways in which the child experienced, explored, and exploited the city—had been a story about boys more than girls, or at least a story in which girls really had been 'in the background'.[122] The images in his chapter on girls tended to support this position. Of nine in total, three dealt with China or Africa and one with London 'street arabs' in the 1890s. Nearly all the photographs, even those whose setting was further afield, offer us images of the girl's connection to a domestic world, including a world of work rather than unfettered play therein. One girl pushes a pram filled with old clothes, and others sort through clothes at a jumble sale. Another, mirroring her mother alongside her, pushes pram and shopping. Two sit, clutching teddies and sucking lollies, on the kitchen floor. One is at play, but hanging from scaffolding right up against the net-curtained windows of home. The Chinese girls are all at work. The Africans are with their mothers at the water pump. Of the contemporary images, only the image of 'practising for the girls' band' fully breaks away, though to a world of institutionalized and gender-demarcated play. In the images throughout the rest of the book, boys predominate. Ward claimed that this simply represented what it was like on the streets of Britain in the 1970s. As such, the neglect of the subject in earlier research on youth culture was perhaps unsurprising. The subculture of girls, only now attracting attention, had been hidden in part because it had been accommodated within the home, requiring only a bedroom, albeit now also a record player, and friends.[123] There was also interest in the possibility of an innate cause of difference, with boys believed to have a stronger visual-spatial ability, though it was accepted that it was likely that an upbringing and an accumulation of environmental experience that encouraged such skills in boys was much more of a factor, as was the continuing tendency to expect girls to contribute to domestic work while at the same time fearing that they were at more danger than boys on the street.[124] There was evidence to support the proposition that this situation was changing, but what was striking was the persistence of a substantial difference. If future study was to address the position of

---

[119] For instance: S. Hall and T. Jefferson (eds), *Resistance through Rituals* (London, 1976).

[120] Ward, for instance, drew on Angela McRobbie and Jenny Garber, 'Girls and Subcultures: An Exploration', in Hall and Jefferson (eds), *Resistance through Rituals*, pp. 209–22.

[121] Ward, *Child in the City*, pp. 152–63.   [122] Ward, *Child in the City*, p. viii.

[123] McRobbie and Garber, 'Girls and Subcultures'.   [124] Ward, *Child in the City*, p. 154.

girls and not just boys, an orientation that was very difficult to avoid given the evidence emerging from feminist study, it would have to be accepted that the idea that there was a single landscape of the child was no longer tenable.[125]

The second shift in thinking was one that in fact echoed aspects of the 1970s radicalism, in particular in the emergence of child-rights thinking, but which nevertheless defined itself in relation to a perceived break in understanding and justified a new discipline of studying children on this basis. Fundamental in this shift—what has been described as a paradigm shift—was the idea that the new child study would take seriously how the child saw the world, and would move from studying children as objects of policy to subjects in their own right.[126] Initially, in the early 1990s, the new field differentiated itself from earlier study of the child through a rejection of psychological emphasis on stages of development and socialization, and a preference instead for approaching childhood as a social construction.[127] As a result, it saw a shift in dominant disciplinary influence, from psychology towards sociology. But as childhood studies followed the successful path of women's studies in defining itself in terms of its object of enquiry, the door was also open to an interdisciplinary approach. The fact that this new academic field came to the fore after a decade of retreat and backlash against the 1970s progressivism and was led by a new generation of academics largely cut off from direct involvement in the radical politics of the 1960s and 1970s, and that it developed within a new context of legitimization of a child's rights agenda following the UN Convention on the Rights of the Child in 1992, all further encouraged a belief in its own novelty. The new field therefore developed with a strong sense that its origins lay in theoretical reorientation, but with less understanding of its relation to the history of its own times or of its lineage with earlier developments and a longer tradition of interest in the perspective of the child that had run alongside countervailing efforts to manage, govern, and protect the child since the Second World War.[128]

As long as it was not pushed too far, the emphasis on listening to the child and recognizing certain rights (which tended to stop short at challenging adult rights and often provided a new language for protection) found itself more acceptable after the 1970s than calls to challenge the nature of a narrowing physical landscape of the child. The strident efforts to create an environment in which children could reclaim the city therefore faded away, partly for ideological and partly for economic reasons.[129] By contrast, the focus on the individual child, for all its often radical intent, was in some ways more comfortably in line with the neo-liberal climate following retreat from the post-war social democratic settlement.

[125] This was reflected in studies of child subjectivity and gender, for instance: C. Steedman, C. Urwin, and V. Walkerdine (eds), *Language, Gender and Childhood* (London, 1985).
[126] For the 'paradigm shift': James and Prout (eds), *Constructing and Reconstructing Childhood*.
[127] Alan Prout later became more critical of this early attempt to set up a dichotomy between the new childhood studies and an older developmental approach, acknowledging that it remained important to consider the nature of childhood as well as its social construction: *The Future of Childhood: Towards the Interdisciplinary Study of Childhood* (London, 2004), pp. 1–2.
[128] See, for instance, the sense of a new field in Mary Jane Kehily (ed.), *An Introduction to Childhood Studies* (Oxford, 2004).
[129] It has been suggested that the retreat was particularly marked in the 1990s: Brendan Gleeson and Neil Spie (eds), *Creating Child Friendly Cities* (New York, 2006), p. 4.

Ironically, the re-emergence of a prominent public debate about the effect of environment on children, a quarter of a century after the period discussed in this chapter, focused on the very effects of this neo-liberalism itself: the results of increased affluence in a toxic cocktail of decreased levels of exercise, an over-rich and processed diet with increased levels of obesity, an increasingly screen-bound existence, and the pressures of living in a culture of consumerism.[130] Jumping on the bandwagon of the new enthusiasm for neuroscience, a 'death of childhood' campaign even suggested that high levels of depression and behavioural problems in children were to be accounted for by the problems of developing brains struggling to cope with the pace of technological cultural change, and without the real food and real play needed for proper development.[131] Rather than centring on radicals, this new critique of a toxic environment was something that in its nostalgia for a lost childhood and lost culture of play, and in its fears of technologically driven social change, attracted not just middle-class parents and liberals guilty about what seemed an impoverished landscape for the child, but also gained the ear of the mainstream political parties and the press.[132] However, the rhetoric of loss, and the creation of new opportunities for protected freedom in summer camps, after-school activities, the fantasy of dangerous books for boys, or even the computer game was far easier than changing the conditions of the physical environment. Government turned to targeting levels of obesity and exercise: things that could be managed and measured. Likewise, in a further reorientation to managing symptoms rather than addressing causes, the economic arguments put forward by Richard Layard helped turn child mental health, like obesity, into a target for major intervention. This sat alongside an ongoing emphasis on the 'feral' child as a key source of danger within society and a punitive orientation at odds with the radical aspirations of the early 1970s. Radical and libertarian academic voices by contrast were more likely to question arguments of toxicity: like Ward in the 1970s, they pointed to the ability of children to overcome and subvert their environment, whether through new ways of populating the spaces of the street or through a critical literacy that enabled them to decode and put in perspective the messages of the media and new technology.[133]

---

[130] For instance: S. Luthar, 'The Culture of Affluence: Psychological Costs of Material Wealth', *Child Development*, 74 (2003), 1581–93. For populist appropriation of this type of argument and language in Britain: Sue Palmer, *Toxic Childhood: How Modern Life is Damaging our Children...and What We Can Do About It* (London, 2006); and her *Detoxing Childhood: What Parents Need to Know to Raise Happy Successful Children* (London, 2007). For the tensions between affluence and protection of children in the post-war period: Avner Offer, *The Challenge of Affluence: Self Control and Well Being in the United States and Britain since 1950* (Oxford, 2006), pp. 339–47.

[131] 'Hold on to Childhood', *Daily Telegraph* (13 September 2006).

[132] See the report on the 'Hold on to Childhood' campaign in the *Daily Telegraph* (13 September 2006), which was signed by 110 academics including childcare guru Penelope Leach and John Bowlby's son, Sir Richard Bowlby. Sue Palmer was one of the organizers. She also spoke at the Conservative Party conference.

[133] For the libertarian position: Frank Furedi, *Culture of Fear: Risk-Taking and the Morality of Low Expectation* (London, 1997). On television: David Buckingham, *After the Death of Childhood: Growing Up in the Age of Electronic Media* (Cambridge, 2000). For a reappraisal of the ability of children to colonize the street: Hugh Matthews, Melanie Limb, and Mark Taylor, *The Street as Thirdspace* (Northampton, 1998).

CONCLUSION

The 1970s, or more accurately the late 1960s and early 1970s, now looks like a rather remarkable period for radical thinking and action in relation to the landscape of the child. This has tended to be hidden from view, perhaps because of the marginal and unrealistic nature of some of this radicalism, or in cases such as child sexual rights its unpalatable nature in retrospect. It has also been overshadowed by a focus on the liberation of adult lives in this period. But the energies directed at child liberation were in fact an essential element of the radical politics of the era, standing alongside and interrelating with the sexual and women's liberation movements that have attracted the attention. Moreover, the significance of this debate and of the resulting practical initiatives went far beyond the radical margins. It was behind a broader progressivism which inspired a generation of teachers, social workers, and parents in their approach to childhood. And it symbolized a problem and line of fracture within the broader post-war settlement. This was a settlement that had largely been predicated on expert calculation of what was best for its subjects, a settlement with an inherently paternalistic orientation. The idea that one had to understand the perspective of the subjects of welfare emerged most clearly in relation to the obviously different psychological position of the child. In what this chapter has described as a landscape turn, social reform and planning, social science, and social politics were all being confronted by this challenge in the late 1960s and early 1970s. This reconfiguration was embraced by the radical supporters of democratization and liberation. However, it also had the potential to provide the basis for a new, more pervasive, form of governance that was alert to the perspective of its individual subjects. In the longer term, this would be just as important a legacy.

As analysis of street photography indicated, nostalgia for the freedom of the street developed well before the 1970s, but evidence from the post-war decades suggests that social scientists, social workers, and even parents had been relatively relaxed about this issue. The early 1970s was the period in which the dangers of house-bound social isolation came to the forefront of concern, and this shifted attention to the way that changes in the urban environment cut down the capacity for healthy child development. As a consequence, the 1970s saw an explosion of fresh thinking about the way to address these problems and a growing consciousness that the child's relationship to a world beyond the home would have to be reclaimed and re-envisaged. Crucially, this reflected the growing appreciation that the landscape of the child was one that needed to be understood from the perspective of the child, and this led to radical experiments in the development of child freedom, rather than moves to increase protection. The focus on children offered a vehicle for bringing together radical epistemology with practical politics in the setting up of sites for play and the subversion of urban space or in challenging the boundaries of authority in social work and social research. And the romance of childhood freedom was one that the young, counter-cultural advocates of liberation could readily, albeit sometimes unrealistically, identify with. The problem with the subject of the child was that pushing the rights and perspective of the child too far led to a clash with deeply entrenched ideas of social order, provoking the backlash that would follow. This is one reason why these efforts now appear so strikingly at odds with the culture of risk management and fear, on the one hand, and of anxieties about the 'feral' child, on the other, that has come to dominate attitudes towards children and child-rearing in our own times.[134]

---

[134] Frank Furedi's influential account of risk culture in Britain thus focuses almost wholly on developments after 1980: *Culture of Fear*. On the emergence of the 'feral' child—the Janus face of overprotection—see footnote 2 in this chapter.

Conclusion

The Introduction of this book introduced three main lines of analysis. This Conclusion will reflect back on each of these in turn in light of the case studies that followed. The first aim of the book was to provide some recent historical context for our feeling that the history of modern British childhood has been one, despite all its positive dimensions, of lost freedom. In doing so, the book has offered insight on a series of social changes that have undoubtedly had an impact on the freedom of children. Road traffic, the volume of which increased spectacularly across the period, would be at the forefront in any list that attempted to calibrate the significance of these factors. But strictly speaking it was the response to road traffic, including a heightened safety consciousness, which led to a loss of freedom. A second factor in any such list would be the threat of sexual molestation, though again the onus here would be on the understanding and response to such a danger as much as the likelihood of falling victim to such acts. In this case, an explosion of alarm came strikingly late, with the 1970s a key turning point. The watching of television also facilitated the shift indoors, with the majority of children spending a not insignificant couple of hours a day in front of the small screen by the 1970s; and in this case the willingness to accept this environment in the end emerges as more striking than alarm about its dangers. However, television also offers an example of the way in which new freedoms could be opened up as others began to close (and it heralded a growing importance of virtual landscapes in the years to come). Its appeal reflected a more general move towards home-centred life, something that was intensified by an emphasis on protection, attachment, and family love that emerged out of the feelings of war, and something that was made easier as a result of an affluence which brought more living space, more toys, and a culture of more play into home life. In this regard, a lost freedom outside the home was compensated for by more emphasis on permissiveness and free play within it. Reflecting the belief that freedom was vital for child development, the period also saw efforts to create new spaces to offer managed freedom, designed with the child's needs in mind. The developmentally calibrated space of children's television can be seen as one of these, even if the reality of what children watched was significantly different. The creation of special play spaces was another, with the adventure playground a striking symbol of the era's interest in child freedom. Such initiatives heralded a future in which an increasingly common response to feelings of lost freedom would be to offer a managed version of such freedom through the institutionalization of protected zones for child play, exploration, and learning. On the other hand, although these post-war responses impress as idealistic attempts to create a sanctuary for extending horizons and nurturing freedom, their limitations are also very apparent. Adventure play provides us with an intriguing symbol of the way in which post-war society could offer some kind of solution to the problem of physical freedom, but it pales into insignificance alongside the dominant story of ceding the urban landscape to the car. Economic development, spreading affluence, individualism, and protection of the liberties of the adult subject were all far too powerful to contain. Television struggled to resist the same forces. Within this context, there was a growing nostalgia for lost childhood freedom, evident, for instance, in photography of working-class street children or in the appeal of the figure of the child playing in the ruins and bombsites of war. This reflected the fact that independent outside play was already on the decline, particularly within the middle classes, but such representation magnified this decline, brought it to attention, and gave it a meaning: all important to the emergence of a consciousness about lost freedom. Nevertheless, what is now far more striking about the period up to the 1970s is the degree of outside freedom that most children still had.

The 1970s emerges as a key decade in changing this situation, less because the dangers of outside play substantially increased at this point, than because of a change in attitudes. One reason for this was that the landscape of home came to be viewed more critically, with a growing feeling that it could trap children in and not just protect and nurture them, and this helped foreground concern about lost freedom. In part, this reflected the fact that a substantial body of research going back to the early 1960s now cast doubt on the degree to which separation of mothers and young children resulted in long-term emotional deprivation. Research pointed instead to the dangers of growing up in homes where the necessary love, security, and opportunities for growth through freedom did not exist. Despite the combination of a welfare state and affluence, it seemed that new social changes were creating new difficulties. There was a feeling that many mothers now found themselves socially isolated, separated from the support of extended families in new estates, or worse still cooped up with their young children in high-rise flats, and were often poorly equipped as a result to provide the necessary love, social relations, and freedom to play demanded by the increased expectations of post-war childcare. There was also a belief that the post-war model of home, family, and maternal attachment was one that could not necessarily be extended to the increasing population of immigrants who may have brought with them a different culture of childcare, and whose children needed not isolation in the home but integration in the broader community. And this was not just a problem of those in the most difficult social and economic circumstances. There was an increasing concern about the difficulties of the house-bound, middle-class mother of young children, and this turned energies towards the setting up of playgroups and playgrounds to supplement home life. For an emerging generation of feminists, the questions of their own freedom and that of children would come to be intimately linked. At the same time, counter-cultural arguments about liberation, forged in relation to thinking about adult lives in the 1960s, now began to be directed at the child. The lost freedom of the child was an issue that young, white, middle-class radicals could directly identify with. For beneficiaries of the post-war welfare state and affluence (and of protected freedom within the home), the idea of lost childhood freedom was symbolic of the feeling within this generation and its descendants that something had nevertheless gone missing in the process. It was also an issue that they could directly act upon as parents, teachers, social workers, and community activists. However, this politics of child liberation would turn out to be just as significant for the hostility it provoked when it went too far. The most striking example of this is the way in which arguments about extending sexual liberation to children ended up stoking widespread public alarm about paedophilia. Indeed, the radical vision of freedom had ultimately mixed results. It did help point the way towards a new era of child-rights thinking. And it saw pioneering ventures in putting forward the child's perspective. On the other hand, it proved difficult to extend a liberationist logic forged in relation to adults into the realm of the child when it clashed with adult interests and a powerful social belief that children were fundamentally different to adults and needed protection not setting free. In the end, although the radicals had questioned the pessimism of the idea of lost freedom, as they looked to unleash the potential of the child to subvert and colonize the spaces of the city, their actions and words ultimately also helped cement it as one of our key modern worries.

The second line of analysis in the book has been to think about the history of post-war childhood in terms of landscape. It has adopted two approaches. Firstly, it has conceptualized the landscape of the child in terms of three symbolic types of space: the home, the institution, and the outside world. And it has examined the changing relationship of these three spaces between the Second World War and the 1970s. The central conclusion of this analysis is that the importance of a landscape of home was consolidated in the period, and that this provided the crucial background for concern over lost freedom regarding access to the outside world. Lying behind this was a more complex process in which the three idealized spaces were played off one another across the period in conceptualizing and debating how to provide a good landscape for the child. For instance, a critique of the landscape of the institution was pivotal in the mid-century argument about the psychological benefits of home. In turn, institutions were directed to become more homely if they were to survive, and this gave institutions an ongoing role but also left them prone to further critique. Home was idealized as all that children needed, but this assumed that it could bring the outside world in through the imagination and the freedom to explore broader horizons through play. Home, therefore, was also a zone in which elevated expectations of childcare, child development, and child protection left it prone to potential criticism regarding the child's access to the world beyond. Of course, there were more subtle variations within this landscape, between different types of institutions, different types of home, and rural and suburban as well as urban outside worlds, and these will need to be addressed in a social history of this subject, but the fundamental conceptual building blocks of debate over the landscape of the child were those which have been set out here.

The second conceptual model for analysis of the landscape of the child has been to distinguish and interrelate three different relationships between individuals and their landscape: a history of where children were situated *in* the landscape; a history of visions and efforts to create a landscape *for* the child; and the history of a landscape *of* the child, of how children saw their world, and of the recognition and consequences of this. Such an approach echoes broader developments within the study of landscape which have taken the field well beyond the traditional terrain of aesthetics and rural vistas. In the field of modern British history, this has opened up a history of the way landscape became an object for control and management so as to shape the subjectivity and citizenship of those who lived within it. But this book has gone one step further to focus on the extent to which contemporaries were already conscious of the subjective dimension of landscape, and to examine the implications of this consciousness. The book has argued that interest in a landscape *of* the child was already evident by mid-century, and became widespread by the 1970s. The book has described this as a move towards landscape thinking. It can be seen not just in psychological theory and in new fields such as environmental psychology; it also spilled over into broader social scientific theory and the thinking of educationalists, human environmentalists, town planners, and criminologists; it was a feature of efforts to represent the child in the arts; it reached considerably further in the popularization of psychological theory in childcare advice to parents; it is even apparent in what children were saying about themselves in radical contexts by the 1970s.

The book has also shown that this landscape turn in understanding subjectivity had important implications when it came to efforts to develop a landscape *for* the child. Initially it provided further justification for systems of protection and welfare and for the role of experts who could understand and respond to the developing perspective of the child. The extraordinary developments and anxieties of war led to a moment of unique opportunity in this regard and drew increasing attention to the child's perspective and feelings. This advance of expertise, regulation, and social welfare has attracted the most attention to date in a history of post-war childhood that centres on action by the state and experts in the name of the child and which points to the increasing governance of subjectivity. As this book has indicated, this is a history that, in fact, extends beyond the role of the state, for instance in the development of children's television and adventure playgrounds, but also in the influence of psychological theory in fostering a culture of post-war childcare. However, it has also indicated the need for caution in relation both to the influence of experts and to the success of governmental aspirations. This was evident, for instance, in the reluctance to draw directly on psychological expertise in the design of children's television programming, and in the muted tones and cautious reception of the Himmelweit report. It was also evident in the translation of the ideas of attachment psychology into a popular idiom in journals like *Parents*. What often seems to have been most important were the more general and popularized psychological messages absorbed by those with real influence as policy makers, figures involved in the representation of children, or those engaged in the delivery of care on the ground. Here, the message about needing to address the child's view did develop into part of the common sense of the era. However, what also needs to be appreciated is that this message did not necessarily sit comfortably with a history that emphasizes increasing regulation and management of subjectivity. The recognition that there was a landscape *of* the child could challenge adult assumptions, values, and interests. It was this otherness of the child that helped turn the post-war child of the city into a symbol of lost freedom: not passive victim, but a more subversive figure that looked back with another point of view. If the landscape of the child was a world that could only be fully comprehended by the child, what did this mean for adult attempts to use landscape design to shape the subjectivity of the child? Perhaps these efforts were doomed to failure? Perhaps they needed to be recast as projects of control rather than welfare? Perhaps real understanding would entail listening to children themselves, and reshaping the landscape accordingly? By the 1970s, such ideas would be taken up by those who wanted to challenge efforts to discipline and manage the child, not just adult supporters of child liberation and critics of an adult environment that deprived the child through its regulations, but there are even signs that the idea and language of perspective was being taken up by some children themselves. Although the book analyses these issues only in relation to the landscape of the child, and although it highlights reasons why such interest was particularly acute in relation to children, phenomena such as human environmentalism, environmental psychology, and the interest in integrating perspective into a democratized form of planning, all point towards the potential significance of such a landscape turn in thinking when it came to adults subjects of the environment too.

The final aim of the book has been to use this subject of the landscape of the child and lost freedom to cast light on broader questions of periodization in twentieth-century British history. Given its focus on the years from the Second World War to the 1970s, it has been particularly interested in offering fresh perspective on our understanding of this as a period that saw the making of a new social contract between state and society: what has been given the shorthand here of the post-war settlement. It has also set out to use the issue of the landscape of the child to explore the degree to which this settlement was challenged in the period up to the 1970s. When it comes to the history of emergence, the book develops a well-established view that the war focused minds on the welfare of children, and in particular on their psychological well-being, and that this was significant for the broader social settlement. Evacuation has attracted most of the attention in such work. Such a focus has been extended here to include studies of the child's response to the Blitz, life in wartime institutions, and the British contribution to a debate about the wartime children of Europe to provide a more complex picture. One of the conclusions emerging from this is that war-stoked anxieties about human nature, which tended to be set aside in post-war British culture, did, in fact, find an outlet in concern about the child and in a resulting emphasis on security, protection, and the importance of attachment to home and family. Indeed, anxiety about child safety and about the human capacity for cruelty reveals a darker side of what has tended to be remembered as a good war and one which cast a long shadow. The evidence about what actually happened to wartime children was in reality much more mixed. Many in fact thrived with the challenge of independence and new freedoms. And their capacity to cope with bombing and a devastated landscape was often remarkable. But it was the image of the withdrawn, unloved child, most notably those discovered in institutions, which attracted spectacular attention, even in the midst of war and its other worries. And it was the psychologists' message of the need for home and family that chimed with the feelings of the post-war population, even if it was in tension with a reality of families and homes damaged and destabilized by war. The post-war debate about child cruelty sits intriguingly in this context, echoing the language of wartime horrors and foregrounding the importance of an idealized landscape of home, but also indicating the difficulty of realizing such a vision. The book has argued that this wartime and post-war mood gave considerable impetus to psychological arguments about the need for a landscape of home. This was one of the reasons why attachment theory became so influential. And it has suggested that the resulting post-war emphasis on the importance of a certain sort of home, family, and maternal care for the child was just as much a part of a post-war social settlement as the advance of the state in other areas of welfare. Moreover, in its emphasis on the importance of environment, social relations, and freedom, the psychologically informed childcare philosophy of the post-war years—what the book has called Bowlbyism—can even be seen as in some respects extending a social democratic ethos associated with some of the public developments of the welfare state into the private realm of the family.

It was the familial and domestic dimension of this post-war social settlement, not just confidence in the achievement and economics of the welfare state, that was faltering and under challenge by the 1970s. In fact the two emerge as being intimately linked. At a time of increasing awareness of problems of poverty and abuse, of instability caused by social change, and of economic crisis, the 1970s would see both sides of the political spectrum considering new diagnoses and solutions in relation to the question of childcare. What also opened up the settlement was the way that the energies of the counter-culture and of feminism were directed at this question in the 1970s. Here, lost childhood freedom provided a symbol for a set of broader misgivings about the post-war settlement. However, rather than despairing at this situation, radicals saw hope in turning back to the child's perspective. Looking at the world from the perspective of the child indicated their resilience, their potential to subvert their environment through play, and the need to give this perspective a voice. And in this democratizing landscape turn of looking at environment from the perspective of its people, there were perhaps more general implications for rethinking social policy, social science, and social politics. This leaves us with a challenge when it comes to periodization. The developments of the 1970s can be read as a precursor to the child-rights thinking of the late twentieth century. However, the shortcomings and contradictions, the collapse and the broader rejection of many of these child liberation movements of the 1970s, but also the significance of the ideological and economic shifts that followed the 1970s are also striking, and this weakens the case for continuities with our own times. The developments of the early 1970s can also be seen in some respects as radical extensions of certain tendencies in understanding and responding to the landscape of the child that had been building since the Second World War, even if before the 1970s an impetus for protection and a logic of psychological difference had tended to override a countervailing recognition of the child's need for freedom. The decade is perhaps best seen as a point of rupture.

In particular, a rejection of the landscape of protection and a desire to push a vision of freedom further than ever before exploded tensions that had hitherto been contained within the post-war settlement.

If the 1970s emerges as a moment of rupture, it also has something to do with the other sort of periodization highlighted in the Introduction of this book: one based on generational change. The impetus to cocoon the child had been fuelled by the emotional legacy of the Second World War, but the force of this legacy had waned by the late 1960s. The generation that now came to the fore was made up of the children who had been recipients of the post-war childcare culture. Unlike their parents, who were more likely to have experienced material and emotional deprivation, whose lives had often been disrupted by war, and whose feelings arising from both these experiences were played out in the protection of the vulnerable child, the radicals of the new generation reacted against protection and paternalism. Writers like B. S. Johnson now looked back to the evacuee experience and expressed anger at the manner of their saving. Photographers turned to the street child as a subject, not for saving, but for celebration of freedom. And the young radicals of the counter-culture found a perfect subject for subversion in children and the politics of play. However, this was only part of the generation. The majority of people were more satisfied with the emotional and material nutrition of their post-war upbringing, they looked now to enjoy the increasing material comforts and the freedoms opened up by affluence and permissive change, and they were often happy to join the outcry against the extension of strident and radical permissiveness to the figure of the child. But there was an irony here. Prosperity, choice, and consumerism (rather than the dreams and visions of advocates of child rights) were the major vehicles for loosening control over a protective landscape for the child. As car ownership extended even further as an expression of this freedom, there was little prospect of reclaiming the city for the child. And as adults embraced a liberalization and commercialization of sex, they were also presenting children with new choices and consequences even if they did not intend to do so. Since the radicals proved a much easier target for critique than individualism or the market, the 1970s would leave the legacy of a mismatched culture of defending childhood innocence (and pathologizing the delinquency of the feral child), on the one hand, while situating these children in a culture of consumption and individualism that undermined a protective landscape settlement, on the other. This is the fundamental contradiction that was bequeathed to the next generation and which has underpinned mounting anxieties about lost freedom. Within this context, it has often proved easier to lament lost freedom than to react against it.

Bibliography

PUBLISHED PRIMARY SOURCES

Adams, Eileen, Bishop, Jeff, and Kean, Joan, 'Children, Environment and Education: Personal Views of Urban Environmental Education in Britain', *Children's Environments*, 9:1 (1992), 49–67.

Adams, Mary, 'Programmes for the Young Viewer', *BBC Quarterly*, 5:2 (Summer 1950), 82–8.

Adams, Paul, Berg, Leila, Berger, Nan, Duane, Michael, Neill, A. S., and Ollendorff, Robert, *Children's Rights* (London, 1971).

Ainsworth, Mary, 'The Effects of Maternal Deprivation: A Review of Findings and Controversy in the Context of Research Strategy', in WHO, *Deprivation of Maternal Care: A Reassessment of its Effects* (Geneva, 1962), pp. 97–165.

Alcock, Theodora, 'Conclusions from Psychiatric Social Work with Evacuated Children', *British Journal of Medical Psychology*, 21 (1948), 181–4.

Allen, Ann, and Morton, Arthur, *This is Your Child: The Story of the National Society for the Prevention of Cruelty to Children* (London, 1961).

Allen, Lady of Hurtwood, *Whose Children?* (London, 1945).

Allen, Lady of Hurtwood, and Jellicoe, Susan, *Gardens: The Things We See (7)* (London, 1953).

Allen, Marjory, and Nicholson, Mary, *Memoirs of an Uneducated Lady* (London, 1975).

Armstrong, Anne, *Planning and Environmental Education: Centre for Environmental Studies*, Occasional Paper 7 (London, 1979).

Arnheim, Mary, and Arnheim, Rudolf, *Phototips on Children: The Psychology, the Technique and the Art of Child Photography* (London, 1939).

Baher, Edwina, et al., *At Risk: An Account of the Work of the Battered Child Research Department, NSPCC* (London, 1976).

Baker, Anthony, and Duncan, Sylvia, 'Child Sexual Abuse: A Study of Prevalence in Great Britain', *Child Abuse and Neglect*, 9 (1985), 457–67.

Baker, Shirley, *Street Photographs: Manchester and Salford* (Newcastle, 1989).

Bartlett, Sheridan, Hart, Roger, Satterthwite, David, Barra, Ximena de la, and Missait, Alfredo, *Cities for Children: Children's Rights, Poverty and Urban Management* (New York, 1999).

Becker, Howard, *The Outsiders* (New York, 1963).

Benjamin, Joe, *Grounds for Play: An Extension of In Search of Adventure* (London, 1974).

Berbaldez, F., Gallardo, D., and Abello, R., 'Children's Landscape Preferences: From Rejection to Attractions', *Journal of Environmental Psychology*, 7 (1987), 169–76.

Berg, Leila, *Look at Kids* (London, 1972).

Bernard, Fritz, 'An Enquiry among a Group of Paedophiles', *Journal of Sex Research*, 11 (1975), 242–55.

Bernard, Fritz, 'Pedophilia: The Consequences for the Child', in Mark Cook and Glenn Wilson (eds), *Love and Attraction: An International Conference* (Oxford, 1979), pp. 499–501.

Bernstein, Basil, 'Education Cannot Compensate for Society', *New Society* (26 February 1970), 344–7.

Bernstein, Basil, *Theoretical Studies towards a Sociology of Language* (London, 1971).

Bone, Margaret, *Pre-School Children and the Need for Day-Care: A Survey Carried out on Behalf of the Department of Health and Social Security* (London, 1977).

Boorman, John, *Adventures of a Suburban Boy* (London, 2003).

Boucher, C. A., 'Accidents in the Home', *Monthly Bulletin of the Ministry of Health* (May 1949).

Bowlby, John, 'Psychology and Democracy', *Political Quarterly*, 17 (1946), 61–76.

Bowlby, John, *Child Care and the Growth of Love* (London, 1971).

Bowlby, John, and Durbin, Evan, *Personal Aggressiveness and War* (London, 1939).

Brongersma, Edward, 'The Meaning of "Indecency" with Respect to Moral Offences involving Children', *British Journal of Criminology*, 20 (1980), 20–32.

Brosse, Thérèse, *Homeless Children: Report of the Conference of Directors of Children's Communities Trogen, Switzerland* (Paris, 1950).

Brosse, Thérèse, *War-Handicapped Children* (Paris, 1950).

Brown, J. M., Henderson, J., and Armstrong, M. P., 'Children's Perceptions of Nuclear Power Stations as Revealed through their Drawings', *JEP*, 7 (1987), 189–99.

Buckingham, David, *Moving Images: Understanding Children's Emotional Responses to Television* (Manchester, 1996).

Buckingham, David, *After the Death of Childhood: Growing Up in the Age of Electronic Media* (Cambridge, 2000).

Buckingham, David, and Allerton, Mark, *Fear, Fright and Distress: A Review of Research on Children's 'Negative' Emotional Response to Television—Prepared for the Broadcasting Standards Council* (London, 1996).

Burlingham, Dorothy, and Freud, Anna, *Young Children in War-Time in a Residential Nursery* (London, 1942).

Burt, Cyril, *The Young Delinquent* (London, 1925).

Burt, Sir Cyril, 'The Psychology of Listeners', *BBC Quarterly*, 4:1 (April, 1948), 7–13.

Burton, Lindy, *Vulnerable Children: Three Studies of Children in Conflict: Accident Involved Children, Sexually Assaulted Children and Children with Asthma* (London, 1968).

Camden Road Safety Campaign, *A Selection of Entries from the Camden Junior Schoolchildren's Short Story Competition* (London, 1974).

Canter, David, *The Psychology of Space* (London, 1977).

Capon, Naomi, 'The Child and the Dragon', *BBC Quarterly*, 6:1 (Spring 1951), 18–26.

Cartland, Barbara, 'Guarding against the Sex Assailant', *Parents*, 13 (June 1958), 40–2.

Case, Paula, *Compensating Child Abuse in England and Wales* (Cambridge, 2007).

Cawson, Pat, Wattam, Corinne, Brooker, Sue, and Kelley, Graham, *Child Maltreatment in the United Kingdom: A Study of the Prevalence of Child Abuse and Neglect* (London, 2000).

Chapman, Jack, 'Ill-Treatment of Children: The Social and Legal Context in England and Wales', in Henry Kempe, Alfred White Franklin, and Christine Cooper (eds), *The Abused Child in the Family and in the Community: Selected Papers from the Second International Congress on Child Abuse and Neglect, London, England*, vol. 1 (Oxford, 1980).

Chesser, Eustace, *Unwanted Children* (London, 1947).

Childs, David, and Whorton, Janet (eds), *Children in War: Reminiscences of the Second World War* (Nottingham, 1989).

Coard, Bernard, *How the West Indian Child is Made Educationally Sub-normal in the British School System* (London, 1971).

Cockburn, Cynthia, *The Local State: Management of Cities and People* (London, 1977).

Cohen, Stanley (ed.), *Images of Deviance* (London, 1971).

Community Work and Caring for Children: A Community Project in an Inner City Local Authority by a Group of Workers from the Harlesden Community Project (Ilkley, 1970).

Constantine, Larry L., 'The Sexual Rights of Children: Implications of a Radical Perspective', in Mark Cook and Glenn Wilson (eds), *Love and Attraction: An International Conference* (Oxford, 1979), pp. 503–8.

Cook, Mark, and Wilson, Glenn (eds), *Love and Attraction: An International Conference* (Oxford, 1979).

Coppard, George, *With a Machine Gunner to Cambrai* (London, 1969).

Cox, C. B., and Dyson, A. E. (eds), *The Black Papers on Education* (London, 1971).

David, Kate, *A Child's War: World War II through the Eyes of Children* (Peterborough, 1989).

Dawson, Gerry [David Widgery], 'The Politics of Pornography', *Socialist Worker* (24 July 1971).

Dean, J. S., *Murder Most Foul: A Study of the Road Deaths Problem* (London, 1947).

DiGuiseppi, C., Roberts, I., and Allen, D. 'Determinants of Car Travel on Daily Journeys to School', *British Medical Journal* (1998), 1426–8.

Diski, Jenny, *The Sixties* (London, 2009).

Douglas, J. W. B., *The Home and the School* (London, 1964).

East, Sir William Norwood, 'Sexual Crime', *Journal of Criminal Science*, 1 (1948), 67–79.

Eglinton, J. Z. [Walter Breen], *Greek Love* (New York, 1964).

Fanning, D. M., 'Families in Flats', *British Medical Journal*, 4 (1967), 382–6.

Field, Mary, *Good Company: The Story of the Children's Entertainment Film Movement in Great Britain, 1943–1950* (London, 1952).

Field, Mary, *Children and Films: A Study of Boys and Girls in the Cinema* (Dunfermline, 1954).

Field, Mary, 'Children's Taste in Cinema', *Quarterly of Film, Radio, and Television*, 11 (1956), 14–23.

Franklin, Alfred White (ed.), *Concerning Child Abuse: Papers Presented by the Tunbridge Wells Study Group on Non-Accidental Injury to Children* (Edinburgh, 1975).

Freeman, Hugh, *Mental Health and Environment* (London, 1984).

Freeman, Kathleen, *If Any Man Build: The History of the Save the Children Fund* (London, 1965).

Freud, Anna, and Burlingham, Dorothy, *Infants without Families: The Case for and against Residential Nurseries* (London, 1965).

Freud, Anna, and Dann, Sophie, 'An Experiment in Group Upbringing', *The Psychoanalytic Study of the Child*, 6 (1951), 127–68.

Fyson, Anthony, *Change the Streets* (Oxford, 1976).

Gavron, Hannah, *The Captive Wife: Conflicts of Housebound Mothers* (London, 1970).

Gibbens, T. C. N., and Price, Joyce, *Child Victims of Sex Offences* (London, 1963).

Gill, Owen, *Luke Street: Housing Policy, Conflict and the Creation of the Delinquent Area* (London, 1977).

Gilloran, J. L., 'Social Health and Problems Associated with "High Living"', *Medical Officer*, 120 (1968), 117–18.

Glover, Edward, *War, Sadism and Pacifism* (London, 1946).

Gollancz, Victor, *Is it Nothing to You?* (London, 1945).

Gollancz, Victor, *Leaving Them to their Fate: The Ethics of Starvation* (London, 1946).

Gollancz, Victor, *Our Threatened Values* (London, 1946).

Goodman, Susan, *Children of War: The Second World War through the Eyes of Generation* (London, 2005).

Greer, Germaine, *Daddy We Hardly Knew You* (London, 1989).

Grubin, Don, *Sex Offending against Children: Understanding the Risk*, Police Research Series Paper 99 (London, 1998).

Hall, Michael, 'Parish Councils for Cities?', *New Society* (29 January 1970), 178–9.

Hall, S. and Jefferson, T. (eds), *Resistance through Rituals* (London, 1976).

Halloran, J. D., Brown, R. L., and Chaney, D. C., *Television and Delinquency* (Leicester, 1970).

Hannay, D. R., 'Mental Health and High Flats', *Journal of Chronic Diseases*, 34 (1981), 431–2.

Hansen, Søren, and Jensen, Jesper, *The Little Red School-Book*, trans. Berit Thornberry (London, 1971).

Hare, E., and Shaw, G., *Mental Health on a New Housing Estate* (London, 1965).

Harris, Mark, Grimshaw, Anna, Ravetz, Amanda, Solomons, Natasha, Liebheit, Melanie, Grasseni, Cristina, Walker, Nicole, Ward, Colin, and Dibb, Mike (eds), *The Child in the City: A Case Study in Experimental Anthropology* (Manchester, 2000).

Hart, Roger, *Children's Participation: From Tokenism to Citizenship* (Florence, 1992).

Hart, Roger, *Children's Participation: The Theory and Practice Of Involving Young Citizens in Community Development and Environmental Care* (New York, 1997).

Hart, Roger, and Petren, Alfhild, 'The Child's Right to Play', in Alfhild Petren and James Himes (eds), *Children's Rights: Turning Principles into Practice* (Stockholm, 2000).

Henriques, Basil, 'Sexual Assaults on Children', *British Medical Journal*, 2 (1961), 1629–31.

Henshaw, Edna, 'Some Psychological Problems of Evacuation', *Mental Health*, 1:1 (1940), 5–10.

Henshaw, Edna, 'Observed Effects of Wartime Conditions on Children', *Mental Health*, 2:4 (1941), 93–102.

Hicklin, Margot, *War Damaged Children: Some Aspects of Recovery* (Thornton Heath, Surrey, 1946).

Himmelweit, Hilde, 'Television Revisited', *New Society* (1 November 1962), 17.

Himmelweit, Hilde, Oppenheim, A. N., and Vince, Pamela, *Television and the Child: An Empirical Study of the Effect of Television on the Young* (London, 1958).

Holman, E. A., and Stokols, D., 'The Environmental Psychology of Child Sexual Abuse', *JEP*, 14 (1994), 237–52.

Howarth, C. I., Routledge, D. A., and Repetto-Wright, R., 'An Analysis of Road Accidents Involving Child Pedestrians', *Ergonomics*, 17 (1974), 319–30.

Howarth, C. I., Routledge, D. A., and Repetto-Wright, R., 'A Comparison of Interviews and Observations to Obtain Measures of Children's Exposure to Risk as Pedestrians', *Ergonomics*, 17 (1974), 623–38.

Howarth, C. I., Routledge, D. A., and Repetto-Wright, R., 'The Exposure of Young Children to Accident Risks as Pedestrians', *Ergonomics*, 17 (1974), 457–80.

Howarth, H. E., 'Impressions of Children in a Heavily Bombed Area', *Mental Health*, 2:4 (1941), 98–101.

Howe, Michael J. A., *Television and Children* (London, 1977).

Housden, Leslie, 'The Effect of Modern Home Conditions on the Rearing of a Family', *Mother and Child*, 19:8 (1948), 176–8.

Hughes, J., 'The Increase in Sexual and Indecency Offences', *Police Journal*, 1:29 (January–March 1956), 54–8.

Ineichen, B., 'High Rise Living and Mental Stress', *Biology and Human Affairs*, 44 (1979), 81–5.

Ineichen, B., and Hooper, D., 'Wives' Mental Health and Children's Behaviour Problems in Contrasting Residential Areas', *Social Science and Medicine*, 8 (1974), 369–74.

Ineichen, B., and Hooper, D., 'Adjustment to Moving: A Follow-Up Study of the Mental Health of Young Families in New Housing', *Social Science and Medicine*, 13 (1979), 163–8.

Ingram, Michael, 'A Study of 92 Cases of Sexual Contact between Adult and Child', *British Journal of Sexual Medicine*, 6:44 (1979), 22; and 6:45 (1979), 24.

Ingram, Michael, *The Owl and the Pussycat: My Autobiography* (Cambridge, 1997).

Ingram, Michael, 'The Participating Victim: A Study of Sexual Offences against Pre-Pubertal Boys', in Mark Cook and Glenn Wilson (eds), *Love and Attraction: An International Conference* (Oxford, 1979), pp. 511–17.

Isaacs, Susan (ed.), *Cambridge Evacuation Survey: A Wartime Study in Social Welfare and Education* (London, 1941).

Isaacs, Susan, 'Fatherless Children', in New Education Fellowship, *Problems of Child Development* (London, 1948), pp. 3–15.

Jackson, Brian, and Jackson, Sonia, *Childminder: A Study in Action Research* (London, 1979).

James, Alison, and Prout, Alan (eds), *Constructing and Reconstructing Childhood: Contemporary Issues in the Sociological Study of Childhood* (1990).

Jellicoe, Geoffrey, and Susan, *The Landscape of Man: Shaping the Environment from Prehistory to the Present Day* (London, 1975).

Jennings, Hilda, *Societies in the Making* (London, 1962).

Jennings, Hilda, and Gill, Winifred, *Broadcasting in Everyday Life: A Survey of the Social Effects of the Coming of Broadcasting* (London, 1939).

Jephcott, Pearl, *A Troubled Area: Notes on Notting Hill* (London, 1964).

Jephcott, Pearl, *Girls Growing Up* (London, 1942).

Jephcott, Pearl, *Homes in High Flats: Some of the Human Problems Involved in Multi-Storey Housing* (Edinburgh, 1971).

Johnson, B. S., *Street Children* (London, 1964).

Johnson, B. S. (ed.), *The Evacuees* (London, 1968).

Kallarackal, A. M., and Herbert, Martin, 'The Happiness of Indian Immigrant Children', *New Society* (26 February 1976).

Kanter, Joel (ed.), *Face to Face with Children: The Life and Work of Clare Winnicott* (London, 2004).

Kehily, Mary Jane (ed.), *An Introduction to Childhood Studies* (Oxford, 2004).

Kempe, Henry, 'Battered-Child Syndrome', *Journal of the American Medical Association*, 181 (1962), 17–24.

Kimmins, C. W., *The Child's Attitude to Life: A Study of Children's Stories* (London, 1926).

Lee, T., 'Urban Neighbourhood as a Socio-Spatial Scheme', *Human Relations*, 21 (1968), 41–67.

Lewinsky, Hilde, 'Psychological Aspects of Cooking for Oneself', *British Journal of Medical Psychology*, 20 (1946), 376–83.

Lewis, Hilda, *Deprived Children: The Mersham Experiment: A Social and Clinical Study* (Oxford, 1954).

Lingstrom, Freda, 'Children and Television', *BBC Quarterly*, 8 (1953), 96.

Lobo, Edwin de H., *Children of Immigrants to Britain: Their Health and Social Problems* (London, 1978).

Lomas, Graham, *The Inner City* (London Council of Social Service, 1975).

Luthar, S., 'The Culture of Affluence: Psychological Costs of Material Wealth', *Child Development*, 74 (2003), 1581–93.

Lynch, Kevin, *The Image of the City* (Cambridge, MA, 1960).

Lynch, Kevin, *Growing up in Cities: Studies of the Spatial Environment of Adolescence in Cracow, Melbourne, Mexico City, Salta, Toluca, and Warsawa* (Cambridge, MA, 1977).

Macardle, Dorothy, *Children of Europe: A Study of the Children of Liberated Countries: Their Wartime Experiences, Their Reactions, and Their Needs, with a note on Germany* (London, 1949).

MacLeod, Mary, and Saraga, Esther, *Child Sexual Abuse: Towards a Feminist Professional Practice* (London, 1987).

McRobbie, Angela, and Garber, Jenny, 'Girls and Subcultures: An Exploration', in Stuart Hall and Tony Jefferson (eds), *Resistance through Rituals* (London, 1976), pp. 209–22.

Madge, Charles, 'Private and Public Spaces', *Human Relations*, 3 (1950), 187–99.

Main, T. F., 'Clinical Problems of Repatriates', *Journal of Mental Science*, 93 (1947), 354–63.

Maizels, Joan, *Two to Five in High Flats* (London, 1961).

Manning, Mary, 'Should We Pity the Paedophile?', *Community Care* (19 October 1977).

Marchant, Sir James (ed.), *Rebuilding Family Life in the Post-War World: An Enquiry with Recommendations* (London, 1945).

Matthews, Hugh, Limb, Melanie, and Taylor, Mark, *The Street as Thirdspace* (Northampton, 1998).

Mayer, J. P., *British Cinemas and Their Audiences* (London, 1948).

Mead, Margaret, 'A Cultural Anthropologist's Approach to Maternal Deprivation', in WHO, *Deprivation of Maternal Care: A Reassessment of its Effects* (Geneva, 1962), pp. 45–62.

Mercer, Charles, 'What Neighbourhood?', *New Society* (22 January 1976), 154–9.

Middleton, Warren (ed.), *The Betrayal of Youth: Radical Perspectives on Childhood Sexuality, Intergenerational Sex, and the Oppression of Children and Young People* (London, 1986).

Miller, E. (ed.), *The Growing Child and its Problems* (London, 1937).

Mitton, Roger, and Morrison, Elizabeth, *A Community Project in Notting Dale* (London, 1972).

Mohr, J. W., Turner, R. E., and Jerry, M. B., *Pedophilia and Exhibitionism* (Toronto, 1964).

Moody, Roger, 'Man/Boy Love on the Left', in Daniel Tsang (ed.), *The Age Taboo: Gay Male Sexuality, Power and Consent* (London, 1981).

Mordaunt, Elinor, *Blitz Kids* (London, 1941).

Morgan, Patricia, *Child Care Sense and Fable* (London, 1975).

Musgrove, Frank, *Youth and the Social Order* (London, 1974).

New Education Fellowship, *Problems of Child Development* (London, 1948).

Newson, John, and Newson, Elizabeth, *Infant Care in an Urban Community* (London, 1963).

Newson, John, and Newson, Elizabeth, *Four Years Old in an Urban Community* (London, 1968).

Newson, John, and Newson, Elizabeth, 'Psychology as a Listening Ear', in G. Bunn, A. D. Lovie, and G. D. Richards (eds), *Psychology in Britain: Historical Essays and Personal Reflections* (Leicester, 2001), pp. 411–21.

Newson, John, and Newson, Elizabeth, *Seven Years Old in the Home Environment* (London, 1976).

Noble, Grant, *Children in Front of the Small Screen* (London, 1975).

O'Carroll, Tom, *Paedophilia: The Radical Case* (London, 1980).

Odlum, Doris, 'Some Wartime Problems of Mental Health', *Mental Health*, 2 (1941), 33–7.

O'Malley, Jan, *The Politics of Community Action: A Decade of Struggle in Notting Hill* (Nottingham, 1977).

Opie, Iona, and Opie, Peter, *Children's Games in Street and Playground* (Oxford, 1969).

Oz, 'School Kids' issue (28 May 1970).

Palmer, Sue, *Toxic Childhood: How Modern Life is Damaging our Children . . . and What We Can Do About It* (London, 2006).

Palmer, Sue, *Detoxing Childhood: What Parents Need to Know to Raise Happy Successful Children* (London, 2007).

Paneth, Marie, *Branch Street: A Sociological Study* (London, 1944).

Panter-Downes, Mollie, 'The Children Who Don't Trust Anybody', *Sunday Dispatch* (7 April 1946).

Parker, Howard, *View from the Boys: A Sociology of Down-Town Adolescents* (London, 1974).

Parker, Tony, *The Twisting Lane: Some Sex Offenders* (London, 1969).

Partington, Frank, and Partington, Molly, *The Art of Photographing Children* (London, 1945).

Payne, M. A., *Oliver Untwisted* (London, 1929).

Pear, T. H., 'Psychology and the Listener', *BBC Quarterly*, 4:4 (Winter 1949–50), 154–9.

Perry, Colin, *Boy in the Blitz* (London, 1972).

Petroleum Films Bureau, *Film Production for Child Audiences—A Psychological Study* (London, 1952).

Pocock, Douglas, and Hudson, Ray, *Images of the Urban Environment* (London, 1978).

Prout, Alan, *The Future of Childhood: Towards the Interdisciplinary Study of Childhood* (London, 2004).

Radcliffe, T. A., 'The Psychological Problems of the Returned Ex-Service Men', *Mental Health*, 7:1 (1947), 2–5.

Radzinowicz, Leon, *Sexual Offences: A Report of the Cambridge Department of Criminal Science* (London, 1957).

Radzinowicz, Leon, *Adventures in Criminology* (London, 1999).

Richman, N., 'Effects of Housing on Preschool Children and their Mothers', *Developmental Medicine and Child Neurology*, 10 (1974), 1–9.

Righton, Peter, 'The Adult', in Brian Taylor (ed.), *Perspectives on Paedophilia* (London, 1981), pp. 24–38.

Ringold, Evelyn S., 'Bringing up Baby in Britain', *New York Times* (13 June 1965).

Robertson, James, *Young Children in Hospital* (1958).

Rooth, Graham, 'Changes in the Conviction Rate for Indecent Exposure', *British Journal of Psychiatry*, 121 (1972), 89–94.

Rooth, Graham, 'Exhibitionism, Sexual Violence and Paedophilia', *British Journal of Psychiatry*, 122 (1973), 705–10.

Rossman, P., *Sexual Experience between Men and Boys* (New York, 1976).

Rotten, Elisabeth, *Children, War's Victims: The Education of the Handicapped* (Paris, 1949).

Rutter, Michael, 'Why are London Children so Disturbed?', *Proceedings of the Royal Society of Medicine*, 66 (1973).

Rutter, Michael, Maughan, Barbara, Mortimore, Peter, Ouston, Janet, and Smith, Alan, *Fifteen Thousand hours: Secondary Schools and their Effects on Children* (London, 1979).

Sadler, Judy (Enquiry for the Road Research Laboratory), *Children and Road Safety: A Survey amongst Mothers, 1969* (London, 1972).

Sandels, Stina, *Children in Traffic* (London, 1975).

Schweitzer, Pam, *Goodnight Children Everywhere: Memories of Evacuation in World War II* (London, 1990).

Searle, Chris, *None but Our Words: Critical Literacy in Classroom and Literacy* (Buckingham, 1997).

Sennett, Richard, *The Uses of Disorder: Personal Identity and City Life* (New York, 1970).

Shepherd, Michael, *The Psychosocial Matrix of Psychiatry* (London, 1983).

Shepherd, Michael, Oppenheim, A. N., and Mitchell, S., *Childhood Behaviour and Mental Health* (London, 1970).

Slater, Eliot, and Woodside, Moya, *Patterns of Marriage: A Study of Marriage Relationships in the Urban Working Classes* (London, 1951).

Smith, Bernard A., 'American Television at the Crossroads', *BBC Quarterly*, 7:3 (Autumn 1952), 129–35.

Smith, Michael, 'The Alternative Press and Teacher Education: A Review', *British Journal of Teacher Education*, 1 (1975), 55–62.

Spencer, David, and Lloyd, John, *A Child's Eye View of Small Heath Birmingham: Perception Studies for Environmental Education* (Birmingham, 1974).

Steedman, C., Urwin, C., and Walkerdine, V. (eds) *Language, Gender and Childhood* (London, 1985).

Stephens, Tom (ed.), *Problem Families: An Experiment in Social Rehabilitation* (London, 1945).

Stewart, W. F. R., *Children in Flats: A Family Study* (London, 1970).

Stott, D., 'The Effects of Separation from the Mother in Early Life', *Lancet*, 1 (1956), 624.

Taylor, Brian (ed.), *Perspectives on Paedophilia* (London, 1981).

Taylor, Stephen, and Chave, Sidney, *Mental Health and Environment* (London, 1964).

Tizard, Jack, Moss, Peter, and Perry, Jane, *All Our Children: Pre-School Services in a Changing Society* (London, 1976).

Tomlinson, Sally, *Ethnic Minorities in British Schools: Review of the Literature* (Aldershot, 1987).

Tudor-Hart, Beatrix, *Toys, Play and Discipline in Childhood* (London, 1955).

Walton, Paul, and Young, Jock (eds), *The New Criminology Revisited* (London, 1998).

Ward, Colin, (ed.), *Vandalism* (London, 1973).

Ward, Colin, *Anarchy in Action* (London, 1973).

Ward, Colin, *The Child in the City* (London, 1978).

Ward, Colin, *Influences: Voices of Creative Dissent* (Bideford, 1991).

Ward, Colin, 'Opportunities for Childhoods in Late Twentieth Century Britain', in B. Mayall (ed.), *Children's Childhoods Observed and Experienced* (London, 1994).

Ward, Colin, and Fyson, Anthony, *Streetwork: The Exploding School* (London, 1973).

Wells, John, *Child Photography* (London, 1927).

West, D. J., *Sexual Crimes and Confrontations: A Study of Victims and Offenders* (Aldershot, 1987).

Wheare, K. C., *Report of the Departmental Committee on Cinema and Children* (London, 1950).

White, L. E., 'The Outdoor Play of Children Living in Flats', in Leo Kuper (ed.), *Living in Towns* (London, 1953), pp. 237–64.

Whitehouse, Mary, *A Most Dangerous Woman* (Tring, 1982).

Wilson, Glenn D. and Cox, David N., *The Child-Lovers: A Study of Paedophiles in Society* (London, 1983).

Wiltshire Schools M4 Motorway Project, *Birth of a Road: A Study in Environmental Education based on the Wiltshire Schools M4 Motorway Project* (London, 1973).

Winnicott, D. W., 'Children's Hostels in War and Peace', in Symposium on 'Lessons for Child Psychiatry', *British Journal of Medical Psychology*, 21 (1948), 175–80.

Winnicott, D. W., *The Child and the Family* (London, 1957).

Winnicott, D. W., *The Child and the Outside World* (London, 1957).

Winnicott, D. W., and Britton, Clare, 'Residential Management as Treatment for Difficult Children', in D. W. Winnicott, Clare Winnicott, et al. (eds), *Deprivation and Delinquency* (London, 1984).

Woodroffe, Caroline, Roberts, Ian, and DiGuiseppi, Carolyn, *The School Run: Blessing or Blight?* (London, 1998).

Wootton, Barbara, 'A Social Scientist's Approach to Maternal Deprivation', in WHO, *Deprivation of Maternal Care: A Reassessment of its Effects* (Geneva, 1962), pp. 63–73.

Wright, J. K., 'Terrae Incognitae: The Place of the Imagination in Geography', *Annals of the Association of American Geographers*, 37 (1947), 1–15.

Yates, Alayne, *Sex without Shame: Encouraging the Child's Healthy Sexual Development* (New York, 1978).

Young, Jock, Taylor, Ian, and Walton, Paul (eds), *The New Criminology* (London, 1973).

Yudkin, Simon, *0–5: A Report on the Care of Pre-School Children* (London, 1968).

Reports: (a) Government

Board of Education and Ministry of Transport, *Report of the Inter-Departmental Committee on Road Safety among School Children* (London, 1936).

Central Advisory Council for Education, *Children and their Primary Schools: A Report of the Central Advisory Council for Education* (London, 1967).

Central Policy Review Staff, *Services for Young Children with Working Mother* (London, 1978).

Department of Education and Science, *Education: A Framework for Expansion* (London, 1972).

Ministry of Transport, *Final Report of the Committee on Road Safety, May 1947* (London, 1953).

Ministry of War Transport, *Interim Report of the Committee on Road Safety, December 1944* (London, 1945).

Report of the Care of the Children Committee Cmd. 6922 (London, 1946).

Report of the Committee on Homosexual Offences and Prostitution (London, 1957).

Report of the Departmental Committee on Sexual Offences against Children and Young Persons in Scotland (London, 1926).

Report of the Departmental Committee on Sexual Offences against Young Persons (London, 1926).

Reports: (b) Non-governmental Organizations

BBC/ITA, *Children and Television Programmes* (London, 1960).

British Medical Association and the Magistrate's Association Joint Committee, *Cruelty to and Neglect of Children* (London, 1956).

National Council of Public Morality, *Cinema Commison of Enquiry: The Cinema: Its Present Position and Future Possibilities* (London, 1917).

A Report of a Conference Held at the Institute of Child Psychology on the Theory and Technique of Direct Objective Therapy (London, 1950).

Royal Institute of British Architects, *A Right to be Children: Designing for the Education of the Under-Fives* (London, 1976).

Royal Society for the Prevention of Accidents, *Road Accident Statistics* (London, 1966).

UNESCO, *Children of Europe* (Paris, 1949).

UNESCO, *The Influence of Home and Community on Children under Thirteen Years of Age* (Paris, 1949).

UNICEF, *Child Poverty in Perspective: An Overview of Child Well-Being in Rich Countries* (New York, 2007).

UNRRA, 'Psychological Problems of Displaced Persons' (June, 1945).

WHO, *Deprivation of Maternal Care: A Reassessment of its Effects* (Geneva, 1962).

Newspapers and Magazines

BBC Quarterly
British Medical Journal
Children's Rights

Daily Mail
Daily Mirror
Daily Telegraph
Guardian
Independent
Lancet
Mental Health
Mother and Child
New Society
New York Times
Nursery World
Observer
Parents
Picture Post
Quarterly of Film, Radio, and Television
The Times

Archival Sources
BBC Written Archives, Caversham:
  WAC R11/51/1–4
  WAC, R34/1155/1, Joint BBC/ITA Committee on 'Television and the Child'
  WAC, R34/1155/5, 'Draft Foreword to the Report of the Joint Committee on Television and the Child', 9 June 1960
  WAC, R44/1/1,057/1, Survey of the press response to the 'Children and Television Programmes' report, 10 August 1960
  WAC T16/46: Commissioned Report on Children's Television, 1951–2
  WAC T16/303: Nuffield Foundation Enquiry, 1953–9
  WAC, T16/304: Nuffield Foundation Enquiry—BBC Study Group, 1958–9
  WAC, T166/689, letters from Hilde Himmelweit to Mr McGivern (Deputy Director of Television Broadcasting) and Kenneth Adam
Mass-Observation Archive, University of Sussex: File Reports: 1910, 1662, 3106.
Modern Records Centre, University of Warwick:
  Papers of Lady Allen of Hurtwood: MSS. 121

PUBLISHED SECONDARY SOURCES

Agajanian, Rowana, ' "Just for Kids?" Saturday Morning Cinema and Britain's Children's Film Foundation in the 1960s', *Historical Journal of Film, Radio and Television*, 18 (1988), 395–409.
Allport, Alan, *Demobbed: Returning Home after World War Two* (London, 2009).
Angelides, Steven, 'Feminism, Child Sexual Abuse, and the Erasure of Child Sexuality', *GLQ: A Journal of Lesbian and Gay Studies*, 10 (2004), 141–77.
Apple, Rima, *Mothers and Medicine: A Social History of Infant Feeding, 1890–1950* (Madison, WI, 1987).
Ariès, Philip, *Centuries of Childhood* (London, 1962).
Aston, Elaine, ' "Transforming" Women's Lives: Bobby Baker's Performances of "Daily Life" ', *New Theatre Quarterly*, 16 (2000), 17–25.
Bailey, Victor, *Delinquency and Citizenship: Reclaiming the Young Offender, 1914–1948* (Oxford, 1987).

Bailey, Victor, and Blackburn, Sheila, 'The Punishment of Incest Act 1908: A Case Study of Law Creation', *Criminal Law Review* (1979), 708–18.

Barthes, Roland, *Camera Lucida* (London, 1982).

Bashford, Alison, and Levine, Philippa (eds), *The Oxford Handbook of the History of Eugenics* (Oxford, 2010).

Bauman, Zygmunt, *Modernity and the Holocaust* (Cambridge, 1989).

Beck, Ulrich, *Risk Society: Towards a New Modernity* (London, 1992).

Behlmer, George K., *Child Abuse and Moral Reform in England, 1870–1908* (Stanford, 1982).

Behlmer, George K., *The Child Protection Movement in England, 1860–1890* (Stanford, 1997).

Behlmer, George K., and Leventhal, F. M. (eds), *Singular Continuities: Tradition, Nostalgia, and Identity in Modern British Culture* (Stanford, 2000).

Bell, Amy, 'Landscapes of Fear: Wartime London, 1939–1945', *Journal of British Studies*, 48 (2009), 153–75.

Bell, Stuart, *When Salem Came to Boro: The True Story of the Cleveland Child Abuse Crisis* (London, 1988).

Bingham, Adrian, *Family Newspapers? Sex, Private Life and the British Popular Press 1918–1978* (Oxford, 2009).

Bingham, Adrian, 'The "K-Bomb": Social Surveys, the popular Press, and British Sexual Culture in the 1940s and 1950s', *Journal of British Studies*, 50 (2011), 156–79.

Birch, Tony, '"These Children Have Been Born in an Abyss": Slum Photography in a Melbourne Suburb', *Australian Historical Studies*, 35 (2004), 1–15.

Birmingham Feminist History Group, 'Feminism as Femininity in the 1950s', *Feminist Review*, 3 (1979).

Black, Lawrence, 'Whose Finger on the Button? British Television and the Politics of Cultural Control', *Historical Journal of Film, Radio, and Television*, 25 (2005), 547–75.

Bourg, Julian, *From Revolution to Ethics: May 1968 and Contemporary French Thought* (Montreal, 2007).

Bourke, Joanna, 'Going Home: The Personal Adjustment of British and American Service-men after the War', in R. Bessel and D. Schumann (eds), *Life after Death: Approaches to a Cultural and Social History during the 1940s and 1950s* (Cambridge, 2003), pp. 149–60.

Bowley, Agatha, *Children at Risk* (London, 1975).

Bradley, Kate, 'Juvenile Delinquency, the Juvenile Courts and the Settlement Movement 1908–1950: Basil Henriques and Toynbee Hall', *Twentieth Century British History*, 19 (2008), 133–55.

Brooke, Stephen, 'Evan Durbin: Reassessing a Labour "Revisionist"', *Twentieth Century British History*, 7 (1996), 27–52.

Buckingham, David, Davies, Hannah, Jones, Ken, and Kelley, Peter, *Children's Television in Britain: History, Discourse and Policy* (London, 1999).

Burke, Catherine, Cunningham, Peter, and Grosvenor, Ian, '"Putting Education in its Place": Space, Place and Materialities in the History of Education', *History of Education*, 39 (2000), 677–80.

Burman, Erica, *Deconstructing Developmental Psychology* (Routledge, 2008).

Calder, Angus, *The People's War, 1939–45* (London, 1969).

Carby, Hazel V., 'Schooling in Babylon', in the Centre for Contemporary Cultural Studies, *The Empire Strikes Back: Race and Racism in 70s Britain* (London, 1982), pp. 183–211.

Carey, John, *William Golding: The Man who Wrote Lord of the Flies* (London, 2009).

Carrey, Normand, 'Interview with Sir Michael Rutter', *Journal of the Canadian Academy of Child and Adolescent Psychiatry*, 19 (2010), 212–17.

Caven, Hannah, 'Horror in Our Time: Images of the Concentration Camps—The British Media, 1945', *Historical Journal of Film, Radio, and Television*, 21 (2001), 205–54.

Ceadel, Martin, *Pacifism in Britain 1914–1945: The Defining of a Faith* (Oxford, 1980).

Chambers, Deborah, 'Family as Place: Family Photograph Albums and the Domestication of Public and Private Space', in Joan M. Schwartz and James M. Ryan (eds), *Picturing Place: Photography and the Geographical Imagination* (New York, 2003), pp. 96–114.

Chawla, Louise, 'Growing Up in Cities: A Report on Research under Way', *Environment and Urbanization*, 9 (1997), 247–51.

Christensen, Pia, and O'Brien, Margaret (eds), *Children in the City: Home, Neighbourhood and Community* (London, 2003).

Coe, Jonathan, *Like a Fiery Elephant: A Life of B. S. Johnson* (London, 2004).

Cohen, Alan, *The Revolution in Post-War Family Casework: The Story of Pacifist Service Units and Family Units, 1940–1959* (Lancaster, 1998).

Colls, Robert, *Identity of England* (Oxford, 2002).

Cooter, Roger (ed.), *In the Name of the Child: Health and Welfare, 1880–1940* (London, 1992).

Cox, Pamela, 'Girls, Deficiency and Delinquency', in David Wright and Anne Digby (eds), *From Idiocy to Mental Deficiency: Historical Perspectives on People with Learning Disabilities* (London, 1996), pp. 184–206.

Cretney, Stephen, *Law, Law Reform and the Family* (Oxford, 1998).

Croall, Jonathan, *Neill of Summerhill—The Permanent Rebel* (London, 1983).

Cronin, James, 'The British State and the Structure of Political Opportunity', *Journal of British Studies*, 27 (1988), 199–231.

Cronin, James, *The Politics of State Expansion* (London, 1991).

Cunningham, Hugh, 'Histories of Childhood', *American Historical Review*, 103 (1998), 1195–208.

Cunningham, Hugh, *Children and Childhood in Western Society since 1500* (London, 2005).

Cunningham, Hugh, *The Invention of Childhood* (London, 2006).

Davies, Andrew, *The Gangs of Manchester: The Story of the Scuttlers, Britain's First Youth Cult* (Preston, 2008).

Davis, John, 'The Inner London Education Authority and the William Tyndale School Affair, 1974–1978', *Oxford Review of Education*, 28 (2002), 275–98.

Deakin, Nicholas, and Edwards, John, *The Enterprise Culture and the Inner City* (London, 1993).

Delany, Paul, *Bill Brandt: A Life* (Stanford, CA, 2004).

Denham, Andrew, and Garnett, Mark, *Keith Joseph* (Chesham, 2001).

Dijken, Suzan van, *John Bowlby: His Early Life: A Biographical Journey into the Roots of Attachment Theory* (London, 1998).

Duniec, Eduardo, and Raz, Mical, 'Vitamins for the Soul: John Bowlby's Thesis of Maternal Deprivation, Biomedical Metaphor, and the Deficiency Model of Disease', *History of Psychiatry*, 22 (2011), 93–107.

Durham, Martin, *Sex and Politics: The Family and Morality in the Thatcher Years* (Basingstoke, 1991).

Edgerton, David, *Warfare State: Britain, 1920–1970* (Cambridge, 2006).

Edwards, Ruth Dudley, *Victor Gollancz: A Biography* (London, 1987).

Egan, Danielle E., and Hawkes, Gail, 'Childhood Sexuality, Normalization and the Social Hygiene Movement in the Anglophone West, 1900–1935', *Social History of Medicine*, 23 (2010), 56–78.

Eley, Geoff, 'Finding the People's War: Film, British Collective Memory and World War II', *American Historical Review*, 106 (2001), 818–38.

Evans, Martin, and Lunn, Ken (eds), *War and Memory in the Twentieth Century* (Oxford, 1997).

Farquharson, John, ' "Emotional but Influential": Victor Gollancz, Richard Stokes and the British Zone of Germany, 1945–9', *Journal of Contemporary History*, 22 (1987), 501–19.

Ferguson, Harry, *Protecting Children in Time* (Basingstoke, 2004).

Finlayson, G., *Citizen, State, and Social Welfare in Britain, 1830–1990* (Oxford, 1990).

Finlayson, G., 'A Moving Frontier: Voluntarism and the State in British Social Welfare, 1911–1949', *Twentieth Century British History*, 1 (1990), 183–206.

Fink, Janet, 'Inside a Hall of Mirrors: Residential Care and the Shifting Constructions of Childhood in Mid-Twentieth Century Britain', *Pedagogia Historica*, 44 (2008), 287–307.

Fishman, S., 'The History of Childhood Sexuality', *Journal of Contemporary History*, 17 (1982), 269–83.

Fowler, David, *Youth Culture in Modern Britain, c.1922–c.1970* (Basingstoke, 2008).

Francis, Martin, 'Set the People Free? Conservatives and the State, 1920–1960', in Ina Zweiniger-Bargielowska and Martin Francis (eds), *The Conservative Party and British Society* (Cardiff, 1996), pp. 56–77.

Frank, Matthew, 'The New Morality—Victor Gollancz, "Save Europe Now" and the German Refugee Crisis, 1945–46', *Twentieth Century British History*, 17 (2006), 230–56.

Friedan, Betty, *The Feminine Mystique* (London, 1971; 1st edn 1963).

Frizzell, Deborah, *Humphrey Spender's Humanist Landscapes: Photo-Documents, 1932–42* (New Haven, CT, 1997).

Furedi, Frank, *Culture of Fear: Risk-Taking and the Morality of Low Expectation* (London, 1997).

Furedi, Frank, *Therapy Culture: Cultivating Vulnerability in an Uncertain Age* (London, 2004).

Fussell, Paul, *The Great War and Modern Memory* (New York, 1977).

Giles, Judy, 'A Home of One's Own: Women and Domesticity in England, 1918–1950', *Women's Studies International Forum*, 16 (1993), 239–53.

Gleeson, Brendan and Spie, Neil (eds.), *Creating Child Friendly Cities* (New York, 2006).

Goodman, Jonathan, *The Moors Murders: The Trial of Myra Hindley and Ian Brady* (London, 1973).

Gregory, Adrian, *The Silence of Memory* (Oxford, 1994).

Gunn, Simon, 'The Buchanan Report, Environment and the Problem of Traffic in 1960s Britain', *Twentieth Century British History*, 22 (2011), 521–42.

Gurjeva, Lyubov, 'Child Health, Commerce and Family Values: The Domestic Production of the Middle Class in Late-Nineteenth and Early-Twentieth Century Britain', in Marijke Gijswijt-Hofstra and Hilary Marland (eds), *Cultures of Child Health in Britain and the Netherlands in the Twentieth Century* (Amsterdam, 2003), pp. 103–26.

Gutman, Marta and de Coninck-Smith, Ning (eds), *Designing Modern Childhoods: History, Space, and the Material Culture of Children* (London, 2008).

Hacking, Ian, 'The Making and Molding of Child Abuse', *Critical Inquiry*, 17 (1991), 253–88.

Hall, Stuart, 'The Social Eye of *Picture Post*', *Working Papers in Cultural Studies*, 2 (Spring 1972), 71–120.

Hampshire, James, 'The Politics of School Sex Education Policy in England and Wales from the 1940s to the 1960s', *Social History of Medicine*, 18 (2005), 87–105.

Hampshire, James, and Lewis, Jane, ' "The Ravages of Permissiveness": Sex Education and the Permissive Society', *Twentieth Century British History*, 15 (2004), 290–312.

Hardyment, Christina, *Dream Babies: Childcare from Locke to Spock* (London, 1983).

Harris, Jose, 'Did British Workers Want the Welfare State? G. D. H. Cole's Survey of 1942', in J. Winter (ed.), *The Working Class in Modern British History: Essays in Honour of Henry Pelling* (Oxford, 1983), pp. 200–14.

Harris, Jose, 'Political Ideas and the Debate on State Welfare 1940–45', in H. Smith (ed.), *War and Social Change* (Manchester, 1986), pp. 233–63.

Harris, Jose, 'Political Thought and the Welfare State 1870–1940: An Intellectual Framework for British Social Policy', *Past and Present*, 135 (1992), 116–41.

Harrison, Brian, 'The Rise, Fall, and Rise of Political Consensus in Britain since 1940', *History*, 84 (1999), 301–24.

Harrison, Martin, *Young Meteors: British Photojournalism: 1957–65* (London, 1998).

Harrisson, Tom, *Living through the Blitz* (London, 1976).

Hawkes, Gail L., and Egan, R. Danielle, 'Developing the Sexual Child', *Journal of Historical Sociology*, 21:4 (2008), 443–65.

Haworth-Booth, Mark (ed.), *The Street Photographs of Roger Mayne* (London, 1993).

Hendrick, Harry, *Images of Youth: Age, Class, and the Male Youth Problem 1880–1920* (Oxford, 1990).

Hendrick, Harry, *Child Welfare: England 1872–1989* (London, 1994).

Hendrick, Harry, *Children, Childhood and English Society, 1880–1990* (Cambridge, 1997).

Hendrick, Harry, *Child Welfare: Historical Dimensions, Contemporary Debate* (Bristol, 2003).

Hendrick, Harry, 'Children's Emotional Well-being and Mental Health in Early Post-Second World War Britain: The Case of Hospital Visiting', in M. Gijswijt-Hofstra and Hilary Marland (eds), *Cultures of Child Health in Britain and the Netherlands in the Twentieth Century* (Amsterdam, 2003), 213–42.

Hewison, Robert, *The Heritage Industry: Britain in a Climate of Decline* (London, 1987).

Heywood, Colin, *A History of Childhood* (Cambridge, 2001).

Higonnet, Anne, *Pictures of Innocence: The History and Crisis of Ideal Childhood* (London, 1998).

Hillman, Mayer, Adams, John, and Whitelegg, John, *One False Move: A Study of Children's Independent Mobility* (London, 1990).

Hinton, James, *Protests and Visions: Peace Politics in Twentieth-Century Britain* (London, 1989).

Hirshch, Marianne, *Family Frames: Photography, Narrative and Postmemory* (Cambridge MA, 1997).

Hoggart, Richard, *The Uses of Literacy* (London, 1959).

Holden, Katherine, 'Other People's Children: Single Women and Residential Childcare in Mid-Twentieth Century England', *Management and Organizational History*, 5 (2010), 314–30.

Holland, Patricia, *Picturing Childhood: The Myth of the Child in Popular Imagery* (London, 2004).

Hollow, Matthew, 'Governmentality on the Park Hill Estate: The Rationality of Public Housing', *Urban History*, 37 (2010), 117–35.

Holmes, Jeremy, *John Bowlby and Attachment Theory* (London, 1993).

Home, Anna, *In the Box of Delights: A History of Children's Television* (London, 1993).

Hopkinson, Tom (ed.), *Picture Post, 1938–50* (London, 1970).

Horst, Frank C. P. van der and Veer, René van der, 'Separation and Divergence: The Untold Story of James Robertson's and John Bowlby's Dispute on Mother–Child Separation', *Journal of the History of the Behavioral Sciences*, 45 (2010), 236–52.

Hubble, Nick, ' "An Evacuee For Ever": B. S. Johnson versus Ego Psychology', in Philip Tew and Glynn White (eds), *Re-Reading B. S. Johnson* (London, 2007), pp. 143–57.

Hulbert, Anne, *Raising America: Experts, Parents, and a Century of Advice about Children* (New York, 2003).

Humphries, Jane, *Childhood and Child Labour in the Industrial Revolution* (Cambridge, 2010).

Humphries, S., *Hooligans or Rebels: An Oral History of Working-Class Childhood and Youth 1889–1939* (Oxford, 1981).

Ishaque, Muhamad M., and Noland, Robert B., 'Making Roads Safe for Pedestrians or Keeping Them Out of the Way?', *Journal of Transport History*, 27/1 (2006), 115–37.

Issroff, Judith, *Donald Winnicott and John Bowlby: Personal and Professional Perspectives* (London, 2005).

Jackson, Louise, *Child Sexual Abuse in Victorian England* (London, 2000).

Jackson, Louise, 'Women Professionals and the Regulation of Violence in Interwar Britain', in Shani De Cruze (ed.), *Everyday Violence in Britain, 1850–1950* (Harlow, 2000), pp. 119–35.

Jackson, Louise, *Women Police: Gender, Welfare and Surveillance in the Twentieth Century* (Manchester, 2006).

Jackson, Louise, and Bartie, Angela, 'Children of the City: Juvenile Justice, Property and Place in England and Scotland, 1945–60', *Economic History Review*, 64 (2011), 88–113.

Jackson, Mark, *The Borderland of Imbecility: Medicine, Society and the Fabrication of the Feeble Mind in Late Victorian and Edwardian England* (Manchester, 2000).

Jay, Margaret, and Doganis, Sally, *Battered: The Abuse of Children* (London, 1987).

Jenkins, Philip, *Changing Concepts of the Child Molester in Modern America* (New Haven, CT, and London, 1998).

Jones, Edgar, Woolven, Robin, Durodié, Bill, and Wessley, Simon, 'Civilian Morale during the Second World War: Responses to the Air Raids Re-Examined', *Social History of Medicine*, 17 (2004), 463–79.

Keating, Jenny, *A Child for Keeps: The History of Adoption in England, 1918–1945* (Basingstoke, 2009).

Kern, Stephen, 'Freud and the Discovery of Child Sexuality', *History of Childhood Quarterly*, 1 (1973), 117–41.

Kern, Stephen, *The Culture of Time and Space, 1880–1918* (London, 1983).

King, Laura, 'Hidden Fathers? The Significance of Fatherhood in Mid-Twentieth-Century Britain', *Contemporary British History* 26:1 (2012), 25–46.

King, Pearl, and Steiner, Ricardo (eds), *The Freud–Klein Controversies, 1941–45* (London, 1991).

Kinkaid, James, *Erotic Innocence: The Culture of Child Molesting* (London, 1998).

Koven, Seth, *Slumming: Sexual and Social Politics in Victorian London* (Princeton, NJ, 2004).

Kozlovsky, Roy, 'Adventure Playgrounds and Postwar Reconstruction', in Marta Gutman and Ning de Conink-Smith (eds), *History, Space and the Material Culture of Children* (New Brunswick, NJ, 2008), pp. 171–90.

Kozlovsky, Roy, 'Urban Play: Intimate Space and Post-War Subjectivity', in Vittoria Di Palma, Diana Periton, and Marina Lathouri (eds), *Intimate Metropolis* (Abingdon, 2009), pp. 195–216.

Kuhn, Annette, *Family Secrets: Acts of Memory and Imagination* (London, 1995).

Kushner, Tony, 'The Impact of the Holocaust on British Society and Culture', *Contemporary British History*, 5 (1991), 349–75.

Kushner, Tony, *The Holocaust and the Liberal Imagination* (Oxford, 1994).

Kynaston, David, *Family Britain, 1951–57* (London, 2009).

Langan, Mary, 'The Rise and Fall of Social Work', in John Clarke (ed.), *A Crisis in Care: Challenges to Social Work* (Milton Keynes, 1993), pp. 48–58.

Langhamer, Claire, 'The Meaning of Home in Post-War Britain', *Journal of Contemporary History*, 40 (2005), 341–62.

Langhamer, Claire, 'Adultery in Postwar Britain', *History Workshop Journal*, 62 (2006), 86–115.

Lee, Nick, 'The Extensions of Childhood: Technologies, Children, and Independence', in Ian Hutchby and Jo Moran Ellis (eds), *Children, Technology and Culture: The Impacts of Technologies in Children's Everyday Lives* (London, 2001), pp. 153–69.

Lefebvre, Henri, *The Production of Space* (Oxford, 1991).

Le Grand, Julian, 'Knights, Knaves or Pawns? Human Behaviour and Social Policy', *Journal of Social Policy*, 26 (1997), 149–62.

Le Grand, Julian, *Motivation, Agency and Public Policy: Of Knights and Knaves, Pawns and Queens* (Oxford, 2003).

Lenman, Robin (ed.), *The Oxford Companion to Photography* (Oxford, 2005).

Levene, Alysa, 'Family Breakdown and the "Welfare Child" in 19th and 20th Century Britain', *History of the Family*, 11 (2006), 67–79.

Lewis, Jane, 'Family Provision of Welfare in the Mixed Economy of Care in the Late Nineteenth and Twentieth Centuries', *Social History of Medicine*, 8 (1995), 1–16.

Lewis, Jane, 'The Failure to Expand Childcare Provision and to Develop a Comprehensive Childcare Policy in Britain during the 1960s and 1970s', *Twentieth Century British History*, 24 (2013), 249–74.

Lewis, Jane, (ed.), *Children, Changing Families and the Welfare State* (Cheltenham, 2006).

Loney, Martin, *Community against Government: The British Community Development Project 1968–78* (London, 1983).

Lowe, Rodney, 'The Second World War: Consensus and the Foundation of the British Welfare State', *Twentieth Century British History*, 1 (1990), 152–82.

Lowe, Rodney, *The Welfare State in Britain since 1945* (Basingstoke, 1993).

Lowe, Roy, *Education in the Post-War Years, 1945–1964* (London, 1988).

Lowe, Rodney, *Schooling and Social Change, 1964–1990* (London, 1996).

Luckin, Bill, 'War on the Roads: Traffic Accidents and Social Tension in Britain, 1939–1945', in Roger Cooter and Bill Luckin (eds), *Accidents in History: Injuries, Fatalities and Social Relations* (Amsterdam, 1997), pp. 234–54,

Lupton, Deborah, *Risk* (London, 1999).

McCormick, John, *The Global Environmental Movement* (London, 1995).

McKibbin, Ross, *The Ideologies of Class: Social Relations in Britain, 1880–1950* (Oxford, 1990).

McKibbin, Ross, *Classes and Cultures in England, 1918–1951* (Oxford, 1994).

Macnicol, John, 'The Effect of Evacuation of School Children on Attitudes to State Intervention', in H. Smith (ed.), *War and Social Change* (Manchester, 1988), pp. 3–31.

Mandler, Peter, 'John Summerson, 1904–1992: The Architectural Critic and the Quest of the Modern', in Susan Pedersen and Peter Mandler (eds), *After the Victorians: Private Conscience and Public Duty in Modern Britain* (London, 1994), pp. 228–45.

Mandler, Peter, *History and National Life* (London, 2002).

Mandler, Peter, 'Margaret Mead amongst the Natives of Great Britain', *Past and Present*, 204 (2009), 195–233.

Mandler, Peter, 'One World, Many Cultures: Margaret Mead and the Limits of Cold War Anthropology', *History Workshop Journal*, 68 (2009), 149–72.

Mandler, Peter, 'Being his Own Rabbit: Geoffrey Gorer and English Culture', in Clare Griffiths, James Nott, and William Whyte (eds), *Classes, Cultures and Politics: Essays on British History for Ross McKibbin* (Oxford, 2011), pp. 192–208.

Marcus, Alan, 'The Child in the City', *History of Photography*, 30 (2006), 119–33.

Marwick, Arthur, *Britain in the Century of Total War* (London, 1968).

Matless, D., *Landscape and Englishness* (London, 1998).

Mause, Lloyd de, *The History of Childhood* (London, 1976).

Mayall, Berry, and Morrow, Virginia, *English Children's Work during the Second World War* (London, 2011).

Mazower, Mark, *Dark Continent: Europe's Twentieth Century* (London, 1997).

Meyer, Anneke, *The Child at Risk: Paedophilia, Media Responses and Public Opinion* (Manchester, 2007).

Moran, Joe, 'Crossing the Road in Britain, 1931–1976', *Historical Journal*, 49 (2006), 477–96.

Morley, David, *Family Television: Cultural Power and Domestic Leisure* (London, 1986).

Morrisett, Lloyd, 'The Age of Television and the Television Age', *Peabody Journal of Education*, 48 (January 1971), 112.

Mulford, Jeremy (ed.), *Worktown People: Photographs from Northern England, 1937–38 by Humphrey Spender* (Bristol, 1982).

Noakes, Lucy, 'Making Histories: Experiencing the Blitz in London's Museums in the 1990s', in Martin Evans and Ken Lunn (eds), *War and Memory in the Twentieth Century* (Oxford, 1997), pp. 89–104.

Nuttall, Jeremy, 'Psychological Socialist: Militant Moderate: Evan Durbin and the Politics of Synthesis', *Labour History Review*, 68 (2003), 235–52.

Nuttall, Jeremy, *Psychological Socialism: The Labour Party and the Qualities of Mind and Character, 1931 to the Present* (Manchester, 2006).

O'Connell, Sean, *The Car in British Society: Class, Gender, and Motoring, 1896–1939* (Manchester, 1998).

Offer, Avner, *The Challenge of Affluence: Self Control and Well Being in the United States and Britain since 1950* (Oxford, 2006).

O'Hara, Glen, *Governing Post-War Britain: The Paradoxes of Progress, 1951–1973* (Basingstoke, 2012).

Ohi, Kevin, 'Molestation 101: Child Abuse, Homophobia, and the Boys of St Vincent', *GLQ: A Journal of Lesbian and Gay Studies*, 6 (2000), 195–248.

Osgerby, Bill, *Youth in Britain since 1945* (Oxford, 1998).

Oswell, David, *Television, Childhood and the Home: A History of the Making of the Child Television Audience in Britain* (Oxford, 2002).

Overy, Richard, *The Morbid Age: Britain between the Wars* (London, 2009).

Pain, Rachel, 'Paranoid Parenting? Rematerializing Risk and Fear for Children', *Social and Cultural Geography*, 7 (2006), 221–43.

Parsons, Martin, *'I'll Take that One': Dispelling the Myths of Civilian Evacuation, 1939–45* (Peterborough, 1998).

Parsons, Martin, and Starns, Penny, *The Evacuation: The True Story* (Peterborough, 1999).

Parton, Nigel, 'The Natural History of Child Abuse: A Study in Social Problem Definition', *British Journal of Social Work*, 9:4 (1979), 431–51.

Parton, Nigel, 'Child Abuse, Social Anxiety and Welfare', *British Journal of Social Work*, 11 (1981), 391–414.

Parton, Nigel, *The Politics of Abuse* (Basingstoke, 1985).

Pimlott, Ben, 'The Myth of Consensus', in L. M. Smith (ed.), *The Making of Britain* (London, 1988), pp. 129–42.

Plowden, William, *The Motor Car and Politics, 1896–1970* (London, 1971).

Plummer, Ken, 'Images of Paedophilia', in Mark Cook and Glenn Wilson (eds), *Love and Attraction: An International Conference* (Oxford, 1979), pp. 537–40.

Pooley, Colin, 'Mobility in the Twentieth Century: Substituting Commuting for Mobility?' in David Gilbert, David Matless, and Brian Short (eds), *Geographies of British Mobility* (Oxford, 2003), pp. 8–99.

Pooley, Colin, and Turnbull, Jean, 'Coping with Congestion: Response to Urban Traffic Problems in British Cities, c. 1920–1960', *Journal of Historical Geography*, 31:1 (2005), 78–93.

Pooley, Colin, Turnbull, Jean, and Adams, Mags, 'The Journey to School in Britain since the 1940s: Continuity and Change', *Area*, 37 (2005), 43–53.

Potter, John Deane, *The Monsters of the Moors: The Full Account of the Brady–Hindley Case* (London, 1966).

Punch, M., *Progressive Retreat* (London, 1977).

Race and Class, special issue on Chris Searle, 51:2 (2009).

Ravetz, Alison, *The Place of the Home: English Domestic Environments, 1964–2000* (London, 1995).

Reeves, Christopher, 'Why Attachment? Whither Attachment?: John Bowlby's Legacy, Past and Future', *Beyond the Couch: The Online Journal of the American Association for Psychoanalysis in Clinical Social Work*, 2 (December 1997): <http://www.beyondthecouch.org/1207/reeves.htm>.

Reinisch, Jessica, 'Internationalism in Relief: The Birth (and Death) of UNRRA', *Past and Present*, 210 (2011), 258–89.

Richards, Martin P. M. (ed.), *The Integration of the Child into a Social World* (Cambridge, 1974).

Riley, Denise, *War in the Nursery: Theories of the Child and Mother* (London, 1983).

Roberts, John, *The Art of Interruption: Realism, Photography and the Everyday* (Manchester, 1998).

Robinson, Lucy, *Gay Men and the Left in Post-War Britain: How the Personal Got Political* (Manchester, 2007).

Roper, Michael, 'Between Manliness and Masculinity: The "War Generation" and the Psychology of Fear in Britain, 1914–1950', *Journal of British Studies*, 44 (2005), 343–62.

Rose, Gillian, 'Practising Photography: An Archive, A Study, Some Photographs and a Researcher', *Journal of Historical Geography*, 26:4 (2000), 555–71.

Rose, Gillian, *Doing Family Photography: The Domestic, The Public and the Politics of Sentiment* (Farnham, 2010).

Rose, Jacqueline, *The Case of Peter Pan or the Impossibility of Children's Fiction* (London, 1984).

Rose, June, *For the Sake of the Children: Inside Dr Barnardo's: 120 Years of Caring for Children* (London, 1987).

Rose, Lionel, *The Massacre of the Innocents: Infanticide in Britain, 1800–1939* (London, 1986).

Rose, Lionel, *The Erosion of Childhood: Child Oppression in Britain, 1860–1918* (London, 1991).

Rose, Nikolas, *Governing the Soul: The Shaping of the Private Self* (London, 1989).

Rose, Sonya, *Which People's War? National Identity and Citizenship in Britain, 1939–1945* (Oxford, 2003).

Rousseau, George (ed.), *Children and Sexuality from the Greeks to the Great War* (Basingstoke, 2007).

Rowland, Wade, *The Plot to Save the World: The Life and Times of the Stockholm Conference on the Human Environment* (Toronto, 1973).

Rudolf, G. De M., 'The Effect of Children's Television on Behaviour', *Mental Health*, 17:2 (Spring 1958), 55–60.

Saint, Andrew, *Towards a Social Architecture: The Role of School Building in Post-War England* (New Haven, 1987).

Samuel, Raphael, *Theatres of Memory* (London, 1996).

Satter, Beryl, 'The Sexual Abuse Paradigm in Historical Perspective: Passivity and Emotion in Mid-Twentieth-Century America', *Journal of the History of Sexuality*, 12 (2003), 424–64.

Sauerteig, Lutz, 'Loss of Innocence: Albert Moll, Sigmund Freud and the Invention of Childhood Sexuality around 1900', in A. H. Maehle and L. Sauerteig (eds), *Sexology, Medical Ethics and Occultism: Albert Moll in Context*, special issue of *Medical History*, 56 (2012), 156–83.

Sauerteig, Lutz, and Davidson, Roger, *Shaping Sexual Knowledge: A Cultural History of Sex Education in 20th Century Europe* (New York, 2008).

Savage, Jon, *Teenage: The Creation of Youth Culture* (London, 2007).

Savage, Mike, *Identities and Social Change in Britain since 1940: The Politics of Method* (Oxford, 2010).

Schulman, Norma, 'Conditions of Their Own Making: An Intellectual History of the Centre for Contemporary Cultural Studies at the University of Birmingham', *Canadian Journal of Communication*, 18:1 (1993), 51–73.

Senn, Milton, 'Interview with John Bowlby', in *Beyond the Couch: The Online Journal of the American Association for Psychoanalysis in Clinical Social Work*, 2 (December 2007).

Shapely, Peter, 'Planning, Housing and Participation in Britain, 1968–1976', *Planning Perspectives*, 26:1 (2011), 75–90.

Shapira, Michal, 'The Psychological Study of Anxiety in the Era of the Second World War', *Twentieth Century British History*, 24 (2013), 31–57.

Shaw, Tom (Scottish Government), *Historical Abuse Systemic Review: Residential Schools and Children's Homes in Scotland 1950 to 1995* (Edinburgh, 2007).

Shephard, Ben, 'Becoming Planning Minded: The Theory and Practice of Relief, 1940–1945', *Journal of Contemporary History*, 43 (2008), 405–19.

Shephard, Ben, *The Long Return Home: The Aftermath of the Second World War* (London, 2010).

Shotton, John, *No Master High or Low: Libertarian Education and Schooling in Britain, 1890–1990* (Bristol, 1993).

Shuttleworth, Sally, *Mind of the Child: Child Development in Literature, Science and Medicine, 1840–1900* (Oxford, 2010).

Silverman, Jan, and Wilson, David, *Innocence Betrayed: Paedophilia, the Media and Society* (Cambridge, 2002).

Simon, Brian, *Education and the Social Order, 1940–1990* (London, 1991).

Sinclair, Andrew, *War Like a Wasp* (London, 1989).

Slater, Don, 'Consuming Kodak', in Jo Spence and Patricia Holland (eds), *Family Snaps: The Meanings of Domestic Photography* (London, 1991), pp. 49–59.

Soothill, K., Francis, B., and Ackerley, E., 'Paedophilia and Paedophiles', *New Law Journal* (1998), 882–3.

Sorlin, Pierre, 'Children as Victims in Postwar European Cinema', in Jay Winter and E. Sivan (eds), *War and Remembrance in the Twentieth Century* (London, 1999), pp. 104–24.

Springhall, J., 'Building Character in the British Boy: The Attempt to Extend Christian Manliness to Working-Class Adolescents, 1880–1914', in J. A. Mangan and James Walvin (eds), *Manliness and Morality: Middle-Class Masculinity in Britain and America 1800–1940* (Manchester, 1991), pp. 52–74.

Stanley, Liz, *Sex Surveyed 1949–1994: From Mass-Observation's 'Little Kinsey' to the National Survey and the Hite Reports* (London, 1995).

Staples, Terry, *All Pals Together: The Story of Children's Cinema* (Edinburgh, 1997).

Stargardt, Nicholas, *Witnesses of War: Children's Lives under the Nazis* (London, 2005).

Stearns, Peter, *Anxious Parents: A History of Modern Childrearing in America* (New York, 2003.

Steedman, Carolyn, *Landscape for a Good Woman* (New Brunswick, NJ, 1986).

Steedman, Carolyn, *Margaret McMillan, Childhood, Culture and Class in Britain* (London, 1990).

Steedman, Carolyn, *Strange Dislocations: Childhood and the Idea of Human Interiority, 1780–1930* (London, 1995).

Stewart, John, 'Child Guidance in Inter-War Scotland: International Context and Domestic Concerns', *Bulletin of the History of Medicine*, 80 (2006), 513–39.

Stone, Dan, 'The Domestication of Violence: Forging a Collective Memory of the Holocaust in Britain, 1945–6', *Patterns of Prejudice*, 33 (1999), 13–29.

Stonebridge, Lyndsey, 'Bombs, Birth, and Trauma: Henry Moore's and D. W. Winnicott's Prehistory Fragments', *Cultural Critique*, 46 (2000), 80–101.

Sutherland, John, *Offensive Literature: Decensorship in Britain, 1960–1982* (Totowa, 1983).

Swanson, Gloria, *Drunk with Glitter: Space, Consumption and Sexual Instability in Modern Urban Culture* (Abingdon, 2007).

Tagg, John, *The Burden of Representation: Essays on Photographies and Histories* (London, 1988).

Taylor, John, *A Dream of England: Landscape Photography and the Tourist's Imagination* (Manchester, 1994).

Thane, Pat, 'Family Life and "Normality" in Postwar British Culture', in Richard Bessel and Dirk Schumann (eds), *Life after Death: Approaches to a Cultural and Social History of Europe during the 1940s and 1950s* (Cambridge, 2003), pp. 193–210.

Thom, Deborah, 'The Healthy Citizen of Empire or Juvenile Delinquent?: Beating and Mental Health in the UK', in Marijke Gijswijt-Hofstra and Hilary Marland (eds), *Cultures of Child Health in Britain and the Netherlands in the Twentieth Century* (Amsterdam, 2003), pp. 189–212.

Thomas, David, *The Making of Community Work* (London, 1983).

Thomson, A., *Anzac Memories: Living with the Legend* (Melbourne, 1994).

Thomson, David, *Try to Tell the Story* (New York, 2009).

Thomson, Mathew, *The Problem of Mental Deficiency: Eugenics, Democracy, and Social Policy in Britain, 1870–1959* (Oxford, 1998).

Thomson, Mathew, *Psychological Subjects: Identity, Culture and Health in Twentieth-Century Britain* (Oxford, 2006).

Thrift, Nigel, 'A Hyperactive World', in R. Johnston, P. Taylor, and M. Watts (eds), *Geographies of Global Change: Remapping the World in the Late Twentieth Century* (Oxford, 1995), pp. 18–35.

Thullier, Rosalind, *Marcus Adams: Photographer Royal* (London, 1985).

Timmins, Nicholas, *The Five Giants: A Biography of the Welfare State* (London, 1995).

Titmuss, Richard, *Problems of Social Policy* (London, 1950).

Turner, Barry, and Rennell, Tony, *When Daddy Came Home: How Family Life Changed Forever in 1945* (London, 1995).

Vernon, James, *Hunger: A Modern History* (Cambridge, MA, 2007).

Vernon, James, 'The Local, the Imperial and the Global: Repositioning Twentieth-Century Britain and the Brief Life of its Social Democracy', *Twentieth Century British History*, 21 (2010), 404–18.

Vicedo, Marga, 'The Social Nature of the Mother's Tie to the Child: John Bowlby's Theory of Attachment in Post-War America', *British Journal for the History of Science*, 44 (2011), 401–26.

Waites, Matthew, 'The Age of Consent and Sexual Consent', in Mark Cowling and Paul Reynolds (eds), *Making Sense of Sexual Consent* (Aldershot, 2004).

Ward, Colin, and Ward, Tim, *Images of Childhood: Old Photographs* (Stroud, 1991).

Warren, Allen, 'Popular Manliness: Baden-Powell, Scouting and the Development of Manly Character', in J. A. Mangan and James Walvin (eds.), *Manliness and Morality: Middle-Class Masculinity in Britain and America 1800–1940* (Manchester, 1991), pp. 199–219.

Waters, Chris, '"Dark Strangers" in our Midst: Discourses of Race and Nation in Britain, 1947–1963', *Journal of British Studies*, 36 (1997), 207–38.

Waters, Chris, 'Autobiography, Nostlagia, and Working-Class Selfhood', in George K. Behlmer and Fred Leventhal (eds), *Singular Continuities: Tradition, Nostalgia and Identity in Modern British Culture* (Stanford, 2000), 178–95.

Webster, Charles, 'Conflict and Consensus: Explaining the British Health Service', *Twentieth Century British History*, 1 (1990), 115–51.

Webster, Richard, *The Great Children's Home Panic* (Oxford, 1998).

Webster, Wendy, *Imagining Home: Gender, Race and National Identity, 1945–64* (London, 1997).

Webster, Wendy, 'There'll always be an England: Representations of Colonial Wars and Immigration, 1948–1968', *Journal of British Studies*, 46 (2001), 557–84.

Weeks, Jeffrey, *Sex, Politics and Society: The Regulation of Sexuality since 1800* (London, 1989).

Welshman, John, 'In Search of the "Problem Family": Public Health and Social Work in England and Wales 1940–70', *Social History of Medicine*, 9 (1996), 447–65.

Welshman, John, 'Evacuation and Social Policy During the Second World War: Myth and Reality', *Twentieth Century British History*, 9 (1998), 28–53.

Welshman, John, 'Ideology, Social Science, and Public Policy: The Debate over Transmitted Deprivation', *Twentieth Century British History*, 16 (2005), 306–41.

Welshman, John, *From Transmitted Deprivation to Social Exclusion: Policy, Poverty, and Parenting* (Bristol, 2007).

Welshman, John, 'From Head Start to Sure Start: Reflections on Policy Transfer', *Children and Society*, 24 (2010), 89–99.

Welshman, John, *Churchill's Children: The Evacuee Experience in Wartime Britain* (Oxford, 2010).

Werner, Emmy E., *Children Witness World War II* (Oxford, 2000).

Westerbeck, Colin, and Meyerowitz, Joel, *Bystander: A History of Street Photography* (London, 1994).

Westwood, Gordon, *A Minority: A Report on the Life of the Male Homosexual in Great Britain* (London, 1960).

Wheeler, Keith, 'The Genesis of Environmental Education', in George C. Martin and Keith Wheeler (eds), *Insights into Environmental Education* (Edinburgh, 1975).

Whitton, Timothy, 'The Impact of the Community Development Projects on Assessing Urban Deprivation', in M. Charlot (ed.), *Britain's Inner Cities* (Paris, 1994), pp. 9–22.

Wills, Abigail, 'Delinquency, Masculinity and Citizenship in England, 1950–1970', *Past and Present*, 187 (2005), 157–85.

Wilson, Dolly Smith, 'A New Look at the Affluent Worker: The Good Working Mother in Post-War Britain', *Twentieth Century British History*, 17 (2006), 206–29.

Winter, Jay, 'Film and the Matrix of Memory', *American Historical Review*, 106 (2001), 104–24.

Wolmar, Christian, *Forgotten Children: The Secret Abuse Scandal in Children's Homes* (London, 2000).

Wooldridge, Adrian, *Measuring the Mind: Education and Psychology in England, c. 1860–1990* (Cambridge, 1990).

Wright, Patrick, *On Living in an Old Country* (London, 1985).

Wylie, John, *Landscape* (Abingdon, 2007).

Young, Robert, Figlio, Karl, and Bowlby, John, 'An Interview with John Bowlby on the Origins and Reception of His Work', *Free Associations*, 6 (1986), 36–64.

Zahra, Tara, 'Lost Children: Displacement, Family, and Nation in Postwar Europe', *Journal of Modern History*, 81 (2009), 45–86.

Zaretsky, Eli, '"One Large Secure, Solid Background": Melanie Klein and the Origins of the British Welfare State', *History and Psychoanalysis*, 1:2 (1999), 136–51.

Zeiher, Helga, 'Shaping Daily Life in Urban Environments', in Pia Christensen and Margaret O'Brien (eds), *Children in the City: Home, Neighbourhood and Community* (London, 2003), pp. 66–81.

Zelizer, V. A., *Pricing the Priceless Child: The Changing Social Value of Children* (New York, 1985).

Websites

Bill Brandt archive: <http://www.billbrandt.com/>

'Children Make a Difference', *Man Alive*, BBC2 (4 January 1967): <http://www.bbc.co.uk/archive/marriage/10512.shtml>

Conway, Joan, 'The Playgroups Movement, 1961–1987', in *Memories of the Playgroup Movement in Wales, 1961–1987*: <http://www.playgroupmemorieswales.org.uk>

Cummins, Gerald, 'The History of Road Safety': <http://www.driveandstayalive.com/info%20section/history/history.htm>

Falsely Accused Carers and Teachers: <http://www.factuk.org/about-us/fact-the-first-decade/>

London Play: <http://www.londonplay.org.uk/document.php?document_id=1198>

Road Accident Casualties 1992–2002: <http://www.statistics.gov.uk>

Royal Society for the Prevention of Accidents: <http://www.rospa.com/about/history/>

Rutter, Michael, interview: <http://www.ucl.ac.uk/histmed/downloads/hist_neuroscience_transcripts/rutter.pdf>

Smith, M. K., 'Community Work', in *The Encyclopedia of Informal Education*: <http://www.infed.org/community/b-comwrk.htm>

Soothill, Keith, 'Opening Doors and Windows for Tony Parker', in *Papers for the British Society of Criminology Conference, Leicester, July 2000* (October, 2001): <http://www.britsoccrim.org/volume4/002.pdf>

Thatcher, Margaret, speeches (Thatcher Foundation): <http://www.margaretthatcher.org>

Tutaev, Belle, interview on the Pre-School Playgroups Association website: <https://www.pre-school.org.uk/about-us/history/1262/interview-with-alliance-founder-belle-tutaev>

Vague, Tom, *Notting Hill History Timeline*, Chapter 11, 'Open the Squares': <http://www.vaguerants.org.uk/wp-content/pageflip/upload/TL/timelinechap11.pdf>

Worktown Photographs (Humphrey Spender): <http://spender.boltonmuseums.org.uk/>

Young, Jock, reflections on the history of the National Deviancy Symposium: <http://www.malcolmread.co.uk/JockYoung/Critical.htm>

Unpublished Sources

Brooke, Stephen, 'Children and Streets: Class, Childhood and the City in 1950s and 1960s Photography', NECBS paper (2009).

Castro, Monica O'Brien, 'On the Privatization of Inner Cities: The British Conservative Government's Urban Policy from 1979 to the 1990s', Paper to Urban History Annual Conference, Reading 2006.

McCarty, Elizabeth Anne, 'Attitudes to Women and Domesticity in England, c. 1939–1955', unpublished DPhil (Oxford, 1994).

Soanes, Stephen, 'Rest and Restitution: Convalescence and the Public Mental Hospital in England, 1919–39', unpublished PhD thesis (University of Warwick, 2011).

Index

Printed and bound by CPI Group (UK) Ltd, Croydon, CR0 4YY